Popular elections are at the heart of representative democracy. Thus, understanding the laws and practices that govern such elections is essential to understanding modern democracy. In this book, Professor Cox views electoral laws as posing a variety of coordination problems that political actors must solve. Under plurality rule, for example, not every leftist aspirant for the presidency can run at once, if the Left is to have a good chance of winning. But although all leftists will benefit from unifying behind a single candidate, they may not agree on which candidate that should be. Analogous coordination problems – and with them the necessity of negotiating withdrawals, strategic voting, and other species of strategic coordination – arise in all electoral systems.

Although the classics of electoral studies have dealt with issues of coordination, this is the first book that employs a unified game-theoretic model to study strategic coordination worldwide and that relies primarily on constituency-level rather than national aggregate data in testing theoretical propositions about the effects of electoral laws. This is also the first book that considers not just what happens when political forces *succeed* in solving the coordination problems inherent in the electoral system they face but also what happens when they fail.

MAKING VOTES COUNT

POLITICAL ECONOMY OF INSTITUTIONS AND DECISIONS

Other books in the series

Alberto Alesina and Howard Rosenthal, *Partisan Politics, Divided Government and the Economy*
Lee J. Alston, Thrainn Eggertsson, and Douglass C. North, *Empirical Studies in Institutional Change*
James E. Alt and Kenneth Shepsle, eds., *Perspectives on Positive Political Economy*
Jeffrey S. Banks and Eric A. Hanushek, *Modern Political Economy: Old Topics, New Directions*
Yoram Barzel, *Economic Analysis of Property Rights, 2nd Edition*
Robert Bates, *Beyond the Miracle of the Market: The Political Economy of Agrarian Development in Kenya*
Peter Cowhey and Mathew McCubbins, *Structure and Policy in Japan and the United States*
Gary W. Cox, *The Efficient Secret: The Cabinet and the Development of Political Parties in Victorian England*
Jean Ensminger, *Making a Market: The Institutional Transformation of an African Society*
Murray Horn, *The Political Economy of Public Administration: Institutional Choice in the Public Sector*
Jack Knight, *Institutions and Social Conflict*
Michael Laver and Kenneth Shepsle, *Making and Breaking Governments*
Michael Laver and Kenneth Shepsle, *Cabinet Ministers and Parliamentary Government*
Brian Levy and Pablo T. Spiller, *Regulations, Institutions, and Commitment*
Leif Lewin, *Ideology and Strategy: A Century of Swedish Politics (English Edition)*
Gary Libecap, *Contracting for Property Rights*
Mathew D. McCubbins and Terry Sullivan, eds., *Congress: Structure and Policy*
Gary J. Miller, *Managerial Dilemmas: The Political Economy of Hierarchy*
Douglass C. North, *Institutions, Institutional Change, and Economic Performance*
Elinor Ostrom, *Governing the Commons: The Evolution of Institutions for Collective Action*
J. Mark Ramseyer, *Odd Markets in Japanese History*
J. Mark Ramseyer and Frances Rosenbluth, *The Politics of Oligarchy: Institutional Choice in Imperial Japan*
Jean-Laurent Rosenthal, *The Fruits of Revolution: Property Rights, Litigation, and French Agriculture*
Charles Stewart III, *Budget Reform Politics: The Design of the Appropriations Process in the House of Representatives, 1865–1921*
George Tsebelis and Jeannette Money, *Bicameralism*
John Waterbury, *Exposed to Innumerable Delusions: Public Enterprise and State Power in Egypt, India, Mexico, and Turkey*
David L. Weimer, *The Political Economy of Property Rights*

R

MAKING VOTES COUNT

STRATEGIC COORDINATION IN THE WORLD'S ELECTORAL SYSTEMS

GARY W. COX
University of California at San Diego

CAMBRIDGE
UNIVERSITY PRESS

)F THE UNIVERSITY OF CAMBRIDGE
ımbridge CB2, 1RP, United Kingdom

CAMBRIDGE UNIVERSITY PRESS
The Edinburgh Building, Cambridge CB2 2RU, United Kingdom
40 West 20th Street, New York, NY 10011-4211, USA
10 Stamford Road, Oakleigh, Melbourne 3166, Australia

First published 1997

Printed in the United States of America

Typeset in Sabon

Library of Congress Cataloging-in-Publication Data

Cox, Gary W.
Making votes count : strategic coordination in the world's electoral systems / Gary W. Cox.

p. cm. – (Political economy of institutions and decisions)

Includes bibliographical references and index.
ISBN 0-521-58516-3 (hardback). – ISBN 0-521-58527-9 (pbk.)
1. Elections. 2. Voting. 3. Comparative government. I. Title
II. Series.

JF1001.C69 1997
324.6 – dc20 96-36254
CIP

A catalog record for this book is available from the British Library

ISBN 0-521-58516-3 Hardback
ISBN 0-521-58527-9 Paperback

To Diane

Contents

PART V
COORDINATION FAILURES AND DEMOCRATIC PERFORMANCE

PART VI
CONCLUSION

APPENDICES

Tables and figures

Tables

Figures

Series Editors' Preface

The Cambridge series on the Political Economy of Institutions and Decisions is built around attempts to answer two central questions: How do institutions evolve in response to individual incentives, strategies, and choices, and how do institutions affect the performance of political and economic systems? The scope of the series is comparative and historical rather than international or specifically American, and the focus is positive rather than normative.

Gary Cox has written a superb, wide-ranging theoretical analysis of the consequences of electoral systems for the way governments are chosen by the mass of citizens. Rooted firmly in the "transaction benefits" theory of political institutions, which holds that a role of institutions is to prevent some collective choices from arising, or otherwise limit the number of enforceable policy outcome, Cox shows how a range of electoral institutions affect the extent and ease with which voters can coordinate (or form electoral coalitions) to provide outcomes or opportunities for transacting that improve on their status quo, but would not happen in the absence of these electoral institutions. In the coalitional equilibria he describes, voters make their votes count by controlling the number of candidates. But the emphasis everywhere is on synthesis, generalization, and unification of theory. Results apply to coalitions whether they are explicitly negotiated by elites or voluntarily coordinated by electors via strategic voting and convergent expectations about the strength of candidates. An unprecedentedly wide range of real-world electoral systems is classified by alliance structure and district structure with respect to the extent to which they facilitate coordination. Duverger's conjectures about the relationships between strategic voting, the proportionality of representation, and the number of effective competitors or parties are reexamined. The research also offers many new proposals about strategic entry and exit of parties, as well as the election of executives in fostering or impeding coordination at the national level.

In its scale and scope, in going beyond taxonomy into analysis, in its relentless testing of the propositions it offers, in its unification of aspects of electoral systems frequently treated as separate, this book is a remarkable achievement. It sets a standard and a challenge for future comparative empirical research on electoral systems.

Preface

This book is about strategic coordination – both strategic voting and strategic attempts to regulate entry – in the world's electoral systems. I assume that readers are familiar with the concept of a coordination game. Those who are not, and are not satisfied with the brief description given below, may wish to consult Lewis (1969), Schelling (1978), or other sources.

The basic idea of a coordination game is simple enough and can be conveyed by considering a classic illustrative game, the Battle of the Sexes. In this game, a man and a woman must independently choose whether to attend a prize fight or a ballet performance. The man prefers the prize fight to the ballet, while the woman has opposite preferences. Both, however, are primarily concerned with having each other's company, so that each prefers going to their dispreferred entertainment with their partner to going to their preferred entertainment alone.

Cultural stereotypes aside, this venerable example lays bare the essence of a coordination problem. The players in the game would prefer to coordinate their actions on some one of two (or more) possibilities but they disagree over which of these possibilities ought to be the one on which they coordinate. There is thus an admixture of common and divergent interests, and the possibility of both *successful* coordination (to the relative advantage of one or more of the players over the others) and *failed* coordination (to the disadvantage of all).

Other than a familiarity with the notion of coordination, I make relatively few assumptions about the reader's background. Doubtless those who are already familiar with electoral studies will find parts of the book easier to follow than those not so familiar. But Chapter 3 of the book gives a self-contained introduction to electoral rules and regulations for those who have not previously considered these matters. Doubtless too those who do not know game theory will find the proofs in Appendix B pretty unintelligible. But the text is written with an eye to making the logic of the proofs in this and other chapters accessible to those who prefer not to wade through the mathematical notation.

This work has benefited from the generosity and insight of a number of scholars. Tom Palfrey and Roger Myerson provided exceptionally valuable comments on some of the papers upon which the book builds. André Blais, Ray Christensen, Skip Lupia, Bing Powell, and Matthew Shugart – along with several anonymous reviewers – read the whole of an early draft and provided detailed comments that helped greatly to improve the final product. I also received valuable comments from Jamie Druckman, Jenn Kuhn, Mat McCubbins, Iain McLean, Mike Molloy, Scott Morgenstern, David Samuels, Robert Schwartz, Steve Swindle, and Frances Rosenbluth. Too many people for me to recall have helped by providing leads to interesting web sites, confirmation of suspicious facts, or ideas about where to look next – but I should mention at least Kathy Bawn, Arend Lijphart, Shaheen Mozaffar, Andy Reynolds, Ron Rogowski, and Matthew Shugart. Finally, several people with whom I have coauthored will find pieces of their work embodied here and there in the text but I should mention in particular Octavio Amorim Neto, as Chapter 11 is but a slightly reworked version of our published work together.

Various people have lent invaluable advice and aid in the process of preparing the final manuscript and shepherding it through the editorial process. At the University of California at San Diego (UCSD), I should thank Jennifer Oh, Ginnah Saunders, and Thad Kousser. Farther afield, I should thank Alex Holzman and Jim Alt.

Funding for various parts of the research program that led to this book has been provided by the National Science Foundation (grants SBR-9422874 and SES-9208753); the Department of Political Science at UCSD (which provided some funds to launch the web site of the Lijphart Elections Archive); and the Committee on Research at UCSD (which partially funded my work with Amorim Neto). I thank all these sources and also the John Simon Guggenheim Foundation for awarding me a Fellowship, during the course of which I completed the manuscript.

Finally, I thank my wife, Diane Lin, and son, Dylan, for their moral support, encouragement, and persistent ability to keep academic endeavors in proper perspective.

PART I

Introduction

1

Introduction

Early in the 1984 presidential primary season in the United States, it was clear that the sitting President, Ronald Reagan, would easily win the Republican nomination and that former Vice President Walter F. Mondale was the front-runner for the Democratic nod. Democratic voters who knew that they disliked Mondale faced a coordination problem: If all of them could agree on a single alternative to Mondale, from among the half-dozen or so candidates languishing in single digits in the opinion polls, they could conceivably deny Mondale the nomination; but if they failed to agree on a single alternative, then Mondale would almost surely win. Although anti-Mondale Democrats shared a dislike of Mondale, they differed substantially in their preferred alternative. Thus, even putting aside the complexities of the American primary process, it was by no means clear *ex ante* that anti-Mondale Democrats could coordinate on an alternative. In the event, although Gary Hart emerged as the focal alternative to Mondale and enjoyed a large and rapid run-up in the polls, his candidacy faltered and Mondale secured the nomination.

Early in the 1990 presidential campaign in Peru, it was clear that Nobel Prize-winning novelist Mario Vargas Llosa was the front-runner. Peruvian voters who knew that they disliked Vargas Llosa faced a coordination problem: If all of them could agree on a single alternative to Vargas Llosa from among the half-dozen or so candidates trailing in the polls, they could conceivably deny Vargas Llosa the presidency; but if they failed to agree on a single alternative, then Vargas Llosa would almost surely win. Although anti-Vargas Llosa voters shared a dislike of Vargas Llosa, they differed substantially in their preferred alternative. Thus, it was by no means clear *ex ante* that anti-Vargas Llosa Peruvians could coordinate on an alternative. In the event, Alberto Fujimori rocketed from obscurity late in the campaign to become the focal anti-Vargas Llosa candidate, securing a strong second-place finish in the first round of voting, then defeating Vargas Llosa in the runoff (Schmidt N.d.).

These two examples illustrate several general features of electoral coordination: the mixture of common and opposed interests; the possibility of success or failure; and the rapidity with which vote intentions change when coordination takes off. The examples' focus on strategic voting in presidential elections is too limited, however. Modern representative democracy presents at its core a *series* of coordination problems that arise as natural consequences of electoral competition for governmental offices. A group with enough votes to elect some number of candidates in a given (legislative or executive) race will in fact elect that number only if it can make its votes count by concentrating them appropriately. One way to avoid spreading votes too thinly is to limit the number of candidates. But which potential candidates, representing what shades of opinion, will withdraw in favor of which others? If attempts to limit the number of candidates fail, another chance to make votes count arises on polling day, when voters can concentrate their votes on a subset of the available candidates. But which candidates will bear the brunt of strategic voting and which will be its beneficiaries?

This is a book about strategic coordination broadly conceived, covering both legislative and executive elections, both strategic entry and strategic voting. It investigates the consequences of strategic coordination and those structural features that determine the nature of the coordination problems that political actors face in differing polities.

The consequences of strategic coordination. Successful electoral coordination reduces the number of electoral competitors. When leftist elites agree to join together into a single leftist party, rather than continuing with some larger number, there are fewer parties nominating fewer legislative candidates. If leftist elites do not coordinate their endorsements sufficiently, leftist voters may complete the coalition that the elites tried but failed to form, by deserting one of the leftist candidates for the other(s). In the process they decrease the effective or vote-weighted number of candidates.[1] Duverger's famous Law – the proposition that "the plurality rule [employed in single-member districts] tends to produce a two-party system" (Duverger 1954:113) – is a claim about how far the processes of reduction can be expected to go in the case of one particular set of electoral rules.

Electoral coordination is not just a matter of reducing the number of parties competing in elections, however, any more than coordination on

[1]Just as an industry with 100 firms, one of which makes 95% of all sales, is essentially a monopoly despite its 100 firms, so one might say that an election with 100 candidates, one of whom garners 95% of the vote, has not much more than one "real" candidate. The notion of an "effective number of parties," due to Laakso and Taagepera (1979), is one attempt to count "real" candidates. If v_j is the vote share of the jth party, then the effective number of parties is $(\sum v_j^2)^{-1}$, the reciprocal of the Hirschman-Herfindahl concentration index.

technical standards is just a matter of reducing the number of such standards. When writers of software programs agree on standards compatible with Microsoft's operating system, this does reduce the sales-weighted number of operating systems, and may even lead to the withdrawal of some operating systems from the market. But, in addition, there are some winners (Microsoft; those who like PCs) and some losers (Apple; those who like Macintoshes). Similarly, when leftist opinion leaders agree to rally around Socialist Party A's candidates, rather than around Socialist Party B's, this does reduce the vote-weighted number of parties, and it may even lead to the disappearance of B from political competition. But, in addition to any gain of seats that the unified socialists may accrue as a whole, there are some relative winners (party A; those who prefer its policies) and losers (party B; those who prefer its policies). To put the point more starkly: Successful electoral coordination necessarily involves a reduction in the number of competitors; but such a reduction just as necessarily entails a selection of which competitors will survive, and this selection potentially has important policy effects.

In this book, I shall consider both the reductive and the redistributive effects of electoral coordination. The reductive effect of strategic coordination is most evident when it succeeds, the redistributive effect most evident when it fails – as will be seen.

The nature of the electoral coordination problem. As regards what determines the nature of the coordination problem that arises in any given system, I shall be principally concerned with three main independent variables: electoral institutions, political motivations, and public expectations. The importance of the first of these factors – electoral institutions – has been alternately asserted and dismissed since Duverger's seminal work in the 1950s (Duverger 1954). Here, electoral institutions – which determine the available opportunities for trading votes in order to win more seats – are taken as largely defining the coordination game that elites and voters must play.

Electoral institutions are not the whole story, however. A second part of the strategic situation is defined by the preferences of the elite and mass actors who must coordinate. If leftists care mostly about policy, and hate each other's policies almost as much as they hate the current government's, then there is little incentive for them to coordinate their actions, even if by so doing they could win more seats. If leftists care substantially about future elections, then it may be a good strategy to play tough in the early rounds, enduring a series of coordination failures in the hopes of emerging eventually as *the* leftist party.

Finally, expectations are crucial in any game of coordination, and electoral coordination is no different. If Socialist Party A believes that B's supporters will vote strategically (for A), in the event that both enter, then A has little incentive to acquiesce in any demands that B might make. If B has opposite beliefs, there is no room for the elites to resolve the coordination problem on the Left. As for the voters, if poll results clearly reveal that A's candidates are ahead, then B's supporters will more likely desert to A than the reverse. If polls are absent, noncredible, or ambiguous, however, then the informational prerequisites of strategic voting may not be satisfied, in which case one again expects a failure of coordination.

Of the three independent variables just mentioned, the first – the nature of the electoral institutions in a polity – is obviously central to comparative electoral studies. The second – the nature of political actors' preferences – is a standard concern, especially of rational choice scholars. The third variable, however, concerning the nature of actors' expectations, may be less obviously relevant to some readers. Before proceeding further, let me say something more about the role that expectations play in elections.

1.1 ELECTORAL SYSTEMS AS SYSTEMS OF EXCHANGE: THE ROLE OF EXPECTATIONS

It is conventional, but no less compelling for that, to express wonder at the vast array of activities that are coordinated by the market and its attendant price system. Somehow, without any central planner dictating that it be so, about the right amount of food descends on New York City, about the right number of flashlights make their way to Omaha, and about the right number of video cassette recorders arrive at Gila Bend.

The key to the process by which consumer demands are anticipated and fulfilled with such enviable accuracy (at least by central planning standards) is the system of prices. Clearly known prices for intermediate and final goods and services allow a vast decentralization of planning and productive activities. *Market-clearing* prices, attained in the hypothetical equilibria of economic models, equate demand and supply. At those prices, the number of widgets that consumers in the aggregate seek to purchase turns out to equal the number of widgets that businesses in the aggregate seek to sell (ignoring inventories and other subtleties).

Political scientists do not usually think of elections as systems of exchange subject to equilibrating mechanisms. But there are some analogies between the exchange of voting support among citizens within the electoral system and the exchange of consumer goods among citizens within the market. Relative to the imaginable extreme in which everyone runs for president and votes for him- or herself, real-world presidential elections are highly concentrated and coordinated affairs. In the United States, everyone expects that only a handful of Republican or Democratic politicians are viable candidates for their parties' nominations, and they act accordingly. Contributors do not contribute to, activists do not volunteer for, and citizens do not vote for hopeless candidates, ensuring that those expected to do poorly, do poorly in fact. Somehow lots of people, with diverse preferences, are willing to contribute in various ways to Bob Dole's candidacy but not to Pete Wilson's. Bob Dole accordingly is willing to continue as a candidate; Pete Wilson is not.

The key to the process by which voter demands are anticipated and fulfilled is the system of expectations. Clearly known common expectations about who is and is not viable are self-fulfilling, and allow a considerable decentralization of planning and vote-productive activities. *Market-clearing* expectations, attained in the hypothetical equilibria of political models, equate demand and supply. At those expectations, the number and type of candidates that voters are willing to vote for turns out to equal the number and type of candidates that are willing and able to stand for election.

Equilibrium, whether economic or political, may of course be a rare bird. Too many entrepreneurs may set up fast-food restaurants in a given (geographical) location, leading to poor (expected or realized) profits and a shake-out in the industry. Too many politicians may set up candidacies at a given (ideological) location, leading to poor (expected or realized) vote totals and a contraction in the field. Developers anticipating a large influx of population may play Chicken against one another in building housing tracts to fulfill the anticipated demand.[2] Groups anticipating a large anticommunist vote in a post-communist eastern European election may play Chicken against one another in launching campaigns to attract the anticipated votes. All of these examples illustrate dynamic adjustment on the supply side, or what happens to the supply of goods or candidacies when prices or expectations are not sufficiently clear.

One could also adduce examples of demand-side informational failures. Consumers are unaware of a spiffy new product that is cheaper and better than a well-advertised alternative that everyone currently uses; it takes some time before word of mouth moves market demand toward the new product. Leftist voters are unclear as to which of two leftist candi-

[2]The original game of Chicken pits two teenagers in hotrods against one another. Both head down the center of the road toward each other, the first to swerve being "chicken." If neither swerves, a very bad outcome results. If one swerves, then the swerver is humiliated while the other is covered with glory. If both swerve, an intermediate payoff results.

dates is ahead (or behind) in a three-way race also including a right-wing candidate. As a result, the leftist vote is split and the rightist wins the seat.

Such evident and important nonequilibrium examples notwithstanding, equilibrium analysis has been fundamental to market economics for some two hundred years. One of the premises of this book is that equilibrium analysis ought also to be fundamental to the understanding of elections. Although there is some work that fits the broad description of equilibrium analysis outlined above, in which expectations play a central role in coordinating electoral activity and choice, there is no book-length treatment of the subject that attempts to explain how different electoral laws affect the nature of market-clearing expectations and electoral coordination. The present work seeks to begin filling that gap.[3]

1.2 PLAN OF THE BOOK

A brief outline of the book can now be given in terms of the three independent variables introduced above – electoral institutions, political motivations, and public expectations. Electoral institutions determine how votes translate into seats. If political actors care mostly about winning seats in the current election, then the influence of electoral institutions on their goals is direct. If, in addition, actors' expectations about each other's vote shares are precise and consensual, then a well-structured coordination game emerges in which the prospects for successful coordination are good. This model corresponds to the standard Duvergerian approach to legislative elections in the electoral studies literature.

Parts II and III of the book formally generalize the Duvergerian model of strategic coordination – both at the level of citizens coordinating votes and elites coordinating endorsements and entry – to legislative electoral systems other than the single-member simple plurality case for which the logic is best developed in the extant literature. Using a formal model forces one to state assumptions explicitly. This leads almost immediately to fairly substantial changes in the way that one understands even so well-known a result as Duverger's Law. For example, although Duverger and the subsequent literature have been quite clear in saying that plurality rule leads to bipartism, the only valid conclusion from the arguments they explicitly advance is that the number of viable parties cannot exceed two. *More generally, in any electoral system the necessity of electoral coordination only implies an upper bound on the number of competitors.*

[3]Perhaps the clearest examples of the kind of equilibrium analysis suggested above are the complete information models of Osborne and Silvinski (1995), Besley and Coate (1995), and Feddersen (1992). In this book, I shall focus more on incomplete information models.

Recognizing this simple fact leads to a number of changes in the way that one thinks about the impact of electoral laws on party systems. For example, I argue in Chapters 7 and 10 that the correct understanding of the institutionalist model implies that the number of parties in a system ought to be an interactive function of electoral and social structure. Many have viewed Duvergerian institutional analysis as reading social cleavages out of the analysis (a point upon which I expand in Chapter 2). But a closer look at what the institutional analysis really entails reads them back in.

Beyond clarifying the general nature of the impact that electoral institutions have – they impose upper bounds, rather than pushing systems toward some specific equilibrium number of parties – this book also identifies what the appropriate upper bounds are. Part II derives the bounds imposed by strategic voting in a range of different electoral systems: single-member simple plurality (SMSP), single nontransferable vote (SNTV), proportional representation (PR), and others. Part III brings strategic entry into view, again focusing on the restraining effect of the electoral system.

Part IV turns to aspects of electoral coordination that hinge on the executive choice procedure, again assuming for the most part that agents are interested primarily in winning office in the current election and that expectations are consistent. Duverger argued that the desire of voters in single-member simple plurality elections to avoid wasting their votes meant only that there would be pressure toward local bipartism in each legislative district. He had an additional argument, developed later by Sartori (1968; 1976), as to why a congeries of potentially unrelated local bipartisms might cumulate into national bipartism. Part IV deals with this systemic part of the institutionalist argument – putting the stress not on the formation of national parties (as did Duverger and Sartori) but instead on competition for executive office.

Part V turns away from the model in which agents are assumed to care primarily about winning seats in the current election and to have aligned expectations about who is best positioned to do so. When other motivations and expectations are entertained – agents that care about current and future policy outcomes, rather than just current seats, for example – the probability of coordination failure increases. The most obvious consequence of coordination failure is not so much that the number, or effective number, of competitors goes up (as it does) but that whichever side of the political spectrum has failed more egregiously to coordinate pays a penalty in seats. If the Left splits in a single-member district, the Right wins the seat. In Part V, I investigate coordination failures and how they affect the quality of representation, the maintenance of dominant parties, and the politics of realignment.

Having briefly sketched the sequence of topics to be dealt with, let me next say something about methodology. This study differs from previous works in comparative electoral studies both in its reliance on formal game theoretic analysis of the incentives set in train by different electoral institutions and in its use of primarily district-level data to test the hypotheses that the theory entails. In Section 1.3, I discuss the use of formal theory in electoral studies, with particular reference to strategic voting. Then, in Section 1.4, I comment briefly on the data that I use in this book.

1.3 THEORIES, FORMAL THEORIES, AND ELECTORAL STUDIES

The study of mass voting systems has been carried on in two distinct theoretical traditions. One tradition, originally a part of mathematical economics and philosophy, can itself be broken down into work in *social choice theory* (e.g., Arrow 1951; Sen 1970; Fishburn 1973; Gibbard 1973; Schwartz 1986), *public choice theory* (e.g., Buchanan and Tullock 1962; Mueller 1989), and *spatial theory* (e.g., Downs 1957; Hinich, Davis, and Ordeshook 1970; Romer and Rosenthal 1979; Palfrey 1984; Cox 1990a; Enelow and Hinich 1990) – to mention only some of the better-known categories. This work uses the tools of formal symbolic logic, mathematical welfare economics, microeconomics, or game theory to get where it is going. A second tradition, the domain of political scientists and sociologists, is characterized by the work of such scholars as Duverger (1954), Rae (1971), Sartori (1976), Lijphart (1984, 1994), and Taagepera and Shugart (1989). It is less formal, more engaged with real-world data, and more interested in concrete political problems – while still being theoretical for all that.

These two traditions seldom speak to one another, as Dummett (1984) and Reeve and Ware (1992) have observed. Research into strategic voting provides an illustrative case of parallel (nonintersecting) development.

Within the electoral studies tradition, concern with strategic voting arose because it was believed to reduce the number of political parties competing in some systems. Duverger's original formulation (1954) seemed to be that strategic voting was *present* in simple plurality systems, acting to push them toward bipartism, whereas it was *absent* in PR and majority runoff elections, which in part explained their tendency toward multipartism. Reacting to Duverger's apparent belief that his "psychological factor" was inoperative under PR systems, Leys (1959:139) and Sartori (1968:278) argued that strategic voting under PR was no different in kind from that found under plurality, differing only in the degree to which it came into play – and, hence, in the degree to which it tended to reduce the number of viable parties in the system.

Sartori's notion of a continuum of systems, from *strong* (in which strategic voting and elite coalitional activity act forcefully to depress the number of parties) to *weak* (in which strategic voting and incentives to form coalitions are largely absent and thus put little downward pressure on the number of competitors), is now standard in the literature.

Within the formal theoretic tradition, concern with strategic voting was sparked by Arrow's theorem, which presumed that social choice processes could operate on the true preferences of the citizenry. The work of Gibbard (1973) and Satterthwaite (1975) demonstrated formally that incentives to vote strategically could arise in any minimally democratic voting system, and the Gibbard-Satterthwaite theorem has since become a benchmark result in the literature.[4]

It is clear that the Leys-Sartori conjecture (they offered no proof of their assertions) and the Gibbard-Satterthwaite theorem are similar: Both assert the general existence of strategic voting incentives across a wide range of voting systems. Nonetheless, neither side cites the other. Gibbard and Satterthwaite were undoubtedly completely unaware of the Leys-Sartori conjecture. No other formal theorists have since recognized Leys and Sartori as precursors. Returning the compliment, one can read the post-Gibbard/Satterthwaite classics of electoral theory, even those which give substantial attention to strategic voting – such as Taagepera and Shugart (1989) or Lijphart (1994) – without finding any mention of Messrs. Gibbard and Satterthwaite.

One might say that this does not matter. After all, if one asks whether Taagepera and Shugart (or Lijphart) exhibit some fundamental flaw in their approach to strategic voting, due to their not using formal theory in their books, the answer is that they do not. If one asks whether Gibbard and Satterthwaite suffered from not having the kind of detailed knowledge upon which Leys and Sartori based their assertions, the answer is that they did not.

Nonetheless, as I am peddling formal theory in this book, and also using the insights of the electoral theory tradition, let me say something about what each has to offer. If one compares the Gibbard-Satterthwaite theorem to the Leys-Sartori conjecture, the theorem wins hands down in terms of rigor and precision. But it is not as useful to political scientists as it might be, because its conclusion is politically ambiguous. The theorem merely alerts one to the possibility that there may be strategic voting under any democratic electoral system, while saying nothing about either the political consequences of that strategic voting, or about how much strategic voting one should expect. In contrast, the Leys-Sartori

[4]I have stated the result loosely. A careful discussion of the Gibbard-Satterthwaite theorem at an elementary level can be found in Ordeshook (1986:82-86).

conjecture focuses on a particular kind of politically relevant strategic voting – the kind that acts to reduce the vote-weighted number of parties – and says something specific about which systems will have a lot and which a little. This greater relevance presumably explains why political scientists who study electoral systems are more likely to use Sartori's distinction between strong and weak systems than they are to cite the Gibbard-Satterthwaite theorem.[5]

In this book, I hope there will be a fruitful combination of traditions. My *interest* is largely in the questions raised by the electoral theorists; my *methods* are largely those of the formal theorist. Thus, although the formal models that I shall use look at strategic voting broadly conceived, including both strategic voting that does and does not depress the number of parties, it is on the former kind that I focus. Moreover, in each model I seek to say something about the equilibrium level of strategic voting. The result, in that part of the book dealing with strategic voting, is a series of formal theorems each of which looks like a version of either Duverger's Law or the Leys-Sartori conjecture, restricted to a specified range of electoral systems.

1.4 DISTRICT-LEVEL DATA

Another gap that the present work seeks to begin filling is that between our electoral theories (mostly district-level) and data (mostly national-level). As Taagepera and Shugart (1989:117) note, "most studies of electoral systems ... have dealt with the whole system rather than with the district level." This book departs from that tradition, in that most of the data employed are district-level rather than national.

A substantial impediment to conducting electoral research with district-level data is, of course, finding the data in a machine-readable form. As part of the research for this work, I have directed an effort to expand and computerize the Lijphart Elections Archive at my home institution, the University of California at San Diego. The result of that effort, along with most of the data used in this book, can be found on the World Wide Web at http://dodgson.ucsd.edu/lij.

[5]Formal theorists have not entirely ignored the issues in which electoral theorists are interested. There is, for example, a large formal literature that investigates how much strategic voting one should expect under different systems. One approach, due to Nurmi (1987), ranks voting systems in terms of the amount of information about preferences that a voter needs in order to cast an intelligent strategic vote. Under simple plurality, one needs to know the vote intentions of the other voters. Under a majority runoff system, one needs to know a bit more: others' vote intentions both in the first and in the second round. Under the single transferable vote system, one needs to know yet more: Bartholdi and Orlin (1991) show that it is "NP-complete" to determine how to vote strategically; colloquially, this means that it is horrendously difficult except in a few special cases.

2

Duverger's propositions

Students of politics have asked how electoral laws affect the formation and survival of political parties since mass elections first became common in the late nineteenth and early twentieth century. Henry Droop, an English advocate of proportional representation (and inventor of the Droop quota), noted as early as 1869 that plurality elections promote what later scholars have called "strategic" or "tactical" voting:[1]

> As success depends upon obtaining a majority of the aggregate votes of all the electors, an election is usually reduced to a contest between the two most popular candidates.... Even if other candidates go to the poll, the electors usually find out that their votes will be thrown away, unless given in favour of one or other of the parties between whom the election really lies (quoted in Riker 1982:756).

Droop was also surely aware of the plurality system's tendency to underrepresent minority parties – a topic generally discussed today under the rubric of "disproportionality," "big-party bias," or the "mechanical effect." In any event, by 1881 he had enunciated a version of what is now called Duverger's Law:

> the only explanation which seems to me to account for [the two-party systems in the United States, United Kingdom, etc.] is that the two opposing parties into which we find politicians divided in each of these countries have been formed and are kept together by majority [what we now call plurality] voting (quoted in Riker 1982:756–7).

Duverger himself originally thought in terms of three propositions, one for each of the main electoral systems in use when he wrote (Duverger 1986:70). Eventually, however, he settled on just two, which

[1]Duverger referred to the same phenomenon under the rubric of the "psychological factor," by which he meant the desire of voters to avoid casting a "wasted vote" for a candidate with no hope of winning.

Riker (1982) has dubbed Duverger's Law and Duverger's Hypothesis. Duverger's Law states that "the simple-majority single-ballot system [i.e., simple plurality rule] favors the two-party system" (Duverger 1954:217). Duverger's Hypothesis states that "the simple-majority system with second ballot and proportional representation favors multipartyism" (Duverger 1954:239).

The rest of this chapter considers Duverger's propositions at length, proceeding as follows. Section 2.1 reviews some well-known criticisms of Duverger's work advanced by those who take a sociological approach to the study of party systems. Since much of the rest of the book is devoted to studying the political consequences of electoral laws, it is important first to address the arguments of those who doubt that these consequences are particularly important. Section 2.2 then clarifies the particular version of Duverger's propositions upon which the first part of the book will focus – a version framed at the district level in terms of the effective number of candidates, rather than at the national level in terms of the actual number of parties. Section 2.3 reviews the standard logic underlying Duverger's propositions, having to do with strategic voting decisions in the mass electorate, on the one hand, and strategic coalition decisions in the elite strata, on the other. Section 2.4 offers a preliminary sketch of when and how strategic voting appears in systems other than simple plurality, with particular attention to how this might place an upper bound on the number of viable candidates. Section 2.5 concludes with an outline of Part II of the book.

2.1 SOCIOLOGICAL CRITIQUES OF DUVERGER'S PROPOSITIONS

Scholarly reaction to Duverger's work has been highly polarized. Two particularly sharp disagreements – one over his research's scientific status, another over its causal validity – illustrate this polarization clearly.

As regards the scientific status of Duverger's propositions, opinion could not be more divided. On the one hand, some question whether Duverger's generalizations serve "any useful function at all" (Jesse 1990:62; cf. Wildavsky 1959:318) or dismiss them on fundamental grounds: the impossibility of summing up complex and reciprocal social interactions in scientific laws (Lavau 1953; Mackenzie 1957; Bogdanor 1983:261). Sartori (1994:30) views this camp as predominant, noting that "the prevailing wisdom of the profession still is ... that comparatively valid generalizations are impossible to achieve." On the other hand, Riker has devoted an entire essay to the thesis that research into Duverger's Law exemplifies scientific progress (Riker 1982). And Sartori

(1994:27), while disagreeing with Riker's specific formulations, asserts that the arguments of those skeptical of the possibility of comparative generalization "are demonstrably wrong."

Scholarly opinion regarding the causal validity of Duverger's propositions is similarly divided. Two main controversies have arisen. First, some argue that Duverger simply mistook the direction of causality. In this view, party systems determine electoral systems, rather than the other way around (Grumm 1958; Eckstein 1963:253; Lipson 1964; Särlvik 1983:123; Fukui 1988:121). The central body of evidence supporting this view has been contested by Duverger and Riker, but a comparison of Riker's (1982) and Bogdanor's (1983) views of the *same* evidence reveals the two sides far from agreeing.

A second (and closely related) challenge to the causal validity of Duverger's work holds that he focused on an unimportant variable. In this view, party systems are determined primarily by the number and type of cleavages in society, with electoral structure playing either an inconsequential, or at least a distinctly secondary and variable, role (Campbell 1958:30-32; Grumm 1958; Lipson 1959; Meisel 1963; Lipson 1964; Lipset and Rokkan 1967; Rokkan 1970; Blondel 1972:237; Nohlen 1981; Beyme 1985; Franco 1986:82–3; Solari 1986:120–21). Lavau (1953:46), for example, in perhaps the earliest retort of this kind to Duverger's theses, opined that "the method of voting remains a rather small consideration among the complex and infinitely diverse factors that, combined differently in each national society ... condition political life." In the purer forms of this school of thought, long-term multiparty systems such as those found in Europe are to be explained by the existence of many strong social cleavages – cleavages which would find expression in the party system even under single-member plurality rules. Conversely, long-term two-party systems such as that in the United States are to be explained either by inherent social dualism (e.g., Charlesworth 1948; Key 1964b:229ff) or by the relative mildness of their social and ideological cleavages (e.g., Lipson 1953; Hartz 1955). Set against the "social determinist" school, especially its purer variants, are a number of scholars who, while admitting (to varying degrees) the importance of social structure, still view electoral structure as having a consistently important independent impact (e.g., Riker 1982; Duverger 1986:71; Taagepera and Shugart 1989:53; Sartori 1994).

The reason that Duverger's Law has stuck in the craw of so many political scientists of a sociological bent is that it seems to set up some sort of "institutional determinism," wherein markedly different social cleavage structures are hypothetically all mashed into one final outcome (a "two-party system") merely upon application of a particular set of electoral laws. Social cleavages thus seem to play no *systematic* role in determining the equilibrium number of parties. They do play a residual role – Duverger states his law as a tendency precisely to allow for the possibility that particularly strong social cleavages might retard the reduction in number of parties that single-member plurality systems promote. But this puts the cart before the horse in the eyes of those who see social cleavages as exogenous and strongly determinative, electoral laws as endogenous and (at best) marginally determinative.

It is no less true that the stronger versions of "social determinism" stick in the craw of institutionalists, especially those with roots in economic rather than sociological theory. A belief that socially defined groups will always be able to organize in the political arena seems to ignore the problem of collective action (Olson 1965), and a belief that they will always organize *as parties* seems to say that "going it alone" is always a better strategy than forging coalitions. Moreover, the number of social cleavages seems large relative to the number of parties in *any* society, so how is one to tell which cleavages are big enough to be party-defining and which are not? Is it obvious, for example, that the cleavage between Finnish and Swedish people in Finland (which gives rise to a separate party) is more intense than that between European-Americans and African-Americans in the United States (which does not)? From an institutionalist perspective, politicians can take socially defined groups and combine or recombine them in many ways for political purposes (Schattschneider 1960). A given set of social cleavages does not imply a unique set of politically activated cleavages, and hence does not imply a unique party system.

Duverger's propositions are obviously controversial and the institutional determinist and social determinist positions are obviously far apart. Yet, despite the wide divergence of views articulated in the literature, the battle between proponents (institutionalists of various stripes) and detractors (mostly political sociologists) has been anything but sustained and focused. In part this has to do with the very size of the disagreement. To the extent that one side of a debate (e.g., Riker 1982) takes social "science" as clearly possible and desirable, while at least some on the other side (e.g., Lavau 1953; Mackenzie 1957) take it as problematic and perhaps not even desirable, it is difficult to find common ground.

I shall not have much to say here about whether scientific study of comparative politics is possible. I certainly hope that it is, but a convincing defense of this hope against more pessimistic views is well beyond the scope of the present work.

One need not take the argument over Duverger's Law all the way to first principles in the philosophy of science, however. The sociological critiques carry weight even if one is committed to a scientific approach to comparative politics. Accordingly, I address these criticisms – concerning the endogeneity of electoral structure and its relative unimportance when compared to social cleavages – before proceeding further. I shall in particular be interested in the degree to which the two views can be reconciled or synthesized.

The endogeneity of electoral structure

Some reconciliation between institutionalist and sociological perspectives is certainly possible in the controversy over whether electoral systems cause party systems or vice versa. Indeed, there is a close symbiotic relationship between these two claims. On the one hand, if electoral laws do indeed affect the ability of political parties to survive as independent organizations, as Duverger's propositions imply, then presumably parties will seek to manipulate those laws to their own advantage when they can. Assuming Duverger is right, in other words, leads naturally to the conclusion that the party system (and the calculations of partisan benefit rattling around within it) may affect the electoral system. On the other hand, the claim that parties tinker with the electoral mechanism in order to ensure their survival, or increase their vote totals, presupposes a belief on their part in electoral engineering. There would be no point in seeking a new electoral system if electoral systems did not matter. Thus, the early sociological attack, if it is to hang together logically, must take for granted that electoral laws confer partisan advantages, or at least that parties believe they do, in order to conclude that parties will attempt to change them.

It is true that the endogeneity of electoral laws can take some of the causal steam out of electoral structure. For, if electoral systems can be changed relatively easily, then one might expect frequent changes for short-term partisan gain, as in Greece, France, or Turkey. Frequent changes – or the anticipation of change – might then undercut the long-term causal effects of electoral law. Consider, for example, a small party facing a single-member plurality system. If such a party believes the electoral system will survive unaltered for a long time, it faces substantial incentives to join or form a coalition capable of securing a plurality. If, on the other hand, the party believes the electoral system can be easily changed, it may simply seek to bring about such change. The strength of the incentive to coalesce produced by an electoral system depends, in other words, on how long that system is expected to last.

This is a good point. It may be what the sociological critics had in mind. But it is not the death knell of the causal validity of Duverger's Law.

I think the main lesson to be learned from the endogeneity of electoral structure is that in some systems, such as Greece and the emerging democracies of Eastern Europe, the perceived changeability of the electoral code may dampen the incentive effects of electoral law. There is some reason to think these cases may not "fit" quite as well with the older, more established electoral systems. Perhaps one could even get some mileage out of these cases in measuring how much perceived changeability affects the reductive strength of a system.[2]

But in fact electoral laws are not everywhere and always easily changed. It is the winners under the current electoral system who (if party discipline holds) must find it in their interest to change the electoral system.[3] Thus – unless there is substantial uncertainty against which even the winners wish to insure themselves;[4] or the winners think the electoral situation has changed, so that the old electoral rules will no longer serve them well, and they can agree on how to manipulate the rules for short-term gain (e.g., France in 1951 and 1986); or the electoral system has come to symbolize an unpopular political regime, so that politicians face intense public pressure to rewrite the code (e.g., the recent reforms in Japan, Italy, and Venezuela) – electoral systems tend to be, and to be perceived as, rather long-lived. As Lijphart (1994:52) puts it, "one of the best-known generalizations about electoral systems is that they tend to be very stable and to resist change." When electoral systems *are* (per-

[2]Even in cases where the electoral code is seen as protean, there may be ways to decide whether electoral structure pushes the party system or vice versa. The problem is a garden-variety one of simultaneous or reciprocal causation. It does indeed make it impossible to infer from a simple bivariate correlation something solid about causation. But there are in principle solutions to such problems. One is to fashion a simultaneous equations model, in which both the electoral system and the number of parties appear as endogenous variables. No one in the literature has attempted to do this, and I do not propose to do so here; but it is not obviously an impossible route to take, merely a very difficult one! Were one to take this route, it would be important to find some variables that predict the adoption of electoral systems that are not endogenous to social structure. In this regard, the findings of Blais and Massicotte (N.d.) are interesting: In a study of the determinants of electoral law in some 166 countries, two of the strongest predictors of a country having a single-member plurality system that they find are "being a former British colony" and "size in km^2." The first is arguably exogenous to indigenous social structure. The second may be a weak proxy for social diversity but in that case the correlation runs in the opposite direction from that which would be predicted from a social determinist perspective.

[3]In some cases, electoral laws can be changed by executive decree (as in Russia 1993) or popular initiative (as in the recent repeal of the senate electoral law in Italy), in which case the "winners" may not control the process of electoral change.

[4]I am thinking here of the uncertainty that European politicians faced upon the introduction of universal suffrage near the turn of the century, an uncertainty that seems to have played an important role in the introduction of PR. Cf. Carstairs (1980); Noiret (1990).

ceived as) hard-to-change and long-lived, however, the incentives they set in train are no longer discounted by the probability that the rules will change.

Social cleavages and the party system

Consider next the importance of social structure. As Taagepera and Grofman (1985:343) note, "it is much harder to find testable propositions" regarding social structure in the literature. Nonetheless, they believe that some in the literature can be taken "as standing for the proposition that 'the more axes of cleavage there are within a society, the greater will be the number of political parties.'" Nohlen (1993:27), for example, offers a thesis in which the number of social cleavages affects not just the number of political parties but also (following Grumm 1958) the nature of the electoral system a given country will possess:

> the greater the social fragmentation, the more probable is the adoption of a proportional [electoral] system and also the rise of a multiparty system. The greater the social homogeneity, the more probable is the adoption of the simple plurality system; but, also, the more probable is the rise of a two-party system ... or of a limited party pluralism.

Although a bit fuzzy, the idea that social cleavages condition the party system has considerable force and has spawned an entire literature in opposition to, or at least in tension with, the institutionalist literature. The prospects for a limited reconciliation of the institutionalist and sociological perspectives are, however, reasonably good. Two points in particular are worth noting at the outset.

First, to assert that social structure matters to the formation and competition of parties – which no one denies, when the point is stated in such a broad fashion – does not imply that electoral structures do not matter. To make this latter point, one has to adopt a rather extreme monocausalist perspective according to which the underlying cleavage structure of a society is so much more important than the details of electoral law that basically the same party system would arise regardless of the electoral system employed (cf. Cairns 1968:78). Does anyone believe that the United States would remain a two-party system, even if it adopted the Israeli electoral system?

Second, to assert that electoral structure affects party competition in important and systematic ways does not imply that social structure is irrelevant. It might appear that this is exactly what Duverger's Law does imply – bipartism in any society merely upon application of single-member districts – but in fact that overstates Duverger's proposition and the institutionalist development of it, where there has been an increasing appreciation of the interaction effects between social and electoral structure.

In the next two subsections, I expand on the two points just made. I first offer some systematic evidence that electoral structure matters, even controlling for social structure. Then I discuss how social and electoral structures might interact in the process of party formation and maintenance.

The importance of electoral institutions. In this section, I compare the number of parties competing (and winning) in elections to the upper and lower houses of those countries that possess elective upper chambers. If social cleavages drive the number of parties competing, with little strategic adjustment to electoral rules, then one should find essentially the same number of parties competing for votes in both house and senate elections, regardless of the electoral systems used in the two bodies. If, on the other hand, groups do adapt to the electoral environment, then there should be predictable differences in the number and effective number of competitors.

Comparing the number of parties in house and senate elections would seem to be a natural method of controlling for social diversity, as the society in which the elections are held is the same. Nonetheless, as far as I know no one has bothered actually to compute the numbers and make the comparisons. I do so by identifying all democratic countries that possessed elective upper chambers circa 1990, analyzing their electoral systems to arrive at an *a priori* expectation regarding the number of parties that should compete in house and senate elections, and then testing these expectations against the empirical record.

Circa 1990 there were 16 democratic countries that possessed elective upper chambers, consisting of 7 Latin American, 5 European, 2 Anglophone, and 2 Asian cases. In Table 2.1, I list these countries, along with a brief characterization of the electoral systems used in each house.[5] The middle column in the table indicates which system should have the larger number (or effective number) of parties. For example, in Australia the house and senate are both elected under single transferable vote (STV) rules but the senate districts all return more than one member, while the house districts are all single-member. Thus, one expects a greater number of parties competing in the Australian senate than in the Australian house.

Before proceeding, I should note four caveats about the predictions listed in Table 2.1. First, Uruguay is too complicated to yield a clear prediction – at least I have not been able to come to a clear *a priori* expectation. Second, the predictions I do make are merely ordinal: They state which chamber should have more parties, without stating how large a

[5]Fuller descriptions of the lower house electoral systems in most of these countries are given in Chapter 3.

difference in number there should be. In some cases, the difference would seem to be fairly large (e.g., Australia) while in others it would seem to be quite small (e.g., Belgium). Third, four of the countries listed employ a fused vote for legislative races. That is, voters have only one vote to cast for a slate that includes both house and senate (and sometimes presidential) candidates. For this reason, the prediction for these systems is necessarily different when it comes to votes as opposed to seats. The parties competing for house and senate seats, and the votes they receive, must be equal in fused vote systems; it is only in the translation of votes into seats that the two chambers can differ. Fourth, one would hardly expect that the party systems for house and senate elections would fully adapt to their respective electoral systems, in splendid isolation from one another. If a party can run and elect candidates under the more permissive system, it may decide to run candidates in the other system as well – not to win seats, perhaps, but to keep its electoral organization in good trim, to establish its blackmail potential, or for other reasons. In this case, the party system in each chamber should be influenced by that of the other, in such a way as to lessen observed differences.

Bearing these caveats in mind, Table 2.2 displays the (effective) number of parties winning seats. As can be seen, of the 15 countries with clear predictions, 14 (93%) show the expected difference in the effective number of parliamentary parties,[6] while 11 (73%) show the expected difference in the scalar number of parliamentary parties.[7] For countries with fused votes, the differences are purely mechanical effects. For the other countries, the difference presumably understates the mechanical effect due to strategic adaptation.

Table 2.3 displays the (effective) number of parties winning votes. Of the 12 countries with predictions, 11 (92%) show the expected difference in the effective number of elective parties, while 10 (83%) show the expected difference in the scalar number of elective parties. If one removes the fused vote systems from the analysis, since they must trivially agree with the prediction of equal numbers, there are 8 countries with predictions, of which 7 (88%) and 6 (75%), respectively, are in conformity with the prediction.

As noted above, not all of the comparisons contrived in Tables 2.2 and 2.3 are such that one expects a large difference in the number of parties; sometimes the electoral systems for house and senate are very simi-

[6]The only exception, the United States, is trivial in that the electoral systems for the house and senate are identical, the only difference (and the reason for the prediction) being that the house has a larger number of districts than the senate.

[7]The exceptions in terms of scalar number of parties are Belgium, Colombia, Poland, and Spain. Belgium is not much of an exception in that the house and senate have very similar electoral systems and are equal in the number of parties competing.

Table 2.1. Comparing the electoral rules for house and senate elections in sixteen countries, circa 1990

Country	*Electoral rules, house*	*Prediction*	*Electoral rules, senate*
Australia	STV with $M = 1$	<	STV with $M > 1$
Belgium	See Chapter 3.	>	Same as lower house system, with lower district magnitudes. Indirectly elected members excluded.
Bolivia[a]	PR with median magnitude = 13.	>	List plurality with $M = 3$.
Brazil	Open list PR with median magnitude = 11.	>	Plurality rule in 1- and 2-seat districts
Chile	Open list PR with $M = 2$. 60 electoral districts.	>	Open list PR with $M = 2$. 19 electoral districts.
Colombia	PR with median magnitude = 6.	<	PR with $M = 100$.
Dom. Republic[a]	PR with median magnitude = 2.	>	Plurality rule with $M = 1$.
Italy	See Chapter 3.	>	Similar to house system, with smaller district magnitudes.
Japan	SNTV with $M =$ 3, 4, or 5.	<	76 seats elected by SNTV with M between 1 and 4. 50 seats elected by PR with $M = 50$.
Philippines	Plurality rule with $M = 1$.	>	Nationwide plurality election of 12 senators. Each voter has 12 votes.
Poland	PR with median magnitude = 10.	>	Mostly 2-seat districts, voters having two votes each (non-cumulative), and the top two vote-getting candidates winning the seats.
Spain	PR with median magnitude = 5.	>	4-seat districts in which each voter casts 3 votes. Some indirectly elected members.
Switzerland	PR with median magnitude = 6.	>	Plurality rule with $M =$ 1 or 2.

Table 2.1. (cont.)

Country	*Electoral rules, house*	*Prediction*	*Electoral rules, senate*
U.S.	Plurality rule with $M = 1$.	>	Plurality rule with $M = 1$.
Uruguay[a]	See Chapter 3.	?	PR with $M = 30$.
Venezuela[a]	PR with district magnitudes varying according to population; up to 5 additional seats awarded on the basis of national vote totals.	>	Same system with lower district magnitudes ($M = 2$), fewer additional seats (3), and fewer total members to be elected.

[a]These countries have fused votes.

lar. This is the case, for example, in Belgium. Thus, although Belgium is technically an exception in terms both of the effective and the scalar number of elective parties, it is not much of an exception. On the other hand, not much difference should be expected in the United States or Chile, either, and so the "successes" there ought to be somewhat discounted too. On the whole, the pattern of evidence is consistent with the notion that different electoral systems do produce different party systems, even when used in the same society at the same time.

The interaction of social and electoral structure. Duverger took social structure more or less as a residual error, something that might perturb a party system away from its central tendency defined by electoral law. Later scholars, however, have considered the possibility that cleavage and electoral structures may interact. For example, two recent papers that take this tack – Kim and Ohn (1992) and Ordeshook and Shvetsova (1994) – both come to the conclusion that Duverger's institutionalist claims are conditioned by the nature of social cleavages.[8]

Kim and Ohn elaborate a point made previously by Sartori (1968), Rae (1971), and Riker (1982) in order to accommodate the Canadian

[8]Another paper that plies the same waters is Taagepera and Grofman (1985). They argue that Duverger's propositions work only if there is one dominant social cleavage, and even then they offer some emendations. The cleavages about which they talk, however, are really *politicized* cleavages, not all cleavages in the society, whether brought into political significance or not. Cf. Ordeshook and Shvetsova (1994:107).

Table 2.2. Comparing the number and effective number of parties winning seats in the house and senate of sixteen countries, circa 1990

Country	*ENPP – house*	*NPP – house*	*Pre-diction*	*ENPP – senate*	*NPP – senate*	*Year of house/ senate election*
Australia	2.03	3	<	2.57	5	1993
Belgium	8.28	13	>	8.24	13	1991
Bolivia[a]	3.92	5	>	3.43	4	1989
Brazil	8.6	19	>	5.5	6	1990
Chile	5.06	10	>	4.68	7	1989
Colombia	2.18	6	<	2.22	5	1990
Dom. Republic[a]	3.06	4	>	2.23	3	1990
Italy	5.60	10	>	3.88	5	1992
Japan	2.46	7	<	3.66	8	1990/ 1989
Philippines	3.46	7	>	2.42	5	1992
Poland	3.88	7	>	3.56	12	1993
Spain	2.67	11	>	2.58	14	1989
Switzerland	6.52	14	>	3.44	7	1987
U.S.	1.94	3	>	1.96	2	1992
Uruguay[a]	3.30	4	?	3.24	4	1989
Venezuela[a]	4.65	8	>	3.98	5	1988

Main Sources: Central Intelligence Agency 1994; Nohlen 1993; Mackie and Rose 1991. Different sources handle independent and minor party candidates or lists differently (e.g., one might group them all in a single 'other' category, another might separate 'independents' from 'minor parties'). These differences mean that one cannot use the data in the table to make confident comparisons between countries. I have tried, however, to ensure that the data for the house and senate from a given country are handled comparably, to ensure that that comparison is meaningful.

[a]These countries have fused votes.

exception to Duverger's Law (Canada has simple plurality elections yet a long-standing multiparty system). They point out that one of the suppositions underlying Duverger's Law – that small parties will be underrepresented under plurality rule in single-member districts – depends for its validity on the geographic distribution of voters. In particular, if a third party's supporters are concentrated in a particular region of the country, then they may be able to compete successfully as one of the two main parties locally, even while remaining a third party nationally. Thus, Duverger's Law holds only if the social cleavage structure is not charac-

Table 2.3. Comparing the number and effective number of parties winning votes in the house and senate races of sixteen countries, circa 1990

Country	*ENPV – house*	*NPV – house*	*Prediction*	*ENPV – senate*	*NPV – senate*	*Year of house/ senate election*
Australia	2.47	4	<	2.61	6	1993
Belgium	9.75	13	>	9.79	13	1991
Bolivia[a]	5.01	10	=	5.01	10	1989
Brazil	9.7	34	>			1990
Chile	7.22	19	>	5.43	17	1989
Colombia	2.22	8	<	2.26	7	1990
Dom. Republic[a]	3.92	4	=	3.92	4	1990
Italy	6.18	10	>	4.10	5	1992
Japan	2.91	8	<	4.47	10	1990/1989
Philippines	3.32	5	>	2.05	4	1992
Poland			>			1993
Spain	4.37	9	>			1989
Switzerland	6.80	18	>			1987
U.S.	2.07	3	>	1.99	2	1992
Uruguay[a]	3.37	5	=	3.37	5	1989
Venezuela[a]	3.36	9	=	3.36	9	1988

Main Sources: See Table 2.2.

[a]These countries have fused votes and therefore the numbers for the house and senate are identical.

terized by geographically concentrated minorities who might form the basis of a successful, albeit localized, third party.

Ordeshook and Shvetsova (1994) reanalyze Lijphart's (1990) data with an eye to clarifying how social structure matters in determining the number of parties. They find that the number of parties in a country increases with the diversity of the social structure and with the proportionality of the electoral structure, but also that these effects interact. Increasing the proportionality of an electoral system in a homogeneous society does not proliferate parties, whereas it does in heterogeneous societies. Similarly, increasing the diversity of the social structure in a non-proportional electoral system does not proliferate parties, whereas it does in a proportional system.

If institutionalists have sometimes explored the importance of social cleavages, it is no less true that those with primary interests in political sociology have also recognized some "institutional" constraints on the formation of parties. Meisel (1974) and Jaensch (1983, ch. 3), for example, are at pains to point out that not all social cleavages become politicized, and that even fewer become *particized* (i.e., made into important lines of partisan division). Both processes – politicization and particization – typically do not just happen; they require someone to push them along, someone with resources who can compete against other political entrepreneurs who may be attempting to prevent the politicization of that particular cleavage, or to activate others instead.

Taking both social cleavage structures and electoral structures into account, there are three key stages to consider when accounting for the level of vote or seat concentration observable in any particular polity. The first stage is the translation of social cleavages (here taken to be exogenous but obviously susceptible to political manipulation[9]) into partisan preferences. The second stage is the translation of partisan preferences into votes. The third stage is the translation of votes into seats.

In some institutionalist models, the first stage is not explored: There is an exogenously given number of parties with clear demarcating features (e.g., the position they adopt along an ideological dimension), so that voters' preferences over parties are easily deducible. No party ever fails to get votes because it is too poor to advertise its position; no would-be party ever fails to materialize because it does not have the organizational substrate (e.g., labor unions, churches) needed to launch a mass party. In an expanded view, of course, the creation of parties and the advertisement of their positions would be key points at which a reduction of the number of political players occurs. The multiplicity of possible or imaginable parties is reduced to an actual number of *launched* parties, then to a smaller number of *known* parties, even before the electorate produces an effective number of vote-getting parties, and the electoral mechanism produces an effective number of seat-winning parties.

The reduction of possible to launched parties depends on many things: the level of preexisting nonpolitical organization that can be turned to political advantage; monetary resources; media access; and so on. Thus, a religious cleavage with well-organized and well-financed churches on both sides (e.g., Evangelicals versus Pietists in the nineteenth-century United States) is more likely to be politically activated, other things equal, than a racial cleavage in which one side is poorly organized and poorly financed (e.g., whites versus Aborigines in Australia).

[9]Ethnic and linguistic identities can be manipulated. Laitin (1994), for example, gives an example of how British colonial policy gave tribal chieftans in Ghana an incentive to accentuate their linguistic differences.

The reduction of launched parties to known parties depends primarily on media access and money. It is unlikely that Screaming Lord Such's party in England would have done much better had it been even more widely known than it was but in principle lack of exposure is a stumbling block for many minor parties. Whether this stumbling block can be overcome may depend partly on strategic decisions by potential contributors: If all of them seek to avoid wasting their contributions on hopeless (because unknown) parties, then the party will remain unknown (because poor), hence helpless.

The reduction of known parties to voted-for parties is the domain of strategic voting. Even if known, a party still has to be viable in order to attract votes.

Finally, the reduction of voted-for parties to seat-winning parties is typically a mechanical feature of the electoral system. The only substantial exceptions occur in systems in which votes are not pooled across all candidates from a given party, as in Taiwan or Colombia. In these systems, the distribution of a party's vote support across its candidates or lists materially affects its seat allocation (Cox and Shugart N.d.).

It is obvious that social cleavages matter. Institutionalists now have a small start toward specifying what kinds of social cleavages matter, and how, under different kinds of electoral systems. If this line of research is continued within the institutionalist paradigm, then institutionalists and political sociologists may have more to say to one another in future. In any event, I think that the interaction between electoral systems and social cleavages merits further research.

2.2 NARROWING THE FOCUS

Having convinced the reader, hopefully, that the sociological critiques of Duverger's propositions do not compel their abandonment, the next step is to clarify the version of these propositions upon which I shall focus in the first part of the book. There are by now a good many versions of Duverger's propositions in the literature and they differ consequentially along at least two dimensions: whether the dependent variable is defined at the national/system level or at the district level; and whether the dependent variable concerns entry deterrence, post-entry winnowing of the field of candidates, or both. I shall discuss these two distinctions in turn.

The national versus the district level

For Duverger, the dependent variable in his Law and Hypothesis was the number of "serious" parties (somehow defined) at the national level. Most political sociologists also take a national view, a fact which may explain why many of them are underwhelmed by the evidence for Duverger's Law. For, if one looks only at the national level for evidence, one finds relatively few examples of electoral systems employing single-member districts and plurality rule. Ignoring small states (below 5,000,000 population), the list would as of 1992 include just seven democratic polities from Chapter 3's list of 77: Bangladesh, Canada, Nepal, New Zealand, the United Kingdom, the United States, and Zambia. To this list, one might add the Philippines and India (which fail to meet the criteria in 1992 but have substantial democratic experience). Of these nine, only the United States has recently had reasonably pure two-party electoral competition. Zambia is dominated by one party. The rest have multiparty electoral competition, and in most the "third" parties succeed in securing a significant presence in the legislature. Thus, by this accounting, there is no empirical regularity to explain.

In contrast to those who concentrate on the national level, there are also those who shift the focus of Duverger's Law to the district level. Duverger himself wrote that "the true effect of the simple-majority system is limited to *local* bi-partism," that is, "the creation of a two-party system inside *the individual constituency;* but the parties opposed may be different in different areas of the country" (Duverger 1955:223; italics added). Nonetheless, he attempted from that beginning to extend the argument to the national level, and of course stated his sociological laws at that level. Leys (1959) and Wildavsky (1959) were perhaps the first to question the validity of Duverger's extension, and to insist that his propositions operated only (in the case of Leys) or at best (in the case of Wildavsky) at the district level.

From a district-level perspective, Duverger's Law is supported every time one finds a district that is dominated by two parties. One can disaggregate even further and look not at a string of elections in a given district over time, and the pattern of party competition that characterizes that period, but instead at individual district elections. At this level of disaggregation (geographically to a single district, temporally to a single election), the relevant prediction is that the top two parties will together garner most of the votes in the election. The district-level evidence is not entirely unproblematic but nonetheless looks a good deal more impressive than does the national-level evidence.

In the first part of this book, I take a completely disaggregated view of electoral systems and their effects. That is, I focus on the processes whereby most district races end up with a limited number of viable candidates (or lists), rather than on the processes whereby polities end up with a limited number of viable parties. Connections between these two levels of analysis (e.g., how the strategies of national parties may perturb district results from what they might be were districts somehow insulated from national forces, how district-level incentives percolate up to the national level, etc.) are considered later.

Pre-entry versus post-entry politics

In addition to focusing on the district rather than the nation, I shall also focus on post-entry rather than pre-entry politics. In the post-entry period, after some number of candidates has entered the fray, the central question concerns the processes that winnow the field out – strategic voting, strategic contributing, and so forth. In the pre-entry period, before candidacies have been announced, the central question concerns the processes that deter entry – the major parties' nomination procedures (which facilitate coordination on a single nominee), the anticipation of failure by third-party and independent candidates, and so forth. Another way to put the distinction is that in the pre-entry period one watches as an indefinitely large field of potential candidates is reduced to a definite field of actual candidates, while in the post-entry period one watches as an actual number of entering candidates is reduced to a smaller effective number of vote-getting candidates.

The effective number of candidates, due to Laakso and Taagepera (1979), is the reciprocal of the Hirschman-Herfindahl index widely used in the industrial organization literature to measure how concentrated sales in a given industry are. It is now the standard measure of how concentrated vote shares are in electoral contests.[10] If there are K actual candidates in a race, the maximum possible effective number of candidates is also K (a value attained when all K candidates garner a 1/K share of the votes). As votes concentrate on a smaller number of candidates, the effective number of parties falls below the actual number. If votes concentrate to the point that only two candidates get any, an extreme version of Duverger's prediction, then the effective number of parties will be bounded above by 2. If voters merely tend to concentrate on two candidates, then the effective number may be somewhat above 2.

2.3 THEORETICAL EXPLANATIONS OF DUVERGER'S PROPOSITIONS

Given our theoretical focus – upon single elections in particular districts, after the field of candidates has been established – the pertinent question

[10] If v_i is the vote share of the *i*th candidate, the effective number of candidates is $1/\Sigma v_i^2$.

for Duverger's Law is as follows. Why do voters in one-seat districts (in which each has a single vote to cast, the candidate with the most votes winning) tend to concentrate their suffrages on only two candidates?

One answer is strategic voting. Instrumentally rational voters eschew wasting their votes on hopeless candidacies, preferring instead to transfer their support to some candidate with a serious chance of winning. As long as everybody agrees on which are the hopeless candidacies, strategic voting will mean that votes concentrate on the serious candidates, of whom there will usually be just two in equilibrium (see Chapter 4).

Another whole set of answers can be generated by noting that *any* class of agents (not just voters but also opinion leaders, contributors, party officials, etc.) will tend to allocate whatever resources they control (not just votes but also endorsements, money, campaign appearances, etc.) to serious rather than to hopeless candidates. All that one needs for this conclusion is that the agents in question be instrumentally rational – that is, motivated primarily by a desire to affect the outcome. For then contributions to hopeless candidacies will be pointless, as they are unlikely to affect the outcome.[11]

Scholars disagree over which of these two causal mechanisms – strategic voting in the mass electorate or strategic contributing in the elite strata – is the more important. On the one hand, some argue that strategic voting is irrational, given the infinitesimal chance that a single vote will affect the outcome, and conclude that most of the action must be at the elite level (see Meehl 1977; Riker 1982:764). On the other hand, there is considerable evidence that voters do behave strategically, and at least one study (Gunther 1989) finds elites bungling their strategic role.

In my view, both kinds of resource concentration are important. Elites typically act first: Contributions and endorsements are sought before votes are. If elites coordinate fully, on just two candidates, then the voters are left with a binary choice and, accordingly, vote sincerely. If the elite strata fail to coordinate fully, then a multicandidate field will typically be further winnowed by strategic voting within the electorate (typically instigated by the prospective elite beneficiaries).

2.4 STRATEGIC VOTING AND THE NUMBER OF VIABLE COMPETITORS

Long ago Leys (1959:139) and Sartori (1968:278) argued that strategic voting should appear even under PR systems, to the extent that those sys-

[11] It is true that contributions large enough to single-handedly convert hopeless into serious candidacies may still be instrumentally rational; but few agents control such resources.

tems embodied significant departures from pure proportionality (due to small district magnitudes, high thresholds, or large premiums awarded to major parties). Leys put the matter as follows: "Although most writers seem to assume that [strategic voting] has no place in the analysis of any PR system, a weakened [form of strategic voting] may be highly plausible" (p. 139). Sartori advanced a very similar thesis, noting that "the influence of PR [through its encouragement of strategic voting] merely represents an enfeeblement of the same influence that is exerted by the plurality systems." Both authors thus placed single-member simple plurality systems and the various real-world PR systems on a continuum as regards their tendency to reduce the number of viable political parties below the theoretical benchmark number that would flourish under a purely proportional system (see also Rae 1971:141–43).

Part II of this book generalizes Leys' and Sartori's claim. Vote concentration due to the strategic diversion of resources away from hopeless candidates is not unique to single-member districts operating under Anglo-American rules. *Any* electoral system can be characterized by an equilibrium upper bound on the number of candidates (or party lists), such that if the actual number exceeds this upper bound there is a tendency for instrumentally rational voters to concentrate on a smaller number. In the remainder of this section, I shall informally sketch out the steps through which one must go in order to identify the equilibrium upper bound of candidates (lists) implied by strategic voting. Following chapters formalize the argument for a certain number of electoral systems.

The first step in identifying the equilibrium number of candidates (lists) for a particular electoral system is to ask how many candidates (or lists) one would expect to be seriously in the running for a seat (or seats). Given instrumentally rational voters, if a candidate (list) is *not* seriously in the running, then he (it) will lose support. Thus, whenever the number of candidates (lists) exceeds the number that can plausibly be seriously in the running for a seat, one expects some of the candidates (lists) to suffer from strategic desertion by their followers.

So how does one decide how many candidates (lists) can be "seriously in the running" in a given electoral system? The most obvious answer regarding candidates running in M-seat districts under plurality rule (top M finishers get seats) is $M + 1$. This answer is defended at length in Chapter 5, but to get a preliminary idea of why $M + 1$ might be the right answer, consider a race between $K > M$ candidates for $M = 5$ seats. Suppose first that the rules of election are those once employed in Japan: Each voter casts a single nontransferable vote, the five candidates with the most votes winning seats. There are two ways that a voter in such a system can "waste" her vote: She can vote for an almost-sure loser; or she can vote for an almost-sure winner. Neither vote is likely to improve the outcome from what it would otherwise have been had the voter abstained. Thus, instrumentally rational voters will avoid both kinds of waste, sending their votes to the "marginal" candidates – those who have, relative to nonmarginal candidates, a large probability of being tied for *M*th, hence of being on the edge between winning and losing.

Imagine now that a random sample of voters is polled and it is found that the proportion of the electorate intending to vote for candidate j is π_j, where candidate labels are chosen so that $\pi_j \geq \pi_j+1$ for all $j < K$. If $\pi_{M+1} > \pi_{M+2}$, and the gap between $M + 1$ and $M + 2$ is large relative to the sampling error in the poll, then $M + 2$'s probability of being tied for *M*th is infinitesimal, relative to $M + 1$'s. Voters can quite confidently count $M + 2$ out (as, for that matter, can contributors, party leaders, and so forth). Any resources controlled by instrumental agents will therefore flow away from $M + 2$ and toward the marginal candidates (which set includes, in equilibrium, the top $M + 1$ candidates). Thus, to the extent that the gap between the first loser ($M + 1$) and the second loser ($M + 2$) is "noticeable," one expects voters (and other contributors) to concentrate their resources on the strongest $M + 1$ candidates.

Now suppose that the rules are changed to largest remainders with the Hagenbach-Bischoff quota ($Q = V/(M + 1)$, where V is the total number of votes cast for all lists). How many lists will be serious contenders? We can again identify the *candidates* in order of their chances at winning a seat and being marginal (tied for *M*th). For example, the lead candidate on a list for which the expected vote share exceeds the quota is likely to win, and becomes virtually certain to win as the sampling error in the poll declines. The third candidate on a list with expected share less than $2Q$ is virtually certain to lose (again, as the sampling error declines). And so forth.

Well-informed instrumental voters in this system will avoid voting for a list that has no chance at a seat. They will concentrate instead on lists in competition for the last-allocated remainder seat, where their votes are most likely to improve the outcome. This leads to a prediction of at most $M + 1$ serious lists.

All of these predictions about the equilibrium number of candidates and lists need to be hedged in various ways. Suffice it to say here that they all depend on two key theoretical assumptions – one an assumption about voters' motivations, one an assumption about voters' expectations. Although closely approximated in some empirical instances, enough to make the theory interesting, these assumptions are certainly not universal. Indeed, part of the value of the formal modeling to follow is that it identifies potentially measurable variables that should, in addition to electoral structure, affect the incidence of strategic voting. All this will be elaborated in the appropriate chapters.

2.5 OUTLINE OF PART II

Part II of the book, which commences with the next chapter, considers strategic voting in each of the three main electoral systems that Duverger originally studied, as well as in various systems that he did not study. Chapter 3 sets the stage for the analysis by discussing electoral systems in general, providing a snapshot of the full range of systems in use circa 1992 in democratic elections, and suggesting informally some of the ways in which different features of these systems facilitate strategic voting or (something which is more pertinent to later parts of the book) strategic entry and alliance formation. Chapters 4, 5, and 6 investigate strategic voting in single-member districts operating under several single-ballot voting procedures (4), multimember districts operating under various forms of proportional representation (5), and single-member districts operating under dual-ballot procedures (6). Each of the analytical chapters includes, in addition to comments on the formal model and associated equilibrium results, a review of relevant literature pertaining to the systems under discussion. Two of the chapters (4 and 5) present original empirical evidence as well.

When put together, the picture that emerges from Part II is very much in accord with the Leys-Sartori conjecture. There is a continuum of systems, ranging from those in which strategic voting imposes a constraining upper bound, to those in which it imposes a rarely-constraining or unconstraining upper bound, on the number of parties.

Part II closes with a discussion (in Chapter 7) of two themes that are largely ignored in the institutionalist view of electoral politics. First, I argue that a proper understanding of the institutionalist results implies that the number of candidates/lists that compete in a system will be an interactive product of both social diversity and the permissiveness of the electoral rules. This leads into the empirical analysis of Chapter 11. Second, I note that there are modalities of strategic voting that do not operate to the detriment of small or weak parties, and that some electoral systems promote these kinds of strategic voting rather than the classic "wasted vote" kind.

PART II

Strategic voting

3

On electoral systems

The primary purpose of this chapter is to develop a consistent set of abstract, non-country-specific terms that can be used to describe and classify electoral systems, especially as regards their coalition-promoting or -retarding properties. Most of the terms I use already appear in the literature, but I have found it necessary to introduce several new terms, or new usages of old terms, for the sake of clarity and consistency. Throughout the chapter, I use the term "structure" to denote a "subsystem" within the electoral system. Thus, I refer to a system's district structure (having to do with the number, size, and nature of electoral districts), its alliance structure (having to do largely with opportunities to pool votes), and even its formulaic structure (having to do with the multiplicity of different electoral formulas that can appear at different levels in a system).

Another purpose of this chapter is to give some idea of the recent state of the art in electoral design. I have taken a "snapshot" sample of the world's democracies: all 77 polities that scored either a 1 or 2 on the "political rights" index in the *Freedom House* survey for 1992-3.[1] This sample excludes some countries with long democratic traditions, such as India and Venezuela, that have hit hard times more recently. It also includes about a dozen countries that have only held free and fair elections very recently, have little democratic experience, and have by no means emerged as consolidated democracies. Examples include Benin, Cape Verde, and Mali in Africa, Bulgaria, Lithuania, and Slovenia in Eastern Europe. Finally, some of the countries in the sample had already slipped below the threshold score (of 2) in the next available *Freedom House* survey for 1993-94: Brazil, the Dominican Republic, Honduras,

[1]For a similarly synoptic description of electoral systems in an even larger sample of nations, see Blais and Massicotte (N.d.). For a pioneering effort to classify the world's electoral systems, that provides generally a greater depth of discussion on each system, see Nohlen (1981). Other sources are cited in the tables and Appendix A.

Nepal, Slovakia, Turkey, and Zambia. The sample thus covers *all* qualifying democracies – whether new and possibly ephemeral, old and presumably stable, or somewhere in between – as of 1992. For each country in the sample, I have attempted to provide a full description of the electoral system.[2]

An "electoral system" is understood here to be a set of laws and party rules that regulate electoral competition between and within parties. Electoral systems have many aspects, and can govern elections to many offices – executive, legislative, and judicial – simultaneously. Here I shall focus on the legislative electoral system and four of its aspects: those laws and rules regulating how parties make their nominations; how citizens vote and how those votes are counted; what the district structure of the polity will be; and how counted votes are translated into seats. The second, third, and fourth of these aspects are determined by electoral law, the first by a combination of law and party regulations.

3.1 HOW PARTIES NOMINATE

In some polities there are no laws regulating how parties make their nominations; everything is left to the parties themselves to decide. This was the case, for example, in the United States for most of the nineteenth century. There are, however, many ways that the state can get involved. Turn-of-the-century laws require U.S. parties to decide their nominations by direct primary elections of various kinds, with profound consequences (cf. Epstein 1986). The German *Wahlgesetz* (Electoral Law) contains detailed prescriptions regarding how parties make nominations, intended to ensure that their procedures are democratic. The Brazilian *candidato nato* clause requires that parties renominate their incumbent federal deputies, should the deputies so wish. As Mainwaring (1991:25) puts it, "a politician can violate all of the party's programmatic concerns, consistently vote against the leadership, and still be guaranteed a place on the ballot."

What features of nomination are relevant depends on the problem at hand. If one is interested in strategic voting and electoral coalition, as here, the relevant laws are those regulating fusion candidacies (in plurality/majority systems) and joint lists (in PR systems). Fusion candidacies,

[2]The rest of the book certainly does not deal with all of the 77 electoral systems canvassed here. Neither is the book limited to these systems. The current chapter provides a systematic overview of the range of electoral possibilities, with later chapters carving out particular parts of this range for deeper scrutiny. Those already familiar with the "range of possibilities" may wish to skim or skip this chapter, using the index when they come across unfamiliar terms in later chapters.

wherein the candidate is nominated by more than one party, were common in state elections in the nineteenth-century United States (Argersinger 1980) and are currently allowed, for example, in New York (Scarrow 1985) and Hungary (Tóka N.d.). Joint lists are similarly those supported by more than one party, typically including candidates from all participating parties.[3] Thus, for example, the Israeli list submitted under the name of *Maarach* (Alignment) in the 1969 elections contained candidates from both *Mapai* and *Achdut Haavoda* (Aronoff 1978:122). Both fusion and joint listing allow small parties to survive in alliance with a partner, as will be seen in succeeding chapters.

In some systems, joint lists face higher threshold requirements than single-party lists. The Czech Republic and Slovakia, for example, both require joint lists to pass a higher threshold than single-party lists before they are eligible to participate in seat distributions above the constituency level (on which, see Section 3.4).

Yet other systems outlaw joint lists. Of course it may not be difficult to create "front" parties that serve the same purpose. Thus, for example, the Chilean system of 1973 banned joint lists, but this just prompted two transparent evasions of the law – in the form of *Unidad Popular* and *el Code,* organizations that Tagle (1993:329) has called *partidos de fachada* (façade parties).

Nonetheless, if it is costly to form a new party, then outlawing joint lists may have some effect. Consider, for example, the costs of forming a new party in Bolivia. Under the electoral reforms passed in 1986 all political parties, fronts, and alliances must register with the *Corte Nacional Electoral,* establishing their status as persons for legal purposes. Whereas previously existing groups polling at least 50,000 votes (a bit less than 3% of the vote) in the preceding election automatically qualified, new groups were required to submit a list of members *certified by a notary public* that showed them to possess a membership equal to at least .5% of the vote in the latest national election. A Bolivian jurist opposed to the reforms has argued that no notary would simply stamp an already completed membership list; they would need to certify the

[3]Joint lists typically appear on the ballot just once, with all the participating parties' names or symbols indicated together. With this ballot format it is not possible to determine where the votes for the joint list are coming from – from party A's supporters? from party B's? – if the list is closed. If the ballot is laid out so that joint lists appear as many times as there are sponsoring parties, however, then voters can vote for the AB joint list either under the A or the B symbol. The vote contributions of the various alliance partners to the joint list can thus be monitored. This system of "multiple-appearance joint listing" is rare but was used, for example, in the 1986 and 1990 elections in the Dominican Republic (and maybe in the 1994 elections as well). I thank Mark Jones for bringing this to my attention.

physical existence of each one of about 8,641 persons (approximately .5% of the last election's total vote) affirming their allegiance to the new party. This would entail about $43,205 in notarial fees, not to mention the logistical difficulties in getting everyone to the notary (or notaries) to begin with (Miranda Pacheco 1986:31-32). Obviously, if this analysis is correct, new parties need to find sympathetic notaries public in Bolivia – willing to give a group rate! For present purposes, however, the point is this: Given the cost of forming a new party, if the Bolivians were to outlaw joint lists, then presumably setting up a front party would not be so attractive an option as it was in Chile in 1973.

3.2 HOW CITIZENS VOTE AND HOW THEIR VOTES ARE COUNTED

There are many different ways to vote. I shall make an initial distinction between single-ballot systems, in which voters vote just once, and multiballot systems, in which two or more rounds of voting may be entailed. Since multiballot methods are built up out of single-ballot methods, I shall begin with the latter.

Voting in single-ballot systems can take a variety of forms: writing out the name of a candidate, checking a box next to a party's name or symbol, pulling a lever, punching a hole in a computer punch card, writing a sequence of numerals in boxes next to candidates' names, and so forth. These different physical actions become abstractly similar when they are counted and thereby reduced to various numerical vote totals. Not all vote totals are created equal, of course. Some totals, such as the sum of all votes cast for candidates whose last names begin with the letter "S," are irrelevant to any further operation of the electoral system. Other vote totals, however, form the basis upon which seats are awarded to candidates, lists, or cartels (on which see below). These vote totals – those that figure in the mathematical operations by which seats are allocated – I shall call *seat-relevant* vote totals.

Three questions are fundamental in sorting through the single-ballot voting methods actually in use, or proposed for use, in democratic elections:

1. For what entities does the voter vote? Sometimes citizens vote for candidates only, sometimes for party lists only, and sometimes they have the option to do either or both.
2. How many votes may each voter cast? The number of *candidate* votes (i.e., votes cast for individual candidates) each voter possesses can range from one to the total number of candidates competing.

Box 3.1: The pooling vote in Finland and Poland

Voters in Finland and Poland cast their votes for individual candidates. Once cast, however, these votes can pool at two different levels. First, candidates join together in lists (known as "electoral alliances" in Finland). Seats are allocated to lists before they are allocated to candidates, on the basis of *list* vote totals arrived at by summing the votes of all candidates within the list. This is the first kind of pooling that can occur. In Poland, *apparentement* (or "blocking") of lists is allowed: Lists can join together in cartels for the purpose of seat distributions (see Section 3.4). Seats are allocated to cartels before they are allocated to the lists within the cartel, on the basis of *cartel* vote totals arrived at by summing the votes of all lists within the cartel. Thus, in Poland, candidate votes can pool at two levels: within lists, and within cartels. The closest approximation to the second kind of pooling in Finland does not entail further vote pooling *sensu strictu*. Finnish parties can run joint lists, with candidates from more than one party on the list. This has some of the same political consequences for small parties as does allowing *apparentement* in Poland.

Similarly, the number of *list* votes each voter possesses can range from one to the total number of lists competing.[4]

3. What seat-relevant vote totals are affected by the vote(s) cast? If each voter casts one vote, then a basic distinction is between votes that affect only a single seat-relevant vote total (exclusive votes) and those that can affect more than one seat-relevant vote total (nonexclusive). If each voter casts more than one vote, then how those votes affect seat-relevant vote totals can be described in terms of whether cumulation, plumping, and/or panachage are allowed.

Further discussion will clarify the meaning of the terms – exclusive vote, cumulative vote, etc. – introduced in the preceding paragraphs. Consider first those systems in which voters cast a single vote for a candidate. An *exclusive* candidate vote is one that benefits *only* the candidate for whom it is cast. Such a vote increases the vote total of the candidate for whom it is cast and never transfers to, or otherwise appears in, any other vote total that is used for purposes of seat allocation. Single exclusive votes are cast in ordinary Anglo-American single-member districts wherever they are used, e.g., in Antigua and Barbuda, India, and

[4]Theoretically, both the number of candidate votes and the number of list votes might exceed the number of candidates or lists competing, but I shall not consider such systems here.

New Zealand. They have also been cast in Japan and South Korea under the name of the single nontransferable vote, and still are in Taiwan.[5]

A *nonexclusive* candidate vote, in addition to appearing in the vote total of the candidate for whom it is cast, also affects other vote totals used in the allocation of legislative seats. There are three main types of nonexclusive vote in current use: the transferable vote, which transfers to the vote total of another individual candidate (who may or may not be politically allied with the candidate originally receiving the vote); the pooling vote, which transfers to the vote total of the party list to which the candidate originally voted for belongs; and the fused vote, which simultaneously affects the vote totals of candidates running for two or more different offices. Nonexclusive candidate votes that transfer to *candidate* vote totals are cast in Australia, Ireland, Malta, and Nepal (in the Senate) under the name of the single transferable vote (STV). Nonexclusive candidate votes that transfer to *list* vote totals are cast in Brazil, Chile (1958–73 and 1989–present), Finland, Liechtenstein, Poland (see Box 3.1), and formerly in West Germany (1949). There is no term for this latter kind of vote in the literature; I shall call it a *pooling* vote.

By a *fused* vote I mean one similar to that long used in Uruguay, where voters cast a single vote for a slate that includes a candidate for the presidency as well as candidates for the Senate and the lower house. The Uruguayan fused vote simultaneously affects three separate vote totals: one relevant to determining who the president will be, one relevant to filling Senate seats, and one relevant to filling House seats. Split-ticket voting, in the sense of supporting one party's presidential candidate while voting for another's congressional candidates, is thus not technically possible. Bolivia and Honduras also currently have fused votes. Venezuela had a fused vote for various legislative offices until the electoral reforms of 1993. The Dominican Republic has used a legislative-executive fused vote frequently in the past. The old party-strip ballot in the United States was similar in that it was difficult for voters to split their votes across statewide offices (Burnham 1965; Rusk 1970; although see Reynolds 1995). And of course the United States still has a (constitutionally mandated) fused vote that links presidential and vice presidential candidates from the same party.

Consider now the possibility that voters cast *multiple* candidate votes. I shall ignore the possibility that different voters dispose of different numbers of votes – as has occurred for example under plural voting provisions in the United Kingdom, Belgium, and the United States – and focus on the issues of plumping, panachage, and cumulation. That *plumping* is

[5]The only other countries that use the single nontransferable vote system, of which I am aware, are Jordan, Malawi (according to Blais and Massicotte N.d.), and possibly Vanuatu (in this case, my sources are not very clear).

Box 3.2: Plumping and panachage (split voting) in nineteenth-century England

Many English constituencies before passage of the third Reform Act in 1884 returned two members to the House of Commons. Each voter possessed two votes that he (the suffrage was restricted to men) could cast in any way he wished, short of cumulation. An example of the possibilities is given in the returns from the election of 1874 in Pontefract (see Cox 1987a:96). Two Conservative candidates, Waterhouse and Pollington, faced a single Liberal, Childers. 699 voters plumped for Childers: that is, they gave one of their votes to Childers, and abstained from using the other. 60 voters plumped for Waterhouse and 37 plumped for Pollington, indicating that some Conservative voters saw significant distinctions between the two Conservative candidates. 619 voters cast a partisan double vote: giving one vote to each of the two Conservative candidates. Another 235 voters took advantage of the possibility of panachage, or splitting their votes across party lines: 182 gave one vote to each of Childers and Waterhouse, while 53 gave one vote to each of Childers and Pollington. (In the event, the Liberal Childers and the more moderate Conservative Waterhouse both won seats, Waterhouse benefiting in particular from the large number of split votes that the two shared.)

allowed means voters need not use all of their votes: they can partially abstain. That *panachage* is allowed means voters need not vote only for candidates of a single party: they can split their votes.[6] That *cumulation* is allowed means voters who cast *m* votes need not vote for *m* candidates: they can give more than one of their votes to a single candidate.

To illustrate these terms, suppose voters can cast as many votes as there are candidates, with plumping and panachage (but not cumulation) allowed. This is the approval voting method in which voters can vote for as many candidates as they "approve," but need not use all their votes, need not confine them to candidates of a given party, and cannot give more than one of them to any single candidate (Brams and Fishburn 1983). Alternatively, suppose voters can cast as many votes as there are seats to be filled, with plumping and panachage (but not cumulation) allowed. Such a system was used, for example, in U.K. parliamentary

[6]The term "panachage" is typically used in regard to systems in which (1) voters can vote for lists as well as candidates; and (2) candidate votes pool to the list level. I extend use of the term here to include systems in which voters vote only for candidates, and candidate votes do not pool. In such systems, panachage is *always* allowed, as far as I know. It would in principle be possible to outlaw it, however.

elections before the third Reform Act (Cox 1987a), in many state elections in the nineteenth- and early twentieth-century United States (Klain 1955; Hamilton 1967), and in India from 1952 to 1957 (in about a third of the districts). Finally, suppose voters can cast as many votes as there are seats to be filled, with panachage (but neither plumping nor cumulation) allowed. This is the system that has been employed in Mauritius since its independence in 1968.[7]

The terms just reviewed are used similarly when speaking of list, rather than candidate, votes. Suppose, for example, that voters possess a single list vote. If this vote affects only the vote total of the list for which it is cast, then it is exclusive. If it affects other vote totals used in the allocation of seats, then it is nonexclusive. The only kind of nonexclusive list vote in current use is of a pooling variety: The vote cast for list X may pool with the votes of other lists – *Y* and *Z*, say – that are allied with *X* in a cartel (on cartels, see Section 3.4). The process is analogous to the pooling *to lists* of votes cast for individuals in Brazil and Finland.

Having described the range of possibilities, I turn now to a description of actual voting practice in the lower houses of the 77 countries judged by *Freedom House* to have democratic elections circa 1992 (Table 3.1). Voting options are described in terms of the number of *candidate* and *list* votes each voter may cast, along with the nature of restrictions on those votes.

Systems with closed lists can be easily identified in Table 3.1 by looking in the "candidate votes" column: If there is a zero in this column, then necessarily there will be a unity in the "list votes" column and, as there will be no basis other than the order of names on the list to decide which candidates get the seats allocated to the list, the list will be closed. Systems with flexible lists are those with at least one candidate vote in addition to a list vote. Finally, systems with open lists have no list vote but a pooling candidate vote. (The terms *closed, flexible,* and *open* are defined in Section 4.3.)

The second column in Table 3.1, labeled "vote type," shows that most candidate votes in lower house elections are exclusive. Transferable votes are cast only in Australia, Ireland, Malta, and Nauru. Pooling votes are cast in Belgium, Brazil, Chile, Denmark, Finland, Hungary, Italy, Liechtenstein, Luxembourg, the Netherlands, Poland, and Switzerland. The candidate votes in the Netherlands and Belgium do truly yeoman service, both pooling to the list level and transferring among candidates

[7]The term "plumping" is used in regard to Mauritian elections (e.g., by Mannick 1989) to mean voting for one or two serious candidates, then wasting the remaining votes (all Mauritian constituencies, Rodrigues aside, are three-member ones) on a clearly hopeless candidate. This accomplishes the same end as would ordinary plumping, in which the voter would be able simply not to use the second or third votes.

Table 3.1. *Voting options in 77 democracies*

Country	*Candidate votes*	*Vote type*	*Panachage?*	*Plumping?*	*Cumulation?*	*List votes*	*Vote type*
ARGENTINA	0					1	exclusive
AUSTRALIA	1	transferable	yes			0	
AUSTRIA	1	exclusive				1	exclusive
Bahamas	1	exclusive				0	
BANGLADESH	1	exclusive				0	
Barbados	1	exclusive				0	
BELGIUM	1[a]	pooling				1	exclusive
Belize	1	exclusive				0	
BENIN	0					1	exclusive
BOLIVIA	0					1	pooling[b]
BOTSWANA	1	exclusive				0	
BRAZIL	1	pooling				1	exclusive
BULGARIA	0					1	exclusive
CANADA	1	exclusive				0	
Cape Verde	0					1	exclusive
CHILE	1	pooling				0	
COLOMBIA	0					1	exclusive
COSTA RICA	0					1	exclusive
Cyprus (Greek)	1-5[c]	exclusive				1	exclusive
CZECH REPUBLIC	4	exclusive				1	exclusive
DENMARK	1	pooling				1	exclusive
Dominica	1	exclusive				0	
DOMINICAN REPUBLIC	0					1	exclusive
ECUADOR	0					1[d]	exclusive
FINLAND	1	pooling				0	
FRANCE	1	exclusive				0	
The Gambia	1	exclusive				0	
GERMANY	1	exclusive				1	exclusive
GREECE	1-3[e]	exclusive				1	exclusive
Grenada	1	exclusive				0	
HONDURAS	0					1	fused[f]
HUNGARY	1	exclusive				1	exclusive
Iceland	0[g]					1	exclusive
IRELAND	1	transferable	yes			0	
ISRAEL	0					1	pooling
ITALY (pre-reform)	3-4[h]	pooling[i]		yes		1	exclusive
JAMAICA	1	exclusive				0	
JAPAN (1947–93)	1	exclusive				0	
Kiribati							
KOREA, SOUTH	1	exclusive				0	
Liechtenstein	1	pooling				1	exclusive

Table 3.1. (cont.)

Country	Candidate votes	Vote type	Panachage?	Plumping?	Cumulation?	List votes	Vote type
LITHUANIA	1	exclusive				1	exclusive
Luxembourg	M	pooling	yes	yes	yes	1	exclusive[j]
MALI	0					1	exclusive
Malta	1	transferable	yes			0	
Marshall Islands							
MAURITIUS	M	exclusive	yes			0	
Micronesia	1	exclusive				0	
NAMIBIA	0					1	exclusive
Nauru	1	transferable	yes			0	
NEPAL	1	exclusive				0	
NETHERLANDS	1	pooling				0	
NEW ZEALAND	1	exclusive				0	
NORWAY	0[k]					1	exclusive
PAPUA NEW GUINEA	1	exclusive				0	
POLAND	1	pooling				0	
PORTUGAL	0					1	exclusive
St. Kitts-Nevis	1	exclusive				0	
St. Lucia	1	exclusive				0	
St. Vincent & the Grenadines	1	exclusive				0	
San Marino						1[l]	exclusive
São Tomé and Príncipe	0					1	exclusive
SLOVAKIA	4	exclusive				1	exclusive
SLOVENIA	1[m]	exclusive				1	exclusive
Solomon Islands	1	exclusive				0	
SPAIN	0					1	exclusive
SWEDEN	0					1	pooling[n]
SWITZERLAND	M	pooling	yes	yes	yes	1	exclusive
TRINIDAD and TOBAGO	1	exclusive				0	
TURKEY	0					1	exclusive
Tuvalu	M	exclusive	yes	yes		0	
UNITED KINGDOM	1	exclusive				0	
UNITED STATES	1	exclusive				0	
URUGUAY	0					1	pooling[o]
Vanuatu	1	exclusive				0	
Western Samoa	1	exclusive				0	
ZAMBIA	1	exclusive				0	

Table 3.1. (cont.)

Notes:

The columns of this table dealing with whether a system allows panachage, plumping, and cumulation are left blank if these options are irrelevant to the system in question, or if the options are relevant but not allowed; a "yes" in these columns indicates that the option is allowed. Countries with populations less than one million are listed with an initial capital letter followed by lower-case letters; larger countries are listed using capital letters throughout.

[a]Voters in Belgium may cast one preferential vote for a list candidate and one preferential vote for a supplemental candidate, so in that sense they have two candidate votes. See Dewachter 1983, p. 95.

[b]Bolivians cast a fused vote: They have one vote, which they cast for a slate including presidential, senatorial, and chamber candidates. See Nohlen 1993.

[c]Greek Cypriot voters have one preference vote for every four seats to be filled in the constituency.

[d]Ecuadorian voters vote once for a provincial list and once for a national list. In this sense they have two list votes.

[e]As of the election of November 5, 1989, preference votes were cast as follows. In the first and second districts of Athens, voters could cast preference votes for one, two, or three candidates. In the first district of Thessaloniki, voters could cast one or two preference votes. In the remaining constituencies, voters were entitled to express one preference. Leaders of parties or alliances and former prime ministers are deemed to have secured as many preference votes as ballots cast for their party lists in the constituency concerned.

[f]Hondurans cast one vote for both the presidential and the congressional election. See Nohlen 1993, p. 396.

[g]Icelandic voters can change the order of the names on the lists presented by their parties, but over half the voters must make the same alterations in order to have any effect. See Helgason 1991.

[h]Italian voters could cast three preference votes in constituencies returning up to 15 members, and four preference votes in larger constituencies.

[i]See Amoroso 1979, p. 164.

[j]The Luxembourg list vote is equivalent to voting once for each of the M candidates on the list. It thus might be said to pool "downward" (to candidates) but it does not pool "upward" (to cartels).

[k]Norwegian voters can change the order of the names on the lists presented by their parties, but over half the voters must make the same alterations in order to have any effect.

[l]The Inter-Parliamentary Union (1993, p. 71) reports that "voters indicate their preferences either for a list or for a maximum of six candidates."

[m]Slovenians cast a kind of fused vote due to the rules governing nominations. Each constituency is divided into *M* "electoral districts," where *M* is the number of seats in the constituency. Each party must, in the simplest case, nominate *M* candidates and legally associate each of them with exactly one of the electoral districts in the constituency. After seats have been allocated to party lists, they are allocated to candidates on the list in order of "their" votes – that is, the votes that the party list got in the district in which the candidate stood.

[n]The vote pooling occurs over multiple lists from a given party, not over lists from different parties. See Särlvik 1983, p. 134.

[o]The vote pooling occurs over multiple lists from a given *sub-lema* (faction), and over *sub-lemas* within a given *lema* (party), not over lists from different parties. The Uruguayan vote is fused, simultaneously affecting the presidential, congressional, and senate races.

service, both pooling to the list level and transferring among candidates on a given list.[8]

The "vote type" column for list votes is read as follows. If the vote type is exclusive, then votes for a given list benefit only that list. If the vote type is pooling, then votes for a given list can pool within "cartels" to which the list belongs, a possibility discussed in greater detail in Section 3.4. As can be seen, pooling list votes are used in Israel, the Netherlands, and Switzerland (where they pool across parties; cf Lijphart 1994:134) and in Sweden and Uruguay (where they pool within parties). In addition, the candidate vote in Poland, as previously noted (Box 3.1), pools not just to the list but also to the cartel level.

3.3 DISTRICT STRUCTURE

The district structure of an electoral system refers to the number and magnitude of all electoral districts used in that system – where an electoral district is defined as a geographic area within which votes are aggregated and seats allocated and a district's magnitude is the number of representatives it is entitled to elect.[9] If a district cannot be partitioned into smaller districts within which votes are aggregated and seats allocated, it is called *primary.* Thus, for example, the districts used in U.S. House elections are all primary. Although these districts are divided into smaller subdistricts for purposes of vote administration and counting (aggregation), no seats are attached to or allocated within the subdistricts, thus they do not count as "electoral districts" as defined here. Systems possessing only primary electoral districts are typically called *single-tier* in the literature.

A secondary electoral district is an electoral district that can be partitioned into two or more primary electoral districts. Usually, seats are allocated first within primary districts, then, if any remain to be allocated, within secondary districts. An example is Belgium, where the prima-

[8]Once seats have been allocated to lists in the Netherlands, they are reallocated to the candidates on those lists as follows. A "list quotient" is calculated, equal to the number of votes obtained by the list divided by the number of seats obtained by the list. "Candidates who have reached the list quotient or above are elected. The votes obtained by these candidates surplus to the list quotient are then transferred," first to candidates whose vote exceeds half the list quotient, then to remaining candidates in list order. The surplus votes transfer only once, not continually as under STV. "If seats still remain to be distributed after the preferential votes procedure has been completed, they are allocated in descending list order to the candidates that have not yet been elected." See Seip (1979:211).

[9]Geographically defined groups of voters are not the only groups that are apportioned seats. Many systems set aside seats for ethnic minorities, e.g., the long-standing Maori seats in New Zealand. I shall focus in the text only on seats apportioned to geographic districts.

ry districts (*arrondissements*) are grouped into secondary districts (provinces), with a second round of seat allocation at the provincial level. The initial allocation of seats occurs as follows. The total number of valid votes cast in an *arrondissement* is divided by the number of seats in the Chamber to which the *arrondissement* is entitled, yielding the Hare quota. Each party then acquires as many seats as there are whole quotas contained in its vote. After this allocation, certain parties qualify for participation in the provincial allocation of seats (those garnering at least 66% of the quota in at least one *arrondissement* in the province, and having formally affiliated the various *arrondissement* lists within the province). Each party's total vote in the province is divided by the number of seats it has won in the *arrondissement* allocations, plus one. The party with the largest quotient (the "highest average") wins the next available seat. Its quotient is then recalculated and the d'Hondt allocation process continues until all seats are allocated. In the final stages of allocation, it is decided how the seats won by the party at the provincial level should be distributed to its *arrondissement* lists, and thence to the candidates on those lists (cf. Hill 1974:57-8).

As the Belgian example suggests, primary and secondary electoral districts are hierarchically ordered, not just in the sense that secondary districts comprise several primary districts but also in the sense that votes and/or seats transfer from the primary to the secondary level for purposes of seat allocation. It is also possible for a system to have geographically overlapping districts that are not hierarchically ordered. In Ecuador, the whole nation serves as a district for the election of *diputados nacionales,* while the provinces serve as districts for the election of *diputados provinciales.* But Ecuadorians have two votes, one for each kind of deputy, and there are no vote transfers between the provinces and the national district. Thus Ecuador has two different kinds of primary district, rather than a hierarchical structure of districts.

Even tertiary districts can exist. In Greece, for example, seat allocations are made to district-based deputies in three stages: in primary districts (*nomoi*), secondary districts ("major districts"), and a single tertiary district (the nation). Tertiary districts, along with secondary districts, are sometimes called *upper tiers* in the literature. Systems possessing them are called *multi-tier* or said to feature complex districting.[10]

A survey of district structures in the 77 countries in the sample appears in Table 3.2. The number of secondary and tertiary districts is visible in the far right-hand columns. As can be seen, only Greece and Germany currently have tertiary districts but thirteen mostly European countries (Austria, Belgium, Bulgaria, the Czech Republic, Hungary, Iceland, Italy, South Korea, Norway, Poland, Slovakia, Slovenia, and Uruguay) have secondary districts.

Table 3.2. District structures in 77 democracies

How to read this table: N1 = number of primary electoral districts. Thus, for example, Argentina has 24 such districts. Of these, none return 1 member, five return 2 members, eleven return 3 members, and so on. *N2* = number of secondary electoral districts. *N3* = number of tertiary electoral districts.

Country (years)	*N1*	*1*	*2*	*3*	*4*	*5*	*6*	*7*	*8*	*9*	*10*	*11*	*12*	*13*	*14*	*15*	*16*	*17*	*18*	*19*	*20*	*>20*	*N2*	*N3*
ARGENTINA	24	0	5	1	2	2	0	0	0	2	0	0	0	1	0	0	0	0	0	0	0	1[a]	0	0
AUSTRALIA (1984–87)	148	148	0	0	0	0	0	0	0	0	0	0	0	0	0	0	0	0	0	0	0	0	0	0
AUSTRIA (1983)	9	0	0	0	0	0	1	1	0	0	1	0	0	2	0	0	0	0	0	0	0	4[b]	2	0
Bahamas	49	49	0	0	0	0	0	0	0	0	0	0	0	0	0	0	0	0	0	0	0	0	0	0
BANGLADESH	300	300	0	0	0	0	0	0	0	0	0	0	0	0	0	0	0	0	0	0	0	0	0	0
Barbados	28	28	0	0	0	0	0	0	0	0	0	0	0	0	0	0	0	0	0	0	0	0	0	0
BELGIUM	30	0	3	4	3	5	6	0	3	1	1	0	1	1	0	0	0	0	0	0	1	1[c]	9	0
Belize	28	28	0	0	0	0	0	0	0	0	0	0	0	0	0	0	0	0	0	0	0	0	0	0
BENIN[d]	6	0	0	0	0	0	0	0	1	0	2	2	0	0	1	0	0	0	0	0	0	0	0	0
BOLIVIA	9	0	0	0	0	0	0	1	0	2	1	0	0	1	0	0	0	1	1	1	0	1[e]	0	0
BOTSWANA	34	34	0	0	0	0	0	0	0	0	0	0	0	0	0	0	0	0	0	0	0	0	0	0
BRAZIL	26	0	0	0	0	0	0	0	10	1	2	0	1	0	0	0	2	1	1	0	0	8[f]	0	0
BULGARIA	31[g]																						1	0
CANADA	295	295	0	0	0	0	0	0	0	0	0	0	0	0	0	0	0	0	0	0	0	0	0	0
Cape Verde	22	0	15	2	0	2	1	0	0	0	0	0	2	0	0	0	0	0	0	0	0	0	0	0
CHILE	60	0	60	0	0	0	0	0	0	0	0	0	0	0	0	0	0	0	0	0	0	0	0	0
COLOMBIA	26	2	3	3	2	2	2	2	5	1	0	1	1	0	0	0	0	0	0	0	0	2[h]	0	0
COSTA RICA	7	0	0	0	2	1	1	1	0	0	1	0	0	0	0	0	0	0	0	0	0	1[i]	0	0
Cyprus (Greek)	6	0	0	1	1	1	0	0	0	0	0	1	1	0	0	0	0	0	0	0	0	1[j]	0	0
CZECH REPUBLIC	8	0	0	0	0	0	0	0	0	0	0	0	0	1	0	0	0	1	0	0	0	6[k]	1	0

DENMARK	19	0	3	0	2	0	0	1	3	2	2	1	1	0	0	0	1	0	2	0	0	1[l]	0	0
Dominica	21	21	0	0	0	0	0	0	0	0	0	0	0	0	0	0	0	0	0	0	0	0	0	0
DOMINICAN REP.	30	0	16	7	1	3	1	0	0	0	0	1	0	0	0	0	0	0	0	0	0	1[m]	0	0
ECUADOR	22	5	4	9	0	1	1	0	0	1	0	0	1[n]	0	0	0	0	0	0	0	0	0	0	0
FINLAND	21	1	0	0	0	0	0	1	2	0	2	0	1	2	0	1	0	1	2	0	1	1[o]	0	0
FRANCE	577	577	0	0	0	0	0	0	0	0	0	0	0	0	0	0	0	0	0	0	0	0	0	0
The Gambia	36	36	0	0	0	0	0	0	0	0	0	0	0	0	0	0	0	0	0	0	0	0	0	0
GERMANY	248	248	0	0	0	0	0	0	0	0	0	0	0	0	0	0	0	0	0	0	0	0	1	1
GREECE[p]	56	5	9	9	10	5	5	4	5	1	0	0	0	1	0	0	0	0	0	0	0	2[q]	14	1
Grenada	15	15	0	0	0	0	0	0	0	0	0	0	0	0	0	0	0	0	0	0	0	0	0	0
HONDURAS	18	2	1	2	2	1	1	3	1	3	0	0	0	0	0	0	0	0	0	0	1	1[r]	0	0
HUNGARY[s]	196	176	0	0	3	4	7	0	2	1	0	1	0	0	1	0	0	0	0	0	0	1[t]	1	0
Iceland	8	0	0	0	0	4	1	1	0	0	0	1	0	0	0	0	0	0	1	0	0	0	1	0
IRELAND	41	0	0	0	13	15	13	0	0	0	0	0	0	0	0	0	0	0	0	0	0	0	0	0
ISRAEL	1	0	0	0	0	0	0	0	0	0	0	0	0	0	0	0	0	0	0	0	0	0	0	0
ITALY	42	1	1	0	1	0	0	2	1	1	1	0	0	0	3	1	2	2	1	0	4	11[v]	1	0
JAMAICA	60	60	0	0	0	0	0	0	0	0	0	0	0	0	0	0	0	0	0	0	0	0	0	0
JAPAN	129	0	8	39	34	46	2	0	0	0	0	0	0	0	0	0	0	0	0	0	0	0	0	0
Kiribati	23	?	?	?	0	0	0	0	0	0	0	0	0	0	0	0	0	0	0	0	0	0	0	0
KOREA, SOUTH[w]	225	225	0	0	0	0	0	0	0	0	0	0	0	0	0	0	0	0	0	0	0	0	1	0
Liechtenstein	2	0	0	0	0	0	0	0	0	0	1	0	0	0	0	1	0	0	0	0	0	0	0	0
LITHUANIA	72	71	0	0	0	0	0	0	0	0	0	0	0	0	0	0	0	0	0	0	0	1[x]	0	0
Luxembourg	4	0	0	0	0	0	0	1	0	1	0	0	0	0	0	0	0	0	0	0	0	2[y]	0	0
MALI[z]	55	19	23	6	4	1	2	0	0	0	0	0	0	0	0	0	0	0	0	0	0	0	0	0
Malta[aa]	13	0	0	0	0	13	0	0	0	0	0	0	0	0	0	0	0	0	0	0	0	0	0	0
Marshall Islands																								
MAURITIUS	21	0	1	20	0	0	0	0	0	0	0	0	0	0	0	0	0	0	0	0	0	0	0	0
Micronesia	14	14	0	0	0	0	0	0	0	0	0	0	0	0	0	0	0	0	0	0	0	0	0	0
NAMIBIA	1	0	0	0	0	0	0	0	0	0	0	0	0	0	0	0	0	0	0	0	0	1[bb]	0	0

Table 3.2. (cont.)

Country (years)	*N1*	*1*	*2*	*3*	*4*	*5*	*6*	*7*	*8*	*9*	*10*	*11*	*12*	*13*	*14*	*15*	*16*	*17*	*18*	*19*	*20*	*>20*	*N2*	*N3*
Nauru[cc]	8	0	7	0	1	0	0	0	0	0	0	0	0	0	0	0	0	0	0	0	0	0	0	0
NEPAL	205	205	0	0	0	0	0	0	0	0	0	0	0	0	0	0	0	0	0	0	0	0	0	0
NETHERLANDS	1	0	0	0	0	0	0	0	0	0	0	0	0	0	0	0	0	0	0	0	0	1[dd]	0	0
NEW ZEALAND	99	99	0	0	0	0	0	0	0	0	0	0	0	0	0	0	0	0	0	0	0	0	0	0
NORWAY	19	0	0	0	2	2	3	3	2	0	3	0	2	0	0	2	0	0	0	0	0	0	1	0
PAPUA NEW GUINEA	109	109	0	0	0	0	0	0	0	0	0	0	0	0	0	0	0	0	0	0	0	0	0	0
POLAND[ee]	37	0	0	0	0	0	0	5	4	3	7	6	4	4	1	1	0	2	0	0	0	0	1	0
PORTUGAL	20	0	0	1	4	3	2	0	1	1	3	0	0	0	1	0	2	0	0	0	0	2[ff]	0	0
St. Kitts and Nevis	11	11	0	0	0	0	0	0	0	0	0	0	0	0	0	0	0	0	0	0	0	0	0	0
St. Lucia	17	17	0	0	0	0	0	0	0	0	0	0	0	0	0	0	0	0	0	0	0	0	0	0
St. Vincent & the Grenadines	15	15	0	0	0	0	0	0	0	0	0	0	0	0	0	0	0	0	0	0	0	0	0	0
San Marino	33																							
São Tomé and Príncipe	12																							
SLOVAKIA	4	0	0	0	0	0	0	0	0	0	0	1	0	0	0	0	0	0	0	0	0	3[gg]	1	0
SLOVENIA	8	0	0	0	0	0	0	0	0	0	0	8	0	0	0	0	0	0	0	0	0	0	1	0
Solomon Islands	38	38	0	0	0	0	0	0	0	0	0	0	0	0	0	0	0	0	0	0	0	0	0	0
SPAIN	52	2	0	8	7	14	4	4	3	4	2	0	1	0	0	0	1	0	0	0	0	2[hh]	0	0
SWEDEN	28	0	1	0	0	1	1	0	1	1	3	6	7	2	0	0	1	1	0	1	0	2[ii]	0	0
SWITZERLAND	26	5	4	1	0	2	3	3	1	1	0	1	1	0	1	0	0	1	0	0	0	2[jj]	0	0
TRINIDAD & TOBAGO	36	36	0	0	0	0	0	0	0	0	0	0	0	0	0	0	0	0	0	0	0	0	0	0

TURKEY[kk]	104	0	0	?	?	?	?	0	0	0	0	0	0	0	0	0	0	0	0	0	0	0	0	0
Tuvalu	8	4	4	0	0	0	0	0	0	0	0	0	0	0	0	0	0	0	0	0	0	0	0	0
UNITED KINGDOM	670	670	0	0	0	0	0	0	0	0	0	0	0	0	0	0	0	0	0	0	0	0	0	0
UNITED STATES	435	435	0	0	0	0	0	0	0	0	0	0	0	0	0	0	0	0	0	0	0	0	0	0
URUGUAY	19	0	11	5	1	0	0	0	0	0	0	1	0	0	0	0	0	0	0	0	0	1[ll]	1	0
Vanuatu	14	0																						
Western Samoa	47	47	0	0	0	0	0	0	0	0	0	0	0	0	0	0	0	0	0	0	0	0	0	0
ZAMBIA	150	150	0	0	0	0	0	0	0	0	0	0	0	0	0	0	0	0	0	0	0	0	0	0

Main Sources: (1) Dick and Natkiel, 1987. (2) Gorwin, 1989. (3) Inter-Parliamentary Union, 1993. (4) Information received from the International Foundation for Electoral Systems, the East-West Center, the Center for the Study of Constitutionalism in Eastern Europe, and various articles, web sites, and scholars.

Notes:

Countries with populations less than one million are listed with an initial capital letter followed by lower-case letters; larger countries are listed using capital letters throughout.

[a]The remaining district returns 35 members.

[b]The remaining 4 districts return 30, 30, 35, and 39 members.

[c]The remaining district returns 33 members.

[d]Allen 1992.

[e]The remaining district returns 28 members.

[f]The remaining 8 districts return 22, 25, 30, 31, 39, 46, 53, and 60 members.

[g]Districts in Bulgaria are not assigned prespecified numbers of seats. How many seats a given district gets depends on turnout in the various districts.

[h]The remaining districts return 26 and 29 members.

[i]The remaining district returns 21 members.

[j]The remaining district returns 21 members.

[k]The remaining six districts return 21, 23, 24, 24, 37, and 40 members. Districts in the Czech Republic are not assigned prespecified numbers of seats. How many seats a given district gets depends on turnout in the various districts. The district magnitudes given are arrived at by multiplying by two-thirds the "maximum number of candidates on lists of candidates" given in appendix 2 of the Czech electoral law.

Notes to Table 3.2 (cont.)

[l]The remaining district returns 21 members.

[m]The remaining district returns 31 members.

[n]This is the nationwide district within which the national deputies are elected.

[o]The remaining district returns 30 members.

[p]My source for these figures is a paper put out by Greece's General Secretariat for Press and Information, "The Electoral System of 5th November 1989."

[q]The remaining two districts return 21 and 32 members. The number of secondary districts includes 13 major districts, plus the nationwide tier within which the state deputies are elected (see the formulaic matrix for Greece in Appendix A).

[r]The remaining district returns 23 members.

[s]Tóka N.d.

[t]The remaining district returns 28 members.

[u]The remaining district returns 120 members.

[v]The remaining 11 districts elect these numbers of members: 23, 23, 25, 25, 26, 27, 30, 36, 42, 51, 53.

[w]Cheng 1993.

[x]The remaining district returns 70 members.

[y]The remaining two districts return 21 and 23 members.

[z]Vengroff 1994.

[aa]Howe 1987.

[bb]The remaining district returns 72 members.

[cc]Inter-Parliamentary Union 1993:61.

[dd]The remaining district returns 150 members.

[ee]From the appendix to "The Act of June 28, 1991 on Election to the Sejm of the Republic of Poland," Law Journal of the Republic of Poland [Dziennik Ustaw Rzeczypospolitej Polskiej], 1991, no. 59, item 252.

[ff]The remaining two districts return 37 and 50 members.

[gg]The remaining three districts return 42, 46, and 51 members.

[hh]The remaining two districts elect 33 and 33 members.

[ii]The remaining two districts elect 26 and 37 members.

[jj]The remaining two districts elect 29 and 35 members.

[kk]Information as of the 1987 election, from Turan 1994. 46 of the districts returned 5 or 6 members. The rest returned 3 or 4 members.

[ll]The remaining district returns 47 members.

Table 3.3. Median magnitudes of primary electoral districts in 72 democracies

PANEL A: MEDIAN MAGNITUDES UP TO 15[a]

N	*Countries whose median district magnitude equals N*
1	AUSTRALIA, Bahamas, BANGLADESH, Barbados, Belize, BOTSWANA, CANADA, Dominica, FRANCE, The Gambia, GERMANY, Grenada, HUNGARY, JAMAICA, KOREA, LITHUANIA, Micronesia, NEPAL, NEW ZEALAND, PAPUA NEW GUINEA, Solomon Islands, St. Kitts & Nevis, St. Lucia, St. Vincent, TRINIDAD, Tuvalu, U.K.,U.S., Western Samoa, ZAMBIA [30]
2	Cape Verde, CHILE, DOMINICAN REPUBLIC, Kiribati, MALI, Nauru, URUGUAY [7]
3	ARGENTINA, EQUADOR, MAURITIUS [3]
4	GREECE, JAPAN, TURKEY [3]
5	BELGIUM, IRELAND, ICELAND, Malta, SPAIN [5]
6	COLOMBIA, COSTA RICA, HONDURAS, SWITZERLAND [4]
7	NORWAY, PORTUGAL [2]
8	Cyprus (Greek) [1]
9	DENMARK [1]
10	BENIN, POLAND [2]
11	BRAZIL, SLOVENIA, SWEDEN [3]
12	—
13	AUSTRIA, BOLIVIA, FINLAND, Liechtenstein [4]
14	—
15	LUXEMBOURG [1]

PANEL B: MEDIAN MAGNITUDES ABOVE 15

N	*Countries whose median district magnitude equals N*
17	ITALY
23.5	CZECH REPUBLIC
44	SLOVAKIA
72	NAMIBIA
120	ISRAEL
150	THE NETHERLANDS

[a]Countries with populations less than one million are listed with an initial capital letter followed by lower-case letters; larger countries are listed using capital letters throughout.

Strategic voting

The median primary district magnitudes for 72 of the 77 countries are indicated in Table 3.3. As can be seen, the median magnitude of primary districts is typically rather low. By far the single largest group of countries are those that rely exclusively or predominantly on single-member districts. Even among countries using multimember districts, however, 18 of 42 (43%) have median magnitudes between 2 and 5. The importance of this for the issues of alliance formation and strategic voting is fairly straightforward: Larger district magnitudes typically make the system more proportional (unless a majoritarian electoral formula such as that in Mali is used), which lessens the pressure both for electoral coalitions and strategic voting.

3.4 HOW VOTES BECOME SEATS

Translating votes into seats is the domain of electoral formulas. In simple systems, such as the United States', there is just one electoral formula in operation. In complex systems, however, such as Germany's, there are several levels at which different electoral formulas operate. In order to trace the process of votes-to-seats translation in complex systems to its final outcome – an allocation of seats among candidates – one must navigate through an entire subsystem of electoral formulas. This subsystem I shall call the formulaic structure. In order to explain this notion more thoroughly, I first review some of the better-known formulas and categories of formulas.

The conventional typology

Electoral formulas are customarily divided into two main families: plurality/majority rules and proportional representation (PR) methods. Plurality rule (which usually applies only in systems in which citizens vote for candidates, not for lists[10]) awards seats in an M-seat district to the top M finishers in the poll. Majority rules of various kinds (which also tend to apply in systems with candidate but without list votes) are discussed in Section 3.5. PR methods can be divided into two chief families, one based on quotas and largest remainders, one based on divisors and largest averages.

The first kind of PR proceeds as follows. An electoral quota, *Q*, is established and each list receives as many seats as there are whole quotas contained in its vote total. Any remaining seats are then allocated in order to the parties with the largest remainders, where a party's remain-

[10]Exceptions include the Bolivian, Mexican, and Argentine Senates and the U.S. Electoral College.

der equals its vote total less the product of (1) the number of quota seats it won in the first round of allocations and (2) the quota Q. One can think of Q as the "price" of a seat, denominated in votes. If a party wins 5 seats, it must "pay" $5Q$ to acquire them, leaving it with a remainder of $v-5Q$ (where v is the party's total vote).

The electoral quota can be calculated in a number of different ways, usually dependent on the district magnitude, M, and the total number of valid votes cast, V. Common quotas include the Hare (or simple) quota, $Q_{Hare} = V/M$; the Droop quota, $Q_{Droop} = [V/(M+1)] + 1$ (where $[x]$ denotes the greatest integer less than or equal to x); and the Hagenbach-Bischoff quota, $Q_{HB} = V/(M + 1)$.[11] Note that with any quota less than or equal to $V/(M + 1)$ it is theoretically possible for each of $M + 1$ parties to amass a quota, hence to allocate more seats than are available in the district. In practice, therefore, quotas at or below the Hagenbach-Bischoff level need auxiliary rules to decide how seats are to be allocated, in case more lists garner quotas than can be given seats.

If seats remain unallocated after each list gets its "quota seats" then the remaining seats are distributed in order to the lists with the largest remainders. Thus, the first unallocated seat goes to the list with the largest remainder, the second unallocated seat goes to the list with the second largest remainder, and so on until all seats are allocated. I shall use the notation "LR-Q" as a shorthand for "the largest remainders method of PR with the Q quota," referring to LR-Hare, LR-Droop, and so forth.

The second main family of PR methods is based on the calculation of ratios (or "averages") that reflect how much each party has paid in votes for its seats. Let $a_i(t)$ denote party i's average at stage t and $s_i(t)$ denote the number of seats allocated to party i in previous stages. The method invented by Viktor d'Hondt sets $a_i(t) = v_i/(s_i(t) + 1)$ for all i and t, where v_i is the vote total for party i. At any stage, one seat is allocated to the party with the highest average. Thus, for example, at the first stage, for which $t = 1$, $s_i(1) = 0$ for all parties (since no seats have yet been allocated) and $a_i(1) = v_i$. Accordingly, the first-stage seat is allocated to the list garnering the most votes. At the second stage, this party's average is now $v_i/2$, all other parties' averages are unchanged, and again the party with the highest average receives a seat. And so forth.

[11]As Taagepera and Shugart (1989:30) and Lijphart (1990:494 n. 5) have noted, the Droop and Hagenbach-Bischoff quotas are technically equivalent in many discussions of quota-and-remainder systems. Nonetheless, in discussions of the so-called Hagenbach-Bischoff variant of the d'Hondt method, used for example in Luxembourg, the quota mentioned is that given in the text. As it is convenient to have separate names for the separate quotas, and not too useful to have two names for the same thing, I shall use the Hagenbach-Bischoff quota as described in divisor systems, rather than the one described in quota-and-remainder systems.

Another divisor method is that invented by A. Sainte-Laguë, which sets $a_i(t) = v_i/(2s_i(t) + 1)$ for all i and t.[12] There are various other methods as well, differing in the sequence of numbers they use to divide parties' vote totals. Regardless of the formula used, the allocation of the next available seat is always to the party with the highest average. I shall use the shorthand "PR-d'Hondt" to refer to "the d'Hondt method of PR," and similarly for other divisor methods.

Having reviewed the mechanics of some of the various electoral formulas in current use, one can ask why the major distinction made among them is that between plurality/majority rules, on the one hand, and PR methods, on the other. The answer is that much of the variance in two of the major variables that electoral systems are thought to influence – namely, the level of disproportionality between each party's vote and seat shares, and the frequency with which a single party is able to win a majority of seats in the national legislature – is explained by this distinction (Rae 1971; Powell 1982; Blais and Carty 1987; Lijphart 1994). Or, more accurately, of the variance in these variables that can be explained by electoral structure at all, much of it is explained by this simple distinction. Plurality/majority rules generally tend to produce more disproportional results and also to raise the likelihood of a single-party majority in parliament. PR methods produce, as the label "proportional representation" would suggest, more proportional results; they also lower the likelihood of single-party majorities (cf. Powell 1982; Blais and Carty 1987; Lijphart 1994).

The distinction between plurality/majority and PR does not exhaust the distinctions to be made. For example, within the category of PR, the d'Hondt method is well known to be the least favorable to small parties. Moreover, some formulas do not fit comfortably in the main categories, prompting the creation of a category of "semiproportional" or "nonlist PR" formulas.[14]

[12]Both the d'Hondt and the Sainte-Laguë methods had been previously invented by Americans (Thomas Jefferson and Daniel Webster, respectively) attempting to deal with the apportionment of representatives to states in the U.S. House of Representatives. See Balinski and Young (1982).

[13]I find the notion of a semiproportional formula misleading. Consider, for example, the single nontransferable vote (SNTV) system, formerly used in Japan. SNTV entails that each voter cast a single vote, for a candidate. Most districts are multimember and, in an M-seat district, the winning candidates are simply the M candidates garnering the most votes. It is very clear that the Japanese *formula,* considered as nothing more than a method of taking a set of vote totals and awarding seats on that basis, uses plurality rule as defined above. But there has been a reluctance to place Japan in the plurality rule column, since its elections have yielded lower indices of disproportionality than typical for plurality rule in single-member districts. Thus,

On electoral systems

The formulaic structure: 1

I shall use the term "electoral formula" to mean a method for translating candidate and/or list vote totals into an allocation of seats among cartels, lists, or candidates. Mathematically, the electoral formula is just a function that takes various vote totals as input and produces a distribution of seats as output. Usually, the process is purely mechanical. That is, given a set of input vote totals, the electoral formula deterministically produces an allocation of seats.[14]

As noted above, many electoral systems have more than one electoral formula. In the Brazilian system, for example, there are two. One electoral formula (d'Hondt) converts list vote totals into an allocation of seats among lists. Another formula (plurality rule) converts the votes cast for candidates on a given list into an allocation of the list's seats (awarded in the first stage) among its candidates.

In addition to electoral formulas as defined above (mappings from votes to seats), some electoral systems also employ other rules in allocating seats. For example, in closed list systems, the method of allocating a list's seats is a mapping from list order (and the number of seats won by the list) to an allocation of seats among the candidates on the list.[15]

many in essence have defined "plurality rule" in multimember districts so as to preserve the essential political features of plurality rule as it operates in single-member districts. Lijphart, for example, writes: "The plurality formula ... stipulates that, in single-member districts, voters can cast one vote each and that the candidate with the most votes wins. (In two-member districts, voters have two votes and the two candidates with the most votes win; and so on.)" (1994:18). I would say that this is a perfectly logical generalization of the one-vote, single-member, plurality rule *system* to the multimember case, in such a way as to preserve the majoritarian nature of the system. I find it confusing, however, to refer to the plurality *formula* as stipulating how many votes each voter casts. In my view, it is clearer to preserve the narrow definition of the plurality rule formula, admit that it clearly existed in Japan, and accommodate the fact that Japanese elections under the 1947–93 system were more proportional than other elections also using plurality rule by reference to the voting options and district magnitudes in force there. The point is really only a terminological one, a plea to reserve the term *formula* for the mechanical translation of votes into seats, and accommodate political reality by reference to the electoral *system*. This avoids conflating two logically separate aspects of electoral systems, formulas and voting options, and puts the emphasis where it belongs in identifying the causal origins of the former Japanese system's greater proportionality: on the voting options and the district magnitude, not on the formula (see Cox 1991).

[14]An exception to this statement occurs under STV in Ireland, where a small element of chance sneaks in, due to the way ballot papers are handled (Harrop and Miller 1987:49).

[15]Of course, the formula allocating seats among candidates on a closed list could be taken as a *constant* function with respect to candidate vote totals (thus making the fact that such vote totals do not really exist irrelevant), or it could be supposed that voters in supporting the list are supporting the order of names on the list, so that list order reflects the voting outcome.

I shall refer to the set of all electoral formulas and other seat allocation rules in a given system, and their interrelationships, as the system's *formulaic structure* (or formulaic subsystem). Knowledge of the formulaic structure by definition allows one to construct a "complete mapping" of votes as initially cast (whether for lists, candidates, or both) into seats for candidates. In Brazil, for example, the complete mapping would take candidate and list votes as input, and produce an allocation of seats among candidates as output. Mathematically, this function would correspond to a *composition* of the various electoral formulas in the formulaic structure.[16]

If one wishes to speak of *the* electoral formula in a complex system, it would either have to be the complete mapping just mentioned or one would have to specify which of the "level-specific" electoral formulas one meant when speaking of *the* formula. I have found it useful to continue current usage in the literature and reserve the term "electoral formula" for votes-to-seats translations at a given level in the system, rather than for the complete mapping of a system. I shall clarify what counts as a "level in the system" throughout the rest of this section. The first step is to discuss the alliance structure of an electoral system.

The alliance structure of an electoral system

Any formulaic structure must eventually allocate all seats to candidates but some arrive at this final outcome via a series of broader allocations. Within a given primary district, seats are always allocated first to cartels (if any), then to lists (if any), and finally to candidates.

In some systems, of course, there are neither cartels nor lists. This is the case in the United Kingdom and Japan, for example, and in both countries there is only one kind of seat allocation – directly to candidates.

In other systems, lists but not cartels exist as entities to which intermediate seat allocations can be made. Usually this means that voters can vote directly for lists, but this is not always the case (e.g., Poland). When intermediate seat allocations are made to lists, then the question arises as to how the list's seats are to be allocated among the candidates on the list. One method is to have the party establish an order of candidates on the list, with the first candidate on the list getting the first seat to which the party is entitled, the second on the list getting the second seat, and so on. This is the *closed* list system (used, for example, in Spain's lower house). Another method is to let the party's voters decide which of its

[16] If g is a function mapping X (e.g., votes) into Y (e.g., seats for parties), and f is a function mapping Y into Z (e.g., seats for candidates), then the composition of g and f – call it h – is such that $h(x) = f(g(x))$.

candidates will win the seats allocated to the party's list. This is the *open* list system (used, for example, in Finland). Finally, there are also intermediate methods that give both party leaders and voters some say in the allocation of a list's seats among its candidates. These are the *flexible* list systems (used, for example, in Greece). A necessary condition for voters to have any influence on list allocations, of course, is that they have the ability to vote for individual candidates (possibly in addition to the ability to vote for lists). Candidate votes that influence seat allocations among the members of a given list are generally referred to as *preference votes* (Marsh 1985; Katz 1986).[17]

In yet other systems, intermediate seat allocations are made both to lists and to cartels. A cartel is a group of lists that are legally allied for purposes of seat allocation. The cartel vote is determined by summing the votes of all lists participating in the cartel. The initial allocation of seats is to the cartel, based on the cartel vote (although at this same stage allocations to unallied parties, if any, will also be made). Naturally, the question arises of how the cartel's seats are to be allocated among its component lists but here the answer is always in terms of votes cast for lists. In practice, citizens do not vote separately for cartels and there are no closed or flexible cartels; they are all open.

Sweden 1911-1952 is an example of a polity in which *apparentement,* i.e., the formation of list cartels, was legal. On the ballot paper, both the name of the party and the name of the cartel to which it belonged (if any) would appear. *Apparentement* was important in that it "allowed the nonsocialist parties to overcome the underrepresentation of small parties that is built into the d'Hondt method" (used in Sweden at that time) without going through the difficulties of an actual merger (Särlvik 1983:127).

In the example just given, the cartels were composed of lists from different parties but the same constituency. Two other possibilities – *apparentement* between lists from the same party and constituency, and between lists from the same parties but different constituencies – have also arisen in practice.

Sweden's contemporary electoral system provides an example of the first possibility: Swedish law allows multiple lists with the same party label in a given constituency, the votes for all these lists being summed for purposes of the initial seat allocation to parties. Which candidates from which lists secure the seats allocated to the party is "determined by the number of votes cast for the various [lists within the party]" (Särlvik 1983:134).

Belgium provides an example of *apparentement* of lists from the same party but different constituencies. Parties must formally affiliate their vari-

[17]In some systems, voters are allowed to alter the order of names on the ballot; I include this possibility under the general rubric of "preference votes."

ous *arrondissement* lists within each province, if they wish to participate in the provincial seat distribution. This creates a cartel of same-party different-constituency lists. Allocation of the seats awarded to the provincial cartel among the cartel's component *arrondissement* lists is by PR-d'Hondt.[18]

The existence or absence of cartels and lists, along with the rules regulating the nature of any cartels and lists that do exist (Are the cartels *partisan* – composed of same-party lists – or *inter-party*? Are the lists open, flexible, or closed? Are joint lists allowed? etc.), together establish what I shall call the *alliance structure* of an electoral system. The alliance structure refers only to the potential relationships that may obtain between candidates and lists, not to any actual pattern of use of the legal options.

Thresholds and bonus seats

Another important wrinkle in discussing electoral formulas concerns the existence of thresholds and bonus seats. Pure electoral formulas may be hedged about by various thresholds that a candidate or list must satisfy before being eligible to receive any seats. Such thresholds are part of the mathematical translation process which converts votes into seats, and thus properly a part of the electoral formula as defined here.

I shall consider two main categories of threshold here: those defined at the level of the primary district, and those defined at the level of the secondary district. Examples of the first are as follows:

- Argentina: Only lists whose vote exceeds 3% of the registered electorate in the district can receive seats.
- Israel: Only lists whose vote exceeds 1.5% of the vote in the district (which in this case coincides with the nation) are eligible to receive seats (the 1.5% threshold came in with the June 1992 election, replacing the older 1% threshold; see Stellman 1993:127).
- Japan: Only candidates whose vote exceeds 25% of the Hare quota are eligible to receive a seat.
- Lithuania: In the first round of a dual-ballot contest (in single-member districts), only candidates whose vote exceeds 50% of the total

[18]In principle, *apparentement* might continue indefinitely: There might be second-order cartels composed of cartels, third-order cartels composed of second-order cartels, and so forth. In practice, few democracies go beyond cartels. One of these is Uruguay. In the terminology used here, Uruguay's *sub-lemas* are cartels (as they are composed of a number of different lists whose votes pool for purposes of seat allocation), while the *lemas* (composed of a number of different *sub-lemas* whose votes pool for purposes of seat allocation) are second-order cartels. Seat allocations occur first to second-order cartels (*lemas*), then to cartels (*sub-lemas*), then to lists, finally to candidates (Taylor 1955; Franco 1986; Gonzalez 1991).

vote are eligible to receive a seat, and then only if turnout in the district exceeds 40% of the registered electorate.

Examples of thresholds that operate at the level of the secondary electoral district are:

- Austria: Only lists associated with parties that have won at least one seat in a primary district contained in the secondary district are eligible to receive a seat.
- Belgium: Only partisan cartels associated with parties that have won at least .66 of a Hare quota in at least one of the primary districts within the secondary district are eligible to receive seats.
- Germany 1949: Only lists associated with parties that had either won at least one seat in a primary district contained in the secondary district, or had won at least 5% of the total vote in the secondary district, were eligible to receive seats.
- Greece 1974-1981: Only lists associated with parties that had won at least 17% of the national vote, or two-party joint lists whose parties won at least 25% of the national vote, or *n*-party joint lists, $n > 2$, whose parties won at least 30% of the national vote, were eligible to receive seats (Clogg 1987:196).

It is conceptually possible, of course, to have threshold requirements both at the primary and at the secondary district level. An example is Iceland, where a party must win at least 2/3 of a Hare quota to win seats in a district, and must win at least one constituency seat in order to be eligible for the national distribution of seats (Helgason 1991).

Whenever there are threshold requirements that actually affect some parties, the unaffected parties will divide 100% of the seats based on less than 100% of the votes. They may divide the resulting "surplus" seats more or less equally, or the surplus may be used to create a bonus in seats for some parties (typically the largest). Even without threshold requirements, a polity may see fit to create bonus seats.

There are only three examples of bonus seats in the 77-country sample described above. In South Korea, if the party winning the most seats in the primary electoral districts does not win a majority of such seats, then it is given a bare majority of 75 nationally-allocated seats.[19] In Malta, if a party wins a majority of first preference votes but fails to win a majority of seats in the legislature, then it is given a sufficient number of adjustment seats to ensure it a parliamentary majority (Lijphart 1994:36). In Turkey, the largest party in districts returning five or more members is entitled to a bonus seat, with the remaining seats distributed by the d'Hondt method of PR (Turan 1994:54).

[19]See Cheng (1993:16-17). This law has been changed recently.

The formulaic structure: 2

The formulaic structure of an electoral system can become rather complex if its district and alliance structure are complex. In working through such systems, I have found it useful to employ a *formulaic matrix,* the rows of which are defined by the various entities to which seat allocations are made (partisan cartels, lists, joint lists, independent candidates, etc.), the columns of which are defined by the electoral district within which the allocation is made (primary, secondary, tertiary). The *i-j* cell in the formulaic matrix, corresponding to the intersection of the *i*th row (or entity) and *j*th column (or level), provides a description of the formula or other rule governing the allocation of seats to the *i*th entity at the *j*th level. Appendix A contains formulaic matrices for most of the 77 countries judged democratic as of 1992.

Consider, as an example, the Belgian system. As can be seen by glancing at the row and column headings of the matrix in Appendix A, seat allocations in Belgium are made to three different kinds of entity (candidates, lists, and partisan cartels) at two different levels (*arrondissements* and provinces). As can be seen by glancing at the cells within the matrix, allocations are not made in every possible cell. Partisan cartels, for example, are not awarded seats at the *arrondissement* level; they take receipt of seats only at the provincial level. Turning now to the non-empty cells, the numerals indicate the sequence of seat allocations. The first allocation of seats is to lists within primary districts, and thus corresponds to the cell at the intersection of the "lists" row and the "primary districts" column. The second allocation of seats is to partisan cartels at the provincial level. The third allocation of seats is to *arrondissement* lists at the provincial level (corresponding, as explained in the cell, to the reallocation of the seats awarded in step 2 to each partisan cartel, among the cartel's component *arrondissement* lists). Finally, the fourth step is the reallocation of seats won by lists in steps 1 and 3 to the candidates on those lists. Each step has its own formula or rule of allocation.

The formulaic matrix forces one to be clear about what entity is receiving seats, on the basis of what votes, and at what level. It also makes certain differences in formulaic structure stand out. Consider, for example, the formulaic matrix for the Czech Republic (to be found in Appendix A). The Czech district structure has two tiers, just like the Belgian, although the second tier there consists of a single national district rather than the provincial districts favored in Belgium. Instead of using partisan cartels, however, the Czechs use national lists. Thus, seats allocated to the parties at the national level are not reallocated to the constituency lists before finally being distributed among the candidates on those lists. Rather, such seats go straight to the candidates on a national list. As it turns out, the candidates on the national list must consist of candidates from the constituency lists who have failed to secure seats in the first allocation (to lists in primary districts). But the distinction may be important insofar as it affects the balance of power between the national party leadership, which must decide on the order of names on the national list, and local party activists, who might be expected to dominate the endorsement process in the constituencies.

The formulaic matrices presented in the Appendix are sometimes not as complicated as they might be, in that potential distinctions – e.g., between independent candidates and candidates on lists, between independent lists and lists allied in cartels, between the various kinds of cartel – are not always made. Sometimes this is due to ignorance on my part of the relevant laws, sometimes to a desire to simplify already-complicated matrices by focusing on the most important distinctions. Even with these simplifications, some 20 of the 77 systems have complex systems entailing seat allocations at more than two stages.

3.5 DUAL-BALLOT SYSTEMS

Another way of voting uses multiple ballots, typically along with a requirement that victors secure a majority of votes cast. The Catholic Church has a long tradition of such voting, which influenced the choice of early electoral institutions in continental Europe. Although multiple ballots are usually employed in single-member districts, this is not always the case. The French have used multiple-ballot multimember systems in the past (Cole and Campbell 1989), while the Swiss upper house (Aubert 1983) and Mali (Vengroff 1994) do currently.

I shall focus initially on *dual*-ballot systems in *single-member* districts. All these systems, it should be noted, are rather simple in terms of their voting options, conversion of votes into seats, and district structure: There is only one vote per voter per round; there are no lists or cartels, only candidates; and there are no secondary electoral districts. These restrictions are not inherent in the nature of dual-ballot voting. It would be possible, for example, to employ approval voting in one or both rounds, or to allow candidates to ally as do presidential candidates in Uruguay. Nonetheless, there is no empirical experience with such systems, and no argument on the table that they should be used. Thus, I shall ignore them here.

Even with these restrictions, there are many different types of dual-ballot single-member systems to consider. They differ in how they decide what a candidate must do to win in the first round, and which candidates are eligible to compete in the second round, absent a first-round winner.

The usual standard for victory in the first round is winning a majority (over 50%) of first-round votes. Some polities, however, require only a plurality that exceeds a given standard – 40% in various U.S. states (cf. Bullock and Johnson 1992) and Costa Rica; 45% under the new Nicaraguan rule. There is also the "double complement" rule, discussed briefly in Chapter 6, which sets yet another standard for victory in the first round.

As regards the qualifications for entering the second round, absent a first-round victor, some systems are very permissive. The French under Napoleon III and again from 1928 to 1936, and the Germans in their presidential elections during the Weimar Republic, let anyone enter the second stage, even if they had not run in the first stage (cf. Nilson 1983; Lakeman 1970:63). I, however, shall focus on systems in which only candidates appearing in the first round are eligible to compete in the second.

Among these *restrictive* runoff systems, there are two basic types. The first type restricts access on the basis of a relative standard: The top N finishers in the first round advance, where N is typically 2 but can in principle be larger. The second type restricts access on the basis of an absolute standard: All and only those candidates getting more than x% of the vote advance, for some x (cf. Greenberg and Shepsle 1987).[20]

Most real-world examples of restrictive majority runoff are top-two systems. This system has a long history in European elections, being used, for example, in nineteenth-century Germany and Italy (Carstairs 1980:163; p. 151), and has come in for more recent European use in Bulgaria (1990 only) and Albania. Top-two majority runoff has also been used since the nineteenth century in U.S. elections, especially in primary contests in the southern states (Wright and Riker 1989; Bullock and Johnson 1992). Finally, all current Latin American presidential runoff elections also restrict runoff access to the top two finishers (Shugart and Taagepera 1994).

Other forms of majority runoff, less restrictive than the top-two variant, have also been used. For example, Norway between 1905 and 1919 allowed any first-round candidate to continue in the second round. With such permissive rules for participation in the second round, the first rounds were really no more than "straw polls," providing information about the relative strengths of the different candidates. Such information could then presumably be used in bargaining over candidate withdrawals and alliances.

[20]There are also mixtures of and variants on these two pure types. An example of a mixed system is that used in the 1990 Hungarian elections, when the top three first-round finishers, plus any candidates exceeding 15%, were admitted to the second poll (Körösényi 1990). An example of a variant on the second or absolute standard system takes "registered voters" instead of "turnout" as the base for the percentage. This is the system used in France.

Finally, as an example of a dual-ballot *multimember* system, consider Mali. The Malian voter casts a single vote for a list of candidates. If any list gains a majority of votes in the first round, then it gets all the seats at stake in the constituency. Otherwise, a runoff election is held between the two lists getting the most votes. In the runoff, the list getting the most votes wins all the seats.

3.6 CONCLUSION

At the beginning of this chapter, I defined an electoral system as a set of laws and party rules that regulate electoral competition between and within parties. These laws and rules can affect many aspects of political competition, including the ideological cast of the policies that parties advocate at election time (e.g., Cox 1990a), the extent to which politicians traffic in pork barrel and other particularistic benefits (e.g., Myerson 1994), and the degree of factionalization of parties (e.g., Kohno 1992). For the purposes of this book, the most important features of electoral systems are those that affect the making of electoral coalitions, whether explicit alliances negotiated between party leaders or tacit alliances worked out among voters through strategic voting.

The essence of both kinds of electoral coalition, at least as conceived in most of the chapters to follow, is the reallocation of votes to produce a more efficient translation of votes into seats. From this perspective, what is crucial in any description of an electoral system is to keep close track of "where the votes go": which vote totals are used for purposes of intermediate or final seat allocations. The new terms and concepts introduced in this chapter are motivated by this need to keep careful track of how votes become seats. Thus, for example, the distinction between an exclusive and nonexclusive vote is cast precisely in terms of how many seat-relevant vote totals the vote in question contributes to. If the answer is just one, then the vote is exclusive; otherwise it is nonexclusive. Similarly, the notion of a formulaic matrix is intended as an aid to mapping out where, when, and with what votes the various seat allocations in a system are made.

Once the "where, when, and with what" of a system are understood, the logic of both explicitly negotiated alliances and tacit (strategic voting) alliances is easier to specify. Explicit alliances reduce the number of entities (whether candidates, lists, or cartels) to which initial seat allocations are made. Thus, for example, fusion candidacies reduce the number of candidates running, joint lists reduce the number of lists running, and *apparentement,* by allowing some lists to combine their votes for purposes of an initial seat distribution, may mean that rather than n lists chasing after seats, one finds $n - 2$ lists and 1 cartel.

It should be stressed that reducing the number of electoral competitors (whether candidates, lists, or cartels) may or may not reduce the number of parties. Outright mergers, such as that between the Liberals and Democrats in Japan, certainly reduce the number of parties. But the whole point of a fusion candidacy or a joint list is that the parties supporting the candidacy or list continue as independent entities. And *apparentement* between lists supported by different parties allows much the same result: a contraction in the number of entities to which seats are legally allocated without a corresponding contraction in the number of parties.

It should also be noted that explicit coalitions depress the need for tacit ones (i.e., for strategic voting), by reducing the number of candidates, lists, or cartels among which voters must choose. If elites fail to coordinate sufficiently, however, "too many" candidates, lists, or cartels may enter the fray and the possibility of a wasted vote thus arises. In this case, the coordination game that began among elites at the level of alliance negotiations may continue at the level of mass voting decisions, as will be discussed in the next four chapters.

4

Strategic voting in single-member single-ballot systems

> *"The evidence renders it undeniable that a large amount of sophisticated voting occurs – mostly to the disadvantage of the third parties nationally – so that the force of Duverger's psychological factor must be considerable."*
>
> William H. Riker (1982:764).

For as long as voting procedures have been used to decide important and controversial issues, there have been legislators and electors willing to vote strategically. Theoretical interest in strategic voting dates at least to Pliny the Younger (see Farquharson 1969) and probably earlier. In this chapter, I build on rather more recent and formal treatments of the strategy of voting: those framed in the decision-theoretic and game-theoretic traditions. Most of this work has appeared in the last thirty years and focuses on the behavior of legislators (e.g., Farquharson 1969; McKelvey and Niemi 1978; Miller 1980; Shepsle and Weingast 1984; Banks 1985; Austen-Smith 1987; Ordeshook and Schwartz 1987). This chapter focuses on the other, less well-trodden, branch of research into strategic voting, that dealing with the behavior of voters in mass elections.

There are of course many ways to conduct a mass election. This chapter deals in particular with elections in electoral districts that satisfy the following criteria: (1) There is one seat to be filled in the district; and (2) there is only one round of voting, after which the victor is decided. There are many electoral systems that satisfy these criteria: the Anglo-American first-past-the-post system; the Australian alternative vote system; the approval voting system; and so on. Not all of these systems are currently used in national elections, of course. For the most part, I shall focus on those that are.

The purpose of this chapter is primarily to specify the theoretical and institutional conditions under which Duverger's Law holds at the local level. In one sense, my findings are largely negative: If one changes any of several institutional features that define ordinary plurality rule (e.g., by allowing fusion candidacies, holding all else constant), then the strategic voting incentives that push toward local bipartism dissipate substantially; if one investigates the theoretical conditions that are necessary to generate a strong local bipartism result, even *given* the right institutional context (i.e., ordinary plurality rule), they appear fairly stringent; and if one investigates the empirical evidence at the district level in countries that use ordinary plurality rule, one finds plenty of cases where more than two candidates enter and receive substantial vote shares, contrary to Duvergerian expectations. On the other hand, my findings are by no means all negative: The institutional conditions can be met (just use ordinary plurality rule), the theoretical conditions are plausible in certain situations, and when the theoretical conditions are approximated in the real world, one finds ample evidence consistent with strategic behavior, as suggested by the quote from William H. Riker that heads this chapter.

The layout of the chapter is as follows. The first section reviews the previous formal literature on strategic voting (leaving the vast informal literature largely untouched). The next four sections consider strategic voting in three particular electoral systems – ordinary plurality rule (Sections 4.2 and 4.3), plurality rule with fusion candidacies allowed (4.4), and the alternative vote (4.5). Section 4.6 concludes.

I should stress before proceeding further that this chapter, as well as the succeeding chapters in this part of the book, all take a post-entry district-level perspective. Duverger's Law claims that use of single-member districts operating under plurality rule will lead to bipartism at the *national* level. To build up to this national-level conclusion, however, Duverger starts at the district level, arguing that strategic voting (and strategic entry) should produce *local* bipartism in each district. How a series of potentially disconnected local two-party systems might cumulate to a national two-party system is a topic for a later chapter (10). In this chapter, I consider the logic of the foundational claim that use of ordinary plurality in single-member districts will lead to local bipartism.

In assessing this claim, it is conventional to note that ordinary plurality mechanically underrepresents small parties at the district level (because the winner takes all) and thereby stimulates two species of strategic adaptation: strategic voting by citizens eager not to waste their votes; and strategic withdrawals by politicians eager not to waste their effort and resources (cf. Blais and Carty 1991:83). In this part of the book, I focus exclusively on the theory and practice of strategic voting (leaving the theory and practice of strategic entry/withdrawal to the next part).

Strategic voting

4.1 PREVIOUS RESEARCH

Formal mathematical study of strategic voting in the last twenty years has had two stages: an early decision-theoretic stage and a more recent game-theoretic stage. The decision-theoretic perspective on strategic voting (see McKelvey and Ordeshook 1972) is, for simple plurality elections, roughly as follows: Some voter, whose favorite candidate has a poor chance of winning, notices that she has a preference between the top two candidates; she then rationally decides to vote for the most preferred of these top two competitors rather than for her overall favorite, because the latter vote has a much smaller chance of actually affecting the outcome than the former. What the decision-theoretic approach adds to common sense is not just greater precision about the assumptions implicit in such reasoning (for example, it is not the probability of victory that matters directly, but the probability of certain ties and near-ties) but also greater generality: The basic model has been extended to illuminate strategic behavior in Borda elections (Ludwin 1978; Dummett 1984), in multimember districts (Cox 1984), in approval voting elections (Niemi 1984), and in a variety of other electoral systems (Hoffman 1982; Dummett 1984; Gutowski and Georges 1993).

Nonetheless, decision-theoretic analyses, both formal and informal, still deal essentially with a single voter in analytic isolation. The logical next step is to consider whether strategic voting by some voters makes such voting by others more or less likely. In particular, suppose a close third-place candidate in a single-member district begins to lose the support of his least committed followers (those who prefer him only slightly to one of the two front-runners). This erosion of support will, if known (perhaps through polls), lead voters to reduce their estimates of the candidate's chances. But, as the candidate's chances are seen to fall, some of his slightly more committed followers may abandon ship for one of the front-runners. The process might in theory continue until the candidate was left with no support.

This line of thinking is game-theoretic. It essentially asks how much strategic voting there is in equilibrium. Should one expect that third-place candidates will always lose all of their support because of strategic decisions among their followers? Or are there general conditions under which this erosion of support is fairly limited or even negligible?

I first addressed these questions in the context of a model in which three candidates compete for a single seat under simple plurality (Cox 1987b). The key assumptions of the analysis were that all voters are short-term instrumentally rational (i.e., they care about whom they vote for only insofar as this affects the outcome of the current election), that voters have incomplete information about each other's preferences over outcomes, and that all voters have "rational" expectations (on which, more later). I showed that in almost all equilibria some voters vote strategically and that the marginal impact of strategic voting was to decrease the effective number of parties (Laakso and Taagepera 1979). The logic of this result is worth sketching, as I shall refer to it again.

Strategic voting in a simple plurality election means voting for a lower-ranked candidate that one believes is stronger, rather than for a higher-ranked candidate that one believes is weaker. The rational expectations condition implies that voter beliefs about which candidates are stronger and weaker will be generally correct. Thus, strategic voting will generally transfer votes from objectively weaker (vote-poorer) to objectively stronger (vote-richer) candidates, with the necessary result that the "effective number of parties" – a measure which is smaller the more concentrated the distribution of votes is – will decline. There are many other electoral systems, it should be noted, for which this result does not hold (see Chapter 7).

Palfrey (1989), exploring essentially the same model, was able to characterize its equilibria in terms of candidate vote shares, showing that they fall into two classes: *Duvergerian* equilibria (in which the level of strategic voting is such that the support of all but two of the candidates is undercut completely) and *non-Duvergerian* equilibria (in which two or more candidates are so nearly tied for second that the voters cannot decide which one to discount, leaving more than two significant candidates in the field). Duvergerian equilibria are so named because they gibe with Duverger's expectations that simple plurality will promote bipartism. The intuition behind the non-Duvergerian equilibria is roughly as follows. Suppose two leftist candidates (say, Charles Goodell and Richard Ottinger) and one rightist (say, James Buckley) are competing for a single post (one of the U.S. Senate seats for New York). The rightist is ahead, the two leftists trailing but close to one another. Under these conditions, leftist voters will have a hard time coordinating on one of the leftist candidates and a non-Duvergerian result can (and did) ensue.[1]

Myerson and Weber (1993) advance a model of voting equilibria applicable in a wide range of single-winner electoral systems – not just simple plurality rule but also approval voting, Borda's method of points, and many other systems as well. Their approach is more general in that, where Cox and Palfrey assume a particular (multinomial) model of voter probability beliefs, Myerson and Weber merely require that these beliefs satisfy a fairly general requirement (the "ordering condition," whereby candidates generally expected to place third or lower in the poll are much less likely to be tied for first than candidates generally expected to

[1]On the theoretical status of the non-Duvergerian equilibria, see Myerson and Weber (1993:106) and Fey (1995).

place first or second in the poll). On the other hand, the Cox-Palfrey approach has the virtue of deriving the ordering condition endogenously as a consequence of more primitive assumptions.

4.2 STRATEGIC VOTING UNDER SIMPLE PLURALITY WITHOUT FUSION

A theoretical model

In this section I sketch out a model of strategic voting in simple plurality elections, based on Cox (1994).[2] Although a few mathematical symbols creep into the text in this and the next section, technical details are left to the footnotes, and the discussion returns to an "English-only" status thereafter.

Imagine K candidates competing for a single seat, with the candidate placing highest in the poll winning. Each voter casts a single exclusive vote and can be characterized by her *preferences* among the candidates, her *beliefs* about the candidate preferences of other voters, and her *expectations* about the likely outcome of the election.

> *Preferences.* I assume that each voter *i* cares about which candidate wins the election, these preferences being formally represented by a von Neumann-Morgenstern utility function u_i.[3] Following standard usage in game theory, I shall sometimes refer to u_i as voter *i*'s *type.*
> *Beliefs.* No voter knows the candidate preferences of other voters with certainty, but each does have beliefs about how frequently the various different types of voter crop up in the electorate as a whole. Formally, these beliefs are encapsulated in a cumulative distribution function F_i.[4]
> *Expectations.* Voters also have beliefs, or *expectations,* about how well each candidate is likely to do in the upcoming election. These expectations are formalized as a vector $\pi_i = (\pi_{i1}, \ldots, \pi_{iK})$, where π_{ij} denotes the proportion of the electorate that *i* expects will vote for *j*. Given preferences (u_i), expectations (π_i), and knowledge of the number of voters (n), voter *i* faces a standard decision problem, the details of which are

[2]This model is essentially the same as that of Palfrey (1989), although the method of proof differs. It is also closely related to the work of Myerson and Weber (1993).

[3]Voters' utilities can be rescaled in the standard fashion so that victory for the voter's most-preferred candidate yields a utility of 1, while victory for her least-preferred candidate yields a utility of 0. After this rescaling, voter *i*'s preferences (or voter i's *type*) can be described by the vector $u_i = (u_{i1}, \ldots, u_{iK})$, an element in the set $U = \{(u_1, \ldots, u_K)$: $\max\{u_j\}=1$ & $\min\{u_j\}=0$ & $u_j=u_k$ only if $j = k\}$.

[4]Given F_i, which is defined over the set U, one can define a distribution over U^n, assuming independence. An alternative approach is to make assumptions directly about the distribution over U^n (over profiles) instead of over U (over individuals).

run through in Cox (1994). The solution to *i*'s problem (i.e., the set of votes that maximize expected utility, given u_i, π_i, and n) is denoted $V(u_i;\pi_i,n)$. $V(u_i;\pi_i,n)$ is simply "the optimal vote for a voter with preferences u_i and expectations π_i" (although in some instances the voter may be indifferent between two or more vote choices, in which case we would need to talk of "the set of optimal votes").

The model is completed with two further assumptions whose joint effect is to restrict the nature and consistency of voter beliefs (about other voters' preferences) and expectations (about how well each candidate will do). First, I assume that $F_i = F$ for all i. In other words, all voters share a common view of the distribution of voter preferences in the electorate.[5] Second, I assume that voters' expectations are publicly generated – by, for example, polls and newspaper analysis of the candidates' chances – so that diversity of expectation among the electorate is minimized. In the discussion that follows, I take this notion to the logical extreme and assume that every voter has the same expectations: $\pi_i = \pi$ for all i. Both of these assumptions can be replaced with weaker ones, under which voters do not agree exactly on how preferences are distributed in the electorate or on what share of the vote each candidate will likely get, without destroying the key result to come.

Given these two postulates, the maintained assumption of voter rationality implies a certain consistency between F and π in equilibrium. For, not all expectations π are "rational" in light of the voters' knowledge of the distribution F of voter preferences. Suppose, to take a three-candidate example, that some voter thought π equaled (1/3, 1/3, 1/3), so that a randomly selected voter was equally likely to vote for any of the candidates. This expectation is not consistent with a distribution of voter preferences in which the proportion of voters ranking candidate 1 last exceeds 2/3. The reason is that voting for 1 is a dominated strategy for voters who rank him last; thus, even if every voter not ranking 1 last intends to vote for him, this still falls short of one-third of the electorate, hence short of the proportion expected under π.

Considerations such as these motivate imposing the following "rational expectations" condition on voter beliefs:

> *Rational expectations condition:* The expectations π are rational with respect to the beliefs F if an electorate whose preferences were in fact distributed according to F, all voting optimally in light of π

[5]Another technical assumption employed about F is that its support set is U. That is, each voter entertains the possibility that there are some voters of any given preference type in the electorate, although they may assign a very low probability to some (or even most) such types.

(i.e., casting a ballot in $V(u_i;\pi, n)$), would in fact produce expected vote shares for the candidates identical to π.

The equilibrium conditions for the model are then two. First, every voter votes so as to maximize her expected utility, given expectations π (and n); that is, every voter of type u votes for candidate $V(u;\pi,n)$. Second, the expectations π satisfy the rational expectations condition.

Voting equilibria and wasted votes

What are the equilibria of the model just sketched? Relabel the candidates, if necessary, so that their labels correspond to their expected rank of finish, i.e., so that $\pi_1 \geq \pi_2 \geq \ldots \geq \pi_K$. Note that with this relabeling one can reasonably assume $\pi_2 > 0$: The candidate expected to place second has a positive expected vote share. Given a distribution F of voter types, I shall say that the expectations π are a limit of rational expectations if and only if arbitrarily large electorates can have rational expectations that are arbitrarily close to π. The point of considering "large electorates" is that expectations in the model become arbitrarily precise in the limit, so that there is a simple relationship between the expected order of finish of the candidates and their probabilities of winning seats. The main result is presented in the following theorem and its corollary.

> *Theorem 1:* Suppose that $0<\pi_j<\pi_2$ for some $j > 2$. Then π is not a limit of rational expectations.
> *Proof:* See Cox 1994.

The basic logic of the proof is this: If $0 < \pi_j < \pi_2$, then candidate j is virtually sure to lose for sufficiently large n, and voting for the most palatable of the candidates most likely to be tied for first yields a higher expected utility than voting for j. A direct consequence of Theorem 1 is:

> *Corollary 1:* If π is a limit of rational expectations, then $\pi_j \in \{0,\pi_2\}$ for all $j > 2$.

The corollary divides equilibria into two classes: (1) Duvergerian equilibria, with two vote-getting candidates; and (2) non-Duvergerian equilibria, with more than two vote-getting candidates. The Duvergerian equilibria entail a single runner-up, all other candidates being reduced to near-zero support. The non-Duvergerian equilibria entail two or more runners-up, whose nearly identical expected vote totals prevent any being winnowed out from the field of viable candidates.

The intuitive motivation for the results just presented is as follows. Imagine a particular expected order of finish between $K = 3$ candidates:

Candidate 1 is expected to finish first, 2 second, and 3 third. Nothing is said about how far ahead of candidate $j + 1$ candidate j is. It might be a small proportional difference, or a large one. If it is small, and the electorate is small, then it is not hard to imagine that $j + 1$ might in fact finish ahead of j. In particular, if 3 is close to 2, then the chances of 1 and 2 tying for first may not be much greater than the chances of 1 and 3 tying for first. As the electorate grows, however, and assuming that the distribution of vote shares collapses around its mean (i.e., π), it becomes less and less plausible that 3 might overhaul 2 and compete with 1 for the seat.[6] Thus, votes for 3 become less and less attractive from the point of view of affecting the outcome, relative to votes for 1 and 2, with the consequence that all short-term instrumental voters desert 3 for either 1 or 2.

Key assumptions

The model discussed in the previous sections embodies one set of assumptions that are sufficient to produce pure local bipartism. Ignoring the non-Duvergerian equilibria for the moment, the Duvergerian equilibria yield a strong version of Duverger's Law: All third parties are reduced to zero support, utterly devastated by strategic voting. This is local bipartism with a vengeance.

What are the assumptions in the model necessary to produce this result? I shall mention the four that seem most important.

Note first that if preferences are not strict, then the reduction of trailing candidates (those expected to place third or lower) to zero is not necessary. Candidate 3's supporters will never desert him if they rank 1 and 2 *equally*. For then there is nothing to choose between the front-runners; any voter who most prefers 3 has a dominant strategy actually to vote for 3. Allowing for the possibility of indifference, one would have to modify the conclusion of Theorem 1: Trailing candidates would be reduced, not to zero support, but to their "hard-core" support (consisting of all those who viewed the front-runners as equally bad alternatives). This is not a terribly important caveat if there are not many voters who are (nearly) indifferent between two or more candidates. But there may be situations in which fairly large numbers of voters do feel intensely about their first choices and relatively weakly about the difference between their second and third choices, in which case the effect of expectations may be relatively small relative to that of preferences.

[6]Even if the probability q_{12} that 1 and 2 tie tends to zero, the probability q_{13} that 1 and 3 tie is so small that q_{13}/q_{12} tends to zero. Put another way, even given the unlikely event that a tie for first occurs, the probability that this tie is between 1 and 3 tends to zero as the electorate increases.

This is the pattern that Blais and Nadeau (N.d.) find in some Canadian elections.

Another technical assumption that is necessary to reduce trailing candidates to zero is that all types of voters are represented in the electorate (the support set of F is U). If one dispenses with this assumption, then it may be that a particular candidate has such an advantage in terms of the distribution of voter preferences that he will win with certainty. Suppose, for example, that there is a unidimensional policy space along which the parties are arrayed; a large centrist party preferred by, say, 45% of the electorate; and a smattering of small parties to the left and right. In this case, assuming that a party's spatial position captures everything about it that voters value and that all voters have single-peaked preferences, it will be common knowledge that the centrist party can defeat any other single party in a pairwise competition. It will not be politically feasible to construct an ends-against-the-center coalition, and the victory of the centrist will be certain. Accordingly, there will be no reason for a voter to desert his or her favorite leftist or rightist party: Small parties will continue, and strategic voting will be minimal, in the face of a Condorcet winner. This is essentially Riker's analysis of the Indian case, with the Congress Party playing the role of the centrist (Riker 1976).

A more pragmatic take on the same point goes as follows. The more obvious it is that a particular candidate is going to win, the less pressure there is to vote strategically. The less obvious it is who will win, the more pressure to vote effectively rather than expressively.

A third, more substantive, assumption that is necessary to preserve the strong local bipartism result derived in Theorem 1 is that all voters are short-term instrumentally rational. This assumption excludes voters who take a long-term, albeit still instrumental, viewpoint: voters, for example, who seek to affect the outcome of future elections by demonstrating stubbornness in this election. (Supporters of the Prohibition Party in the turn-of-the-century United States may have believed that by demonstrating a willingness to incur the cost of a bad outcome this time, they could convince their most likely major-party partner to adopt their viewpoint on liquor. Similarly, perhaps those who voted for the richest of the three candidates in the 1992 U.S. presidential election can be characterized as "waiting for Perot," rather than as miscalculating the then-relevant electoral probabilities. Such speculations cast an interesting light on the notion of electoral realignment but are not pursued here.) Assuming short-term instrumental rationality also excludes voters who derive a direct consumption value from the act of voting for one or another candidate: voters, for example, who use their vote to affirm allegiance to a political cause. Introducing voters who are not short-term instrumentally rational into the model modifies the result of Theorem 1 roughly as follows: Trailing candidates are deserted, not by all voters, but by all short-term instrumentally rational voters (cf. Cox 1994). The more short-term instrumentally rational voters there are, then, the more closely does the theoretically predicted result approximate that of the baseline model.

A fourth condition necessary to generate pure local bipartism is that the identity of trailing and front-running candidates is common knowledge. The extent to which this knowledge is public keeps all instrumental voters on the same page of the playbook: They *all* desert the (publicly identified) trailing candidates in order to focus on the (publicly identified) front-running candidates. (There are several assumptions in the model that contribute to this certainty and consensus on the part of voters regarding candidate chances but two are particularly important: first, that voters' expectations are rational; second, that in the limit voters can be virtually certain about the candidates' order of finish.)

One might argue for the reasonableness of the common knowledge assumption by noting the self-fulfilling character of voter expectations. If every voter *believes* that candidate *j* is out of the running, then he will in fact *be* out of the running. Moreover, if some voters, who previously intended to vote for *j*, come to believe that he is behind, they will desert him, thereby making it more likely that he is behind.

The arguments just given do not really justify *assuming* that the identity of trailing candidates is common knowledge, however; they only justify a belief that, in equilibrium, the identity of trailing candidates will probably be common knowledge. To simply assume the common knowledge condition is similar to assuming that the players in a two-person Battle of the Sexes game will coordinate on one of the two pure-strategy Nash equilibria.

If who trails is not common knowledge, then an extra degree of freedom is opened up in the model. In the extreme, the analyst can stipulate (possibly inconsistent) expectations for each voter. This degree of analytical latitude would be enough to make any pattern of aggregate vote returns consistent with some equilibrium of the model. On the other hand, placing limits on the extent to which voters' expectations differed would begin to restore some "bite" to the model's predictions.

These observations motivate asking how voters learn about the candidates' expected vote shares. In the real world, the forces generating common knowledge of candidate chances are polls, news analyses, candidate statements, and other bits of essentially free information (cf. Johnston et al. 1992:197–211). It has to be free information because rationally ignorant voters will not exert any effort in determining who is ahead, for the same reason that they will not research candidate positions carefully (Downs 1957). Thus, the extent to which the real world approximates the model's strictures should depend on the availability and clarity of free information regarding the relative standing of the candidates. If voters are exposed to lots of free information (e.g., frequently published polls) which reveals some candidates to be clearly trailing the others, and this information seeps out to a large proportion of the instrumental electorate, then one expects that trailing candidates will be left with not much more than their noninstrumental support. If voters have no information regarding candidate chances (and diffuse priors), then sincere voting is consistent with expected utility maximization, and one does not expect objectively trailing candidates (those who have fewer voters ranking them first) to lose their instrumental support. If, to take a third example, voters have conflicting information regarding candidate chances, then strategic voting by some voters may "cancel out" strategic voting by others, leaving little or no observable impact on the aggregate distribution of votes.

One reasonable reaction to the list of conditions necessary to produce pure local bipartism might be that they illuminate the *limits* to Duverger's reasoning. That there are such limits Duverger himself emphasized: that is why he stated his law as only a tendency. The advantage of the formal model is that it specifies some of the limitations. In particular, the model suggests that failures to achieve the drastic reduction in third party vote totals predicted by Theorem 1 can flow from (1) the presence of voters who are not short-term instrumentally rational; (2) lack of public information about voter preferences and vote intentions (hence about which candidates are likely to be "out of the running"); (3) public belief that a particular candidate will win with certainty; or (4) the presence of many voters who care intensely about their first choice and are nearly indifferent between their second and lower choices.

Although quite a few assumptions are needed to generate a pure local bipartism result, it should be noted that much less is needed to generate appropriate comparative statics results. To generate a tendency toward bipartism it is sufficient, for example, to posit (1) short-term instrumentally rational voters; (2) reasonably accurate and publicly available information on candidate standings (π); and (3) myopic ("price-taking") adjustment. Such a dynamic adjustment model will converge to a Duvergerian equilibrium. Consider, for example, a situation in which the percentage of voters ranking Candidate 1 first is 36%, the percentage ranking 2 first is also 36%, and the percentage ranking 3 first is 28%. A sequence of r random-sample polls is taken, each with a margin of error of +/– 1%. If all voters answer the first poll sincerely and then respond truthfully regarding their current vote intentions, it will rapidly become evident that the chance of 3 tying for first is small relative to that of 1 and 2 tying for first. Thus, 3's least-committed supporters – for whom 1 or 2 are good substitutes –

will desert him. The next poll will reflect this desertion and lower the chance of 3 tying for first even more, and so on (cf. Fey 1995).[7]

4.3 STRATEGIC VOTING AS AN EXPLANATION OF REAL-WORLD PHENOMENA

In this section, I consider the empirical usefulness of the results just sketched. There is no question that short-term instrumentally rational agents of the type stipulated, with rational expectations, will behave in a very precise fashion. But of course it is possible to doubt that real people are entirely instrumentally motivated, or that they have rational expectations, hence to doubt the result that strategic voting will devastate third parties.

Overly precise predictions are typical of highly abstract models and a typical (often unstated) assumption of theoreticians is that the model's predictions could fairly easily be made more reasonable, without changing their qualitative nature, by adding a bit of "noise" or "friction" to the model. I have suggested what some of the noise to be added might be above. Even if adding noise, say in the form of noninstrumental voters or of voters whose expectations are inconsistent, can in principle produce predictions that tend toward local bipartism without going all the way, there is still interest in two questions: First, do real-world data conform sufficiently closely to the model's predicted equilibria so that one might believe that a model essentially similar to this one (just adding noise) might tally with real-world patterns? Second, even if the real world conforms to stylized versions of the model's equilibria, are there other explanations that predict the same patterns? I shall examine each of these topics – empirical patterns and alternative explanations – in turn.

Empirical patterns: The literature

The main pattern that the model predicts is the strategic desertion of trailing candidates by their instrumental supporters. Empirically, there is substantial evidence in the literature that real voters do vote strategically in simple plurality contests for legislative office, whether one talks of elections to the German *Bundestag* (see below), the British House of Commons (see below), the Liverpool City Council (Laver 1987), the Canadian House of Commons (Blais, Renaut, and Desrosiers 1974; Black 1978, 1980; Bowler and Lanoue 1992; Blais and Nadeau N.d.), or

[7]Even if one allows voters to answer polls strategically, this should not change the outcome much. What might change the result is if the margin of error in the poll were large relative to the difference in support between candidates.

the New Zealand House of Commons (Vowles and Aimer 1993:25, 157; Catt 1991; Rydon 1989:137; Levine and Roberts 1991).[8]

To give an idea of what is, and is not, in the literature, I shall consider the German and British evidence in more detail. One might question whether the German evidence really belongs in the simple plurality column. It is true that voters in each constituency possess a single exclusive vote and that plurality rule determines the winner. But Germans also have a second vote which they may cast for a list within their *Land,* and it is the list votes that determine how many seats each party will receive. So why would German voters care who won in their district? One way to think of it is in terms of the *Überhangmandat* clause, whereby parties that win more constituency seats than their list votes would be entitled to nonetheless keep their "extra" seats. In light of this rule, electing another Christian Democrat as a constituency candidate may make sense to a Free Democrat (FDP) voter who detests the major alternative, the Social Democrats (SPD). Readers who believe that this explanation demands too much of the German voter may find another idea more plausible: that the identity of the local representative is valued in itself, above and beyond the balance of party forces in the *Bundestag.* Either way, strategic voting in German constituencies should be similar to that in English constituencies.

Strategic voting in Germany. The (English-language) literature has four main pieces on "ordinary" strategic voting in West Germany – Barnes et al. (1962), Fisher (1973), Jesse (1988), and Bawn (1993) – all employing essentially the same methodology. Each takes the difference between a candidate's *own* vote total (cast for him or her in a given constituency) and a candidate's *party's* vote total (cast for the party list in the same constituency) as a measure of strategic voting.[9] In particular, a candidate whose own vote falls short of his or her party's vote is taken to have been strategically deserted. In each case, substantial desertion of small parties is found. For example, Fisher (1973:297–8) reports that 13.5% of the FDP's list voters deserted the party in the single-member district contests in 1961, with the comparable figure being 29.7% in 1965, and 38.0% in 1969. Jesse's more extensive study finds FDP desertion rates as high as 61.8% in 1972, 70.9% in 1983, and 61.3% in 1987.

[8] There is also evidence on strategic voting in executive elections. On U.S. presidential elections (not strictly plurality rule but comparable), see e.g. Brody and Page (1973), Abramson et al. 1995. On mayoral elections in Taipei, see Hsieh, Niou, and Paolino (1995). On presidential elections in Mexico and Peru, see Magaloni Kerpel (1994) and Schmidt (1996, N.d.), respectively.

[9] The candidate votes are called *Erststimme* (or "first votes"), the list votes *Zweitstimme* (or "second votes"). Similar analyses also appear in German; see, e.g., Ritter and Niehuss (1987:177-78).

Casting a list vote for the FDP and a candidate vote for, say, the Christian Democratic Union (CDU) is not unambiguous evidence of "ordinary" strategic voting, however. It may be that the voter truly prefers the CDU, casts a sincere vote for the CDU candidate, but casts her list vote strategically for the FDP, because the FDP is both in alliance with the CDU and in danger of falling below the 5% national threshold (in which case the FDP would get no seats and the CDU might not be able to form a government). There is substantial evidence that supporters of the FDP's senior coalition partner have deserted their favored party in order to support the FDP (reviewed in Chapter 10). So how is one to tell whether some component of the discrepancy between the FDP's candidate and list votes is due to "ordinary" strategic voting, intended to avoid wasting the constituency vote?

One approach is to look at surveys that ask voters if they cast split votes and, if so, why. These lend some support to the idea that there is local strategic voting (cf. Roberts 1988:330). Another approach is to look at the district-by-district election returns. If those who give the FDP their list but not their candidate votes are acting for local strategic reasons, then desertion rates should be higher in districts where the contest for the seat is closer. But there is no reason that strategic *list* votes should be cast differentially in constituencies that are close in terms of the candidate votes. Thus, if there is a systematic relationship between the closeness of the constituency race and the FDP desertion rate in each constituency, then this suggests that there are locally strategic voters in Germany too.[10]

To investigate this possibility, let the FDP's percent of the total candidate vote in a given constituency be denoted FDP1, with the FDP's percent of the total list vote in that same constituency denoted FDP2. Similarly, let GREEN1 and GREEN2 denote the percent of candidate and list votes won by the Greens. The dependent variables in the analyses presented below are two: FDPLOSS = FDP2 – FDP1, measuring the loss the FDP candidate suffers from the baseline set by the party's list vote; and GRLOSS = GREEN2 – GREEN1, a similar term for the Greens. I regressed each of these dependent variables on MARGIN, the absolute difference between the top two candidates' vote percentages in the constituency, for the 1987 and 1990 elections. As MARGIN gets larger, the margin of victory in the district gets larger, and the temptation to desert one's first choice wanes. Thus, a negative coefficient is expected in both cases.[11]

[10]Another reason often suggested as to why German voters split their votes is that they misunderstand the importance of the *Zweitstimmen*, or "second vote." There is no reason why this misunderstanding should correlate with the closeness of the constituency race, however.

[11]The data for this analysis, along with relevant SAS programs, can be found on the Lijphart Elections Archive's web site (http://dodgson.ucsd.edu/lij) by following the link to "publication-related datasets."

Table 4.1. Loss of votes by small German parties in constituency contests, relative to list contests

	Dependent variable and year of election			
Independent variables	*FDPLOSS 1987*	*FDPLOSS 1990*	*GRLOSS 1987*	*GRLOSS 1990*
CONSTANT	5.02 (33.5)	4.36 (27.8)	2.04 (20.3)	–.45 (5.5)
MARGIN	–.04 (5.3)	–.04 (5.1)	–.05 (10.7)	–.02 (4.7)
N =	247	254	247	254
adjusted R^2 =	.10	.09	.32	.08

As can be seen in Table 4.1, the coefficient on MARGIN is negative and significant in all four regressions. Not all of this effect is necessarily conventional strategic voting, wherein those who truly rank the third parties first desert them when the district race gets close. Some of it may be due to protest voting by major party voters: If the constituency result is a foregone conclusion, one can take the opportunity to send a pro-environment message to the major parties by voting for the Green candidate.

Strategic voting in Great Britain. The literature on strategic voting in Britain is by far the largest in the world. Much of this literature deals with the elections of the 1980s, when the Alliance surged to near-parity in votes with the Labour Party. Johnston and Pattie (1991) estimate that 5.1% of all voters voted tactically in 1983, with 7.7% doing so in 1987. Heath et al. (1991:54) estimate that "6.5% of major party voters" voted tactically in 1987. Lanoue and Bowler (1992) opine that 5.8% of all voters in 1983, and 6.6% of all voters in 1987, voted tactically. Niemi, Whitten, and Franklin (1992) find these estimates, especially those for 1987, "surprisingly low ... in the light of the efforts of various groups to encourage tactical voting in order to avoid fragmentation of the anti-Thatcher vote." Interpreting survey responses differently, they estimate that about 17% of all voters were tactical in 1987, a figure which is in accord with an ITN/Harris Exit Poll conducted on election night.[12] Another high-end estimate is offered by Crewe (1987:55), who notes that "among the 23 percent of respondents who claimed to have voted or seriously considered voting Alliance, before deciding against, the

[12]See Evans and Heath (1993) for a critique, and Niemi, Whitten, and Franklin (1993) for a defense of the Niemi, Whitten, and Franklin (1992) methodology.

overwhelming reason given was some variation of the classic 'wasted vote' argument." Estimates of the percentage of voters that would "consider" voting tactically also vary widely, from an average Gallup figure in 1986–87 of 15% to an average BBC Newsnight figure of 41% (Catt 1989). Even taking the low estimates both of voters that did cast, and voters that would consider casting, a tactical vote, the impact in terms of seats is potentially significant. Butler and Kavanagh (1988:266), for example, reckon that the Conservatives would have won 16 more seats than they did in 1987, had there been no strategic voting.

In addition to estimating the extent of tactical voting, the British literature also explores the determinants of such voting. Lanoue and Bowler (1992) and Niemi, Whitten, and Franklin (1992) both run probit analyses of the probability that individual survey respondents will (report having) cast a tactical vote. Both find that individuals with intense partisan attachments are less likely to vote strategically. This makes sense since intense attachments to one party make it more likely that the other two will be viewed as almost equally bad, which approximates one of the theoretical conditions under which strategic voting is unlikely. Niemi, Whitten, and Franklin also find that respondents whose favorite party was further from contending for the seat, who were better educated, who recalled knowing which party was expected to win, and who had negative feelings about the winning party, were more likely to vote tactically. All these findings fit comfortably with the model of tactical voting expounded above. Voters whose favorite parties ended up out of the running, who were better educated, and who knew before the election who was likely to win in their constituencies, were more likely to know (before the election) that their party was trailing and to have heard the relevant wasted vote argument: hence more likely to have voted strategically. Voters who had negative feelings about the winning party, especially if intense, were more likely to view their second-ranked party as an acceptable vehicle with which to defeat their last-ranked (and clearly threatening) party.

The importance of there being a clear ordering of the second and third candidates is also documented by Galbraith and Rae (1989). Focusing on districts won by the Conservatives in 1983, they find that the swing to Labour (resp. the Alliance) in 1987 was significantly larger if Labour (the Alliance) finished second in 1983. The Alliance swing, for example, was 5.3 percentage points larger on average when the Alliance finished second in 1983 than when Labour did.[13] Johnston and Pattie (1991)

[13]Galbraith and Rae (1989) find a larger swing to the Alliance despite an artifactual reason to expect a smaller swing. The artifactual reason is this: If the Alliance finished second in 1983, rather than third, then its vote percentage in 1983 was on average larger. A larger 1983 vote percentage, *ceteris paribus,* means a *smaller* swing in 1987.

replicate these findings using a finer-grained measurement of tactical voting and actual vote margins in 1983, rather than just place of finish.

Strategic voting in other countries. In contrast to the plethora of studies of tactical voting in Britain, very little has been written on other countries employing simple plurality, even those whose political conditions approximate those of Britain in the 1980s. There are a few studies of the Canadian and New Zealand experience (cited above), but none that I know concerning India, Trinidad and Tobago, or other developing countries that also use simple plurality.

A brief consideration of the Papua New Guinean experience suffices to show that even simple plurality may not be strong enough to force a sharply divided society into a two-party mold. Papua New Guinea, which became independent of Australia in 1975, has some 700 tribes speaking over 1,000 languages. Its elections, albeit held in single-member districts under simple plurality rules, have not produced any tendencies toward local bipartism. In the 1987 elections, 1,515 candidates chased after 109 seats, with the vote often being fairly evenly divided among the contestants. In the Kerowagi constituency, for example, the winner came in with 7.9% of the poll in a field of 45 candidates. Overall, 41 of the 109 members elected won with less than 20% of the vote (Dorney 1990:57-8). The conditions in Papua New Guinea are almost perfectly designed to discourage strategic voting. With huge fields of candidates, no reliable constituency-level polls, and strong social pressures upon voters to support their own tribes, every candidate (not unreasonably) thinks he may sneak in with a win in a crowded field. Interestingly, what strategic manipulation there is pushes the system toward further fractionalization: "the nomination of 'friendly' candidates to split a powerful opponent's clan vote is a common tactic" (Dorney 1990:59).

Empirical patterns: The bimodality hypothesis

The prediction that third-place candidates will be deserted really holds only in Duvergerian equilibria. What of the non-Duvergerian equilibria? These equilibria all entail that the first and second losers receive nearly the same number of votes. Thus, a theoretically interesting statistic is the ratio of the second to the first loser's vote total – what I shall refer to as the SF ratio. Under Duvergerian equilibria, the SF ratio will be near zero. Under non-Duvergerian equilibria, the SF ratio will be near unity. Thus, if one were to compute the ratio for a number of districts and plot the resulting distribution, one should find a spike at zero and a spike at one.

Allowing for some frictions in the model – e.g., some noninstrumental voters, some disagreement about which candidates are trailing and which are front-running – the prediction is softened. The SF ratio should either be close to unity (when second losers are so close in the polls to first losers that they do not lose their support due to strategic voting) or close to zero (when second losers are sufficiently far behind first losers that strategic voting kicks in and they are reduced to their non-instrumental support level, which I assume to be close to zero for most candidates). The SF distribution, in other words, should be bimodal.

A possible real-world example of a non-Duvergerian equilibrium, with an SF ratio near unity, may have occurred in the Ross and Cromarty district of the United Kingdom in its 1970 general election. The final figures were:

Gray	Conservative	6,418
Mackenzie	Liberal	5,617
MacLean	Labour	5,023
Nicholson	Scottish Nationalist	2,268

It is possible, of course, that these figures are the net product of all sorts of strategic calculations by voters – cross-cutting, erroneous, shrewd, etc. Interpreting these results as if they stemmed from a non-Duvergerian equilibrium entails believing the following two points. First, the Liberal and Labour candidates were so close that, before the poll was actually held, it was not at all clear who was in third and who in second; thus, Mackenzie's and MacLean's supporters stuck with them: Neither suffered from strategic desertion. Second, Nicholson did lose his "non-fanatical" support, if any, due to his being obviously out of the running. The 2,264 voters who stuck with him were perhaps those who felt so strongly about the single issue of Scottish independence that they were virtually indifferent between the other three candidates. Alternatively, these voters may have been making an investment in the future, hoping to establish the Scottish Nationalists in their district for a more realistic run at a later time. In either case, they were not short-term instrumentally rational.

I have tested the bimodality hypothesis empirically using data from British elections 1983–1992. Some results, which focus on the behavior of Labour voters, are presented in Figures 4.1 to 4.3. The procedure was as follows. First, I computed the ratio of the vote total of the second loser (third-place candidate) to the vote total of the first loser (second-place candidate) for all districts in which the Conservatives and the Alliance (or its successor, the Liberal Democrats) finished one-two (in some

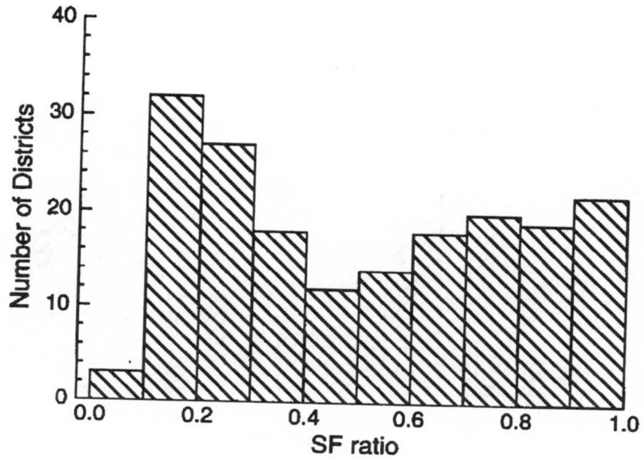

Figure 4.1. Testing the bimodality hypothesis in moderately close districts: British elections, 1983–1992

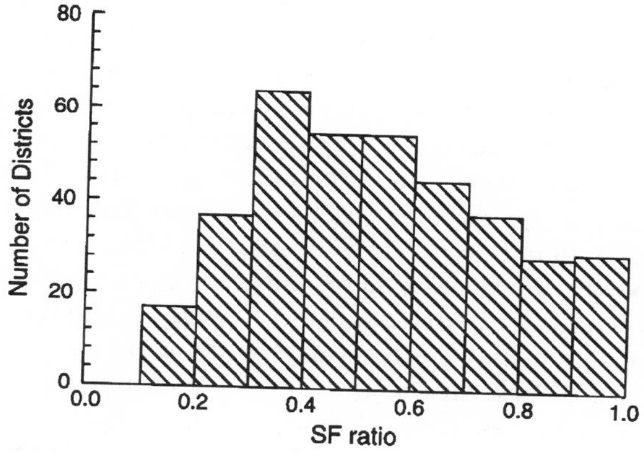

Figure 4.2. Testing the bimodality hypothesis in districts that were not closely contested: British elections, 1983–1992

order), with Labour finishing third.[14] Then I produced a histogram to summarize the distribution of the resulting SF ratios, subject to three different restrictions on the margin of victory in the previous race in the dis-

[14]Note that in principle there is a sample selection bias that militates against finding any strategic voting. Only those districts in which third parties decided to field candidates enter the sample. If third parties decide to enter where they think they can hold on to their votes, then the level of strategic voting in the sample will not be representative of the level that would appear were entry decisions exogenous. In practice, this does not appear to be too important, since third parties enter in most U.K. districts.

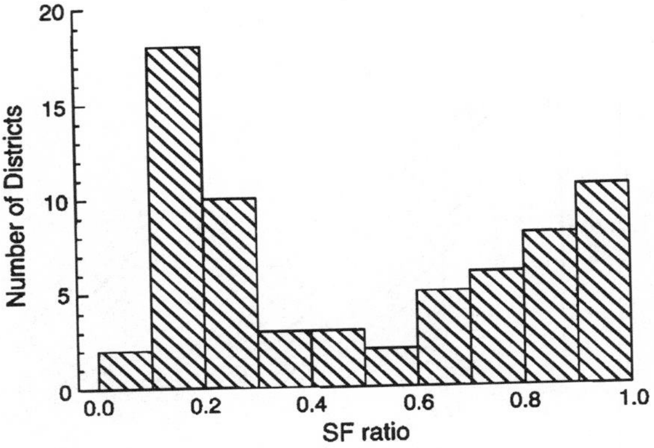

Figure 4.3. Testing the bimodality hypothesis in very close districts: British elections, 1983–1992

trict: that the margin was less than 20% (Figure 4.1), greater than 20% (Figure 4.2), or less than 10% (Figure 4.3).

As can be seen in Figure 4.1, the distribution of SF ratios is bimodal in districts in which Labour ran third and there had been a "close" race (margin less than 20%) the previous time out. In these districts, Labour held on to its support if its candidate was a close enough third, but lost substantial support if its candidate fell too far behind. In contrast, Figure 4.2 shows the SF distribution for districts which, while also featuring a third-place Labour finish, had not been "close" in the previous election. There is no hint of bimodality in the distribution, suggesting that voters do not bother to vote strategically in noncompetitive districts. The importance of a common perception that the race may be close is further suggested by Figure 4.3, which looks just at districts in which the previous race was "very close" (margin less than 10%). As can be seen, the dip in the middle of the SF distribution is even more pronounced in these "very close" districts, suggesting that voters were more willing to vote strategically in more competitive districts. These results comport with previous analyses of the 1983 and 1987 elections (reviewed above) using survey data.

Although the evidence just discussed does indicate there is strategic voting in *some* British constituencies, the constituencies chosen for inclusion in the analysis were those in which it would have made sense for voters to consider a tactical vote (the strategy of investigation here is similar to that in Blais and Nadeau N.d.). If one looks at other districts, one finds much less evidence of strategic voting. Just as the survey evidence shows a distinct minority of the electorate voting strategically – many not being in a position that would logically call for a strategic vote – the aggregate evidence shows a distinct minority of districts with substantial levels of strategic voting – many not being in a position that would produce larger levels.

Alternative explanations

Although the model of strategic voting generates empirically testable predictions, some of which are new, in the sense that they have not been noticed in the previous literature, there are also some obvious alternative explanations that might explain the pattern of evidence uncovered in the previous section. The problem is that *any* class of agents who care about the outcome of the election – not just voters but also activists, contributors, and candidates – will tend to allocate whatever resources they control (labor, money, etc.) to front-running candidates, where they are more likely to affect the outcome, rather than to trailing candidates, where they are less likely to affect the outcome. Moreover, allocation or reallocation of resources to front-running candidates should produce the clearest aggregate results (trailing candidates deprived of all instrumental support) when who is trailing and who is not is widely agreed and the margin of victory is small. Thus, the empirical evidence adduced above is far from proving that a significant proportion of the electorate votes strategically. It may be that contributors give only (or mostly) to front-running candidates, or that trailing candidates try to sell their endorsement to front-runners.

The elite-level hypotheses are attractive in that it is more plausible that elite actors, having larger stakes in the outcome, will pay attention to how close the race is and respond by diverting resources to front-running candidates. Put negatively, it is unlikely that ordinary voters will pay any attention at all, since their single votes have an infinitesimal chance of affecting the outcome. If it is at all costly to find out who is trailing or to calculate expected utilities, rational voters should avoid these costs, since bearing them has virtually no impact on the outcome (Meehl 1977; Riker 1982).

Nonetheless, despite the apparent advantages of elite-based models, it is not clear that one can reject the voter-based model. The informational and cognitive costs of strategic voting are modest and may be borne entirely as by-products of everyday activities, such as reading the newspaper, watching TV, or attending college courses in politics. Information on the relative standings of candidates is sometimes published in polls; it does not take a rocket scientist to understand traditional wasted vote arguments; and these arguments are sometimes hard to avoid, being urged by concerned elites.

The sensitivity of elite actors to the possibility of strategic voting can be seen in three observations. First, during the 1987 general election in the United Kingdom, a group called TV87 formed whose sole purpose was to instruct voters how best to cast a tactical anti-Conservative vote. Their activities consisted primarily in identifying which of the non-Conservative candidates in each constituency were ahead in the latest polls and urging anti-Conservative voters to coordinate on these candidates (Lanoue and Bowler 1992; Catt 1989).

Second, candidates trailing in multicandidate races tend to dispute the accuracy of the polls that show them trailing, to claim to have different results in proprietary polling, and to urge voters to ignore the polls. All these actions make good sense from the point of view of preventing their last-place status from becoming common knowledge. These trailing candidates find allies in their attempts to avoid the logic of the wasted vote in front-runners who expect a net loss should the trailing candidacy go down the tubes (recall, for example, Ronald Reagan's support of John Anderson's candidacy in 1980), and foes in front-runners who expect a net gain of support (recall Jimmy Carter's persistent reminders to voters not to waste their vote on Anderson).

Third, candidates who believe they are breaking out of the non-Duvergerian pack into a clear second-place position tend to advertise this fact ostentatiously. Thus, for example, George Bush's crowing about "Big Mo" in the 1980 presidential primaries after his strong finish in the early contests (Bartels 1988) or Merrill Cook's heavy advertising of his second-place poll finishes (as an independent running for the governorship in Utah; see Magleby and Monson 1995).

All this suggests that voters in the real world may strategically desert weak candidates for essentially the reasons stylized in the model. It is true that the whole process is mediated by elites: They point out that the race is close and that votes on weak candidates are wasted (or attempt to obfuscate this fact). But the voters do the rest: They buy the argument and act accordingly. Empirically, I think that there is substantial evidence that voters have voted strategically in this sense (some of it reviewed above). The question of the relative importance of strategic reallocation of votes in the mass electorate as opposed to strategic reallocation of other resources in the elite strata remains open, however.

4.4 NOMINATION RULES AND STRATEGIC VOTING

Perhaps the clearest example of electoral rules that nullify the alliance-promoting (party-reducing) effect of single-member districts, *even when plurality rule is used,* is encountered in New York state. New York has had a stable multiparty system since the 1940s, despite using plurality rule in single-member districts. The explanation lies in its peculiar mix of rules governing cross-filing, cross-endorsement, and ballot format.

Cross-filing occurs when a candidate for office files not just for his own party's primary but also for one or more others' as well. If a state allows cross-filing, factions within the major parties can open up shop as separate parties without necessarily sacrificing any influence they have in their original party: Their candidates can run in both the minor party's primary and in the major party's primary. California's Progressives took this route in the early part of the century (Scarrow 1986:250).

Cross-endorsement, or fusion, occurs when more than one party nominates the same candidate (and the endorsements appear on the general election ballot). This feature too can provide small parties with an electoral niche to occupy; by regularly nominating one of the major parties' candidates as their own, and stipulating in advance the criteria that will be used in choosing, small parties can influence big parties.[15]

The success of this tactic of "auctioning" the small party's endorsement may depend on ballot structure. If a state uses the party-column format, in which all candidates endorsed by a given party appear in a single column with the offices forming the rows, then a cross-endorsed candidate will appear once on the ballot for each party that endorsed him. This allows minor parties to document the size of their voting blocs, since a candidate's total vote will be the sum of his votes in each party's column. In a series of close races, when their support is crucial, this can give small parties considerable bargaining power. If a state uses the office-block format, in which all candidates for a given office appear in a single area of the ballot, together with all their party endorsements, the vote total for the candidate cannot be broken down into subtotals due to each party. The nomination of a small party may still be valuable, but its value is harder to assess.

Since 1947, New York has restricted cross-filing to those who can get the permission of the relevant party's executive committee, allowed unlimited cross-endorsement, and employed a party-column ballot. These three features interact to produce a system quite favorable to the formation and maintenance of minor parties. Small parties can document the size of their vote at general elections and essentially "sell" it (in return for policy or particularistic considerations) to the highest major-party bidder. Thus, what would ordinarily be the left wing of the Democratic party in New York has broken off to form the Liberal party and what would ordinarily be the right wing of the Republican party has broken off to form the Conservative party. Other small parties, of the

[15]Currently, ten states allow fusion in state and national elections: Arkansas, Connecticut, Delaware, Idaho, Mississippi, New York, South Carolina, South Dakota, Utah, and Vermont. See Kirschner (1995). I am unaware of any systematic study of the consequences of fusion outside of the New York case, however, except for the important historical studies of Argersinger (e.g., 1980).

single-issue variety, have found viable niches to occupy as well (Mazmanian 1974; Scarrow 1986).

From the voter's point of view, the New York system can remove any fear of wasting votes by casting them for small parties. So long as a small party supports a viable *candidate,* one also nominated by a major party, their supporters can just as well vote for that candidate under the small party's label as under the major party's label: The candidate's viability is unaffected.

New York shows rather clearly that a single-member plurality system in the general election is no guarantee of "ordinary" bipartism, in which third parties are evanescent and/or politically ineffective. One might argue, then, that the statement of the law needs to be modified to include some explicit conditions on nomination rules; perhaps: "the use of a single exclusive vote in single-member districts operating under plurality rule, together with laws preventing cross-filing and cross-endorsement, tends to produce bipartism." Alternatively, one could simply stress that the logic behind Duverger's Law really does not apply to parties, but rather to candidates, the objects of choice with which voters are directly faced.

4.5 THE ALTERNATIVE VOTE AND MULTIPARTISM

Another way to mitigate the concentrating tendencies of simple plurality rule is to switch from an exclusive to a nonexclusive vote. The effects of such a switch can be seen in elections to Australia's lower house, where the alternative vote (AV) allows a citizen's vote to transfer from one candidate's vote total to another's. The procedure is as follows. As in simple plurality, elections are held in single-member constituencies without secondary districts. Each citizen is required to rank *all* candidates seeking election, from first to last.[16] The returning officer first sorts the ballot papers according to which candidate is ranked first. If at this stage any one candidate has a majority of the votes, he or she is declared elected. Otherwise, the candidate with the fewest first-place preferences is declared defeated. The returning officer then transfers the votes of the defeated candidate's supporters to whichever of the remaining candidates they have marked as their next preference, again checking to see if any candidate has achieved a majority of all votes. This process continues

[16]Certain kinds of "mistakes" in ranking candidates are allowed: "A House of Representatives ballot paper is now formal so long as it shows a unique first preference for a candidate and numbers, any numbers, against all the other candidates, or against all the other candidates but one, with the square next to that candidate left blank. Consequently, ballot-papers may be admitted to the scrutiny even when they do not exhibit fully correct numbering, and therefore fail to indicate preferences for all candidates" (McAllister et al. 1990:57).

until some candidate does attain a majority, whereupon he or she is declared elected.

The alternative vote in Australia, like fusion in New York, allows small parties to document their contribution to a larger party's success. It is thus possible, even for parties that virtually never win seats on their own, to play a significant role. Jaensch (1983:21–2) points to three aspects of the Australian electoral system – compulsory attendance at the polls, compulsory ranking of all candidates, and the alternative vote method of translating votes into seats – as underpinning the "blackmail potential" of minor parties. Compulsory attendance at the polls means that minor parties' potential clientele will turn out and, given that few Australians choose purposely to spoil their ballots, vote. Compulsory ranking of all candidates means that those ranking a minor party's candidate first will rank *someone* second. This opens the door for the minor party to influence the outcome of the election by issuing "how to vote" cards urging their supporters to adopt a particular ranking of candidates below first. As Jaensch (*ibid.*) puts it, "a minor party which offers (electoral) support in return for (legislative or policy or electoral) concessions, or which threatens electoral retribution if some concession is not offered, must be able to guarantee the allocation of a high proportion of its preferences." Finally, the AV procedure of counting votes and translating them into seats means that minor party supporters whose party is doomed to elimination at the first round have no reason not to rank their favorite party first. If some party wins on the first count, then they would have done so even had the voter not ranked a hopeless minor party candidate first. If no party wins on the first count, then the voter's vote will transfer to a more viable candidate.

An example of the viability of very small parties in the Australian system is provided by the Democratic Labor Party (DLP), which flourished 1955-74. Although the party never won a seat in the Australian House of Representatives, "Mackerras (1970) calculated that 81.5 per cent of all DLP second preferences followed the direction of the party and were transferred to the Liberal-Country Party coalition candidates. Further, DLP preferences were instrumental in deciding which party should govern in at least two elections, 1961 and 1969. On both occasions, the coalition government was a 'second-preference government,' depending on the DLP" (Jaensch 1983:22).

Despite the hospitality to small parties exhibited by the Australian version of the alternative vote, it would be erroneous to conclude, as is sometimes hinted in the literature, that AV produces no incentives to vote strategically. This conclusion would of course run afoul of the Gibbard-Satterthwaite Theorem's general guarantee that any democratic voting procedure can generate incentives to vote strategically. Dummett (1984), who has considered exactly how strategic voting might arise under AV, points to two main possibilities. First, perhaps one's favorite candidate, while having enough votes to survive the first round, will lose in the second round against one prospective opponent, but probably win against another. In such a case, it behooves one to ensure that the "beatable" opponent is not eliminated in the first round of counting: Thus one may not vote for one's favorite, instead voting for the weaker of two major opponents. Second, perhaps candidate A, who has lots of first preferences and is virtually certain to survive the first round, can defeat your favorite candidate handily but might lose to your second-favorite candidate, who unfortunately has fewer first preferences and is likely therefore to be eliminated in the first round. In this case, it behooves one to vote for one's second-favorite rather than one's favorite.

Note that the first kind of strategic voting under AV, in which one attempts to set up the second round so that one's favorite can win it, does not decrease the effective number of candidates in the first round. Rather just the opposite: One's incentive is to divert votes from a stronger candidate (in terms of first preferences) to a weaker. The second kind of strategic voting, in which one attempts to ensure that a weaker candidate (in terms of first preferences) survives to the second round, may either decrease, leave unchanged, or increase the effective number of candidates. To see this, suppose that one's favorite candidate, C, has 40% of the first preferences, if everyone votes sincerely, while A (whom C cannot beat) also has 40% and B (who can defeat A) has 20%. Suppose also that almost everyone ranking C or A first ranks B second. Depending on whether less than half (but more than one-fourth), exactly half, or more than half of the C-supporters "desert" C and rank B first, the effective number of candidates in the first round will increase, stay the same, or decrease. All three of these cases yield identical *outcomes:* B makes it into the second round, and then defeats C. Thus there is nothing to distinguish them in terms of payoffs. They are all equilibria to the particular game envisioned.

Should we expect strategic voting under AV in practice? On the one hand, voters need more information in order to cast a strategic vote under AV than under ordinary plurality (see Bartholdi and Orlin 1991). On the other hand, some argue that voters will be able to acquire the necessary information and manipulate the system. Dummett (1984:229), discussing the first case above, in which it is necessary to vote for some candidate B in order to prevent another, say C, from surviving the first count, has this to say: "With detailed and reasonably accurate information about the intentions of the voters, such as can be obtained from well-conducted opinion polls, and with a thorough canvass to identify its own supporters, an organized group such as a political party ... can instruct sufficiently many supporters to list A highest to ensure that A is not eliminated at stage 1, and instruct the rest to list B highest, in order to bring about the elimination of A's principal rival C." He thinks it is "not far-fetched to imagine a political organization's acting in this way," citing the activities of the Birmingham Caucus as a real-world example (albeit under another electoral system). Colin Hughes, co-author of one of the standard references on Australian politics (Hughes and Graham 1968), opines that "tactical voting for partisan purposes is readily understood e.g. when it is advisable to run third so that preferences will be distributed to the less undesirable alternative rather than run second and have that candidate's preferences distributed and go to the more undesirable who would then win" (Hughes 1993:5). I am not aware of any systematic evidence that bears on the frequency of strategic voting of this or other kinds in Australian elections, however.

All told, the case would appear as follows. There is certainly the theoretical opportunity for strategic voting under AV, and there is some expert opinion that it appears in practice. But more information is needed to vote strategically under AV than under simple plurality. And, whereas strategic voting always acts to decrease the effective number of candidates under simple plurality, it is as likely to increase as to decrease this figure under AV. Thus, small parties can be viable under AV where they would not be under simple plurality. AV does not exert as strong a reductive influence on the party system as does simple plurality.

4.6 CONCLUSION

This chapter has investigated strategic voting in single-seat elections held under a variety of single-ballot procedures. In the process, I have sought to specify the theoretical and institutional conditions under which Duverger's Law does and does not hold at the local level. My conclusions can be summarized as follows:

Institutional limits on Duverger's Law. In the last three sections, I have considered the U.S. system (a single, exclusive, non-fused candidate vote; cast in a single-member district without secondary districts; decided by plurality rule; with fusion candidacies outlawed), the New York system (identical to the U.S. system except that fusion candidacies are allowed), and the Australian system (identical to the U.S. system except that the vote is nonexclusive and a majority is required for election). It is not usual to describe an electoral system by listing such a long train of features. But each item in the list is arguably necessary to produce local bipartism. Approval voting differs only in that there are multiple votes; and many believe that it would lead to multipartism, although there is no empirical evidence on this score. The Australian alternative vote system differs only in that the vote is nonexclusive (and in the use of majority, rather than plurality, rule); and Australia has more than two significant parties. The SNTV system used formerly in Japan differs only in that the districts were multimember rather than single-member; and postwar Japan has had a multiparty system except briefly in the midfifties. The system used in Germany in 1949 differs only in that there were secondary districts; and Germany at that time had a multiparty system. It is hard to imagine changing the electoral formula holding all else constant. Ignoring differences in the voting options available to voters, however, one might say that the French system differs only in that runoff elections are held if no candidate garners an absolute majority of votes, rather than awarding the seat to the candidate with a relative majority (i.e., a plurality); and France has a multiparty system. Finally, New York's system differs only in that fusion candidacies are allowed; and New York has a multiparty system.

One possible lesson of this exercise is that Duverger's Law really pertains to a quite specific system and is not very robust to small changes in that system. Another possible lesson is that there are many ways one might improve the prospects of smaller parties, and hence promote multipartism. Some ways (increasing the primary district magnitude, or adding a secondary district) entail also improving the overall proportionality of the system. Some ways (making the vote nonexclusive, introducing runoffs, allowing fusion candidacies) do not. Finally, one might conclude that the importance of the plurality formula in promoting bipartism has been exaggerated. It is obviously not a sufficient condition for bipartism (witness New York or West Germany 1949). Nor, in light of Austria, Malta, Colombia, and Uruguay – all of which have had long spells of two-partyism, despite having one form or another of PR – is plurality a necessary condition.

Theoretical limits on Duverger's Law. Suppose that one focuses on the ordinary plurality system originally considered by Duverger. Does the logic of strategic voting play out at the local level as he suggested? Many in the literature take this for granted, convinced by the usual wasted vote argument. In this chapter, I have specified the preconditions that must be met for strategic voting to have much impact and also noted that strategic voting need not necessarily appear in equilibrium in three-candidate races.

Consider the behavioral preconditions of the model first. The model shows that the extent to which strategic voting winnows out weak candidates depends on how many short-term instrumentally motivated voters there are and on how consistent their expectations about the relative standings of the candidates are. The empirical approximation of both these conditions plausibly depends on elite action and propaganda.

American third-party movements (Ross Perot included) frequently emphasize *future* election outcomes: "We may have no real chance this time," they say, "but vote for us anyway, send a message, and help restructure American politics." The established party most hurt by the third party's appeals, in turn, is apt to emphasize the electoral here and now – the instrumental motivations highlighted in the present model. Similarly, elite actions determine how consistent voter beliefs are regarding who is winning and losing. If clear information about candidate chances is provided, one can expect substantial levels of strategic voting and a consequent reduction in the number of viable candidacies. If little (or conflicting) information is provided, then greater amounts of sincere voting (or cross-cutting strategic voting) can be expected, and the tendency toward two viable candidates will be weaker.

Consider next some preconditions of the model concerning the structure of partisan preferences and competition. One such precondition stipulates that not too many voters can have a clear first choice but be essentially indifferent between the rest of the field (since such voters have no incentive to vote strategically). Another precondition, first noted by Riker (1976), forbids the existence of a party that is a sure winner. As one example of when sure winners might arise, consider a polity in which the structure of political competition is really unidimensional, and the largest single party stands athwart the median position in most constituencies. In this case, leftist and rightist voters are "stuck." Even if a supporter of a leftist party notes that her party is out of the running, supporting a larger rightist party does not further her interests and supporting a larger leftist party will still leave that party in, at best, second place (either because the centrist party has enough votes on its own to defeat a coalition of parties on the left, or because, if it does not, it will attract sufficient right-wing support to defeat the leftist challenge). Thus, voters facing such a structure of competition might as well vote sincerely.

Even if all the preconditions of the model are met, the result that follows is still a bit more hedged than the typical formulation in the literature. It is true that the most likely equilibrium in the pure model is a Duvergerian one, in which third parties are devastated by strategic voting. But non-Duvergerian equilibria can arise when two or more candidates are tied for second, because in this case neither will be obviously "out of the running," and hence their supporters will have no clear incentives to desert them. In the pure model these non-Duvergerian equilibria arise only with precise ties for second, and appear to be generally unstable (Fey 1995). But if voters perceive larger variances in candidates' vote shares than they do in the pure model, then near ties (where what counts as "near" is defined relative to the perceived variance in candidate vote totals) may suffice to forestall any clear shaking out of the field of candidates. The present model thus provides specific and empirically testable predictions about what kind of exceptions to local bipartism one should expect – something that has not previously been done in a systematic fashion.

Empirical evidence for local bipartism. Most of the evidence adduced in the literature relating to Duverger's Law has been national-level and, as noted in Chapter 2, the evidence is not very supportive. What is pertinent in assessing the local bipartism argument, of course, is evidence at the constituency level. Here it is certainly possible to find contrary evidence: In recent general elections in Britain and New Zealand, for example, three or more candidates have received significant vote shares in a number of districts. But it is also possible to find ample positive evidence of strategic voting playing the vote-concentrating role attributed to it in the standard view, when key conditions are met. Thus, although there are clear theoretical conditions that limit the force of the local bipartism argument, these conditions can be and are met or approximated sufficiently often to make strategic voting an important force, pushing party systems toward bipartism as Duverger argued.

There are of course other possible avenues to explore in explaining local bipartism. Duverger appropriately suggested that elites may get into the act. Meehl (1977) and Riker (1982) argue that voters have too small a stake in elections to motivate strategic voting, and emphasize elite actors even more strongly. Here, I have noted that strategic reallocation of resources by outcome-oriented elite actors (activists, contributors, candidates) should produce many of the same aggregate patterns as identified in the voters-only model. My personal bias is strongly toward the elite-level hypotheses, as it is in the study of turnout (Cox and Munger 1989). I think strategic voting survives, both in theory and in practice, because one of the things outcome-oriented elites can do in close races to reallocate resources from trailing to front-running candidates is flood the mass media with "wasted vote" arguments (including therein both the relevant evidence on candidate standings and the basic logic motivating a strategic vote).

Beyond bipartism. Finally, I should note that the wasted vote arguement does not imply local bipartism, as Duverger and others in the literature have asserted. The argument does provide a reason to expect downward pressure on the number of competitors, in case there are more than two, as shown in this chapter. But, although I have spoken here of the "local bipartism" result, the wasted vote argument does not in fact provide any reason to expect upward pressure on the number of competitors, in case there is only one. I elaborate on this point in the next chapter.

5

Strategic voting in multimember districts

Compared to the attention they have lavished on strategic voting in single-member simple plurality elections, scholars have neglected strategic voting in multimember districts. We do have the Leys-Sartori conjecture – the thesis that strategic voting will be politically significant, acting to reduce the number of competitors, under PR systems with low district magnitudes, high thresholds, or other features that militate against the success of small parties. But there is not much systematic empirical evidence to back this claim up. Indeed, neither Leys nor Sartori cite or adduce any evidence at all; their conjecture is based on their own insight and an informal appeal to logic.

In this chapter, I consider three different multimember electoral systems: the single nontransferable vote (SNTV) system; the largest-remainders proportional representation (LRPR) system; and the divisor-based proportional representation (DBPR) system. For each system, I show how one can adapt the model of strategic voting used in the previous chapter to cover multimember elections. Key assumptions about voters remain the same. What changes are the rules of the election in which voters participate.

The main goals of this chapter are two. First, I will show that, for each of the multimember systems considered, a direct generalization of Duverger's Law, which I call the "$M + 1$ rule," exists. The $M + 1$ rule states that no more than $M + 1$ candidates (in the case of SNTV) or lists (in the case of LRPR and DBPR) can be viable – i.e., proof against strategic voting – in an M-seat district. When $M = 1$, this yields the local version of Duverger's Law developed in the previous chapter (because all three systems reduce to plurality rule in single-member districts). For $M > 1$, the PR results provide a specific quantitative version of the Leys-Sartori conjecture, while the SNTV results formalize a thesis first advanced by Reed (1991).

Second, I shall provide empirical evidence that strategic voting does in practice play the role assigned to it in theory. In particular, relevant data are marshaled from multimember districts in Japan (SNTV), Colombia (LRPR), and Spain (DBPR).

Three subsidiary themes of this chapter are as follows. First, I shall show that strategic voting need not necessarily have a reductive impact. That is, there exist modalities of strategic voting that do not have the classical vote-concentrating effect upon which Duverger and the subsequent literature have focused. An extended consideration of one kind of "nonstandard" strategic voting is undertaken for the case of Chile.

Second, I shall emphasize that, even when strategic voting does exert a reductive influence, it only imposes an upper bound on the number of viable candidates or lists.[1] The local version of Duverger's Law states that ordinary plurality elections usually lead to *two* viable candidates. But the only explicit argument in favor of this prediction is that third-party candidates will suffer substantially from strategic voting (and hence may not enter to begin with). This argument only says that there cannot be three or more: It puts an upper bound on the number of viable candidates, not a lower bound.

Third, I shall argue that strategic voting ought to fade out in multimember districts when the district magnitude gets much above five. The logic behind this argument is simply that it gets harder and harder to satisfy the informational assumptions of the model as district magnitude increases. This does not provide a very precise idea about when strategic voting ought to fade out, but empirically (in Japan, Colombia, and Spain at least) it seems to be above magnitude 5.

The layout of the chapter is structural rather than thematic. That is, I consider each of the three main multimember electoral systems – SNTV, LRPR, and DBPR – in turn, running through the five themes just highlighted for each system (rather than marching down the themes, with comments on each system under the thematic headings).

5.1 SNTV

Perhaps the simplest way to describe SNTV is to say that it is identical in all respects to the Anglo-American system of single-member districts operating under plurality rule, except that the district magnitude (the

[1] I believe that the first person to make a point along these lines was Wildavsky (1959:307, n. 11): "At best, however, Duverger's law argues for the discouragement of local multipartism rather than necessarily for the maintenance of local bipartism. Communities ... may well find sufficient political expression through a single party."

number of members elected from each district) is not fixed at one but instead is larger. In both systems, the nation is divided into a number of geographically defined constituencies from each of which a prespecified number of representatives are returned. In both systems, each voter has one (nontransferable) vote to cast. In both systems, the winning candidates in each district are the top M vote-getters, where M is the district magnitude.[2] From this perspective, the SMSP system of voting can be thought of as a special case of SNTV, corresponding to $M = 1$.

This formal similarity between SMSP and SNTV extends to the nature of strategic voting incentives under the two systems. Steven Reed (1991) was the first to note this in his article extending Duverger's Law to the Japanese case. In Reed's formulation, both strategic voting in the mass electorate and prudent withdrawals by candidates (those who fear bearing the brunt of strategic voting) serve to push the number of viable candidates in M-seat Japanese districts toward $M + 1$. In previous work, I have formalized the strategic voting part of Reed's argument, showing that in the equilibria of a pure model – with short-term instrumentally rational voters possessed of rational expectations, as in Chapter 4 – typically at most $M + 1$ candidates can expect to get positive vote shares (Cox 1994).

The reason for saying that "*typically* at most $M + 1$ candidates can expect to get positive vote shares" is that strategic voting equilibria under SNTV come in both Duvergerian and non-Duvergerian varieties, just as do equilibria under SMSP. Duvergerian equilibria correspond to situations in which there is a clear gap separating the first from the second loser, so that the latter is perceived as having virtually no chance of competing for the last-allocated seat, and hence suffers strategic desertion. Non-Duvergerian equilibria correspond to situations in which it is not clear *ex ante* who will be the first loser and who the second, with the result that neither suffers from strategic desertion, and the number of viable candidates exceeds $M + 1$.

The reason for saying "*at most* $M + 1$ candidates can expect to get positive vote shares" is to emphasize that all a consideration of strategic voting gets one is an upper bound on the number of competitors. Reed, like Duverger, offers his $M + 1$ rule as a point estimate of the number of competitors, not an upper bound. But if all one appeals to is the wasted vote argument, then having just M candidates is certainly an allowable

[2]The Japanese did impose an additional requirement: In order to win a seat, a candidate had to garner more than a legally defined "minimum vote." The minimum was set at such a low value, however, that no candidate who finished in the top M places in a district failed to attain it. Taiwan has a similar requirement.

outcome (when there are just M candidates, all of them will win and voters have no incentives to vote strategically). It is true that there is a plausible auxiliary argument, having nothing to do with strategic voting, that suggests that there will be more than M candidates. After all, if there are only M candidates then a potential entrant might very well see his or her chances of securing a seat as pretty good, and therefore enter.

I would just note three things about this auxiliary argument. First, neither Duverger nor Reed make this argument explicitly, nor does anyone else in the electoral studies literature, as far as I know. Second, in the $M = 1$ case, there have been pockets of one-party rule in the U.S. in which uncontested races are not particularly rare. Third, Greenberg and Shepsle (1987) show that M-candidate equilibria can in principle arise under SNTV. The logic of their model is that M candidates, the current entrants, may have adopted positions such that no new entrant can win a seat. In this case, no new competitor (at least of the seat-seeking kind) will wish to enter. The Greenberg-Shepsle model thus constitutes a theoretical criticism of the implicit argument upon which Reed and Duverger rely, in that they do find conditions under which just M candidates enter.[3]

Having noted how the $M + 1$ rule generalizes from the SMSP case to SNTV, I can now note one way in which strategic voting under SNTV differs from that under SMSP: It need not always benefit stronger candidates at the expense of their weaker opponents. Votes cast for candidates with more votes than they need to guarantee a seat are also wasted, from a short-term instrumentally rational voter's point of view. She could divert her vote from such a strong candidate, without causing that candidate to lose, and instead cast it for the best of the *marginal* candidates (i.e., those competing for the marginal or last-allocated seat).[4] Such a decision is risky, in that if too many supporters of the strong candidate think in this way, then the "strong" candidate may lose! Thus, there is some reason to expect that voters will be a bit timid in deserting supermarginal candidates. Nonetheless, there is also some temptation to do so, and so another type of strategic voting is at least theoretically possible under SNTV: the strategic desertion of strong or supermarginal candidates.

[3]In practice, this argument does not seem to be important, at least in the Japanese case, but it is not clear to me that it can be dismissed in general. I should also note that for PR systems the argument that there should be at least $M + 1$ entrants is substantially less compelling (because the entrants in the PR case would be lists, not candidates).

[4]In the case of single-member districts, of course, the "marginal" candidates are simply the two front-runners. More generally, the marginal candidates are those on the boundary between winning and losing: the last winner and the first loser.

Strategic voting in multimember districts

Is there in fact evidence that voters in Japan vote strategically, deserting either weak or strong candidates? The answer is affirmative. I shall consider in turn the evidence marshaled by Reed (1991), Cox (1994), and Cox and Shugart (1995).

Runners-up and second runners-up

Reed uses a test, similar to that employed by Galbraith and Rae (1989) in the British case, that focuses on the percentage of candidates whose vote totals decline, by their order of finish in the previous poll. As Reed (p. 351) notes, "a model of sophisticated voting would predict that second runners-up and lower finishers should lose votes," if they run again, because "they have little chance of winning," hence "some of their voters [will] abandon them." As it turns out, aggregate electoral statistics from postwar elections (down to 1986) confirm this expectation: "Whereas no more than half of the runners-up lose votes, over 70 per cent of the second runners-up lose ground. Runners-up tend to gain votes but second runners-up almost always decline."

The bimodality hypothesis

As noted above, a pure model of strategic voting admits of both Duvergerian and non-Duvergerian equilibria, corresponding to situations in which voters do and do not fully coordinate their strategies, and in which the second loser does and does not fall substantially behind the first loser. In light of this, a theoretically interesting statistic is the ratio of the second to the first loser's vote total, the SF ratio introduced in Chapter 4. Under Duvergerian equilibria, the SF ratio will be near zero. Under non-Duvergerian equilibria, the SF ratio will be near unity. Thus, if one were to compute the ratio for a number of districts, the resulting distribution of SF values should be bimodal.

I have tested this bimodality hypothesis empirically in the case of Japan, using district-level electoral returns over the period 1958–1990.[5] The procedure, in the case of 3-seat districts, was as follows. First, I computed the ratio of the vote total of the second loser (fifth-place candidate) to the vote total of the first loser (fourth-place candidate), for all districts with at least five candidates. Then, I produced a histogram to summarize the distribution of the resulting SF ratios (Figure 5.1). Results for 4- and 5-seat districts (the other frequently occurring types of district in Japan) are given in Figures 5.2 and 5.3.

[5]The data used in this analysis are from Steven Reed's compendium *Japan Election Data: The House of Representatives 1947-1990* (Ann Arbor: Center for Japanese Studies, 1992). A machine-readable version of the dataset can be found on the web site of the Lijphart Elections Archive at http://dodgson.ucsd.edu/lij.

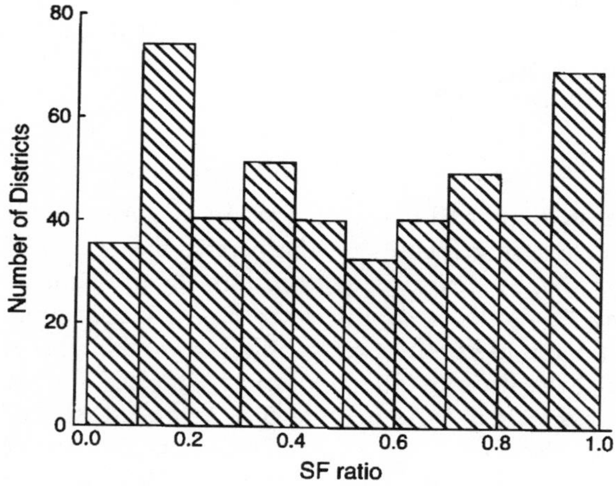

Figure 5.1. Testing the bimodality hypothesis in 3-seat districts: Japanese lower house elections, 1958–1990

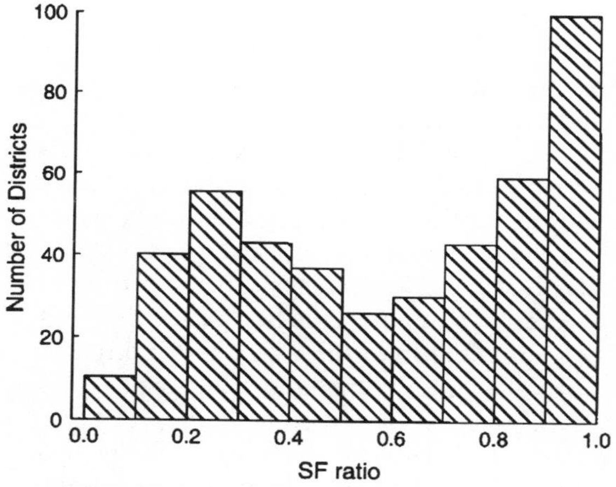

Figure 5.2. Testing the bimodality hypothesis in 4-seat districts: Japanese lower house elections, 1958–1990

As can be seen, the SF distribution appears to be bimodal in each case. SF values near .5 are rare, relative to those near 1 or 0. That is, it is much more common to have either a close or a distant second loser than an "in-between" second loser. Moreover, the closer is the first loser to the last winner, hence the more likely it is that a few more votes might change the outcome, the further from .5 is the SF ratio (i.e., the stronger is the tendency for the ratio to be either near 1 or near 0).

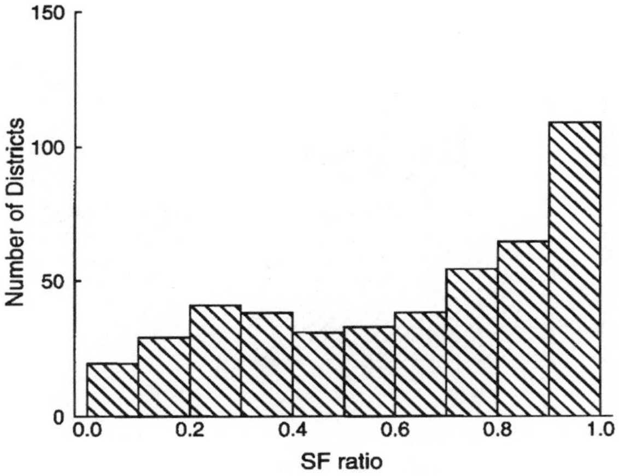

Figure 5.3. Testing the bimodality hypothesis in 5-seat districts: Japanese lower house elections, 1958–1990

Are the distributions displayed in Figures 5.1, 5.2, and 5.3 significantly bimodal? One can reject the null hypothesis that the distribution is *uni*modal in the first two cases, but not at conventional levels of significance in the third. One cannot reject the null hypothesis that the distribution is *bi*modal, in favor of the alternative that it is multimodal, in any of the cases.[6] All told the evidence is as it appears to be to the naked eye: The first two figures really are bimodal; the third is harder to call but has some tendency toward bimodality.

A second-order pattern apparent in the data is that the height of the mode near zero – i.e., the mode that corresponds to Duvergerian equilibria in which strategic voting has a substantial impact – declines as district magnitude increases. My interpretation of this is that the quality of voter information regarding candidate chances declines with district magnitude. In particular, it is harder to be sure who is trailing in a more crowded field in which small vote percentages can win a seat. Think, in the extreme, of a high-magnitude system like Israel's, in which a party needs

[6]I used dip or depth tests (see Hartigan and Hartigan 1985) to test unimodality. In the third case, the probability of observing the degree of bimodality visible in Figure 5.3 is a bit below .2, under the null hypothesis that the distribution is really unimodal. I used a kernel density-based test proposed by Silverman (1981) to pit the null hypothesis of bimodality against the compound alternative of more than two modes, finding p-values of .22, .26, and .98 for the first, second, and third figures respectively.

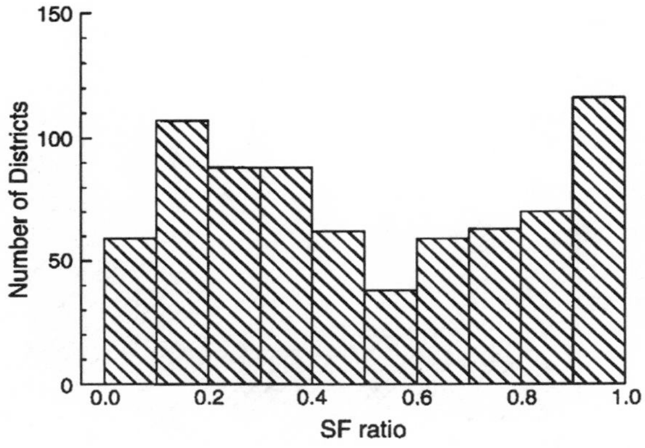

Figure 5.4. Testing the bimodality hypothesis in low-turnover districts: Japanese lower house elections, 1960–1993

only 1.5% of the vote to win a seat. 1.5% is less than the sampling error of almost all polls and so it is hard to see how Israeli voters could be extremely confident that a party with, say, 1% support in the polls was in fact hopeless. Absent consistent beliefs about a party's hopelessness, however, incentives to strategically desert this party dissipate. Thus, large-magnitude systems should in general depress the level of strategic voting, by destroying the primary informational prerequisite of such voting.[7]

Strategic desertion of the strong

Evidence that Japanese voters strategically desert leading candidates – those with more support than they need – is much less compelling than that they desert weak candidates. Nonetheless, there is some evidence consistent with the model. First, there is an over-time trend within the dominant Japanese party, the Liberal Democrats, toward fewer seats being lost on account of votes "wasted" on strong candidates (Cox and Niou 1994). Second, there is a statistically significant tendency for fewer votes to be "wasted" on leading candidates when the margin of victory of the last winning candidate is narrower, indicating that votes switched from leading to marginal candidates are more likely to affect the outcome (see Cox 1994).

[7]In Chapter 10 I will consider some evidence that Israeli voters do vote strategically, but for different reasons than those modeled here.

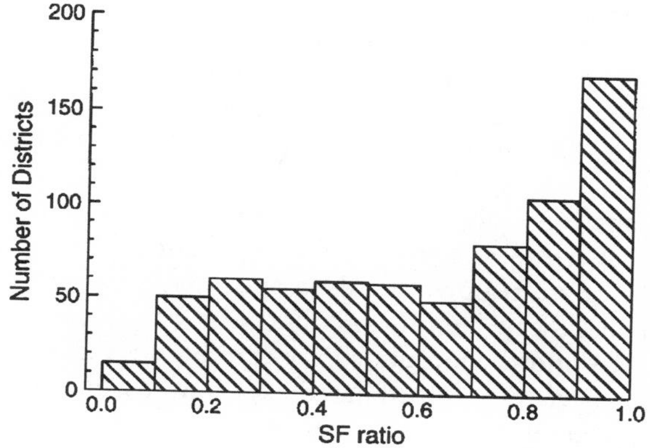

Figure 5.5. Testing the bimodality hypothesis in high-turnover districts: Japanese lower house elections, 1960–1993

The informational prerequisites of strategic voting

If voters have little information about the electoral prospects of the various candidates, then one should expect little strategic voting because it will never be clear who is trailing. In this section, I test this idea by examining the role of electoral history in stabilizing and coordinating electoral expectations. If voters are faced with little change in the field of candidates running from election to election, so that everyone can simply extrapolate from "last time" to "this time," then the informational requirements of the model are more likely to be met than if the field of candidates changes substantially.

Do the data conform to the expectation just articulated? Cox and Shugart (1995) have explored this question both graphically and via probit analysis, using Japanese lower house electoral data from 1960 to 1993.

Consider the graphical approach first. Let NEWPER_{jt} be the number of *new* candidates in district *j* at election *t* (i.e., candidates who did not run in the same district at $t - 1$), divided by the district magnitude. The mean value of NEWPER in the 1,487 district elections held 1960–1993 is .5, or half a new candidate per seat in the typical contest. If one divides the Japanese observations into two categories, those with NEWPER > .5 (indicating an above-average level of turnover in candidates) and those with NEWPER ≤ .5 (indicating a below-average level of candidate turnover), one finds a much more marked bimodality in the SF distributions for the low turnover races than for the high turnover races (see Figures 5.4 and 5.5).[8]

To back up the visual impression conveyed by Figure 5.4, Cox and Shugart ran a probit analysis of the probability that a particular contest would produce a low SF value, controlling for the district magnitude and the total number of candidates running. They find that more candidates of any kind, and especially more new candidates, significantly reduce the probability that the second loser will be well out of the running.

The theory of strategic voting developed here implies that races that are easier to handicap should also be those in which the electorate's expectations are more coordinated concerning who does and does not have a chance at victory. Coordinated expectations, in turn, should lead to greater strategic desertion of weak lists/candidates, leading to low SF ratios. The analysis of Japanese elections lends credence to this chain of reasoning. Races that are plausibly more difficult to handicap – with more candidates per seat, and especially more new candidates per seat – are also those in which the SF ratio tends to be high. The findings regarding new candidates corroborate experimental evidence provided by Forsythe et al. (1993) on the importance of election histories in facilitating voter coordination.

5.2 LRPR

Under closed-list LRPR, votes are converted into seats as follows. The electoral quota, Q, is multiplied by the total number of valid votes cast in the district, V, to produce a quota or "price" denominated in votes.[9] Seats are then allocated to lists in two stages. In the first stage, each list "buys" as many seats as its vote total permits, given the "price" per seat, QV. This leaves each list with a certain number of seats and a certain

[8]This result is consistent with a rational entry model in which candidates *anticipate* strategic voting, and thereby obviate its necessity in practice. Under this view, some districts are pretty cut-and-dried at the time at which entry decisions must be made, with little chance of a challenger unseating an incumbent. In such districts, few challengers with high opportunity costs, which is to say few strong challengers, enter the race. The second loser is thus typically a weak candidate, the strong ones having decided not to risk strategic desertion, and this produces a low SF ratio. In contrast, other districts may have several open seats or otherwise look to be good opportunities. Here, there will typically be several strong challengers among whom it is difficult to distinguish, and the SF ratio will accordingly end up near unity. I do not have the information that would be needed to separate this story from the strategic voting story told in the text.

[9]Thus, as used here, Q is a proportional quota (where it is assumed that $1/(M + 1) < Q \leq 1$), with QV denoting the "raw votes quota." In practice, many systems start with a specification of the raw votes quota.

balance of unexpended votes, called the remainder. In the second stage, seats not allocated in the first stage are allocated, one to a customer, to the lists with the largest remainders. After seats have been allocated to the lists, they are reallocated to the candidates on the lists in accord with the order of appearance of the names on each list. Thus, if list *j* gets 5 seats, the first 5 candidates on that list receive seats.

Applying LRPR in single-member districts ($M = 1$) is equivalent to SMSP, if $Q > 1/(M + 1)$. For, given that $Q > 1/(M + 1) = 1/2$, the only seat at stake in the district will go to the candidate with the most votes, either in the first stage (if that candidate commands a sufficient majority of votes) or in the second stage (if he does not). Thus, SMSP elections can be thought of as a special case of LRPR.

Applying LRPR with a large quota ($Q = 1$) is equivalent to SNTV. With a quota equal to unity, no seats are allocated in the first stage (unless one candidate gets all the votes, a possibility I shall ignore) and each list's remainder is simply its vote total. Thus, the second-stage allocation of seats to the lists with the largest remainders is equivalent to allocation by plurality rule: The top *M* vote-getting lists will win the seats at stake. Those seats then go to the top name on each winning list. As this is essentially the allocation rule used under SNTV, one can consider SNTV to be LRPR with a quota $Q = 1$.[10]

The formal similarity of SNTV and LRPR elections helps one to extend several of the results obtained in the previous section for SNTV to the case of LRPR (cf. Cox and Shugart 1995).[11] In particular, under LRPR there are still two different kinds of strategic vote: one in which voters abandon hopeless or submarginal lists (those that are expected neither to win a quota seat nor to be competitive for the last-allocated remainder seat), and one in which they abandon strong or supermarginal lists (those that have remainders above the expected least winning remainder).[12] There are also still two kinds of equilibria: Duvergerian

[10]The only difference is that, under LRPR, the top-of-list candidates do have running mates below them on the list, while in SNTV each candidate runs his own campaign. As none of the lists win more than one seat, however, it is essentially an SNTV contest between the tops-of-list.

[11]It is not too misleading to think of the matter in the following way (although this does not turn out to work cleanly for the proofs): In an LRPR contest in which expected vote shares are known with considerable precision, everyone can calculate the number of quota seats that each list is expected to win, and the number of remainder seats, say μ, that will be left to be allocated in the second stage. The allocation of these seats will then look essentially like the allocation of (seats in an SNTV election, with each party's expected remainder taking the place of its expected vote in the SNTV model.

[12]Tsebelis (1986) is the first paper of which I am aware that stresses the latter kind of strategic voting.

equilibria, in which the M+2nd list (ranked in order of vote totals) is clearly behind the M + 1st list, and thus suffers the loss of all instrumental support; and non-Duvergerian equilibria, in which the M+2nd list is close enough to the M + 1st as to be indistinguishable, and thus holds on to its instrumental supporters. Finally, there is still an upper bound implied on the number of viable lists, on the assumption that Duvergerian equilibria are more common: There should generally be no more than M + 1 viable lists.[13]

What differs between the SNTV and LRPR cases is the practical meaning of the results generated. For SNTV, the results apply to candidates and the M + 1 upper bound has some bite to it: The number of candidates is always at least M, so a prediction that the effective number should be at most M + 1 is both non-obvious and constraining. For LRPR, the results apply to lists and because lists can win more than one seat the upper bound has much less bite to it, especially as the district magnitude increases. Taagepera and Shugart (1989:144) have found that most real-world observations fall within +/–1 of the equation $N_{eff} = 2.5 + 1.25 log_{10} M$ (where N_{eff} is the effective number of parties competing). If we ignore several facts – that their data include mostly non-LRPR systems, that they compute the effective number of parties at the national rather than district level, that they use an *effective* magnitude for each system (a kind of adjusted average of the district magnitudes) rather than the actual magnitude defined at the district level – this suggests that the M + 1 upper bound will rarely be binding in districts of magnitude greater than three (since for $M > 3$, $M + 1 < (2.5 + 1.25 log_{10} M) + 1$). Thus, something else other than strategic voting must explain the reduction of the effective number of parties below M + 1 observed in most large-magnitude PR systems.[14]

[13]For, suppose that $K > M + 1$. Then (absent non-Duvergerian equilibria) there will necessarily exist at least $K - M \geq 2$ lists that are expected to win neither a quota nor a remainder seat, and Theorem 2 in Cox and Shugart (1995) applies to show that all but one of these lists must have zero expected vote shares.

[14]The pure model refers to the "number of lists/candidates that receive positive vote shares," and it has been suggested to me that this is what should be counted in empirical tests. But if one entertains the notion that the model's assumptions might not be met perfectly, as I think one must, then one wants to count the "number of parties that get a positive share of the vote from the short-term instrumentally rational part of the electorate." I do not pretend to know how to do this, but looking at the effective number of parties seems a reasonable first cut. Thus, I have compared the theoretical upper bounds in the text to Taagepera and Shugart's estimates of the effective number of parties.

What might this "something else" be? On the one hand, it might involve the direct response of other agents – contributors, potential entrants, activists – to the particular electoral structure in which they find themselves. If so, then one could continue to think of the features of the electoral system alone as producing the relationship between M and N_{eff}. On the other hand, the factors that reduce N_{eff} well below $M + 1$ might not be directly tied to particular electoral structures at all. Perhaps, for example, there are economies of scale in advertising and/or creating habitual attachments in the electorate, and these kick in independently of electoral structure to limit the effective number of lists. By this accounting, strategic voting would be a more limiting factor than would be the problem of overcoming voter ignorance at low district magnitudes, while just the reverse would be true at high district magnitudes. Complementing this economies-of-scale view would be consideration of the cleavage structure of society, with societies divided into larger numbers of pre-existing, cohesive, and hence easily mobilized, groups producing more parties than those with fewer such cleavages, especially at high district magnitudes (see Chapter 11).

Strategic voting in Colombia

In this section, I consider the empirical usefulness of the results just sketched.[15] There are two main patterns that the model predicts strategic voting will produce: First, trailing lists will be deserted by all supporters; second, leading lists will be deserted by excess supporters. In examining how these two predictions fare, I shall look at Colombian electoral data from the period 1974–1990.

Why Colombia? As explained in Cox and Shugart (1995), it is not easy to find an appropriate LRPR case for analysis. Most PR systems use a divisor formula (e.g., d'Hondt's). Many of those that do use LRPR couple it with upper tiers or other complicating features. Colombia is a good case because all seats are allocated at the district level, each party regularly presents multiple lists in each district (at both House and Senate elections), and most lists do not win quota seats. Thus, Colombian LRPR contests are similar to SNTV contests between the heads of each list, so that the correspondence to the formal conditions required in the theorems (Cox and Shugart 1995) is fairly close.

[15]Before proceeding I should note a caveat analogous to that registered in Chapter 4: Even if the model's predictions are borne out, this will not prove that strategic voting is the primary causal agent. The problem is that *any* class of agents who care about the outcome of the election will tend to allocate whatever resources they control to marginal lists.

The bimodality hypothesis

I shall again investigate the SF ratio. Under Duvergerian equilibria, the SF ratio will be zero, since the second losing remainder will be pushed down to zero by strategic desertion,[16] while under non-Duvergerian equilibria the SF ratio will be unity, since the first and second lists with losing remainders will have virtually identical remainders. Thus, the prediction is that the SF distribution will be bimodal, with one mode near unity and another near zero. Lists that are not ahead of the list expected to have the greatest losing remainder either will be "close enough" so that they are still seen as having a chance at the last remainder seat, in which case they will hold on to their support and produce a large value of the SF ratio, or will be "too far" behind, in which case all their *instrumental* supporters will desert them, leaving only a rump of noninstrumental support.

In analyzing the Colombian data, we present detailed results only for districts of magnitude one to five, pooling 55 districts from the House with 88 districts from the Senate. At higher district magnitudes in Colombia, there is very little evidence of strategic voting. This is consistent with the trends observable in the Japanese data and again suggests that strategic voting phenomena fade out rapidly as the district magnitude increases past five (cf. Sartori 1968:279).

A histogram of SF values from 143 elections held in small-magnitude Colombian House and Senate districts over the period 1974-1990 is presented in Figure 5.6. As can be seen, it appears to be bimodal, although the mode near zero is considerably smaller than that near unity.

Does the degree of bimodality observed in Figure 5.6 pass some threshold of statistical significance? If one thought that, with everyone voting sincerely, the SF ratio ought to be uniform, or unimodal with a peak near .5, then these nulls could be rejected at conventional levels of significance. One can also reject other null hypotheses that entail at least as many observations with SF ratios in the middle tertile as there are in the upper or lower tertiles.

As another benchmark, consider the ratio r_{j-1}/r_j: the (j–1)*th* list's remainder divided by the j*th* list's remainder. When $j = M + 1$, this is the SF ratio. But for $j \neq M + 1$, we have other ratios. As it turns out, for $j < M + 1$ all of the ratios r_{j-1}/r_j are distributed unimodally with considerably thinner tails than posited in the hardest-to-reject scenario. I propose testing the null hypothesis that the distribution of the SF ratio is no different than the distribution of r_{j-1}/r_j, for some $j < M + 1$ (which $j < M + 1$

[16]This is true only if the list expected to have the second largest losing remainder has a lower expected vote total than the list expected to have the largest losing remainder. Most of the Colombian data, as it turns out, satisfy this condition.

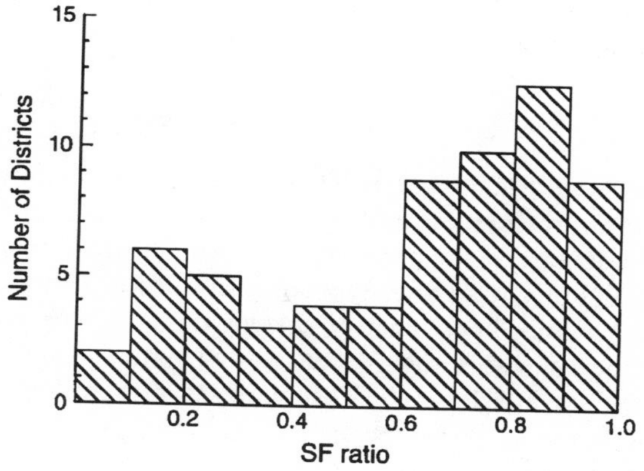

Figure 5.6. Testing the bimodality hypothesis in low-magnitude districts: Colombian lower house elections, 1974–1990

is selected turns out not to matter). The null hypothesis, in other words, says that there is nothing unusual or special about the SF ratio as compared to other remainder ratios involving adjacent candidates.

One can reject this null hypothesis at conventional levels of statistical significance. The distribution in Figure 5.6, in other words, is not like the other remainder ratio distributions. Where they have thin and declining tails toward zero, the SF distribution has at least a very thick tail and probably what it appears in the figure to have: a second mode near zero. We interpret this difference as evidence of strategic voting. (I should note that an analogous test for the Japanese case comes to a similar conclusion. For example, the ratio of the second-place candidate's vote total to the first-place candidate's vote total is distributed in a thoroughly unimodal fashion.)

Is there any other evidence consistent with the idea that Colombians vote strategically in their small-magnitude districts? It turns out that the closer is the least winning remainder to the greatest losing remainder, hence the more likely that a few more votes might change the outcome, the stronger is the tendency for the SF ratio to be either near 1 or near 0. One way to document this is to regress the absolute value of the difference between the SF ratio and .5 on the percentage margin separating the last winning and first losing remainders. Theorem 1 (of Cox and Shugart) suggests that SF values near .5 should be particularly unlikely if the race for the last seat is a close one. The results from such a regression (controlling for district magnitude) show that SF values from closer races do tend to be further from .5 on average than those from less close races.

An effect of the magnitude found would be expected under the null hypothesis of no effect about six times in a hundred.

Strategic desertion of strong lists

Evidence that Colombian voters strategically desert leading lists is much weaker than the evidence for strategic desertion of trailing lists.[17] There is a mild decline in the percentage of votes wasted on leading lists from 1974 to 1986 (with 1990, when the dominant Liberal party was divided over a proposed constitutional revision, reverting to earlier levels). And, if one regresses the percentage of votes wasted on leading lists on the "margin of victory" (least winning remainder minus greatest losing remainder, as a percentage of total vote), one finds a positive effect. Unlike in Japan, however, this effect is not statistically discernible from zero.

5.3 DBPR

I conjecture that PR systems operating under a divisor-based seat allocation formula, such as the d'Hondt method, are similar in their strategic voting equilibria to those operating under a largest-remainders formula. In particular, DBPR elections should obey an $M + 1$ rule, whereby there are rarely more than $M + 1$ viable lists, just as LRPR elections do. This point is potentially important because a fair number of the world's PR systems (especially in Latin America) are low-magnitude divisor systems, in which the $M + 1$ upper bound might be constraining.[18]

In this section, I propose to do three things. First, I shall review evidence from the Spanish case that voters under low-magnitude DBPR do vote strategically to the detriment of smaller parties, consistent with the $M + 1$ rule. Second, I consider the nature of strategic voting under the open-list DBPR system of Chile, where typically the number of lists falls below $M + 1$ and yet, as will be seen, opportunities to vote strategically still arise. The point of this investigation is to highlight modes of strategic voting that do not have the concentrative effect upon which students of electoral systems since Duverger have typically focused. Third, I also briefly note some opportunities for strategic voting that arose under the open-list system of election once used in French labor elections (again with fewer lists than the upper bound of $M + 1$, again without a clear concentrative effect).

[17]In part this may be because the relevant conditions of the formal theorems in Cox and Shugart (1995) are met in the sample only about 75% of the time.

[18]Tables 3.1–3.3 show that Argentina, Cape Verde, Chile, the Dominican Republic, Ecuador, Spain, and Turkey all combine PR-d'Hondt with median magnitudes below 6.

Strategic voting in Spain

The Spanish electoral system adopted in 1977 is a good example of a PR system in which larger parties regularly get larger seat shares than vote shares (cf. Gunther and Montero 1994). Over the period 1979–1989, Spain's has consistently been among the least proportional of all European electoral systems. The primary features that fuel this disproportionality are the use of the d'Hondt method of seat allocation (which is more favorable to large parties than most other PR allocation formulas), the presence of many districts of small magnitude (31 districts with magnitude 5 or smaller), the absence of any upper tiers, and the use of a 3% threshold at the district level. In the smaller Spanish districts, one might expect to see strategic voting similar to that seen in the smaller Japanese districts (operating under SNTV) or the smaller Colombian districts (operating under LRPR).

And in fact strategic voting does appear to be substantial in the smaller Spanish districts. The best evidence of this is provided by Gunther (1989), based on surveys conducted after the general elections in 1979 and 1982. Examining the reported votes of respondents with strong partisan preferences, Gunther finds that relatively large percentages of those preferring the large parties reported voting for them, while relatively small percentages of those preferring the small parties reported voting for them. Moreover,

> This *prima facie* case for the presence of sophisticated voting is strongly corroborated when the voting behavior of these respondents is broken down by province in accord with the number of deputies sent to the *Cortes* from each district. Respondents with highly-favorable attitudes toward the third- and fourth-place parties in large provinces were about twice as likely to vote for them as sympathizers of those same parties in small provinces (Gunther 1989:842).

Gunther's definition of what counts as a "large" and "small" province depends in a natural way on the size of the party being investigated. The Communist Party of Spain (PCE), for example, had a national vote total which, if replicated in each district, would have given it a seat in districts of magnitude five or above, but no seats in the smaller districts. The smaller Popular Alliance (AP) could only expect to get a seat in districts electing six or more deputies (again, on the assumption that it would get its national level of support in each district). Thus, the dividing line between "small" districts (in which a party's supporters should have feared wasting their votes) and "large" districts (in which a party's supporters should not have feared wasting their votes) varied systematically across parties, depending on their national vote shares.

What is striking about Gunther's results, as he notes, is the Spanish voter's apparent ability to figure out these rational cutpoints.

It is possible, of course, that Spanish voters in some of the "small" districts knew that their party had stronger support there than it did in the nation as a whole, and accordingly did not desert. Alternatively, some voters in "large" districts may have known that their party was weaker than it was in the nation as a whole, and accordingly voted strategically. So Gunther's analysis may understate the true ability of Spanish voters to calculate the right time to cast a strategic vote. Can a district-level analysis of SF ratios, similar to that performed for Japan and Colombia above, provide any corroborating evidence?

In a d'Hondt system, the SF ratio refers to the ratio of the second losing quotient to the first losing quotient. But in the Spanish data, the list possessing the second losing quotient won seats in all but six provinces in 1986. This is in sharp contrast to the Colombian data, where most of the second losing remainders were owned by lists that had *not* won a seat (and in even sharper contrast to the Japanese data, where all of the candidates owning the second losing vote totals of course did not win seats). As argued briefly in the Colombian case, there is less reason to expect bimodality in the SF distribution if the second losing remainder or quotient is owned by a list that has won seats. If the list with the second largest remainder or quotient does not win seats, then one can imagine that polling results before the election might have indicated this. Voters then have an easy calculation: "My list is so small that my votes are wasted on it." (This is the calculation that Gunther imputes to his survey respondents.) But if one's favorite list is a large list, clearly expected to win one or more seats, then one has to calculate the expected distribution of seats to *each* party, calculate the first and second losing quotients in the district, and discover that one's party owns the second losing quotient.[19] Even then, one might worry that if too many copartisans decide to desert the favored party, in order to use their wasted votes elsewhere, then the party will lose one of the seats that it was expected to win. So it is not obvious that we should expect any bimodality in the SF ratios in Spain; the prediction is similar to the weak prediction in the Japanese and Colombian cases that lists with "excess" votes will be relieved of them.

As it turns out, the SF distributions for Spain from the 1982, 1986, and 1989 elections are all distinctly unimodal. And there are really too few cases in which the second losing quotient was owned by a losing

[19]As noted before in the text, elites might get into the act and publicize the logic of the wasted vote. But they certainly have a harder sell in the case under consideration than if the list is small.

party (21) to yield much of a test.[20] There is thus no aggregate evidence in the PR-d'Hondt case comparable to that from the SNTV and LRPR cases. For this case, then, one has to rely on Gunther's surveys, which provide more direct evidence of strategic voting in any event.

Strategic voting in Chile

The Chilean electoral system (for the lower house) uses two-seat districts. Each Chilean voter has one vote to cast, which she must cast for an individual candidate. Candidates are grouped for purposes of seat allocation into lists, each list having two candidates. Votes are counted, and seats allocated, in two stages. First, the votes for all candidates on a given list are summed, to give a list vote total. These vote totals are then translated into an allocation of seats among the lists by the d'Hondt divisor method of PR (on which, more presently). Second, plurality rule is used to allocate each list's seats among that list's candidates. Typically, a Chilean list will win only one seat, in which case that seat goes to the candidate on that list receiving the greatest number of votes.

An example may help to clarify matters. Suppose that there are two candidates on the A list (A1 and A2) and two candidates on the B list (B1 and B2). The vote totals for these candidates are 15,000, 16,000, 7,000, and 20,000, respectively. In this case, list A's vote total is 31,000, while list B's is 27,000. The d'Hondt method of seat allocation proceeds as follows. First, one divides each list's vote total by the numbers from 1 to M, to produce a number of quotients equal to the number of lists times the district magnitude. In this case, there are two lists chasing after $M = 2$ seats, and so list A's quotients are 31,000 and 15,500; while list B's quotients are 27,000 and 13,500. Second, one takes the M largest quotients produced in the first stage, and allocates one seat per quotient to the party owning each such quotient. In the present case, that means that each list is given a single seat: List A gets a seat by virtue of its first quotient being the largest, list B by virtue of its first quotient being the second largest. Candidate A2 gets the seat awarded to list A, because he has more votes than his running mate. Similarly, candidate B2 gets the seat awarded to list B.

The Chilean system gives a strong incentive to coalition and in practice has given rise to two large alliances, the *Unión por El Progreso*, con-

[20]In these 21 cases it turns out that the SF ratio is always greater than .7. This is not strongly inconsistent with the bimodality hypothesis, in that there are no observations in the midrange (.4 to .6). But on the other hand there is no *aggregate* evidence of strategic voting, either.

sisting of center-right and right-wing parties; and the *Concertación*, consisting of the center-left and left-wing parties. The nature of the incentive to coalesce can be seen by considering a case in which two conservative parties, that together garner 60% of the vote, offer a joint list. Suppose that there are two liberal parties, that garner 25% and 15% of the vote, respectively. If the liberal parties offer a joint list, then that list will win a seat (because 25+15 = 40, which is more than half of 60). But if each liberal party runs its own list, then the conservative alliance will win both seats in the district (because the two largest quotients will be 60 and 60/2 = 30, both owned by the conservative list).

What is the nature of strategic voting incentives under the Chilean rules? I shall focus upon the typical situation, in which the main contenders are a joint list from the *Unión por El Progreso,* on the right, and a joint list from the *Concertación,* on the left.

It will help to introduce a little notation to structure the discussion. Let L_1 and L_2 denote the number of voters who most prefer the first and second leftist candidates, with $L_1 \geq L_2$; and C_1 and C_2 denote the number of voters who most prefer the first and second conservative candidates, with $C_1 \geq C_2$. Assume that all voters have a unique most-preferred candidate and let $L = L_1 + L_2$, $C = C_1 + C_2$. So the total number of voters is $T = L + C$. Each voter j must choose a strategy v_j from the set {Vote for the first leftist, Vote for the second leftist, Vote for the first conservative, Vote for the second conservative}.

Some insight into strategic voting under the Chilean system can be had without developing a full incomplete-information model of the kind used hitherto. Indeed, I shall focus on a simpler (complete-information) model and a simpler question: When will the situation in which all voters vote sincerely (which I shall denote by $v^* = (v_1^*, \ldots, v_T^*)$) be a strong equilibrium (or core point)?

A vector of voting strategies $v = (v_1, \ldots, v_T)$ is a strong equilibrium if no coalition of voters can alter their voting strategies in such a way as to make all of them better off, on the assumption that all other voters continue to act as specified in v. I shall further simplify the analysis by assuming that all voters have separable preferences: They either rank the two leftist candidates one-two (which leftist is ranked first being unconstrained), or they rank them three-four. Even with this restriction, there still turn out to be strategic voting incentives.[21]

One situation in which an incentive to vote strategically can arise occurs when $.5C < L < 2C$ and $2/3(L - .5C) > C_1 - C_2$. The first condition guarantees that both the conservative and the leftist list will win one seat, if everyone votes sincerely. The second condition says that the leftists

[21]Without this restriction other possibilities open up as well.

have $2/3(L - .5C)$ excess votes which they could give to the second conservative.[22] How would this gambit affect the outcome? The leftist list would still win a seat, since $L-2/3(L - .5C) > C+2/3(L - .5C)$. The $2/3(L - .5C)$ leftist voters could be chosen, moreover, so that the allocation of the leftist seat was unaffected. (For example, taking at least as many votes from the second as from the first leftist to finance the "raid" on the conservatives would leave the first leftist winning the leftist seat.) Finally, the $2/3(L - .5C)$ extra votes for the second conservative would be sufficient to at least put him into a tie with his running mate, and possibly to elect him over that running mate, because $2/3(L - .5C) > C_1 - C_2$.[23] Thus, *if* leftist voters generally prefer the second conservative to the first, they have an incentive to "raid" the conservative list.[24]

Of course, this strategy is quite risky if the parties are not sure of their vote totals. It would be particularly risky if one list attempted to transfer nearly all of their excess votes to the other, in an attempt to affect which candidate there won, because this would leave the raiding list with just over half the votes of the raided list. A little miscalculation in the total votes received by each list would then give both seats to the raided list.

With the restriction to two lists and separable preferences, the case just considered is essentially the only one in which incentives to vote strategically arise, as the following proposition goes some way toward establishing:

> *Proposition:* The sincere strategy vector v^* is a strong equilibrium if either:
> (1) $L < .5C$; or
> (2) $L > 2C$; or
> (3) $L = .5C$; or
> (4) $L = 2C$; or
> (5) $.5C < L < 2C$ and $2/3(L - .5C) < C_1 - C_2$ and $2/3(C - .5L) < L_1 - L_2$.

A sketch proof of this assertion for the main cases, (1), (2), and (5), goes as follows. In case (1), the two conservative candidates will win under v^*. There is nothing that the leftist voters can do to alter this and the

[22] More precisely, they could take the integer portion of $2/3(L-.5C)$, if this is nonintegral, or the next lowest integer, if this is integral. These votes are "excess" in the sense that transferring them from one list to the other leaves both lists winning just one seat.

[23] If $2/3(L - .5C)$ is an integer, one larger than $C_1 - C_2$, then the leftists can only spare $2/3(L - .5C)$-1 votes and thus can only put the weaker Conservative into a tie.

[24] A symmetric case arises regarding conservative incentives to "raid" the leftist list. Again, the key consideration is whether the conservatives have enough *surplus* votes (more than needed to secure their seat under the d'Hondt allocation rule) to affect the allocation of the leftist seat among the leftist candidates.

conservative voters have no incentive to do so, as the outcome corresponds to their most-preferred outcome. So everyone may as well vote sincerely. Case (2) is symmetric, with the leftists and conservatives switching roles. In case (5), the leftist list and the conservative list will each win one seat. Leftist voters do not have enough surplus votes to "raid" the conservative list (because $L - .5C < C_1 - C_2$) and similarly for the conservatives.[25]

Is there any evidence of strategic raiding of the kind suggested above in Chilean elections? In the 1989 elections, the larger list was in a position to raid the smaller (having more excess votes than separated the candidates on the second-place list) in only about half the districts. Moreover, there were only ten cases where the larger list would have needed to use only a small percentage (less than 10%) of its excess votes in order to affect who won the smaller list's seat, and in several of these districts the larger list either won both seats or was near to doing so, which would obviously remove any incentive to raid. All told, then, there were only about five districts in which the conditions for strategic raiding were favorable. And in these five cases supporters of the larger lists may not have cared much who won the other list's seat; or may not have had enough information about the lists' relative standings to act on the strategic opportunity they faced. The only case that I know of where strategic calculations are alleged to have come into play – the 1993 election in the *Las Condes* constituency – involved national considerations.[26]

Strategic voting in French labor elections

Rosenthal (1974) describes a species of strategic voting under open-list DBPR in which French labor unions attempt to raid one another's lists in a fashion somewhat similar to the Chilean case. The elections concern who will serve as factory representatives for the workforce. Rival unions put up lists, typically with as many names on the list as there are representatives to be elected from a given factory. Workers select a single list, but are then allowed to strike out as many names on the list as they see

[25]The proposition states a sufficient condition for the sincere strategy vector v^* to be a strong equilibrium. It is almost a necessary condition as well, except for some messy minor cases that I will not go into.

[26]In this constituency, the leader of the more moderate right-wing party faced stiff opposition from a strong candidate of the more extreme right-wing party, as well as an incumbent candidate of one of the *Concertación* parties. Faced with the prospect of a parliament in which the more moderate opposition leader was not present, it is alleged that leftist voters who were not from the party of the left-wing incumbent voted in sufficient numbers to give both seats to the right. See Lagos (1996).

fit.[27] Seats are allocated first to the union lists, by PR-d'Hondt;[28] and then to the candidates on each list, by plurality rule (with ties broken by list order). Thus, for example, if a list wins 3 seats, the 3 candidates on the list receiving the most votes win the seats, where a candidate's vote total equals the number of voters selecting the candidate's list, less the number that have struck out his or her name.

How do unions manipulate this system? As described in Rosenthal (1974), a union may instruct a small band of its militants to support another union's list but to strike out the top names. The result, if the other union's supporters typically strike no one off, is that the top names (i.e., the union leaders) are defeated. The total number of seats that the other union wins is not changed but the occupants of those seats are altered. In order to protect against this strategy, the to-be-raided union may instruct its members to strike off the last names on the list. The bulk of Rosenthal's analysis concerns the equilibrium to this game of strategy, which apparently the French unions have been playing for some time.

5.4 CONCLUSION

This chapter has investigated strategic voting equilibria in three main electoral systems: SNTV, LRPR, and DBPR. In multimember districts operating under SNTV or PR, strategic voting can refer to the strategic desertion of both candidates/lists that are "too weak" and candidates/lists that are "too strong." Outcome-oriented voters in multimember districts desert weak candidates/lists for the same reason that they do in single-member districts – a fear of wasting their votes (cf. Leys 1959; Sartori 1968). They desert strong candidates/lists when those candidates/lists have one or more of the M seats sewn up but there are other seats still up for grabs; for then the voter's vote has a much greater chance of affecting the outcome if cast for one of the "marginal" candidates/lists: those on the edge between winning and losing the last-allocated seat.

The equilibrium levels of strategic voting entailed in a pure model imply that all three systems – SNTV, LRPR, and DBPR – impose the same upper bound on the number of viable competitors, K: namely, $K \leq M + 1$.[29] For SNTV, this is in accordance with Reed's "$M + 1$ rule" (Reed

[27] Thus, in effect, each worker selects a list and then casts approval votes for the candidates on the list. Cf. Brams and Fishburn (1983).

[28] Each list's vote total is roughly equal to the number of workers selecting the list; for details see Rosenthal (1974).

[29] How to measure the "number of viable competitors" operationally is another matter. See footnote 14.

1991); for PR, the upper bound provides a quantification of the Leys-Sartori conjecture.

There is evidence that elections held in small-magnitude Japanese (SNTV), Colombian (LRPR), and Spanish (DBPR) districts have followed the $M + 1$ rule (or tended toward agreement with it). In the case of large-magnitude PR, however, the $M + 1$ upper bound appears not to be binding, revealing that empirically observed effective numbers of lists are depressed below this upper bound by forces other than strategic voting.

I have also stressed three subsidiary themes in this chapter: First, that the logic of strategic voting leads only to an upper bound on the number of candidates or lists, as taken for granted above; second, that there are nonstandard modalities of strategic voting that do not have the classical vote-concentrating effects assumed by Duverger and the subsequent literature in electoral studies; third, that strategic voting fades out in multimember districts when the district magnitude gets above five. The last of these points relates to the informational requirements of the model, and in particular the rational expectations assumption.

Violations of the rational expectations assumption are largely a matter of the level of information about electoral prospects in the election at hand. Strategic voting should decline as voters' expectations about who will win and who will lose are less clear and less coordinated. Voters' expectations should be less clear and coordinated: (1) the greater is electoral volatility (so that expectations about "this time" cannot be grounded in simple extrapolations from "last time"); (2) the fewer are the relevant polls published in the mass media (so that expectations cannot be grounded on simple extrapolations from polls);[30] and (3) the larger is the district magnitude (since a given vote percentage means more, in terms of a chance at a seat, as district magnitude increases, a voter requires more information to become confident that a given list is really out of the running as M increases). The first two points, concerning the usefulness of electoral history and contemporaneous polls in coordinating voters' expectations, have been validated by a series of interesting experiments conducted by Forsythe et al. (1993). The last point, concerning the impact of district magnitude, points to a conclusion similar to that drawn by Sartori (1968:279): "The general rule is that the progression from maximal manipulative impact [via strategic voting] to sheer ineffectiveness follows, more than anything else, the size of the constituency."

[30]Many countries outlaw the publication of polling results during some portion of the campaign, e.g., France (last 7 days), Italy, Spain, Peru, Portugal, Belgium, Japan, Lithuania (throughout the campaign), Bulgaria (last 14 days), the Czech Republic (last 7 days), and Poland (last 7 days). The more such laws are actually observed, the more difficult it may be for voters to vote strategically, at least if who is ahead and who behind has not become clear before the ban on polls begins.

6

Strategic voting in single-member dual-ballot systems

In the last two chapters, I have investigated strategic voting equilibria in SMSP and in PR elections, two of the three electoral systems that Duverger originally explored in his seminal work in the 1950s. In this chapter, I consider the dual-ballot system, the subject of what was originally Duverger's third proposition.

For dual-ballot systems, Duverger makes no specific claim regarding an equilibrium number of parties. He does argue that such systems produce no incentives to vote strategically in the first round, concluding that "the variety of parties having much in common does not adversely affect the total number of seats they gain since in this system they can always regroup for the second ballot" (Duverger 1954: 240). But this leads only to an expectation that there will be "more than two" parties. The literature on electoral systems has not since produced any more specific prediction and, in a recent survey, Sartori (1994:67) opines that "the reductive effects on the number of parties of the double ballot cannot be generally predicted with any precision" (an opinion shared by Bartolini 1984:118).

This chapter explores the possibility of saying something more precise about the dual ballot's effect. I shall argue two main theoretical points. First, when voters are concerned only with the outcome of the current election and have rational expectations, strategic voting plays a role in dual-ballot elections similar to that it plays in single-ballot plurality elections: acting to limit the number of viable first-round candidates. Second, the limit theoretically applied on the number of first-round candidates is $M + 1$, where M refers to the number of first-round candidates that can legally qualify for the second. This is the limit suggested by Shugart and Taagepera (1994), based on their reading of Cox (1994). It is also, of course, the same limit as found in the previous two cases, if one thinks of the "number of first-round candidates that can legally qualify for the second" in a runoff system as equivalent to the district magnitude in other systems.

In addition to further generalizing the $M + 1$ rule, I shall also argue that in practice strategic voting in the first round of runoff elections is probably much rarer than the theoretical benchmark established by the model. This is partly because the informational preconditions of rational expectations are greater, and partly because optimal strategies are more complex in dual-ballot than in single-ballot systems. Thus, practically speaking, it may be more difficult to predict the number of parties under dual-ballot systems, as Bartolini and Sartori assert.[1]

The rest of the chapter proceeds as follows. Section 6.1 notes in a preliminary way the existence of strategic voting incentives under majority runoff provisions. Section 6.2 presents a formal model of strategic voting under a top-two majority runoff system, when voters care only about the outcome of the current election and have rational expectations. Section 6.3 analyzes the kinds of equilibrium phenomena that the model supports. I find, in the pure model, that there are always voters in whose interest it is to vote strategically when there are three or more candidates – consistent with the Gibbard-Satterthwaite theorem (Gibbard 1973; Satterthwaite 1975) but contrary to the thrust of Duverger's discussion – and that strategic voting acts in top-two runoff elections to limit the number of viable candidates to three, just as it limits the number of viable candidates in plurality elections to two. Section 6.4 discusses various relaxations of the pure model's assumptions. Section 6.5 concludes.

6.1. STRATEGIC VOTING IN RESTRICTIVE MAJORITY RUNOFF ELECTIONS

Duverger's theoretical discussion as to why there should be more than two parties in dual-ballot systems is very brief. It consists of little more than the single sentence quoted above, according to which "the variety of parties having much in common does not adversely affect the total number of seats they gain since in this system they can always regroup for the second ballot" (Duverger 1954:240). Looked at closely, this comment fails to convince in the case of top-two runoffs.[2]

To see this, consider the following unidimensional spatial example: There are two center parties (A and B), one left party (L), and one right party (R) competing for one seat under a top-two majority runoff system.

[1]Strategic voting in the *second* round of a runoff race is a different matter. If more than two candidates survive to the second round (which is held under plurality), then there may be a substantial amount of strategic voting, since the first round results have provided excellent information on the relative standings of the candidates. In this chapter, I focus on the first-round incentives.

[2]Duverger, of course, was thinking of the Third Republic's more permissive system when he wrote in the 1950s.

The percentages of voters in the electorate who support each party are as follows: L – 31%, A – 25%, B – 15%, and R – 29%. In this case, it is easy to see that, if each center party puts up a candidate (and its voters follow the cue of the leadership and vote for this candidate), then L and R will make it to the second round, leaving the center parties (and voters) with a poor choice. On the other hand, if the two center parties coalesce in the first round, then they will make it to the second round with L, and then win the runoff. So, in this case, "the variety of parties having much in common" *does* "adversely affect the total number of seats they gain." Party elites have an incentive to coalesce (up to a point) and, if they fail to, voters who favor B have an incentive to vote strategically for A.

In fact, incentives to vote strategically in the first round of a majority runoff election can occur even with only three candidates and even under more permissive systems. This much is known from the very general social choice theorems of Gibbard (1973), Satterthwaite (1975), and Schwartz (1982). Nonetheless, these general theorems do not tell us anything about the nature, frequency, or plausibility of strategic voting in majority runoff elections. The only guidance in the literature is provided by Sartori (1994:63), who asserts the following:

> At the first round of voting the voter can and does freely express his first preference. His freedom is maximal when there is no threshold (or only a minimal barrier) for admission of the candidates to the second ballot .... On the other hand, the calculating voter's freedom is "less free" when the admission to the run-off is filtered by relatively high thresholds, especially when only the two front runners are admitted to the second round.

To investigate further the theoretical nature and frequency of strategic voting in dual-ballot systems, I develop in the next section a game-theoretic model of strategic voting in a top-two majority runoff election. As will be seen, the model's equilibria are consistent with Sartori's intuitive insights.

6.2 A TOP-TWO MAJORITY RUNOFF ELECTION WITH *K* CANDIDATES

Now it is time to describe the model. Because there are (potentially) two rounds of voting under runoff rules, the model here is not as direct a generalization of the SMSP model as was the case for SNTV and LRPR in Chapter 5. Nonetheless, the model does follow the same lines as the SMSP model, *mutatis mutandis*.

Imagine K candidates competing in a single-member district under top-two majority runoff rules. After first-round votes have been cast, either a majority winner exists and is given the seat, or the top two finishers go on to meet in a runoff election. The candidate with the most votes wins the runoff, if any is held.

There are *n* voters in the district. I assume that voting is costless (or compulsory), thus focusing attention on vote choice rather than turnout. I also assume that voters care only about who wins the seat at stake in the election. This last assumption rules out, among other things, voters who care about: the margin by which the seat is won; who makes the runoff (beyond the effect that this has on who ultimately wins the seat); or the outcome of other elections that may be affected indirectly by the voters' choices in the current election (e.g., future elections in their own district or contemporaneous or future elections in other districts). I discuss voters who care about more than the outcome of the current election below.[3]

Although each voter knows her own preferences, she is uncertain about the preferences (or type) of other voters. I model this uncertainty formally by assuming that there exists a commonly known distribution function, *F*, defined over voter types.[4]

Each voter chooses her vote in order to maximize her expected utility, something that depends not just on her preferences over candidates but also on her *expectations* about how well each candidate will do in the first round. For example, suppose a voter thinks that there is no chance that any candidate will win a majority in the first round; that candidate 1 will top the polls in the first round; and that, conditional on *some* candidates being tied for second, it will almost certainly be candidates 2 and 3. Such a voter is presented with only one real chance of affecting the outcome: She should vote in such a way so as to produce the better of the two most likely runoff pairings, which pit 1 versus 2 and 1 versus 3. Which of these pairings is better of course depends both on her preferences among candidates 1, 2, and 3 *and* on her estimates of who will win in the two pairings.

If voters believe that, conditional on there being any tie for second at all, there are *many* different pairs of candidates who might be tied with

[3]Formally, each voter i assigns a Von Neumann-Morgenstern utility u_{ik} to the outcome "candidate k wins the seat." Voter utilities can be rescaled in the standard fashion so that victory of the most-preferred candidate yields a utility of 1, while victory of the least-preferred candidate yields a utility of 0. After this rescaling, voter i's preferences (or voter i's *type*) can be described by the vector $u_i=(u_{i1}, \ldots ,u_{iK})$, an element in the set $U = \{u \in R^K: \max\{u_k\}=1 \;\&\; \min\{u_k\} = 0 \;\&\; u_k = u_j \text{ only if } k = j\}$. (Note that the definition of the set U rules out voter indifference between outcomes. This is a convenient but inessential assumption.)

[4]I follow Palfrey (1989) and Cox (1994) in assuming that *F* has no mass points. Myerson and Weber's work (1993) shows that this assumption is not crucial. Note that from the perspective of a given voter, any other voter is an independent draw from *U*.

non-negligible probability, then their expected utility calculations are rather complex (see Appendix B). However, just as in plurality elections it often becomes clear who is in the running for the seat (who might be tied for first), so in runoff elections it may become clear who is in the running for the second runoff spot (who might be tied for second). And, just as in plurality elections outcome-oriented voters may strategically desert hopeless candidates in order to secure a better victor, so in runoff elections outcome-oriented voters may desert hopeless candidates in order to secure a better runoff pairing, i.e., a better lottery over final outcomes.

Given the model's postulates, voter rationality implies a certain consistency between a voter's beliefs about other voters' preferences and her expectations about the likely outcome. If everyone is supposed to entertain the same expectations about what the outcome will be, and everyone acts rationally, then there should be an equality between (1) the expected vote share for candidate j and (2) the vote share for candidate j implied by optimal behavior on the part of all voters in reaction to what everyone expects. That is, expectations are assumed to be "rational" in this model as in Chapter 4.

A final (and dispensable) condition on voter expectations that I shall impose limits the races covered to those in which a first-round majority is not in the cards. Formally, I shall assume that the probability of the event "candidate j is one vote shy of a majority" is negligible relative to the probability of the most likely second-place tie. Thus, instrumental voters do not worry about their vote putting a favored candidate over the top in the first round; they only worry about their vote deciding who will be in the runoff. I consider the general case in Appendix B and briefly in Section 6.3.

The (symmetric Bayes-Nash) equilibrium conditions for the model are then two. First, every voter votes so as to maximize her expected utility, given expectations. Second, the expectations satisfy the rational expectations condition.

6.3 SOME EQUILIBRIUM RESULTS

In this section, I describe some general characteristics of strategic voting equilibria under top-two runoff rules.[5] I shall assume throughout that voters are uncertain as to who will win any given runoff pairing. Formally, denoting by p_{jk} the probability of candidate j winning a runoff,

[5]Existence of equilibrium is not a problem. A formal proof of existence is given in Myerson and Weber (1993). Although stated for single-ballot systems, the same proof works (*mutatis mutandis*) for dual-ballot systems as well.

when pitted against candidate k, I assume that $0 < p_{jk} < 1$ for all j,k. Note that because the distribution F is common knowledge, the parameters $\{p_{jk}\}$ are also (see Appendix B).

Four is a crowd

The first theoretical result I wish to note concerning strategic voting in the first round of elections held under top-two majority runoff rules is that fourth- and lower-place candidates will often be ruined by strategic voting in the first round. To demonstrate this, consider first how a purely outcome-oriented voter, of the type under study here, thinks about an election. Such a voter essentially asks: When could my one vote affect the outcome? The answer is that there are only two ways that one vote can affect the outcome. First, that one vote can put some candidate over the top in the first round. As I have assumed that the probability of any candidate being one vote shy of a majority is negligible, this possibility can be ignored. Second, one vote can break or make a tie for second place, thus affecting who gets into the runoff election. Since I have assumed that the probability of the event "candidate j is tied for second" is *negligible* in comparison to the probability of the event "candidate 3 is tied for second," whenever $\pi_j < \pi_3$ and n is sufficiently large, voting for any candidate $j > 3$ (such that $\pi_j < \pi_3$) is almost certain not to affect the outcome in large electorates. Such a vote is, in other words, negligibly different from abstaining, *even conditional on a tie of some sort occurring.* Accordingly, in order to prove the claim made above, one need only show that the voter is strictly better off voting for one of the top three candidates (1, 2, or 3) than abstaining. This is an elementary consequence of the assumptions that all voters have strict preference rankings of the candidates and that voting is costless. Thus we have:

> *Proposition 1:* For large enough electorates, the expected vote shares garnered by candidates expected to finish fourth or lower converge to zero.

In other words, for large enough electorates, it becomes obvious that any fourth- or lower-place candidate is out of the running for a runoff spot, at which point no outcome-oriented voter has any reason to vote for them. So, speaking loosely (because dynamically in the context of a static model), if a candidate falls to fourth, strategic voting kicks in and reduces him to a zero vote share.

There are two kinds of limit equilibria that Proposition 1 allows in large electorates. One type, which I shall call *Duvergerian* equilibria, are such that all candidates expected to finish fourth or lower have negligible vote shares. That is, only 3 of the K candidates end up with non-negligible vote shares, the rest being reduced nearly to zero by strategic voting. A second type, the *non-Duvergerian* equilibria, entail ties for third between two or more candidates. None of these third-place candidates suffers from strategic desertion because each has as good a chance as any of the others at making the runoff (or, more precisely, at tying for second).

A dynamic story that provides either a justification or a critique, depending on one's point of view, of the static result just articulated is the following. Imagine a candidate who falls into fourth or lower place in the polls leading up to the first-round election. In response to the poll, some of the candidate's least-committed supporters desert him. This pushes him lower in the (next) polls and causes more supporters (those a bit more committed) to desert. The unraveling continues until the candidate has no instrumental support left. This story does not require a huge electorate and invocation of a law of large numbers. It requires many polls, myopic adjustment, and an opportunity for "momentum" to build for certain candidates at the expense of others (cf. Johnston et al. 1992:222; Forsythe et al. 1993; Fey 1995).

Strategic desertion of first-place candidates

Under majority runoff procedures, it may sometimes be advantageous to desert a stronger and more preferred candidate for a weaker and less preferred candidate in the first round. Suppose, for example, that there are three candidates, that a voter prefers candidate 1 to 2 to 3, and that the candidates' expected vote shares are $\pi_1 > \pi_2 \geq \pi_3$. Under the conditions of the model, the only situation in which a single vote is decisive that need be considered in large electorates occurs when candidates 2 and 3 tie for second, with candidate 1 in first place. Given that this event occurs, the voter would vote for candidate 2, if she preferred that 1 face 2 in the runoff; and for candidate 3, if she preferred that 1 face 3 in the runoff; and indifferently for any candidate if she was indifferent between the runoff pairings. Thus, she might end up voting for her least-favored candidate (3) in the first round, if that ensured a victory for her most-favored candidate (1) in the runoff.

The general point as far as what expectations can be (limits of) rational expectations is embodied in the following proposition:

> *Proposition 2:* For large enough electorates, the expected vote shares of the candidates expected to finish first and second must be equal.
> *Proof:* Similar to that of Proposition 1.

A candidate who has more votes than he needs to get into the runoff will, in other words, be relieved of those votes by strategic voters.

It should be stressed that voters who desert a first-place candidate who has "too many" votes (yet not enough to have a shot at winning in the first round) adopt a risky strategy: If too many of 1's supporters desert him in the first round, seeking to help the "weaker" of his two closest first-round competitors get into the runoff with him, so to ensure his ultimate victory, then 1 may fail to get into the runoff to begin with. The current equilibrium concept (Bayes-Nash) does not deal with these aspects of "Chicken" particularly well (about as well as the Nash concept deals with coordination problems in the Battle of the Sexes; on which see Farrell 1987).

When a first-round majority is in view

What happens if one relaxes the assumption that no voter thinks the chance of a first-round majority need be considered? Does relaxing this assumption affect the results in Proposition 1 concerning strategic desertion of hopeless candidates? If some candidate is certain to win a majority in the first round, then outcome-oriented voters have no reason to desert their first preferences, even if they rank low in the polls. Aside from this extreme situation, however, the results do not change. A fourth- or lower-place candidate who does not have a significant chance at tying for second will also not have a significant chance at winning outright in the first round. Thus, there will not be any new reason to support him, just because some other candidate might win the seat in the first round.[6]

The possibility of a first-round majority similarly seems to have little effect upon the strategic desertion of first-place candidates. If a first-round majority for 1 were possible, would his supporters have a new reason to stick with him? Putting 1 over the top in the first round is valuable, from the point of view of the final outcome, only if he might lose the runoff. But, conditional on 1's having enough support to win a majority in the first round, he cannot lose the runoff. Thus, the only situations that matter are those in which 1 does not have enough votes to win a majority, in which case there *will* be a runoff in which he *might* be vulnerable. Thus, the need to assure the best possible runoff pairing remains paramount (for purely outcome-oriented voters) as long as there is any chance of a runoff.

[6]This conclusion assumes away the possibility that the probability function g_n (on which see Appendix B) is such that candidate 4 will finish either one vote shy of a majority, or much lower, on average coming in fourth.

Strategic voting in single-member dual-ballot systems

An M+1 rule for top-M majority runoff systems

It is possible to generalize the model presented above from top-2 to top-M systems.[7] The general rule, as far as the strategic desertion of weak candidates goes, is this: If the top M finishers in the first round get to go on in the second, then no more than $M + 1$ candidates are expected to get positive vote shares in the first round (in Duvergerian equilibria).

6.4 VIOLATING SOME ASSUMPTIONS

The results of the pure model presented above provide a theoretical benchmark against which one might judge real-world elections. Voters in the model are highly informed and have arrived at a (self-fulfilling) consensus that certain candidates are out of the running. Caring only about the outcome of the current election, they therefore have no reason to vote for such candidates. In this section, I consider a variety of ways in which real-world voters and elections might depart from this idealized world, and speculate on the consequences as far as strategic voting goes.

Voters who care about more than who wins the current election

It is obvious that the results stated above are sensitive to relaxing the assumption that voters care only about who wins the current election. If, for example, some voters derive a consumption value from voting for their favored party in the first round, then such consumption values will overwhelm any instrumental values in large electorates (because the probability of one vote affecting the outcome is infinitesimal). Noninstrumental voters of this kind will therefore not vote strategically. It remains true, however, that those voters who *are* outcome-oriented will desert hopeless candidacies. So the result of Proposition 1 becomes: Candidates expected to place no better than fourth lose all their *instrumental* supporters in large electorates.

A different kind of instrumental voter would be one who did not look ahead to the runoff, instead treating the first round as an election in which there were two equally valuable prizes – *viz.*, the runoff spots – to be awarded. This case may not be *formally* different from that consid-

[7]In top-M systems, $M > 2$, it is no longer possible to deduce analogs to the probabilities $\{p_{jk}\}$. Moreover, whereas under top-2 rules voters can assume sincere voting in the second round, under top-M rules they may have to anticipate the nature of the strategic voting equilibrium in the second round. Nonetheless, one can take the analogs to the p_{jk} probabilities as primitives, or take voter preferences over runoff fields as primitives, and proceed as in the current model.

ered here: In a zero-foresight model, voters continue to have a utility ranking over runoff pairings; it is just that this ranking does not depend on their beliefs about who will win the runoff. Substantively, however, there may be some important differences, as I discuss later.

Yet another kind of voter would care about the margins of victory compiled in the first round. It is plausible that voters might care about margins, because these could affect elite bargaining between the first and second round. In a top-two system, a hard-left voter who thought it virtually certain that a center-left and a right candidate would make it to the runoff, might hope to strengthen the hard-left candidate's bargaining position (in dealing second-round support for policy concessions or pork) by continuing to vote for her, even if the hard-left vote total was too small to figure in the first-round outcome. Such considerations obviously may substantially affect patterns of strategic voting.

A final kind of instrumental voter might care about "other elections" (e.g., those held in other districts). I shall say little about other elections except to note that they are clearly relevant, especially when the issue of entry is brought into view. To mention the case of France, which uses not a top-two but a more complicated runoff system, one finds that the Right put up only one candidate in almost all districts in the 1988 elections, having divided the constituencies up beforehand (Cole and Campbell 1989:161).

Nonrational expectations

In practice, voters have virtually no instrumental incentive to pay attention to politics (Downs 1957; Popkin 1991). Learning more about candidates or about candidates' chances will simply produce a better vote; in order actually to produce a better outcome, the voter's vote would have to be decisive, something that is extremely unlikely. One expects, therefore, that many voters will lack well-developed perceptions of the candidates' chances.

Looking at the matter pragmatically, when would one expect any approximation of the rational expectations condition? Consider two cases: where there is a single clear leader in the first round, with a close race for the second spot; and where there is a close three-way race.

In the first case, if it becomes clear *to voters* that A is ahead, with B and C in a dead heat for second, will this motivate strategic voting? It depends on what voters think about the likely runoff pairings (A vs. B and A vs. C). If everyone expects A to win no matter which of B or C make it to the runoff, then there is little point, from the perspective of affecting the outcome, of deserting a hopeless first choice in the first round. This is true even for an elite actor who has a substantial chance of affecting the first-round outcome, or for a voter with greatly exaggerated impressions of her own electoral importance. If everyone expects A to *lose* no matter which of B or C make it to the runoff, on the other hand, then there is a substantial reason to vote strategically: The first round is really a choice of the ultimate victor. Finally, if everyone expects A to win against B but to lose against C then there is again a substantial reason to vote strategically, especially if B and C are ideologically closer to one another than either is to A.

Schmidt (1996, N.d.) argues that something like this last scenario played out in the fateful Peruvian presidential election of 1990. The common expectation in the final week of the campaign was that A (Vargas Llosa, the right-wing candidate) could beat B (Alva Castro, one of two centrist candidates vying for second place in the first round) but probably not C (Fujimori, the other viable centrist candidate). On the assumption that these were in fact the operative expectations just before the election, Vargas Llosa should have held his support and Fujimori should have benefited from a sizable strategic vote as the anti-Vargas Llosa forces coordinated on the best available vehicle to defeat him. The rapidity with which Fujimori was transformed from an obscure minor-party candidate with apparently no chance to the strongest challenger to Vargas Llosa – reminiscent of the rapidity with which presidential candidacies are made and unmade during the U.S. primary season (Bartels 1988) – is strong *prima facie* evidence that coordination among the anti-Vargas Llosa forces was the key to his rise. But Schmidt goes beyond this *prima facie* evidence. He uses disaggregated electoral returns to show that Vargas Llosa did indeed hold onto his support and that Fujimori did indeed benefit substantially from strategic voting. In addition, he provides some interview-based evidence that key elite actors actively fomented this strategic coordination.

Another case similar to the Peruvian was the enormously important Russian presidential election of 1996. In February 1996, the communist Gennadi Zyuganov led all other presidential aspirants in the polls, while the sitting President, Boris Yeltsin, languished in single digits. Yeltsin then hired a team of American campaign consultants who advocated the following strategy in a memo dated March 2: "There exists only one very simple strategy for winning: first, becoming the only alternative to the Communists; and second, making the people see that the Communists must be stopped at all costs" (Kramer 1996:33). This of course is precisely the strategy that one would pursue in order to ensure that strategic coordination acted to one's benefit rather than to one's detriment. While there were numerous bumps in the road, this strategy appears to have contributed substantially to Yeltsin's victory (Kramer 1996).

What about the other case mentioned above? In close three-way contests, will there be plausible incentives to vote strategically? Elites again will have incentives to promote strategic behavior, but whether they will succeed is less clear. Suppose, for example, that A is highly likely to defeat either B or C in a runoff, and that B is highly likely to beat C. While supporters of weak parties who prefer A to B have an obvious strategy – vote for A – those who prefer B to A must ensure that A does not make the runoff, which entails *equalizing the vote between B and C.* It is not obvious that elites will be able to orchestrate the necessary balancing between B and C. At minimum, it seems a more difficult educational task than the usual "wasted vote" exhortations.

Things do not get any clearer if there is not a Condorcet winner – if, in other words, there is a cycle among A, B, and C. Taking the case of an "A beats B, B beats C, C beats A" cycle, many agents need to engage in an equalization strategy. Elites who prefer A, for example, will seek to maximize the probability that candidate C (who would beat A in a runoff) does not make the runoff, since this leaves A against B and leads to a victory for A. In order to maximize this probability, they must ensure that both A and B exceed C's vote total, which entails equalizing their expected votes.

One might again wonder whether elites could convince voters to go along with the vote balancing act they suggested. There are cases in which fairly exact equalization of votes has occurred under electoral systems different from top-*M* runoff. The nineteenth-century Birmingham Liberals, for example, sent voting instructions to their followers in each ward of the city in order to equalize their candidates' votes under the limited vote system then in operation (Ostrogorski 1902). But this feat of vote equalization occurred among voters of the same party and the theoretically required equalizations in runoff systems can cross party (or even left/right coalitional) boundaries.

Suppose one posits that voters will never cross the left/right boundary. Then something like what Duverger (1986) describes in French politics as bipolar multipartism would be in equilibrium under top-two runoff rules (N.B. These are *not* the French rules, which are less restrictive). The logic would be as follows. As long as one party from the left and one party from the right are expected to make it into the runoff, there is no pressure on either the left or the right to coalesce. This condition is certainly met when, as in 1988, the right puts up only one first-round candidate in most constituencies, with the left putting up two (Cole and Campbell 1989:161). It is also possibly met when there are two candidates from each party, as long as neither side is so strong that their parties finish one-two (in which case the ultimate outcome is probably a foregone conclusion anyway). But *lopsided* bipolar multipartism, say the

Left running three or more candidates to the Right's two, would present some clear pressures for consolidation on the Left: It would be likely, especially if the Left was not much larger than the Right, and the Left and Right candidates split their respective votes equally, that the two rightist candidates would finish in the top two spots in the first round. Anticipation of this result should prompt leftist elites to arrange withdrawals in the first round, or failing that, to provide the necessary information and cues to voters to produce a strategic desertion of one of the leftist candidates.

From this perspective it is interesting to note that, in the 1988 French elections, candidates on the far right (associated with Le Pen) did enter in substantial numbers. One reason for the traditional Right's decision to divide the seats up before the first round in that year may have been a desire to avoid splitting the Right's vote three ways.[8]

Shortsighted voters

I noted above that voters who do not look ahead to the runoff outcome may produce substantively different results from the farsighted voters considered here. Now it is time to show how this may be so. Consider again the case of a close three-way race between A, B, and C, with A a Condorcet winner, B beating C. With farsighted voters, any minor party supporters should desert their favored party and vote either for A, if they prefer A to B, or so as to equalize the vote totals of B and C, if they prefer B to A. With shortsighted voters (operationally taken to be those with additively separable preferences over candidates, who act simply to add the most-preferred first-round candidates to the runoff pair that they can, without considering his chances in the runoff), minor party supporters should also desert their favored party but they should vote for whichever of the three top candidates – A, B, or C – they most prefer. No equalization strategy is entailed; just a straight vote for the most-favored of the viable first-round candidates. Thus, if every candidate is seen as having an equally good chance of winning any runoff he happens to get into – or runoff probabilities do not even figure in voter calculations,

[8]With the actual French rules, which require a first-round vote exceeding 12.5% of the registered electorate to gain admission to the second round, there may be room for three parties on the Right, even if the Left puts up two. Suppose the Right collectively holds 51% of the voters in a given constituency, and splits those votes equally among three candidates, with the Left splitting equally between two candidates. If the turnout rate in the constituency exceeds about 73.5%, then all three Right candidates will make it into the second round (as will the two leftists). But if turnout falls below 73.5% (and above about 51%), then the two leftists will be the only ones to qualify for the second round.

because voters are myopic – then strategic voting under top-*M* procedures will look very similar to strategic voting under *M*-seat districts operating under the single nontransferable vote.

6.5 STRATEGIC VOTING IN NON-MAJORITARIAN RUNOFF SYSTEMS

As noted above, some dual-ballot systems are non-majoritarian: They do not require that a candidate win a majority of all votes cast in order to win a seat in the first round of voting. In this section, I briefly consider two such systems: the 40% rule used in Costa Rica (and elsewhere) and the double-complement rule proposed by Shugart and Taagepera (1994).

Under the 40% rule, any candidate who finishes first in the first round of voting *and* garners at least 40% of the first-round vote is declared elected. The 40% rule is thus a combination of a relative standard (the vote must exceed all others) and an absolute standard (the vote must exceed 40%). The impact of substituting the 40% rule for the more usual majority rule depends on whether there is a likely first-round winner or not. Suppose first that there is no such prospective winner, e.g., there are five candidates splitting the vote 25%, 25%, 20%, 20%, 10%. In this case, the two rules, 40% and majority rule, are likely to produce identical outcomes (a runoff between the two strongest first-round finishers) and so should induce similar patterns of strategic voting in anticipation of this outcome, aimed at producing the most favorable possible runoff pairing. Suppose next that a first-round winner looks likely, e.g., there are three candidates splitting the vote 44%, 35%, 21%. In this case, the 40% rule will likely produce the same outcome as ordinary plurality rule (victory for the strongest first-round candidate) and so should induce a similar pattern of strategic voting in anticipation of this outcome, with the third-place candidate suffering substantial desertions.

Another non-majoritarian runoff system, the double-complement rule of Shugart and Taagepera (1994), averages the relative standard required by plurality rule (i.e., $v_1 > v_2$, where v_1 and v_2 represent the vote percentages of the first and second candidates, respectively) and the absolute standard required by majority rule (i.e., $v_1 > 50\%$) to yield $v_1 > (v_2 + 50)/2$. This differs from the 40% rule in that, for example, a 40% vote share would win in the first round only if the second-place candidate garnered less than 30% of the vote. But the consequences for strategic voting are similar. If under the double-complement rule there is no likely first-round winner – e.g., there are three candidates with vote shares 42%, 41%, and 17% – then both the likely outcome and the strategic voting incentives set in train by anticipation of that outcome are similar to those under majority runoff. If, on the other hand, there is a likely first-round victor, then one expects some concentration of the vote, at least until it is no longer clear that there will be a first-round winner.

6.6 CONCLUSION

Duverger (1954) was wrong if, in his discussion of runoff elections, he meant to say that there were typically no reasons for voters to vote strategically. In top-two majority runoff elections with three or more candidates, voters *always* face incentives to vote strategically. And when there are four or more candidates, these incentives (in a frictionless model) destroy candidacies not in the running for a runoff spot, just as in plurality elections they destroy candidacies not in the running for a seat (in accordance with Duverger's Law). As a more general rule, top-M runoff elections can have at most $M + 1$ viable candidates, at least in the "Duvergerian" equilibria of the pure model.

Duverger was on better ground if he was merely asserting that as a practical matter voters under runoff rules do not vote strategically very often (or, as often as they do under plurality). Compare the information that a voter (or an elite agent) needs in order to cast a strategic vote under runoff and plurality rules. Under both systems, the voter needs to know that his favorite candidate is "out of the running," whether for first place in a plurality election, or for first or second place in the first-round of a runoff election. Voters in runoff elections will, in addition, probably want to know something about the likely outcome of the various possible runoff pairings, something that is hard to predict and unnecessary to predict under plurality rule. Consider also the nature of the strategy required. Under plurality rule, strategic voting is simple: It means voting for one's most-favored *viable* candidate. Under runoff rules, in contrast, strategic voting is often more complicated: It entails voting so as to equalize the vote totals of two viable candidates, so as to minimize the probability that a third viable candidate will make the runoff. Such fine balancing usually requires a substantial and sophisticated party organization to accomplish. In a nutshell, under runoff rules it is more difficult for elite actors to discern when it is in their interests to foment strategic voting, and, conditional on their deciding that it is worthwhile, it is more difficult to implement the appropriate strategy.

Having said this, however, there are still situations when strategic voting in top-two runoffs seems a plausible bet. And, as under plurality rule, anticipation of strategic voting in such situations ought to prevent the situations from arising in the first place. Two examples of this kind of effect were discussed in particular: the case of the divided center, and the case of lopsided bipolar multipartism.

The first of these cases involves unidimensional politics with a unified Left, a large Center split into two parties, and a unified Right. If the Center puts up two candidates in the first round, neither will make it to the runoff, leaving Center voters with a poor choice. If the Center coordinates, the unified Center candidate will make it to the runoff and win. The incentives in this case are fairly clear and the strategy straightforward. One expects, therefore, that either there will not be two Center parties at all (fusion), or that the two Center parties will negotiate which of them puts up a candidate in each district (nomination agreements), or that voters will supply the defect of elite coordination and vote strategically.

The second case is similar. The point here is that a Left coalition of, say, five parties may fail to secure one of the runoff spots if they all run and the Right runs two evenly-matched candidates. So lopsided bipolar multipartism, similarly to divided Centers, ought to end in fusion, nomination agreements, or strategic voting.[9]

Finally, I should note that the focus of concern here has been the number of parties that will compete under majority runoff rules. A related issue is the *kind* of party that will prosper (i.e., win seats). Here the conventional wisdom, clearly articulated by Sartori (1994), is that anti-system and extremist parties will be disadvantaged by runoff rules, since they will typically be poorly positioned in the bargaining that goes on between first and second rounds.[10] The point here is reminiscent of one frequently made in the literature on coalition governments, whereby centrally located parties have an advantage, at least when parties are to some extent policy-motivated (cf. Laver and Schofield 1990).

[9] Something of the incentives that runoff elections provide for fusion, in the top-two case, can be seen in the Russian presidential race of 1996. By April and May of 1996, the situation seemed to be one in which Yeltsin and Zyuganov would be the only two to make the runoff. This led to some talk about a "third force" primary that would involve three of the major players left out in the cold by the anticipated result. If they could arrange a primary, with the winner taking the sum of the third-force votes, then *ex ante* they could transform a situation in which each had no chance of making the runoff into one in which each had some positive probability of doing so. Yeltsin's American advisers, consistent with their overall strategy of making Yeltsin the focal alternative to Zyuganov, advocated disrupting the attempt at third force unity (Kramer 1996:36).

[10] Evidence that this is indeed the case is provided by Fisichella (1984); Blais and Carty (1989).

7

Some concluding comments on strategic voting

In the last three chapters, I have focused on the nature of strategic voting equilibria in the three electoral systems that featured in Duverger's original propositions: SMSP, single-tier PR, and majority runoff. The main conclusion has been that all three systems obey the $M + 1$ rule, according to which the number of viable candidates or lists in each system cannot exceed $M + 1$ (where M refers to the district magnitude for SMSP and PR, and to the number of first-round competitors who can advance to the second round for majority runoff). I have also considered three broad theoretical limits on the $M + 1$ result: First, if the electoral institutions do not correspond to one of those specified above, then nonstandard varieties of strategic voting may arise, that do not systematically concentrate the distribution of votes; second, even if one considers one of the electoral systems listed above, there are still a number of key assumptions about voters that must be met in order for strategic voting to have a strong effect; third, even if the electoral institutions are "right" and the voters obey all the model's assumptions, only an upper bound is imposed in Duvergerian equilibria. In this chapter, I consider the first and third of these hitherto subsidiary issues in greater detail. I make two main points. First, the fact that strategic voting only imposes an upper bound on the effective number of competitors, when it has any reductive impact at all, has some clear consequences for how we think about doing electoral research. Second, strategic voting under some systems has no general reductive impact.

7.1 STRATEGIC VOTING ONLY IMPOSES AN UPPER BOUND

I have already noted that the $M + 1$ rule only imposes an upper bound on the effective number of competitors that will appear in equilibrium. I shall now explore four issues related to this fact, pertaining to whether the upper bound is constraining or not, what factors might explain the equilibrium number of competitors when the upper bound is not constraining, the interaction of social and electoral structure, and electoral competition viewed as a coordination game.

Does the upper bound bind? One consequence is that adopting a more permissive system will not necessarily multiply the number of parties. If electoral system A imposes an upper bound U_A, and system B imposes a bound U_B, then one may say that A is stronger than B (or that B is more permissive than A) if $U_A < U_B$. But if country X changes from system A to system B the number of parties will increase only if the upper bound under system A really was consequential, in the sense that it was preventing the emergence or success of some would-be parties. If the "natural" number of parties in country X, defined in terms of its social cleavages or on some other grounds, falls below U_A, then increasing the permissiveness of the electoral system will have no effect. It is only if the natural number is above U_A that making the electoral system more permissive should matter.

There are two further consequences of the observations just made. First, they provide a *district-level* justification for those who argue that PR systems have no multiplying effects (e.g., Sartori 1994:47). Second, they suggest some caution in interpreting what are otherwise quite natural research designs. Consider, for example, Lijphart's (1994) magisterial examination of changes in post-war democratic electoral systems and the subsequent changes in number of parties. Often he found that increases in the permissiveness of an electoral system did not subsequently give rise to an increase in the number of parties. On a purely institutionalist account, this would count against the importance of electoral law. Taking account of the interaction between social and electoral structure, however, finding no increase in the number of parties after increasing the permissiveness of the electoral system counts as evidence against the importance of electoral structure only if one believes that the previous electoral system had impeded the exploitation of extant cleavages in the society, so that it was actually holding the number of parties below what it would be with a more permissive system. Absent such a belief, one would not expect a weakening of the electoral system to lead to increases in the number of parties, and so one would not count failure to observe such an increase as evidence of the unimportance of electoral laws in conditioning political life.[1] Similarly, finding that an increase in the strength of an electoral system does not pro-

[1]Another interesting study that is similar to Lijphart's, hence open to the criticism made in the text, is Shamir (1985).

duce a contraction in the party system is telling evidence only if the number of parties under the old system exceeds the "carrying capacity" of the new system.

Equilibration below the upper bound. Another point related to the fact that strategic voting only imposes an upper bound on the number of competitors can be developed as follows. Recall first that, in SNTV systems and in LRPR systems that are like SNTV, strategic voting phenomena seem to fade out rapidly for district magnitudes above 5. The main reason for this is that the larger the magnitude, the smaller are the vote percentages that separate winners from losers, hence the harder it is to be sure who is out of the running. Recall also that for PR systems generally, the effective number of lists falls well below the $M + 1$ upper bound, for M above 4. If one puts these two observations together, the conclusion seems to be that strategic voting does not explain much about the number of parties in districts of magnitude above about 5.

This observation suggests some redirection of the research agenda in electoral studies. Taagepera and Shugart's "generalized Duverger's law" – embodied in their equation $N_{eff} = 2.5 + 1.25 log_{10}M$ – may be an *empirical* generalization of Duverger's law/hypothesis, but it does not generalize his logic. Whatever it is that explains why so few lists appear in large-magnitude districts operating under PR, it is not systematic downward pressure derived from the fear of wasting votes. So, we should look elsewhere: to economies of scale in advertising, raising funds, securing portfolios, supplying policy benefits, and so on.

The interaction of social and electoral structure. A third point is that the logic of strategic voting, properly understood, suggests an interaction between social and electoral structure. In Chapter 2, I noted that some political sociologists seem to regard Duverger's Law as a species of institutional determinism, something to be rejected on the obvious grounds that social cleavages are key in understanding where parties come from and how many there will be. But the logic of strategic voting leads only to each system having a certain "carrying capacity." If the number of lists or candidates exceeds that carrying capacity, then one can expect strategic decisions by the voters to winnow the field. But exactly how many candidates or lists there will be is not determined: It just has to be below the upper bound. In systems with multimember districts, this leaves plenty of room for social diversity to determine the precise number of competitors. A homogeneous society may have only two parties even if the electoral system allows for more. A heterogeneous society with the same electoral system may hit up against the upper bound. Thus, if we adopt the simple notion that the more cleavages there are in a society, the more parties it will have, but modify it by appeal to the institutionally imposed upper bound articulated by the $M + 1$ rule, we should expect that the number of competitors, N, will be an *interactive* function of electoral and social structure: N will be low if either the electoral system is strong or social diversity is low; N will be high only if the electoral system is permissive and social diversity is high. I provide evidence that this is indeed the case in Chapter 11.

Elections as coordination games. A final point is that the logic of strategic voting suggests what characteristics successful players of the electoral game will possess. The simplest form of the institutionalist perspective – and here I step beyond the exclusive focus on voters that has characterized this part of the book and informally include elites as well – merely asserts that each electoral system faces social actors with a giant coordination game of a more or less constraining nature. In strong systems, the amount of coordination needed to guarantee a seat is rather large and the penalties for failure to coordinate are large. In less strong systems, both the amount of coordination needed and the penalties for failure are milder.

Who will be well-positioned to succeed in giant coordination games of the kind that strong electoral systems in particular pose? In order to answer this question, let us first consider a central feature of coordination games well known to game theorists: It helps to be able to make the first move, or to precommit to a particular move. Consider, for example, a SMSP contest in which two leftists contemplate entering against a single rightist. Either can defeat the rightist in a pairwise contest, but neither will win if both enter and stay in the race to the end. In this situation, if one of the leftists credibly commits to entering and staying in the race till the end, the other leftist's best move would be to stay out of the race, and the first leftist would therefore win the seat. If both leftists had the ability to make such commitments, then whichever of them succeeded in making the commitment first would win the election. So, being able publicly to commit to a future course of action and being able to move nimbly when the difficulty first becomes clear are both valuable in coordination problems.

What kinds of social groups possess these features? In the context of large-n coordination games – as for example the problem of strategic coordination among voters in a mass election – social groups that are organized, that have leaders who can speak for their interests in an authoritative and public fashion, and that are perceived as usually voting as a bloc are more likely to be able publicly to commit to future courses of action (and to move nimbly when the need arises). Such groups, of which ethnic, linguistic, or religious minorities might be leading examples, are more likely to be successful in steering the outcome of large coordination games toward their preferred equilibrium. They are therefore more likely to appear as the central social underpinnings of endogenously created factions, parties, or alliances than are less organized groups.

The argument just given is informal. But I think it is sufficient to suggest that the appropriate understanding of the logic of strategic voting does not deal out the social interests, it deals them in.

7.2 WHEN WILL STRATEGIC VOTING RESTRICT THE EFFECTIVE NUMBER OF PARTIES?

Thus far in this book we have encountered several electoral systems – SMSP, majority runoff, SNTV, and PR – in which strategic voting puts an upper bound of $M + 1$ on the effective number of competitors (candidates in the first three cases, lists in the last case). What do these voting procedures have in common? All of these systems give voters a single exclusive vote (recall that a vote is exclusive if for purposes of seat allocation it affects only the vote total of the list or candidate for whom it is cast). All are also first-place rewarding rather than last-place punishing systems. (First-place rewarding systems are those in which voters are able, via their ballot options, to make a sharp distinction in favor of their top-ranked alternative(s), without being able to distinguish very sharply between lower-ranked alternatives; last-place punishing systems are those in which voters are able to sharply discriminate against their least-favored alternative, but cannot distinguish much between higher-ranked alternatives.)[2] Do systems that have a reductive impact on the party system necessarily have a single exclusive vote? Are they necessarily first-place rewarding? Or is some other condition key to distinguishing between those systems that do and those that do not restrict the effective number of competitors?

I shall approach these questions by first considering single-vote systems in which the vote is not exclusive; then single-vote systems that are last-place punishing rather than first-place rewarding; then multiple-vote systems of various kinds.

Single nonexclusive vote systems

There are two main types of system that give voters a single nonexclusive candidate vote: the single transferable vote (STV) system used, for example, in Ireland and Malta; and the single pooling vote (SPV) used, for example, in Chile and Finland.

[2]A more complete definition of the notion of a "first-place rewarding" system is given, for the case of scoring rules, in Cox (1987c).

Strategic voting under STV can lead to a deconcentration of votes, as can be seen by recalling an example given in Chapter 4. In this example, there is one seat at stake and three candidates compete for it. If a voter's favorite candidate, while leading the polls and having enough votes to survive the first round, will lose in the second round against one prospective opponent, but win against the other, then it is optimal to rank the "beatable" opponent first and one's favorite second. But this entails redirecting votes from a vote-rich to a vote-poorer candidate, thereby deconcentrating the distribution of (first-preference) votes.

Suppose there were four candidates, instead of three, chasing after a single seat under STV rules. Could it ever be optimal to rank a clearly weakest candidate (in terms of expected first preferences) first? The answer, by analogy to the discussion in Chapter 6 of runoff elections, should be no. In the first round, one should be trying to set up the best possible second round. Voting for candidates who are expected to have too few first preferences to make it to the second round cannot affect who makes it to the second round, hence cannot affect the ultimate outcome. One might conjecture, then, that the alternative vote should be like a top-two runoff system, as regards strategic voting. In particular, the upper bound ought to be $M + 1$ in a pure model, with perhaps $M + 2$ in a bipolar system (see Chapter 6).

Strategic voting under SPV can also lead to a deconcentration of votes. Consider the Chilean example given in Section 5.3, in which a leftist and a rightist list, each with two candidates, chase after two seats. If neither list doubles the other's vote, and the two conservative candidates are expected to get about the same number of votes, then the leftist voters may be able to determine which of the two conservatives wins. If the leftist list's expected vote total exceeded the conservative list's, then this would entail a transfer of votes from a stronger list to a weaker, deconcentrating the distribution of votes across lists.

Could there be more than $M + 1$ lists under SPV? I would conjecture that there cannot be, again because voting for a list that has no hope of winning a seat cannot affect the outcome (in large electorates), hence cannot be something that a short-term instrumentally rational voter would do. So there ought to be an $M + 1$ rule for SPV, too. (It should be stressed that this rule applies to lists, not parties. The possibility of joint listing means that even if there are typically fewer than $M + 1$ lists, there may typically be more than $M + 1$ parties, as in Chile, for example).

If both STV and SPV obey the $M + 1$ rule, then it cannot be the exclusivity of the vote that is key to underpinning the emergence of this rule. What of the first-place rewarding nature of the systems considered thus far? Does that matter?

Last-place punishing systems

In last-place punishing systems, candidates' incentives are to avoid being ranked last, or low, in a voter's preference ordering, rather than to rank first or near the top. Consider the most extreme case, negative plurality voting. Under negative plurality voting, each voter casts a single vote for a candidate, and the candidate with the *fewest* votes wins. Equivalently, one can think of voters as casting negative votes (that add –1 to the voted-for candidate's vote total), with ordinary plurality rule deciding the winner.

In this system, a sincere vote would entail giving –1 to the candidate that the voter ranked last (hence giving 0 to all the rest of the candidates). Rational behavior under negative plurality, however, entails giving –1 to one's least-preferred *marginal* candidate. So the top two candidates should become the target of more negative votes, until their vote totals fall to near-equality with that of the third-place candidate.

An example may help to clarify matters. Suppose that three candidates, A, B, and C, compete for a single seat under negative plurality rules. Suppose also that half of the voters in this election rank A first and B second; while the other half rank B first and A second. Suppose finally that for both groups candidate C is not only third but a distant, repugnant third. In this example, sincere voting would mean that everyone gave –1 to the repugnant C, yielding a tie between candidates A and B, both of whom would get zero votes (C getting $-n$ votes, where n is the total number of voters). BAC voters could profit by diverting some of their negative votes from C to A, thereby electing B. ABC voters could similarly profit by giving B some negative votes, in order to elect A.

More generally, BAC voters could always profit by diverting their votes from C to A, if the current allocation of votes satisfied: $V_A \geq V_B > V_C$ but $V_B - V_C - 1 > V_A - V_B$. For then $V_B - V_C - 1$ of the BAC voters could divert their votes from C to A and change the outcome in B's favor. Similarly, ABC voters could always profit if $V_B \geq V_A > V_C$ but $V_A - V_C - 1 > V_B - V_A$. Thus, if there are any strong Nash equilibria in the model (i.e., situations in which no coalition of voters can make themselves better off by jointly changing their strategies), they necessarily entail that a substantial number of voters do not vote sincerely.

In fact, strong Nash equilibria do exist for this example. For example, any situation in which $V_A > V_C \geq V_B$ (and no voters employ dominated strategies) is a strong Nash equilibrium: The ABC voters get their first choice, while the BAC voters can only make matters worse for themselves by voting for A rather than C. Thus, strategic voting under negative plurality voting would lead, in this equilibrium outcome, to a candidate who is ranked last by all voters finishing at least in a tie for second.[3]

What is interesting about this example is that votes are substantially deconcentrated in the strategic voting equilibrium vis-à-vis the sincere voting outcome. Voters are willing to offer the repugnant candidate C tacit support, by giving him a zero instead of a –1, as long as they believe that this will not in fact elect C. The advantage of giving this tacit support is that the voters are then free to cast their –1 vote for the candidate who is most threatening to their favorite. To put it another way, because the voting system essentially forces voters to give two 0's and one –1, it is sometimes useful to give one of the high votes to a hopeless candidate, in order to avoid giving it to a viable candidate that one wishes to defeat. Is this "turkey-raising" a general feature of some class of voting systems?

Multiple-vote systems

In this section, I shall consider two classes of voting procedure that give voters many votes but require that the voter use all these votes. The first kind of voting procedure is one that was once frequently employed in U.S. local elections and still is employed in Mauritian national elections. In this system, voters are given as many votes to cast as there are seats to be awarded in the district. In Mauritius, for example, this means voters have three votes to cast. They can cast these votes for any three candidates of their choosing, but may neither cumulate (vote more than once for a given candidate) nor partially abstain (fail to cast one of their votes).[4] Thus, if there are only four candidates, the Mauritian system is equivalent to negative plurality voting: Negative plurality would force voters to give -1 to one candidate and 0 to three; the Mauritian system would force voters to give 0 to one candidate and 1 to three; so any distinction that can be made under one system can be made under the other as well.

Even if there are more than four candidates, the possibility for turkey-raising arises in Mauritius. Suppose that a voter wishes to elect candidate A, who faces stiff competition from B, C, and D. If the voter votes for A and two of the three others, then she helps some of those most likely to prevent A from winning. What to do? Such a voter may wish to park her extra votes on two hopeless candidates, say E and F, who are far out of the running and will pose no threat to A. Thus, the Mauritian system

[3]A similar result could be obtained for an incomplete information model, in which voters respond to pivot probabilities.

[4]If voters can partially abstain, then the system is similar to that used throughout most of the nineteenth century in Great Britain, except that the district magnitude then was typically two rather than three. On strategic voting under this system, see Cox (1984).

gives voters an incentive in some circumstances to vote for submarginal candidates. Because of this feature, it is not clear that strategic voting in this system would impose any kind of upper bound on the effective number of candidates.

But is it really the similarity of the Mauritian system to negative plurality (a last-place punishing system) that is key? It would seem not, because a similar kind of turkey-raising can occur under *any* monotonic scoring rule, last-place punishing or not.

A scoring rule is a method of voting in which voters are required to submit full rank orderings of the candidates, these ranks are then awarded points (e.g., 5 points for first, 3 for second, etc.), and the candidate with the most points wins. A scoring rule is monotonic if every rank is awarded a number of points that is strictly less than the next higher rank. Strategic voting under such scoring rules often entails putting a candidate whom one really ranks fairly high, but who threatens a yet-higher candidate's chances of winning, at the end of one's submitted ordering of candidates. This is done in order to make as large a distinction as possible between one's favorite and one's least-favorite marginal candidates. Some high ranks then necessarily go to candidates who are unlikely to win. And, indeed, in the allocation of these ranks the highest should go to those candidates who are most hopeless, and therefore least likely to upset one's best laid plans.

Myerson and Weber (1993) provide an extended example of strategic voting under the most famous of monotonic scoring rules, the Borda Count (which is not last-place punishing). Their example has three candidates, two leftists (both supported by .3 of the population) facing a single rightist (with .4). In equilibrium they find that the three candidates' vote shares are equalized. Thus, the equilibrium effective number of candidates is 3, while the corresponding figure given sincere voting is 2.94. Strategic voting again deconcentrates the distribution of votes.

Some general conjectures about turkey-raising

The general point seems to be this: If under a given electoral system it can be useful to raise turkeys (vote for hopeless candidates), then the system will not impose an upper bound on the effective number of competitors. When will it be useful to raise turkeys? All monotonic scoring rules entail turkey-raising. So do multiple vote systems with bans on partial abstention. So do last-place punishing single-vote systems. In all of these systems, voters wishing to make a maximal distinction between their most-preferred and least-preferred marginal candidates (say A and B) must sometimes, as a side effect of strategically demoting B, give some other candidate an intermediate number of points or votes.

Strategic voting

Voters are usually thought not to vote for hopeless candidates because such votes cannot change the outcome. But sometimes voting for a hopeless candidate or list can be a necessary part of a larger strategy – one that can affect the outcome. When this is true, the political consequences of strategic voting will be quite different from those first identified by Duverger (1954), Leys (1959), and Sartori (1968).

7.3 A FINAL WORD

In this chapter, I have summarized the nature of strategic voting's political impact, noting first that it only imposes an upper bound on the effective number of competitors (as opposed to implying a point prediction for this number), and then only in systems that do not make it profitable for voters to raise turkeys.

As a final word, I should note that all of the models of strategic voting in this part of the book are constructed in the shadow of other possibilities. There are many instrumentally rational agents in elections – candidates, activists, contributors – and all of them may respond in ways that overwhelm or accentuate the strategic responses of voters. I have already suggested that candidates and other elites may play a key role in providing voters with the necessary information to vote strategically. In Part III of the book, I investigate strategic entry decisions by candidates and parties, taken in light of the likely strategic voting consequences.

PART III

Strategic entry

8

Strategic voting, party labels, and entry

Part II of this book investigated the nature and incidence of strategic voting in a variety of electoral systems, with particular emphasis on strategic desertion of weak candidates and lists. Duverger, and many after him, have argued that elite anticipation of strategic voting should lead to prudent withdrawals and hence a reduction in the number of competitors entering the field of battle. In particular, those elites who foresee that their own candidates or lists will bear the brunt of strategic desertion are likely to decide that mounting a (hopeless) campaign is not worth the cost, and seek instead to throw their support behind more viable candidates or lists (presumably for a price). To the extent that withdrawals of this sort do occur, the number of competitors will of course decrease.

In this chapter, I note that this argument about prudent withdrawals is theoretically limited in some of the same ways that the Duvergerian argument about strategic voting is limited. First, the argument presupposes that it will be clear *at the time at which entry decisions must be made* which candidate(s) or list(s) are doomed to be perceived as nonviable on the day of the election, hence shunned by instrumentally rational voters. So, just as voters must have consistent beliefs ("rational expectations") about who is trailing, elites must have consistent beliefs about who *will be* trailing and hence be the victim of strategic voting. Second, the prudent withdrawals argument also presupposes that elites are motivated primarily by the prospect of victory in the current election. Thus, just as voters must be short-term instrumentally rational, so must elites, for the argument to work.

In order to clarify these points, I first consider what happens when it is *not* clear, at the time at which entry decisions must be made, who will be perceived as nonviable. There are, of course, real-world situations in which such clarity is plausibly lacking: Think, for example, of elections held in new democracies or in polities with unstructured party systems.[1] Here, I shall consider some formal models of entry that take things to the logical extreme: Every potential entrant is perceived (at the time entry must be decided) to have an equal chance of dodging the bullet of strategic desertion or, to put it the other way around, an equal chance of getting hit by it, should they in fact enter. To anticipate the result, such models show that the number of entrants is not limited by anticipations of strategic voting when everyone has an *ex ante* equal chance of suffering (or benefiting) from it. The only limits that are placed on the number of entrants in equilibrium have to do with the costs of entry and the benefits of office.

In Section 8.2, I consider another way in which Duverger's argument about prudent withdrawals might go awry, even if the issue of short-term viability is clear. I simply note various different kinds of possible long-term payoffs that might motivate elites, making them less likely than voters to coordinate.

In Section 8.3, I consider the case that is most favorable to the Duvergerian logic on entry: when all politicians are primarily concerned with doing well in the current election and a certain subset of potential entrants are clearly viable, with everyone else clearly nonviable. In this case, there is a sound reason not to enter if one is (consensually predicted to be) nonviable: One will probably face strategic desertion and lose badly, so why bother if the current election is all that one cares about? There will thus be an $M + 1$ rule at the level of candidate entry, if expectations are clear enough. But the real question is how it becomes so clear that large numbers of potential entrants have no chance of winning. Section 8.3 elaborates the role of party labels in coordinating expectations of viability and suggests that there may be an $M + 1$ rule governing the number of party labels as well.

Section 8.4 investigates the nature of entry in situations in which clear viability advantages exist for certain parties, due to their possession of valuable labels. Candidates value possession of these labels both because they convey a certain number of habitual voters into their camp and because they publicly certify the candidates' viability, thus insuring them against strategic desertion.

Given that candidates value labels with an established following in the electorate, at least two things follow. First, would-be career politicians will compete for the established labels that exist, as their chances of win-

[1] Sartori (1968:281, 293-4) defines a structured party system as one in which the established parties possess nationwide organizations and, more importantly for current purposes, command habitual allegiances in the electorate.

ning with such a label are typically far better than their chances as an independent or a new party's endorsee. Second, political groups, movements, and would-be parties will often find it more advantageous to join one of the viable parties, rather than setting up a new party of their own or joining a party that is not viable. In Section 8.4, I focus on the latter point, although of course the two are closely related.

8.1 NEUTRAL ENTRY MODELS

In this section I consider entry under conditions of extreme symmetry, with every potential entrant perceived, at the time of entry, as having as good a chance as any other to win. To capture such a situation, I turn to extant efforts in the literature based on a two-stage spatial model in which potential candidates first decide whether or not to enter the race and then, after some number have actually entered, compete by adopting positions somewhere along a left-right continuum (Palfrey 1984; Greenberg and Shepsle 1987; Ferejohn and Noll 1988; Feddersen, Sened, and Wright 1990; Weber 1990, 1992a, 1992b; Osborne 1993; Osborne and Silvinski 1995; Shvetsova 1995; Wada N.d.; see also Brams and Straffin 1982).[2] All such studies considered here employ the technical assumptions of neutrality and deterministic spatial voting, which together imply that the only characteristic of candidates that voters care about is their adopted left-right position, which voters know with certainty.[3] Assuming neutrality and deterministic voting means that voters are not "rationally ignorant" (Downs 1957) and accordingly need not utilize party labels as informational shortcuts (cf. Popkin 1991; Fiorina 1977) or make "standing decisions" in favor of candidates bearing a particular label (Key 1964b). Another way to put it is that candidates, and the parties that endorse them, have no spatial (i.e., ideological or policy) reputations to live down or build up. Assuming neutrality also means that voters have no cues, such as incumbency or

[2]Not all of the studies take exactly this form. For example, in Palfrey (1984) the entry stage is set up exogenously, with exactly two candidates entering; these two then take positions knowing that a third candidate will enter after they take their positions.

[3]A spatial model is *neutral* if, whenever candidates A and B switch spatial positions (all other candidates' positions held constant, if there are any other candidates), then they switch expected vote shares and probabilities of victory. The meaning of *deterministic voting* (as opposed to probabilistic voting; on which see Coughlin 1992) can most easily be explained in the case of two-candidate competition, say between A and B. If, whenever a voter prefers candidate A's policy position, then he or she votes for candidate A with certainty, then voting is deterministic. If A's superior spatial position makes it more likely that the voter will support A, but not certain, then voting is probabilistic.

past electoral history, that might tell them which candidates are viable and which are not. All the players are on a level playing field. This is in direct contrast to the more empirically-oriented decision-theoretic literature, in which the scare-off or entry-deterring effect of incumbency is often taken for granted.[4]

Four neutral entry models

In this section, I discuss four neutral entry models from the literature. The four models differ in various respects but all impose an upper bound on the number of entrants in equilibrium. The *existence* of an upper bound is reminiscent of Duverger's Law but, as will be seen, the *reasons* for the upper bound are quite different from what Duverger had in mind.

The first model I consider is that of Feddersen, Sened, and Wright (1990). In this model (of a simple plurality election), citizens vote strategically and a party can either enter a political contest at a specific spatial location, paying a cost of entry to do so, or decide not to enter at all. If a party sits the election out, it receives a payoff of zero. If, on the other hand, the party enters the fray, then its payoff equals its probability of winning (p), times the benefit of holding office (b), less the cost of entry (c). Thus, in equilibrium, no party will enter unless $pb \geq c$. In part because of the neutrality assumption, the equilibrium value of p turns out to equal $1/n$, where n is the number of entrants. That is, every entrant

[4]The decision-theoretic branch of the literature focuses on explaining the entry and exit decisions of individual candidates. Some, for example, investigate why incumbent legislators decide to retire or seek higher office, rather than seek reelection. Others investigate why nonincumbents seek legislative office to begin with. In both kinds of study, typical findings show that opportunity costs and chances of victory matter in a straightforward manner. As regards incumbents, for example, the literature shows that Republicans in the U.S. House of Representatives have sought higher office more frequently than their Democratic colleagues throughout the post-war era, because their party's perennial (albeit recently ended) minority status meant that they had little chance of attaining a committee or subcommittee chair (Gilmour and Rothstein 1993; Schansberg 1994); that U.S. Representatives from small states have sought statewide office more frequently than their large-state colleagues, because their House districts comprise a larger portion of the state electorate in which they must compete and they face less competition from other upwardly mobile House members (Rohde 1979; Brace 1984; Kiewiet and Zeng 1993:933); and that U.S. Representatives who kited more checks in the House banking scandal of 1991–2, plausibly reducing their (perceived) chances of reelection, were more likely to retire (Groseclose and Krehbiel 1994; Jacobson and Dimock 1994). As regards the scare-off effect of incumbency, Squire (1989:284) finds that only 4% of open seats in U.S. House elections were uncontested in the period 1978-88, whereas 14% of all seats were uncontested; Cox and Morgenstern (1993) find that the probability of a contested election in U.S. state legislative districts is from .02 to .14 greater if the seat is open than if it is defended by an incumbent (after controlling for relative party strengths in the district).

has an equal shot at winning in equilibrium. Thus, the condition $pb \geq c$ turns into $b/c \geq n$: *The number of entrants, n, is bounded above by the benefit-cost ratio, b/c.*

If one assumes that $b/c < 3$, then an upper bound similar to that claimed by Duverger's Law arises: In equilibrium, there will be at most two entrants. But the immediate reason for this equilibrium prediction is simply the assumption that $b/c < 3$. As Shepsle (1991:75; cf. Ferejohn and Noll 1988:15) puts it, "entry costs and office valuations drive the equilibrium number of entrants." But an emphasis on costs of entry and benefits of office has no obvious connection to Duverger's line of reasoning, which focused on elite anticipations of strategic voting. Feddersen, Sened, and Wright's approach puts one in mind of onerous signature requirements to get on the ballot in the United States, or the advantages given to "permanent" lemas in Uruguay (Gonzalez 1991), or the costs of television advertising in France (Duverger 1986:81). Duverger's approach centers around anticipations of strategic voting. Absent some reason to believe that the benefit-cost ratio *is* generally less than three, the Feddersen-Sened-Wright entry model does not lead to a result consistent with Duverger's Law, although it certainly does point to an important set of factors that might affect the equilibrium number of entrants in a given polity.

A second model of entry in simple plurality elections, due to Weber (1992b), differs from that of Feddersen, Sened, and Wright in a number of ways: parties maximize their share of the vote, not their expected utility; voters vote sincerely, not strategically; entry is sequential, not simultaneous. Yet the gist of the result on entry remains quite similar.

Weber posits that n established parties play simultaneously against one another, while anticipating the possible entry of a single potential entrant. The potential entrant will enter if and only if it can secure a share of the vote that exceeds a prespecified level, q. One interpretation of this is that the potential entrant derives utility from getting votes (possibly due to the probability that votes translate into seats, but possibly for other reasons as well), but also incurs a cost of entry. The level q is then simply the cost of entry expressed as a proportion of the total vote.

One result in Weber's model is that, if the cost of entry is sufficiently high (at least .25 expressed in share of vote terms), then two established parties will be able to deter entry by a third.[5] This prediction is the same as that made in Duverger's Law but, as with the Feddersen, Sened, and Wright result, depends purely on entry costs. Indeed, the absence of any reliance on elite anticipations of strategic voting is made even more obvious in this model by the stipulation that citizens vote sincerely.

[5]The mechanics of entry deterrence are similar to those in Palfrey (1984).

A third entry model, due to Shvetsova (1995), also envisions a number of established parties playing simultaneously against one another, while anticipating the possible entry of a single additional candidate. Shvetsova's model, however, investigates entry under SNTV electoral rules in an *M*-seat district; the electoral structure is thus more general than that considered by Palfrey or Weber.

Shvetsova posits that all candidates maximize their probability of winning a seat, and that the potential entrant will enter if and only if it can secure a positive probability of winning. She also assumes that voters vote sincerely, not strategically.

One question Shvetsova asks (cf. Greenberg and Shepsle 1987) is whether an *M*-equilibrium exists: a situation in which *M* candidates have adopted spatial positions such that (1) these positions constitute a Nash equilibrium for the *M* prespecified entrants; and (2) the one potential entrant is deterred from entering. She also asks whether $M + 1$-equilibria, defined analogously, exist (cf. Weber 1992a). She finds that *M*-equilibria exist under stringent conditions (symmetric convex preference distributions and $M \leq 3$), that $M + 1$-equilibria exist for somewhat less stringent conditions (symmetric unimodal preference distributions), and that either an *M* – or an $M + 1$-equilibrium must exist under yet less stringent conditions (unimodal preference distributions).

If one believes that preference distributions tend to be unimodal, then these results gibe to some extent with Duverger's Law and Reed's extension of it, in that the prediction is that there will be no more than $M + 1$ parties. The mechanism producing this result, however, has nothing to do with strategic voting, since voters in the model are assumed to behave sincerely. Instead, the result depends on the ability of the already-entered parties to collude, as it were, occupying all the attractive electoral niches and leaving no room for an $(M + 2)$nd entrant to eke out a positive probability of winning a seat.[6]

A final model that yields a result pertinent to Duverger's Law (Osborne and Silvinski 1995) compares entry under plurality rule and majority runoff. The model assumes that candidates value policy as well as the spoils of office and must pay a cost to enter the contest. In addition to finding that the number of candidates who enter (under either plurality or majority runoff) is sensitive to the cost of entry and benefit of winning, Osborne and Silvinski are able to show that the conditions under which

[6]Viewed more broadly, Shvetsova's result is essentially similar to those of Weber and Feddersen, Sened and Wright. Although the notion of a cost of entry is not explicitly introduced, her results can be interpreted as assuming that entry is costly, but that a positive probability of victory is sufficient to overcome this cost. (The model does not support arbitrarily small probabilities of victory in equilibrium, so in fact the assumed entry cost is not infinitesimal.)

a two-candidate equilibrium can be sustained under majority runoff are strictly more demanding than the analogous conditions for plurality rule. Thus, although the model does not support the conclusion that two-candidate equilibria are the only possible or likely equilibria under plurality rule (as Duverger's Law would suggest), it does show that two-candidate equilibria are more likely under plurality than under majority runoff. This result, however, has nothing to do with elite anticipations of strategic voting, since voters in the model are assumed to vote sincerely.

Discussion

The four models just reviewed all focus on the same basic mechanism as key in putting an upper bound on the number of entrants: Entry is costly and so new candidates will enter the fray only if their probabilities of victory (or vote shares) are large enough to justify the cost. This approach is not inconsistent with an emphasis on strategic voting: One can imagine building a model in which candidates estimate their probabilities of victory in part by anticipating who will bear the brunt of strategic voting. But in fact none of the models does this.

The only attempt in the literature to consider incorporating strategic voting as a factor influencing parties' perceptions of their chances of victory is due to Palfrey (1989), who merely notes (pp. 84-85) that a *neutral* entry model with strategic voting is "essentially indeterminate." If the model maintains neutrality, then before entry decisions are made, every party views itself as having as good a chance as any other in the position-taking subgame that will ensue post-entry. That is, no party has any reason to believe that *it* will be the likely victim of strategic voting, even though all believe that there will be victims. Thus, anticipations of strategic voting do nothing in a neutral entry model to change pre-entry (or even post-entry, pre-position taking) probabilities of victory, and hence do nothing to drive down the number of entrants.

How might an entry model incorporate elite anticipations of strategic voting? Taking the expected utility formulation of Feddersen, Sened, and Wright, the simplest way to incorporate anticipations of strategic voting would be via assumptions about the probability of victory. Parties would no longer calculate probabilities of victory, conditional on entry, by assuming voter neutrality and deterministic spatial voting. Instead, all parties would know that some of them had a nonspatial advantage, in that voters perceived them as more likely to be seriously in the running. The equilibrium result, in the voting subgame, would then be that disadvantaged candidates would likely bear the brunt of strategic voting and receive a zero vote share. Anticipating this, foreseeably disadvantaged candidates would not enter in the first place.

Thus, *if* it is clear at the time of entry who is viable and who is not, then entry by nonviable candidates should be deterred (to the extent that their entry is motivated by the chance of winning the current election). But how does it become clear who is nonviable? One answer is that it becomes clear from electoral history: Those who have won in the past become focal in any coordination games that ensue in subsequent elections (cf. Forsythe et al. 1993). The answer that I shall pursue later (Section 8.3) is that possessing the endorsement of a major party confers viability advantages.

8.2 WHEN POLITICIANS HAVE LONG-TERM PERSPECTIVES

Even if it is clear that a particular politician is likely to bear the brunt of strategic voting, were she to enter the race, she may still do so if she believes that entering will redound to her benefit in the future. Perhaps she believes that entering will cause a particular other candidate to lose the race, thereby demonstrating that her group's support is crucial and winning policy concessions. (This may have been the motivation of the Prohibitionist candidates in turn-of-the-century U.S. politics, for example.) Perhaps she believes that she will post a respectable showing, positioning herself for a more serious run at office next time. (Bernard Sanders, the lone Socialist in the U.S. House of Representatives, was able to establish credibility as a third-party candidate by first placing second, ahead of a weak Democratic candidate; cf. Endersby and Thomason 1994.) Perhaps she is a young British Conservative and understands that running well in a safe Labour district is a good way to get nominated in a better (more winnable) district next time.

If all politicians have long-term perspectives, then the coordination game between them is more complicated than Duverger implicitly assumed. Instead of being a one-stage coordination game, in which potential entrants jostle for position in the context of well-established expectations about viability, it is a multistage coordination game, in which an indefinite string of future elections is to be held, and expectations of viability may either be well-established (e.g., the Social Democratic Party (SDP) in the United Kingdom trying to supplant Labour) or not (e.g., a new democracy holding its first elections). In what follows, I shall focus on the case in which expectations are not well-formed.

In such games, it certainly makes sense to enter in the first round: By assumption, one has as good a chance as anyone else at winning seats and establishing focalness for later elections, or at least it is not clear that one does not. It also makes sense to "sound tough." If one can convince others that one is unalterably committed to entering in perpetuity, then others who seek to fill a similar niche in the field of candidates may be deterred from entering. Just *saying* that one is committed, however, should not be very persuasive. The most obvious signal of commitment that has some credibility is to enter the first few rounds of competition, even if one's prospects are not good. The most natural equilibria of these kinds of multistage coordination games, then, are those in which there are a lot of entrants in the early rounds and a lot of huffing about long-term commitments.

From this perspective, the typical scenario in emerging democracies, whereby a great number of parties spring up in the first elections, and there is a relatively slow winnowing out process, makes sense. A large number spring up in the first election because it is not clear who will be viable and who not. As information is revealed about voter preferences, the more serious groups will continue to enter, even against poor short-term odds, in the hopes of convincing less committed competitors to drop out. The reward for such short-term sacrifice is establishing the clear expectation for future elections that one's group is the viable representative of a particular niche of electoral opinion.

8.3 ON THE VALUE OF PARTY ENDORSEMENTS AS COORDINATION DEVICES

If politicians are concerned primarily with the current election, and it is clear to all who the viable candidates are and who the nonviable candidates are, then coordination at the elite level will be easy and one expects no more than $M + 1$ candidates (or lists, in the case of PR) to enter. The $M + 1$ result at the level of strategic voting, in other words, induces an $M + 1$ result at the level of entry, if elites fully anticipate who will bear the brunt of strategic voting. The real question, then, is how "reputations for viability" are established or conferred. The answer in this section will be in terms of party endorsements.

Party endorsements can be valuable to voters in two main ways. The typical source of value noted in the literature is that endorsements can indicate, with variable precision, where the candidate receiving the endorsement stands on the issues (Key 1964b; Fiorina 1977). Another, less often noted, source of value lies in the endorsement's usefulness as a coordination device: If there were no nomination stage and no public endorsements, groups of like-minded voters might end up splitting their votes sub-optimally among a superabundance of similar candidates.

Party endorsements that are valuable to voters will for that reason also be valuable to candidates. To the extent that they convey information regarding the policy beliefs of candidates, and voters are rationally ignorant, they will carry along with them a certain mass of habitual followers. To the extent that the endorsement holds sway as a focal coordination device among some set of voters, it insulates endorsees from strategic desertion, and, indeed, operates to make them a net beneficiary of strategic voting.

How can the value of a party's label be established or maintained? The label's value as a policy cue can be promoted by consistency and homogeneity of belief within the party. Then the party endorsement "means something" in terms of policy. The label's value as a coordination device is partly in the nature of a self-fulfilling prophecy. If all leftists believe that all leftists will cue on the Democratic party's endorsement, then it is rational for them to do so, rather than cueing on some other endorsement by some other group. Otherwise the Republicans, fewer in number but better coordinated, let us say, may steal the election.

Another way to put the last point is that a label must be focal in order to be valuable as a coordination device. It must have established a *monopoly* on endorsing within a given segment of opinion, having beaten out or coopted all the other would-be coordination devices.[7] If it has not beaten out the others, then voters are in the position of the subjects in Schelling's (1960) famous experiments, with too many bases on which to coordinate. Too many endorsements may thus be just as bad as none at all.

The preceding discussion has taken for granted that the end result of successful coordination is that the endorsee has a real shot at winning a seat. This in turn presumes a certain size. Successful coordination between a tiny minority of voters merely produces a voting bloc; it does not produce seats. Assuming that a payoff in seats is necessary to maintain a viable label, a maximum number of such labels is implied.

What this maximum is depends both on electoral structure and on how one defines viable. Consider first the main electoral systems considered in Part I, for which there are formally developed strategic voting models. There cannot generally be more than $M + 1$ candidates expected to be "in the running" for a seat in these systems, where M refers either to the district magnitude (in the case of plurality rule and proportional representation) or to the number of candidates that can qualify for the runoff (in the case of dual ballot systems). Defining a "viable" or "established" label to mean one whose top candidate has a shot at win-

[7]How *party* endorsements come to be preeminent, eclipsing endorsements by newspapers, prominent businesspersons, and so forth, is a fascinating question. My own hunch, based on a reading of the historical literature on the development of nomination procedures in the U.S., is that party nominations are constructed to be more persuasive about underlying strength in the electorate than are the endorsements that an interest group can issue.

ning every election, the maximum number of viable party labels competing in a given district is $M + 1$.[8]

Another way to think about this upper bound on the number of viable labels is in terms of the minimum viable size of a party. Certainly a party that can regularly attain or approximate the threshold of exclusion in a system will qualify as viable. As district magnitude increases, the threshold of exclusion, and hence the minimum viable size for a party, declines, so that the maximum number of viable labels increases.[9]

Moving beyond the purely electoral factors, being small will be less feasible if there are substantial economies of scale in purchasing television advertising, raising campaign funds, or securing government portfolios and other positions of power. There may thus be reason to expect that the number of viable *labels* will fall short, perhaps well short, of the number of viable *candidates*.

8.4 ENTRY IN THE PRESENCE OF ESTABLISHED LABELS

In the previous section, I argued that the maximum possible number of viable labels in a given district (operating under one of the electoral systems considered in Part I) would be $M + 1$. This upper bound comes essentially from a consideration of rational behavior on the part of voters under alternative electoral conditions.

Can one say anything more about the equilibrium number of labels, other than that it will not exceed $M + 1$? In this section, I imagine that there are a certain number of established labels, and consider the options of a "new" group that might wish to enter electoral politics. From an analysis of the group's decision in the face of these options, some further insight into the features of an equilibrium number of labels may be gained.

Assuming for present purposes that candidates running under established labels have an advantage (and not a disadvantage as recently in

[8]If a somewhat lower standard for viability were adopted, then of course the equilibrium upper bound on the number of viable labels would increase.

[9]Moving beyond the main electoral systems discussed in Part I, note that the minimum viable size of a party also declines with any other electoral manipulations – e.g., lowering legal thresholds, changing to a more proportional electoral formula, setting up upper tiers – that lower the threshold of exclusion. Being small is also made more feasible when electoral law facilitates either within-district vote trading (via *apparentement* or transferable-vote provisions) or joint nominating agreements (via joint listing or fusion provisions). In either case, parties below the minimum viable size can avoid paying any electoral penalty for their suboptimal size by allying with other parties. They can thus accrue the benefits of smallness-cum-consistency without sacrificing viability. Systems with intradistrict vote trading or joint nominating provisions thus may have more than $M + 1$ viable labels.

Italy), new political forces that seek to achieve power or influence in the short- or medium-term will be faced with a choice among four basic *electoral* options: (1) They can do nothing on the electoral front, perhaps discouraged by the high costs and low probabilities of success, and instead focus on nonelectoral strategies, e.g., lobbying the elected members of one or more of the established parties;[10] (2) they can seek to achieve influence over the endorsement process in one of the established parties, thereby securing safe list positions or safe constituencies for the candidates that they sponsor; (3) they can start a new party, motivated by a belief that they will be able to establish the new party's viability; or (4) even if they feel that there is no more room for another viable label in the system, they can become a "protest" or "blackmail" party, inflicting short-term damage on both themselves and one of the established labels, in the hopes of eventual concessions. In order to examine this four-way choice a bit more formally, it is useful to imagine a (unitary) group of some kind pondering its options in an M-seat district in which there are $m \leq M + 1$ established parties. To begin with, I shall consider only groups with very short time horizons, who would not consider the fourth option, nor the third if there was no *immediate* prospect of winning seats. Such groups thus choose among sitting the election out, seeking influence within one of the established parties, and running an independent or new-party slate of candidates.

I shall assume that each established party nominates at most M candidates, and that the nominees from party i can be ordered from 1 to n_i, where $n_i \leq M$.[11] The general interpretation of this ordered list of candidates (for which I shall use the term "slate") is that candidate 1 has a better (or at least no worse) endorsement position than candidate 2, who in turn is at least as favored as candidate 3, and so on. In closed-list systems of PR, the ordering corresponds simply to list position. In open- and flexible-list systems of PR (including STV), the idea that there is an ordered "slate" of names may have a natural analogue – in the Netherlands, for example, there is a party-determined order of names which substantially influences which candidates fill the list's seats – or it may not – in Finland, for example, I am not aware that the parties can differentially benefit their various candidates by allocating more and less favorable ballot positions; in this case, the formal notion of a "slate" has no real analogue and the ordering of candidates referred to above can be chosen at random. In Japan's system of SNTV, there is of course nothing that

[10] I shall assume that the group already pursues these nonelectoral stratagems at some optimal level, and is considering *adding* an electoral component to their overall strategy. Thus, the "do nothing" strategy can be taken to yield a utility increment of zero.

[11] Many of the world's polities limit the number of nominees in this fashion, but some do not.

would colloquially be called a "slate" but there may nonetheless be an advantage to having one's endorsement announced earlier rather than later. The Liberal Democratic Party (LDP), for example, typically announces the candidates that it will endorse in several rounds, and it may be advantageous to be in the first rather than second round. If so, then the formal notion of slate order would correspond to the chronological sequence in which nominations are announced. If, as is possible, order of announcement confers no systematic advantage, then the formal slate order can be chosen at random. In a single-member district, the issue of ordering does not arise.

Let e_{ij} be a dummy variable, equal to one if the group under consideration secures the *j*th position on party *i*'s slate for one of its candidates, equal to zero otherwise. The vector $e_i = (e_{i1}, \ldots, e_{iM})$ then describes the overall success of the group in securing endorsement positions from party *i*, and the variable $e = (e_1, \ldots, e_m)$ describes the success of the group in securing endorsement positions from each of the *m* established parties. I shall assume that no group can secure endorsements from more than one established party. Thus, e_i is non-zero for at most one party *i*. If a group strikes out completely, whether through lack of trying or through being rebuffed, $e = \mathbf{0}$, where $\mathbf{0}$ is a vector of *mM* zeroes.

Let $s(e)$ be the expected number of seats that the group will win, given that it secures the endorsement positions described in *e* and runs a candidate in each secured position. Thus, for example, in a three-member Spanish district with two established parties, perhaps $e = (0,1,0;0,0,0)$ – the group gets the second spot on party 1's list – and $s(0,1,0;0,0,0) = .5$ – the second spot is competitive in this district. If $e = \mathbf{0}$, I shall interpret $s(\mathbf{0})$ as the expected number of seats the group will win if it runs an "optimal" number of candidates on an independent or new-party slate (the issue of optimal nomination arises, e.g., in limited vote systems).

The group cannot, of course, guarantee itself the endorsement positions that it wants. It is costly to enter party *i*'s endorsement process and, even if the group can afford the costs of entry, it may not be successful in securing the spots it wants (or indeed any spots at all). To reflect these costs and uncertainties, let c_{ni} be the cost to the group of competing, at an optimal level of effort, in whatever process allocates nominations in party *i*, and let $p_i(e_i)$ equal the probability that the group will secure the endorsement positions e_i if it enters party *i*'s nomination process and exerts its optimal effort.[12]

[12]As in the work of Black (1972) on progressive ambition, the expected utility calculation could be generalized to take explicit account of the effort level. As such refinements do not affect the basic points I am trying to make, I dispense with them here.

The decision problem facing the group can now be described in greater detail. The group must first decide whether or not to enter the endorsement process of one of the established parties and, if so, which one. If the group participates in an established party's process, then it must decide what to do next, in light of the endorsement positions that it secures. It may decide that the positions secured are not worth the costs of running in a general election or it may be denied any positions at all. In either of these cases, it would then face the problem of deciding whether to run as an independent or to sit the general election out. Alternatively, it may decide that the positions secured are good enough to be worth the costs of running in the general election, and proceed to do just that.

The expected utility of *not* entering *any* established party's endorsement process is expressed as follows:

$$\text{EU(Not Enter)} = \max\{s(0) - c_g(0), 0\} \tag{1}$$

where $c_g(0)$ represents the cost (denominated in seat-equivalents) of running an independent or new-party slate in a general election.[13] The logic behind this equation is simple: If the group under consideration does not compete for endorsement slots on the slate of any established party, then it will, come the general election, have a choice between launching an independent or new-party slate of its own, yielding an expected payoff of $s(0) - c_g(0)$, or sitting the election out, yielding a normalized payoff of zero. One might write the expected utility of running an independent or new-party slate as $s(0)b - c_g(0)$, where b is the value, in some unit of accounting, of a single seat. I have chosen the normalization $b = 1$, so that the cost function c_g is, as noted above, denominated in seat-equivalents.

The expected utility to the (risk-neutral) group of entering party i's endorsement process can be expressed formally as follows:

$$\text{EU(Enter } i) = \sum_{e_i \in E} p_i(e_i) \max\{s(e_i;0) - c_g(e_i;0), s(0) - c_g(0), 0\} - c_{ni} \tag{2}$$

where $E = \{0,1\}^M$ is the set of all possible sets of endorsement positions garnered by the group; the notation $(e_i;0)$ indicates that the group received no endorsement positions from parties other than i, while receiving the positions listed in e_i from i; and $c_g(e_i;0)$ represents the expected cost of running in a general election with the endorsement positions denoted by $(e_i;0)$.

[13] I assume that the focal group could run an independent or a new-party slate without bearing any costs analogous to the cost c_{ni} of entering party i's endorsement process; and I ignore the possibility of the group seeking to put its candidates on the slate of some other, already existing but nonviable, party.

The way to read equation (2) is as follows. For any given $e_i \in E$, the group under consideration has some probability $p_i(e_i)$ of securing the endorsement positions listed in e_i. Conditional on receiving those endorsement positions, the group can choose to sit the election out (yielding a normalized payoff of zero); to refuse the proffered nominations and run an independent or new-party slate (yielding a payoff of $s(0) - c_g(0)$); or to compete in the general election with the nominations garnered from party i (yielding a payoff of $s(e_i;0) - c_g(e_i;0)$). Regardless of which postnomination option the group chooses, it will have incurred the cost c_{ni} of participating in party i's nomination process, thus the last term on the right-hand side.

The group's decision between entering party i's nomination process and entering no process at all is governed by the sign of EU(Enter i) – EU(Not Enter): If this expression is positive, the group prefers entering i's process to entering none; if zero, the group is indifferent; if negative, the group prefers not entering any process to entering i's. Using equations (1) and (2), EU(Enter i) – EU(Not Enter) equals

$$\sum_{e_i \in C_i} p_i(e_i)[s(e_i;0) - c_g(e_i;0) - \max\{s(0) - c_g(0),0\}] - c_{ni} \qquad (3)$$

where $C_i = \{e_i \in E: s(e_i;0) - c_g(e_i;0) > \max\{s(0) - c_g(0),0\}\}$ is the set of all endorsement offers from party i that the group finds attractive, in the sense that it prefers running under party i's label in whatever positions it is given to its other options.

The entry decision as portrayed thus far focuses on current payoffs only. Future payoffs might be brought partially into view, albeit in a purely decision-theoretic way, simply by positing some discounted present value for the blackmail or protest option, and specifying continuation values for the other options as well. I will not develop this extension formally. The results stated below thus go beyond what is demonstrable in the confines of the formally developed model when they refer to the fourth option.

With that said, one can proceed to characterize the group's choice among the four options outlined above. The easiest case to consider is that of single-member plurality ($M = 1$) systems. In this case, $E = \{0,1\}$, $C_i = \{1\}$, and – assuming that $s(1;0) - c_g(1;0) - \max\{s(0) - c_g(0),0\} > 0$ – expression (3) reduces to $p_i(1)[s(1;0) - c_g(1;0) - \max\{s(0) - c_g(0),0\}] - c_{ni}$. From this expression we have:

> *Proposition 1:* In single-member plurality systems, the probability that an office-seeking group will attempt to take over an established party's nomination process, rather than sit the election out, or enter the fray as a new party, increases with:

(a) The *permeability* of the major parties' endorsement processes (measured directly for party i by $p_i(1)$, the probability that the group can capture i's nomination for its own candidate, if it tries; and inversely by c_{ni}, the perceived costs of trying);
(b) The *advantage* of possessing one of the major parties' labels (measured for party i by $s(1;0) - c_g(1;0) - \max\{s(0) - c_g(0),0\}$, the expected value in seat-equivalents of the group's candidate campaigning *with* party i's endorsement, rather than *without* it).

The meaning of this proposition can be clarified by considering a few special cases that have already been noted in the literature.

Consider first the case where $s(1;0) \cong 1$, so that party 1 is dominant – indeed, virtually certain to win the general election – and the benefit of securing its label is maximal. In such a district, there is no (current seat-maximizing) reason to run under any other than the dominant label. Would-be career politicians will either enter the dominant party's endorsement process, or not at all. Groups that seek control of legislative power will similarly seek to take over the dominant party's endorsement process, or satisfy themselves with lobbying activities.[14]

These expectations of course correspond closely to conventional wisdom concerning the old "solid South" in the United States. There being no chance that a Republican might win, real political competition was diverted almost entirely into the Democratic primary (Key 1964a). As Epstein (1986:129) put the theoretical point: "Those who seek office [in one-party states] may perceive the primary of the dominant party as a more advantageous vehicle for success than entry, however easy, as candidates of a minority party. Protests, along with ambition, talent, and interest, are thus attracted to a single party." Grimm (1983:316) has noted a similar tendency in Germany for nomination contests to arise more frequently in districts that are "safe" for one or the other of the major parties (with the contest arising of course within the dominant party).

A separate claim often made about the South is that adoption of the direct primary helped to perpetuate one-partyism (cf. Epstein 1986:129-131). In terms of Proposition 1, this is a claim that a more permeable endorsement process – the direct primary as opposed to delegate caucuses or conventions – attracted more competition.[15]

Consider next the case in which $s(1;0) \cong s(0;1)$ and $s(0) - c_g(0) \leq 0$. This is a district in which two parties have a shot at winning the seat

[14]Blackmail parties of the kind described above will not be viable, because by assumption there is no chance that a third party could tip the election to the second party. There would thus be no pain inflicted and no reason to grant concessions.

[15]As an aside, it might be noted that when candidates *do* contest districts under a hopeless label, there are payoffs from doing so other than the prospect of winning the seat currently at stake or forcing policy concessions in the medium-term. In

but in which third parties and independents stand a sufficiently poor chance in the general election that it is not worth their effort to try (solely for the chance at the current seat). One result here is similar to that of the first case and depends on the substantial *advantage* of a major-party label: There is no (current seat-maximizing) reason to enter this district as anything other than one of the major-party candidates. Thus, new electoral forces (with short time horizons) will either try and force their way into one of the major's endorsement processes or sit the election out.

Another result in this case corresponds to Espstein's (1986:131-32) well-known argument that the widespread adoption of the direct primary in the United States, an eminently permeable endorsement process, contributes to the "distinctively American weakness of third parties." "The reasoning," Epstein notes, "is that third-party efforts are discouraged by the opportunity to capture the label of one or the other major party in a primary" (p. 131) and that "early abandonment of evidently failing third parties may be encouraged by the same ... opportunity that appears to make third parties less useful in the first place" (p. 132).

The logic underlying Proposition 1 is not limited to single-member plurality ($M = 1$) systems. A similar proposition holds for systems with $M > 1$ – whether top-M runoff systems in single-member districts, or PR and SNTV systems in multimember districts. The only complicating factor is that the permeability and benefit factors may not be nicely separable as in the $M = 1$ case. We may talk of $q = \sum_{e_i \in C_i} p_i(e_i)$ as the chance of getting a favorable set of endorsement spots, and of $B = \frac{1}{|C_i|} \sum_{e_i \in C_i} [s(e_i;0) - c_g(e_i;0) - \max\{s(0) - c_g(0),0\}]$ as the average advantage of a favorable set of endorsement spots, but we cannot simply multiply q and B to recover the expected benefit, as we could in the $M = 1$ case. Nonetheless, it is not too misleading to talk as if these terms were separable. If one does, then a more general version of Proposition 1 can be stated as follows:

Proposition 2: The probability that an office-seeking group will attempt to take over an established party's nomination process,

for example, contesting hopeless seats is an accepted means of demonstrating one's campaigning skills, and puts one in good stead for a better district next time. (The British example also points out a distinction between a label that is not viable in a particular district and one that is not viable anywhere. One reason that British third parties have trouble fielding good candidates in all districts is that they do not have enough safe and marginal constituencies to dangle as rewards for slogging into the more unpromising ones.)

rather than sit the election out, or enter the fray as a new party, increases with:

(a) The *permeability* of the established parties' endorsement processes (measured directly for party *i* by the probability *q* that the group can, if it tries, capture some good positions on *i*'s slate for its own candidate(s); and inversely by c_{ni}, the perceived costs of trying);

(b) The *advantage* of possessing one of the major parties' labels (measured for party *i* by the average gain from having a favorable set of major-party endorsement spots, rather than running without them).

This proposition too can be clarified by considering some examples.

Consider first the cases of Uruguay and Colombia. Both elect their lower houses in multimember districts (ranging in magnitude from 2 to 29 in Colombia, from 2 to 47 in Uruguay).[16] Yet both have had long spells of democratic two-party politics (e.g., from 1974 to present in Colombia, from 1911 to 1971 in Uruguay). A reason for this similarity suggested by Proposition 2 is that in both countries the two major parties are very highly permeable.

Colombia is the simpler system to explain. All seats are allocated at the district level (no upper tiers or additional seats) using the largest-remainders method of PR with (usually) the Hare quota. There are, however, no legal restrictions on using the label of the two main parties, the Liberals and Conservatives. Anyone can run a list of candidates and call it a Liberal list, even if there are already Liberal lists in the field. The party label is thus a common good: exhaustible but nonexcludable. One result of this peculiar status of the major party labels in Colombia is that multiple lists bearing the same major-party label routinely appear in most districts. As votes for the various Liberal (or Conservative) lists do not pool for purposes of seat allocation, the system is similar to Japan's SNTV (cf. Cox and Shugart N.d.). Another result, related to the first, is that independent and third-party lists have been rare in Colombia (until the introduction in 1991 of a national list for the Senate, along with a new ballot format and party registration procedures, fueled an expansion). The rarity of such lists may have been partly due to the influence of the presidential race: Taking the Liberal (Conservative) label, rather than inventing some new one, associated a legislative list with a presidential candidate (hence, with the possibility of executive patronage and other favors).

The story in Uruguay is theoretically similar but more difficult to explain. Before the onset of military rule in 1971, a two-party system

[16]And both countries have long electoral and democratic traditions, albeit interrupted by civil war (in Colombia) and military rule (in Uruguay).

was maintained in Uruguay by, among other things, electoral laws that simultaneously ensured that both major parties would be highly *permeable* and that there would be a substantial *advantage* to running within an established party. The benefit of running within an established party (a "permanent" *lema*) was that all votes for lists running under the party label (under the *lema*) were pooled for purposes of seat allocations to the party, whereas no such advantage was offered to new groups. The advantage to running as a factional (or *sub-lema*) list within an established party (*lema*) was thus substantial.

Both major parties in Uruguay were also highly permeable. Both did maintain legal control of their labels but, precisely because all votes under the party label were pooled, party leaders had little incentive to deny the label to any group wishing to participate.

Colombia and Uruguay do not appear to be idiosyncratic. Shugart (1995) compared the effective number of legislative parties in seven countries (including Colombia but not Uruguay) that held their legislative and presidential elections concurrently. He found that those countries with more decentralized endorsement processes had significantly lower effective numbers of legislative parties. Shugart's interpretation of the data is that legislative candidates in concurrent elections are eager to align themselves with a presidential candidate, thus producing, in countries whose decentralized endorsement processes allow it, a reduction in the effective number of legislative parties.[17]

Although Propositions 1 and 2 speak of the permeability of a party's endorsement process, it is possible to interpret the theoretical parameters $\{p_i(e_i;0)\colon e_i \in C_i\}$ differently. Taken strictly, these are simply the probabilities that the group will secure various endorsements from group *i*. For an external group, these probabilities may well reflect the permeability or penetrability of the party. For a group that has already penetrated the party and is an active participant in it, however, these probabilities may reflect the balance of power within the party as much as or more than the permeability of the party.

Suppose one stipulates a relatively nonpermeable party and focuses on the *exit* decisions of intra-party factions. In this case, Proposition 2 suggests that a faction will exit whenever its likely endorsement placement(s) on the party slate yield fewer (expected) seats (net of costs) than would a run as an independent or new-party slate. The party as a whole, then, is more likely to hold together as (1) electoral life outside the party

[17]Shugart's evidence is not all positive. Looking at cases in which legislative and presidential elections were not held concurrently, he finds that countries with more decentralized endorsement processes had significantly *higher* effective numbers of legislative parties. It is not clear why this should be the case.

is less pleasant in prospect; and (2) there is less "underrepresentation" of factions in the endorsement process (whereby some factions take more than their proportional share of the endorsements, in view of their voting strengths, leaving others with less). These last comments may help explain why many of the world's stably factionalized parties either allocate endorsements proportionally to strength in the party conference (e.g., the Christian People's Party of Belgium, the Christian Democrats of Italy, the Union for French Democracy and Socialist Party of France) or "freeze" each faction's share (e.g., the Israel Labor Party in 1973).[18]

8.5 CONCLUSION

This chapter has considered several issues relating to political entry decisions and how they are conditioned by the anticipation of strategic voting. Duverger's original argument about entry in plurality elections was simply that would-be third-party candidates would anticipate their candidacies being ruined by strategic voting, and therefore not enter. The first task of this chapter has been to note some logical restrictions on the scope of this logic.

One restriction has to do with the clarity of expectations regarding viability. If, at the time at which entry decisions must be made, everyone is thought to be equally susceptible to strategic desertion, then no one in particular will be deterred from entering. It is only if it is clear, at the time of entry, who will probably suffer from strategic desertion that entry (by those unfortunates) will be deterred.

Another restriction has to do with politicians' goals. If they are concerned only with winning the current election, then the logic goes through. But if they are willing to suffer a string of losses in the hopes of eventual victory, or policy concessions, then it does not.

The force of the Duvergerian entry argument thus depends on whether these two conditions are generally met in a particular polity, or not. I do not have much to say about when politicians will have longer or shorter time horizons but I have suggested that generating clear expectations about viability is a matter mostly of electoral history and party labels. Once party labels have been established, and have the properties of (1) conveying a certain number of habitual votes into a candidate's total and (2) certifying the candidacy as "viable," then new candidacies that might compete for the voters that are aligned to the label are deterred. Such candidacies face a rather substantial coordination problem in competing with

[18]Japan's LDP has departed to a limited degree from this norm; see Cox and Rosenbluth (N.d.). If factions are risk-averse, then proportional allocation rules also provide some "insurance" benefits.

the nominee of the established label, with all of the advantages of focalness belonging to the nominee. If one views Duverger's Law as depending on two causal mechanisms – strategic voting, which reduces the effective number of candidates if more than two enter; and strategic entry, which reduces the number of candidates who actually enter to two – then the point can be restated as follows: The entry reduction part of the argument goes through if there is a structured party system in Sartori's sense of the term, but may not if there is not a structured party system.[19]

If indeed party labels are the primary devices of long-term coordination in most electoral systems, then the question arises of how many viable labels a given electoral system can sustain. Stating a unique optimal size for a party in a given electoral system is difficult. Being *small* is best for maintaining ideological consistency and making the party endorsement mean something in terms of policy. Being *big* is best for making a candidate or list focal and certifying that she, he, or it is viable; and for accruing any economies of scale in advertising, fund-raising, and government formation. At what size the overall profit from maintaining the label is maximized is hard to say.

One can say, however, something about what the minimum viable size of a party is. This depends more straightforwardly on thresholds of exclusion, which in turn are well understood functions of electoral structure (cf. Lijphart and Gibberd 1977). Dividing the minimum viable size into unity yields a maximum number of viable labels. This number is simply $M + 1$ for the three main electoral systems of Part II: plurality rule in M-seat districts, PR in M-seat districts, and top-M runoffs. In practice, the number of viable labels may well be smaller than this upper bound, if there are significant economies of scale in advertising, fund-raising, or government formation.[20]

[19]Sartori seems to take for granted that both parts of the district-level argument will go through in unstructured party systems. This may be true if there are other focal arbiters in the system: local oligarchs in prereform England, for example. But absent such alternative methods of certifying which candidates are viable (and which not), entry will not be deterred. So Duverger's Law would not operate fully even at the local level.

[20]This raises the question of what happens when the number of labels, m, falls short of $M + 1$, and new cleavages arise in the system. This is essentially asking whether an equilibrium in which $m < M + 1$ can be stable. Some possible responses to a new cleavage are compatible with maintaining the number of viable labels at m: if one of the major labels coopts the new issue, for example, or if activists seeking to push the issue onto the political agenda choose to infiltrate one of the major parties rather than start a new one (which decision would depend on the permeability of the various major parties' endorsement processes, *inter alia*). Another response, the creation of a protest or blackmail party designed to force issue cooptation or a favorable allocation of endorsements, suggests a short-term deviation from m, followed by a return. Finally, a third response, the creation of a new party, intended to be viable,

Strategic entry

If party labels confer viability and viability is otherwise hard to establish, then ambitious politicians who wish to win office may try to get a major party's endorsement rather than launch a new party or independent candidacy. The more valuable is running with a major-party label rather than without, and the more permeable is the major party's nomination process, the more likely are new groups or would-be candidates to "infiltrate" the major party, rather than start a new party, in accord with the old adage: If you can't beat them, join them.

increases the number of viable labels if successful (assuming that, because $m < M + 1$, there is actually room for another viable label and the creation of a new one will not simply displace an old one). Thus, when $m < M$, there is at least the logical possibility of the system accommodating some turbulence in electoral preferences without the creation of a new party. If, on the other hand, new cleavages arise in a system with $m = M + 1$, then the options are more limited. Cooptation, infiltration, and blackmail are still options but starting a new party with the idea that it will become viable is a much longer shot. If none of these strategies produce satisfaction, pressure to change the electoral system may mount, which can be considered a structural facilitation of new entry by would-be viable parties (e.g., New Zealand?). Of course, a desire to *consolidate* parties can also motivate electoral tinkering (as in Japan; cf. Christensen 1994).

9

Rational entry and the conservation of disproportionality: Evidence from Japan

In this brief chapter I provide some district-level evidence pertinent to Taagepera and Shugart's Law of Conservation of Disproportionality, a proposition articulated at the system level that hinges on rational entry decisions. Both Taagepera and Shugart (1989:123) and Lijphart (1994:97), among others, have noted that the bivariate correlation between a system's proportionality and its number of parties reflects a reciprocal causal mechanism at work. Increasing the number of contestants (beyond some threshold determined by the electoral system's capacity to dispense seats proportionally, and holding all else constant) decreases measured proportionality. *Anticipated* deviations from proportionality, however, tend to depress the number of parties. For, if everyone anticipates a disproportional outcome, and everyone agrees that party A will be on the short end of this disproportional outcome, then party A has reason to drop out of the race. But if A does drop out, then the correspondence between votes and seats actually obtained will be less distorted than had been anticipated.[1]

The lesson that Lijphart (p. 97) draws from the reciprocal causation between the number of parties and the proportionality of the electoral outcome is that proportionality measured on the basis of actual vote shares will overestimate proportionality measured on the basis of true preferences: "Assuming that many voters cast their votes for larger parties because they do not want to waste their votes on small parties with poor chances of being elected, the parties' seat shares deviate much more from the pattern of the voters' true preferences than from the actual vote shares." The lesson that Taagepera and Shugart (p. 123) draw, essentially similar, is that measured proportionality will not respond as much to changes in electoral structure – in particular, increases in district magni-

[1]Sartori (1985:66, n. 12) is another who makes this kind of point, in his criticism of Rose (1983).

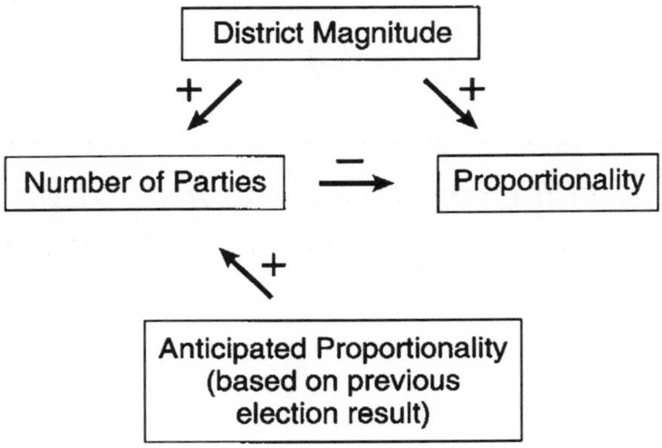

Figure 9.1. Conserving disproportionality

tude – as it would were no strategic adjustments to take place: thus their law of conservation of disproportionality.

The reasoning behind this law is straightforward. Higher district magnitudes boost the proportionality of a system but also tend to increase the number of parties competing. Increases in the number of parties, however, depress proportionality. Thus the direct positive effect of district magnitude on proportionality is partially offset by an indirect negative effect (via increases in the number of competitors).

Of course, as noted above, if parties *anticipate* a disproportional result at their own expense then they may well withdraw their candidate(s). The structure of relationships is thus as it appears in Figure 9.1: The number of parties is positively related to both district magnitude and anticipated proportionality; while actual proportionality is positively related to district magnitude but negatively related to the number of parties.

Plausible though the argument for a conservation of disproportionality may be, its empirical importance hinges on two conditions that may or may not be met in any given election. First, entry decisions must be sensitive to anticipated defeat (or underrepresentation) in the current election. This seems a natural condition to assume but it should be noted that the degree to which disproportionality is conserved depends on how sensitive party entry decisions are to variations in current electoral prospects. The level of sensitivity might be rather low for parties that take a long-term view and seek an eventual realignment of forces or change of regime (e.g., post-war communist parties).

Even if all parties in the system do base their entry decisions on their assessment of how well they can convert their votes into seats, a second condition is also necessary before any conservation of disproportionality is to be expected: The parties must agree on who it is that is likely to suffer underrepresentation. If party A thinks only party B will suffer underrepesentation, and party B thinks only party A will, then both may enter. But then there will be no (or diminished) conservation of disproportionality.

All told, then, the theoretical expectation that there should be a conservation of disproportionality requires both that parties be short-term instrumentally rational, i.e., concerned substantially with converting their votes into seats in the current election, and that they have common expectations about the likely outcome of the current election. What is the empirical evidence for this proposition?

The only evidence of which I am aware takes advantage of a unique feature of Venezuela's former electoral law, under which Venezuelans cast a fused vote, but only for legislative races (Shugart 1985; Taagepera and Shugart 1989:120–125). There is not much opportunity to replicate Shugart's research design elsewhere because few other systems employ fused votes, and those that do include the presidential race. In this chapter, I offer an alternative research design that may be easier to apply to other systems.

This alternative approach uses district-level data (in this case, from Japan) to estimate a system of two equations that approximates the structure of forces postulated in Figure 9.1. In equation (1), proportionality is predicted as a function of district magnitude and the number of parties competing. In equation (2), the number of parties is predicted as a function of district magnitude, *past* proportionality (a proxy for *anticipated* proportionality), and the district's ruralness (introduced as a control variable).

Operationally, the analysis focuses on a measure of *dis*proportionality, rather than proportionality. The dependent variable in the first equation is $\text{EXCESS}_{it} = \text{ENPV}_{it}/\text{ENPS}_{it}$, where ENPV_{it} is the effective number of elective parties in district *i*, election *t*, and ENPS_{it} is the effective number of parliamentary parties in district *i*, election *t*. Large values of EXCESS indicate that there are substantially more parties chasing votes than winning seats, hence that there is a disproportion between vote and seat shares. Results are similar if a more conventional measure of disproportionality, e.g., Rae's, is used.

Table 9.1 displays the results of regressing EXCESS first on district magnitude alone (Model 1), then on magnitude plus the number of parties competing (Model 2), finally on both these variables and the lagged value of EXCESS (Model 3). The first model shows a weak negative bivariate relationship: Larger-magnitude districts have less disproportional results. The second model shows that the relationship between magnitude and disproportionality is substantially stronger when one controls for the number of parties competing. Thus, the impact of elec-

Table 9.1. The law of conservation of disproportionality: Japan, 1960–90

Dependent variable: $EXCESS_{it}$

Independent variables	*Model 1*		*Model 2*		*Model 3*	
	Param.	*Std. err.*	*Param.*	*Std. err.*	*Param.*	*Std. err.*
CONSTANT	1.32	0.032	1.16	0.031	1.01	0.044
$MAGNITUDE_{it}$	–.033	0.008	–.074	0.008	–.067	0.008
N OF $PARTIES_{it}$	—	—	0.101	0.007	0.095	0.007
$EXCESS_{i,t-1}$	—	—			0.123	0.026
R SQUARED	.01		.16		.17	
N OF OBS	1324		1324		1324	
DW STATISTIC	1.60		1.67		1.90	

Notes: The dependent variable, $EXCESS_{it}$, is a measure of disproportionality in the ith district at election *t*, equal to $ENPV_{it}/ENPS_{it}$, where $ENPV_{it}$ is the effective number of elective parties in district *i*, election *t*, and $ENPS_{it}$ is the effective number of parliamentary parties in district *i*, election *t*. Large values of EXCESS indicate that there are substantially more parties chasing votes than winning seats. $MAGNITUDE_{it}$ is the number of members elected from district *i*, election *t*. N OF $PARTIES_{it}$ is the number of parties running candidates in district *i*, election *t*. The estimation was performed using OLS.

toral structure on disproportionality is greater when strategic adjustments (entry and exit decisions as reflected in the number of parties competing) are held constant: Taagepera and Shugart's Law of Conservation of Disproportionality holds at the district level, at least in Japan. The final model is included because the first two suffer from positive autocorrelation. Including the lagged dependent variable takes care of this problem, while leaving the key regression coefficient (measuring the impact of district magnitude) unchanged.

The dependent variable in the second equation (see Table 9.2) is the number of parties competing in district *i*, election *t*. The regressors are the lagged number of parties (included to deal with autocorrelation), the district magnitude, the lagged value of EXCESS in the district, a measure of the ruralness of the district, and a series of year dummies. As can be seen, all of the independent variables of primary interest have statistically significant effects of the expected sign. The important result for present purposes is that districts that had more disproportional outcomes in the previous election – presumably those in which high levels of disproportionality would be expected, were the same cast of parties to enter the

Table 9.2. Predicting the number of parties: Japan, 1960–90

Dependent variable: N OF PARTIES$_{it}$

Independent variables	*Coeff. est.*	*Standard errors*
CONSTANT	0.52	0.14
N OF PARTIES$_{i,t-1}$	0.57	0.02
MAGNITUDE$_{it}$	0.18	0.02
EXCESS$_{i,t-1}$	–.19	0.08
PURBE$_{it}$	0.01	0.00
YEAR63	–.86	0.08
YEAR67	–.44	0.08
YEAR69	–.19	0.08
YEAR72	–.51	0.08
YEAR76	–.26	0.08
YEAR79	–.46	0.09
YEAR80	–.61	0.08
YEAR83	–.60	0.08
YEAR86	–.65	0.08
YEAR90	–.62	0.08
R SQUARED	.60	
N OF OBSERVATIONS	1323	
DURBIN-WATSON	2.25	

Notes: The estimation was performed using OLS. PURBE$_{it}$ is the percentage of all electors in the district who reside in urban areas. The variables YEARxx are all dummy variables, equal to one for observations occurring in year xx, equal to zero otherwise. See Table 9.1 for definitions of the other variables.

fray again – had fewer parties, *ceteris paribus*. The inference is that some parties, with reasonably significant vote totals but no seats last time, decided not to run again. Presumably, they traded their votes for reciprocal treatment in another district or for some other concession.

To return to the issue of conservation of disproportionality, the results indicate that a unit increase in district magnitude would directly *decrease* disproportionality by .067; but would indirectly *increase* disproportionality by .017 (because larger magnitudes lead to more competitors, and more competitors lead to more disproportional results).[2] Hence, the

[2]The .067 is the coefficient of MAGNITUDE in Model 3, Table 9.1. The .017 equals the coefficient of MAGNITUDE in Table 9.2 (.18) times the coefficient of N OF PARTIES in Model 3, Table 9.1 (.095).

overall effect of a unit increase in magnitude (the sum of the direct and indirect effects) is to decrease disproportionality by .050.[3] By these numbers, then, the direct effect of the change in magnitude, what we would like to measure, is about 1.34 times larger than the overall effect, what has usually been measured in the literature. To put the point another way, by failing to account for the strategic adjustment of parties, we underestimate the direct effect of changing the district magnitude by .017/.067 = 25%.[4]

The two-equation model presented here is not fully simultaneous, with current disproportionality and current number of parties both endogenous. It takes the view that (1) there is a temporal sequence in which the variables are determined: the number of parties is determined first, then the election is held, producing a disproportionality score of some value; and (2) the only basis on which parties might forecast disproportionality, at the time they are deciding whether to enter the race or not, is what happened last time. If there are other, contemporaneous sources of information available to parties regarding what the level of disproportionality might be, then a more fully simultaneous treatment might be appropriate.[5] But the current results do illustrate the interconnections between disproportionality, anticipated disproportionality, and number of parties in a somewhat finer-grained fashion than previous work at the system level has done.

[3]This estimate of the overall effect (–.050) is larger in magnitude than the estimate of the overall effect derived from Model 1, Table 9.1 (–.033). The discrepancy between these two estimates may indicate some misspecification of the model.

[4]Another way to interpret the results presented here is as describing dynamic adjustment paths over time. For a district of given magnitude (say 3) and urbanness (say 66% urban, the median for Japanese districts), in a given year (say 1983, by which time, judging from the string of similar year effects observed in Table 9.2, the system may have hit a steady state), the equations estimated in Tables 9.1 and 9.2 reduce to (dropping the *i* subscripts and letting *E* stand for EXCESS and N for N OF PARTIES):

$$E_t = 1.01 - .067(3) + .095N_{t-1} + .123E_{t-1} = .81 + .095N_{t-1} + .123E_{t-1}$$

$$N_t = 1.13 + .57N_{t-1} - .19E_{t-1}$$

If we assume that the system has hit a steady state, at which $N_t = N_{t-1} = N$ and $E_t = E_{t-1} = E$, then we have a system of two equations in two unknowns. Solving, we find that (approximately) $E = 1.27$ and $N = 2.07$.

[5]The econometric model is consistent with a rational expectations approach if the only systematic information that potential candidates possess about the likely outcome of the current election, when they must make their entry decisions, is the last electoral result in the district.

PART IV

Electoral coordination at the system level

10

Putting the constituencies together

Thus far, this book has dealt with issues of local coordination: how voters in a given electoral district coordinate their suffrages; how candidates and parties, again at the district level, coordinate their entry decisions. Scholarly arguments about the effect of electoral systems on party systems, from Duverger onward, have not stopped with these district-level considerations. Instead, they have gone further and claimed that electoral rules also affect the larger stage of national politics, because national parties link politicians from many electoral districts together for purposes of electoral campaigning and governance.

In this chapter, I consider this appeal to the existence of national parties, and the phenomenon of cross-district linkage of legislative candidates more generally. I shall argue that the standard linkage argument, in particular, that advanced in support of Duverger's Law, fails; and that better linkage arguments entail the same kinds of social and institutional considerations encountered previously in the book. Under the heading of "institutional considerations" I stress in particular the importance of the rules determining the selection and power of the chief executive (whether president or prime minister). This discussion sets the stage for the empirical analysis presented in Chapter 11.

A second topic that I investigate in this chapter concerns how taking a multi-district view of things might affect the topics considered in the previous two parts of the book: strategic voting and strategic entry. Will voters vote with an eye to affecting the formation of governments, rather than merely the allocation of seats in their particular electoral constituency, thereby changing the nature of strategic voting effects? Will a national market in which candidacies and withdrawals are traded emerge, thereby changing the character of the coordination problem at the district level? As it turns out, answers to both these questions again come back to the politics of choosing a chief executive.

10.1 LINKAGE AND DUVERGER'S LAW

Duverger clearly recognized that the wasted vote argument applied only at the district level, as did his arguments about prudent entry decisions by potential candidates: "the true effect of the simple-majority system is limited to *local* bipartism" (Duverger 1954:223; my italics). This left open the question of how an argument that predicted local bipartism might lead to a conclusion that entailed systemic or national bipartism. Why, in other words, would the same two parties necessarily compete in all districts, even if the method of election ensured local bipartism in every district?

Duverger (p. 228) had a rather cryptic answer to this question, whereby the "increased centralization of organization within the parties and the consequent tendency to see political problems from the wider, national standpoint tend of themselves to project on to the entire country the localized two-party system brought about by the ballot procedure ..." Both Wildavsky (1959) and Leys (1959) appropriately argued that this projection argument essentially assumed what was to be shown.

Given that this step in Duverger's argument, explaining how local bipartism "projects" into national bipartism, is absolutely crucial in establishing his law as a *systemic* rather than a merely *local* one, it is amazing how little attention has been paid to it in the subsequent literature. The projection argument is a natural point at which those preferring a sociological theory of party systems might have focused their attacks, but as far as I know no one has done this. Indeed, to my knowledge only Leys and Sartori offer any extended attempts to provide a better projection argument. In this section, I consider their proposals.

Leys' projection argument

The key to Leys' projection argument is the assumption that strategic voting "occurs in favour *not* of the two parties which are in the lead locally, but *in favour of the two parties which have the largest number of seats in Parliament, regardless of their local strength*" (Leys 1959:142; italics in original). Voters, in other words, focus on the outcome in the national legislature, seeking to vote in such a way as to affect which party wins a majority of seats, rather than merely which candidate wins the seat at stake in the constituency. This national focus, according to Leys, leads to the abandonment of nationally uncompetitive parties.

Leys had in mind the British case, where voters are generally believed to be nationally oriented, but even here he clearly overstated the importance of national as opposed to local viability. This can be seen by noting two points. First, voting for a locally hopeless party never makes instrumental sense, even if it is nationally competitive and voters care only about the disposition of forces in parliament. The reason is that a vote that cannot change the local outcome cannot *a fortiori* change the national outcome, and thus has no instrumental value either at the local or the national level. Second, voting for a nationally hopeless party (i.e., one that has no hope of securing a majority of legislative seats) may make sense, so long as it is locally competitive. The reason is that electing a nationally hopeless party's candidate increases the probability of a hung parliament (and thus perhaps the probability of participation in a coalition government), and decreases the probability that one of the nationally competitive parties will secure a majority, both things that some instrumentally motivated voters may want to do.

I shall return to Leys' argument later, when discussing strategic voting that aims to affect the formation of governments rather than the allocation of seats within a given electoral district. But for now the point is simply that his argument does not succeed in providing an adequate projection argument that might allow Duverger's Law to be seen as a systemic proposition.

Sartori's projection argument

In this section, I consider Sartori's (1968; 1976) attempt to explain how single-member plurality elections can have a more-than-local effect, which I view as an elaboration and clarification of the brief Duvergerian argument noted above. Sartori begins by asserting that "plurality systems have no influence (beyond the district) until the party system becomes structured ..." (1968:281). One learns elsewhere that a party system is structured when it is composed of at least some mass parties, and that a mass party is characterized by "(1) the development of a stable and extensive ... organization throughout the country, and (2) the fact that it presents itself to the electorate as an abstract entity (ideologically or programmatically qualified) that allows stable identifications" (p. 293). Substituting the definitions of "structured party system" and "mass party" into the original formulation, one gets the claim that plurality rule will have no effect beyond the district until there are parties that have both nationwide organizations and ideological reputations that command a habitual following in the electorate. If what is to be explained is the knitting together of district parties (the establishment of "nationwide organization"), then Sartori simply assumes the consequent. But if the explanandum is the existence of national bipartism, then Sartori's approach is not circular in that it does not assume national bipartism.

Unfortunately, however, Sartori gives no theoretical argument that having a structured party system should allow the effect of single-member plurality elections to be felt *fully* at the national level, thus unleashing national bipartism. If we take as given that the local effect of the electoral system will be to drive every district toward (at most) two viable parties (which might just be district-specific "nominating committees" that have successfully structured local electoral choice), then the theoretical maximum number of parties in the system is $2D$: 2 parties from each of D districts. The argument that Sartori makes just suggests that the more nationalized are the parties, the fewer there will be.

The point can be made formally as follows. Consider a single-member plurality system in which there are D districts. Suppose there are N parties in this system which on average put up C candidates for election. If each district has only two viable parties, and if each party puts up candidates only in districts where it is viable, then the relation between N, C, and D must satisfy $NC = 2D$. If we take C as a measure of the nationalization of the parties in the system, then we can clearly say that the more nationalized are the parties (the larger is C), the fewer parties there must be (the smaller is N).

Sartori's argument leaves us with just the following: If there are reasons for politicians to link across districts, and they therefore do link across districts, then this will reduce the number of parties from $2D$. But the number remaining after reduction may still be well above 2, unless the definition of a 'national party' is that it fields candidates in every district (in terms of the example, unless $C = D$). If we do not assume that national parties field candidates in every district, then how close the national party system gets to the theoretical minimum of 2 (or, how far away it gets from the theoretical maximum of $2D$) depends on something other than the district-level electoral structure.

Before leaving Sartori's argument, I should note one feature of it that has been neglected thus far: the emphasis that he puts on literacy. The notion is that loyalty to a party "as an abstract entity (ideologically or programmatically qualified)," as opposed to loyalty to persons, requires an electorate capable of abstraction. Thus, the "mass party stage cannot be entered until an adequate spread of literacy allows 'capacity for abstraction'" (Sartori 1968:293).

This argument implies that one simply *cannot* profitably link politicians across districts, absent literacy, if the source of the profit is something to do (economies of scale in electoral advertising and propaganda?) with the party label. One may *try* to popularize a party label and cultivate mass loyalty to it but, with an illiterate electorate, one will fail.

I doubt the empirical accuracy of this claim. Business firms have been successful in cultivating brand-name recognition and loyalty in illiterate societies, so why could not political parties in principle succeed as well? In the English case, the nineteenth-century parties built up a mass following to abstract principles among illiterate and literate citizens alike. More generally, the response of political parties to illiteracy in the electorate seems to be competition over the symbols that might appeal to such voters. In South Africa, for example, the leader of the Zulus (Mangosuthu Buthelezi) was perturbed to discover that, in a book that proposed the use of animal symbols on the ballot to identify candidates, he had been allocated the hyena (!) while one of Nelson Mandela's associates had drawn the lion. In India, Prime Minister P.V. Narasimha Rao tried in 1993 to ban the use of religious symbols on the ballot, in an apparent attempt to lessen the growing influence of right-wing Hindu parties. And other examples of "symbolic politics" in illiterate societies might be cited as well (see Reynolds 1995).[1]

In the absence of a projection argument

The bottom line is that none of the major projection arguments work. These arguments are intended to explain how the logic of strategic voting and strategic entry, which is clear enough at the district level, "projects" onto the national stage. Both Duverger and Sartori begin their arguments by *assuming* that parties have nationalized, i.e., that the groups in each district have seen fit to link together into larger national entities. But this assumes most of what is to be shown. And whatever variables might explain why district groups do link together to form larger parties, they appear to have little to do with district-level electoral structure.

I think we ought clearly to recognize that Duverger's Law has a different status as a systemic proposition than it does as a district-level proposition. At the district level there are clearly specifiable theoretical models of strategic voting and of entry that predict local bipartism (or unipartism) as an equilibrium; and there is pretty good evidence that the theory works essentially as specified. At the national level, there is no

[1]Even if one accepts the claim that illiteracy makes the development of party identification in the mass electorate impossible, or prohibitively costly, this does not necessarily mean that there are no incentives to forge cross-district links. Economies of scale in converting votes into seats, due to upper tiers, for example, would provide a clear impetus to the formation of national or regional parties, as would the other factors discussed below.

clearly specified way in which district forces translate to the national level. That is, there is nothing in the original district-level logic (regarding either strategic voting or strategic entry) that allows one to conclude that there will be two parties nationally. There may be factors that push the system toward national bipartism but these factors do not depend on local electoral structure, and no one has offered any argument that says the equilibrium of these forces necessarily pushes *to* bipartism. Thus, Duverger's Law at the district level is a theoretical proposition, while Duverger's Law at the national level is an empirical generalization, and one to which there are many exceptions at that.

10.2 WHY LINK?

Where are we then in terms of explaining the character of *national* party systems? The local argument does provide an upper bound on the number of parties nationally. A system with nothing but single-member plurality elections, for example, should have no more than $2D$ parties, where D is the number of districts; a system with nothing but M-seat PR or SNTV elections should have no more than $(M + 1)D$ parties; and so forth. But this upper bound is not much use. In order to get any further, one needs an argument that explains not only why district-based groups would seek to link together to form multi-district parties but also something about the equilibrium level of such linkage. For example, if one can fashion a theoretical argument that shows that linkage should typically extend to all districts in a single-member plurality system, when conditions X, Y, and Z are met, then one has some reason to expect national bipartism. So the question becomes, why do politicians seeking election to the national legislature from different districts find it useful to run under a common party label, as opposed to running separate campaigns? And how far do such incentives go – what is the equilibrium extent of linkage?

There are many conceivable reasons that politicians from different districts might link together under a common party label. The most important reasons all pertain to economies of scale and have a similar abstract form: Some preexisting group, that is already of national scope or perspective, seeks to accomplish a task that requires the help of a large number of legislators or legislative candidates; this group therefore seeks to induce would-be legislators from many different districts to participate in a larger organization. I shall consider five versions of this story in which the "task that requires the help of a large number of legislators or legislative candidates" is either enacting laws, electing a president, electing a prime minister, securing seats distributed in a national upper tier, or securing campaign finance.

In pursuit of national policy

Well-known versions of the story just limned appear in the historical literature on party origins (cf. Duverger 1954; LaPalombara and Weiner 1966). In the case of "interior" parties, groups of parliamentarians have allied at the national level, in pursuit of some collective policy goal, and then sought to enhance their alliance's prospects by organizing the electorate more thoroughly. In the case of "exterior" parties, a group that is already nationally organized, such as a peak association of labor unions or a religious sect, launches a political party. In another exterior pattern, various interest groups from around the nation form a political party to further their respective interests (cf. Vincent 1966). In all these cases, the group that forms the party is already of national (or at least regional) scope, and the motivation for forming a party seems directly related to the prospect of controlling governmental policy.

In pursuit of the presidency

An abstractly similar story is sometimes told about the role of presidential elections: Would-be presidents must necessarily gather votes *nationwide* and often organizing groups of would-be legislators is a natural strategy in pursuit of that goal. If presidential elections are held regularly in conjunction with legislative elections, presidential ambitions may have substantial effects on the legislative party system. Let us consider three different versions of this story, from the United States, France, and Latin America.

The level of linkage in U.S. House elections during the 1820s was relatively low. The Federalist party was largely defunct, leaving a number of candidates who were either loosely associated with any party or overtly independent. The four-way contest for the presidency in 1824 further increased the number of legislative groups. This is evident, for example, in the large number of different labels under which candidates ran for election in the 1820s. Although the various kinds of Democrats (or Federalists) cooperated once they got into the House, by the criterion of what label they ran under the system was far from being a two-party one at the national level: The effective number of party labels in the House of Representatives in the 1820s averaged 3.63. After Andrew Jackson's election to the presidency in 1828, the effective number of labels in the House trends downward, averaging 3.03 in the 1830s, 2.29 in the 1840s, bumping back up to about 2.5 in the 1850s and 1860s, and finally settling down for good to about 2 in the 1870s.[2] McCormick (1975) has argued that the motive force creating the second American party system was competition for the presidency and this is certainly reflected in the nationalization of party labels during this period.[3]

France is a similar example of the linking power of presidential campaigns. During the Third Republic, there was a single-member district system with two rounds. Almost all of the local races had only one or two viable candidates but, because these candidates were not fully linked, there was a multiparty parliamentary system (Campbell and Cole 1989:19). Although the labor movement did launch a national party early in the twentieth century, which linked many candidates on the left, candidates on the right and center remained largely unlinked until the Gaullist Rally for the Republic (RPR) appeared in 1951. Even then, a substantial number of independents continued to compete on the right and center. After de Gaulle successfully forced the parliament to accept a directly elected president in 1962, however, almost all seats have been won by candidates linked to national parties.[4]

More extreme instances of the power of presidential elections to stimulate legislative linkage appear in several Latin American systems that use fused votes: Bolivia, the Dominican Republic, Honduras, and Uruguay. In Uruguay, for example, voters cast a single fused vote for a slate that includes a candidate for the presidency, a list of candidates for the senate, and a list of candidates seeking to represent the particular district in which the voter resides in the chamber of deputies. Because of this fused vote, the process of winning seats in the lower house in Uruguay is pretty thoroughly entangled with the process of winning the presidency. More to the current point, the Uruguayan ballot is such that every list of candidates for the lower house under a given presidential candidate,

[2]The figure for the 1850s is about 2.5 if one excludes the 34th Congress, during which the Republican party supplanted the Whigs. If this congress is included the decadal average is almost 2.9.

[3]The numbers reported in the text are my calculations from Inter-university Consortium for Political and Social Research, and Carroll McKibbin. 1989. *Roster of United States Congressional Officeholders and Bibliographical Characteristics of Members of the United States Congress, 1789–1989: Merged Data [Computer file]*. 7th ICPSR ed. Ann Arbor, MI: Inter-university Consortium for Political and Social Research [producer and distributor].

[4]As Wilson (1980:540) puts it: "When the presidency became the chief prize of political competition, the entire party system was affected. No longer could small parties hope to play key roles in politics by holding a strategic center position, as the Radical party had done throughout the Third and Fourth Republics. Instead, parties had to generate national electoral support for one candidate in order to control the government." Thus, political parties, especially those in the center and on the right, changed from loose alliances of "notables with firm local support" to allow a "focus on a handful of national figures who might be regarded as presidential contenders" (p. 537).

regardless of district, automatically runs under the same party (and factional) label: Linkage is thus a built-in feature of the system that candidates for the chamber cannot avoid.

The examples above make it clear that presidential elections have sometimes been key factors driving the linkage of legislative candidates across districts. But only the U.S. example shows cross-district linkage being pushed to the point that national bipartism emerges. So the question arises: When will presidential elections drive the legislative party system to (or toward) national bipartism?

This question is analogous to asking when district-level electoral systems will create local bipartism and, by analogy with the district-level answer, an answer along the following lines is suggested: Presidential elections will drive the system toward national bipartism to the extent that the presidency is a single nondivisible prize elected by rules that approximate a straight plurality fight. This answer suggests that the *presidential* party system will be bipolar. If two-partyism is to reach the legislative system, then we also need to consider the nature of legislative elections and the connections between executive and legislative elections.

All told then, there are four key conditions that must be met to maximize the push toward national legislative bipartism that presidential elections can impart. First, the presidency must be a big prize, worth considerable effort to attain. The greater the concentration of powers within the presidency, and the more the system approximates an elective kingship, the more the whole politics of the nation ought to organize themselves around the battle for this one prize. Second, the presidential election must be held under rules that allow only two viable candidates. Third, the presidential election must be strongly linked to the legislative elections. Fourth, the legislative elections must themselves be held under a strong electoral system. Let us consider each of the first three conditions in a bit more detail:

1. *Presidential power.* Shugart and Carey (1992) make clear that the powers of presidents vary in important ways from country to country. They note, for example, variations in the president's veto power, decree authority, budgetary control, ability to form and dismiss cabinets, and ability to dissolve the legislature. It is clear from their work that there are substantial differences between, say, the strong presidencies of Paraguay or Brazil (1988), the intermediate-strength presidencies of the United States or Nigeria, and the weak presidencies of France or Finland. It may be that the presidency is sufficiently attractive a prize even in France and Finland to provide a strong organizing push to legislative elections. But the prize should be worth even more effort in Brazil and Paraguay, and hence pursuit of that prize should be even more likely to affect legislative elections there (*ceteris paribus*).

2. *Strength of the presidential election procedure.* The strongest presidential election procedures are those that approximate plurality rule. The U.S. Electoral College, for example, roughly approximates a straight plurality fight and has regularly produced just two viable candidates (exceptions occurring in 1824 and 1912). Many other countries use a runoff system, with a consequent weakening of the incentives to coalesce in presidential elections. Weaker incentives yet are produced when there are plural executives, as in Switzerland and formerly in Uruguay, because the election procedure then takes on a proportional character.
3. *Executive-legislative electoral linkage.* The link between presidential and legislative elections depends on two main factors: (1) whether the two elections are held concurrently or not; and (2) whether a fused executive-legislative vote is used or not. Many presidential elections are held concurrently with legislative elections but some are not, and research reviewed in Chapter 11 shows that this can have a substantial impact on the legislative party system. Most presidential systems do not use a fused vote but, as noted above, some do, and those that do maximize the possibility of influence between presidential and legislative electoral politics.

If all four conditions are met – (1) a powerful presidency, (2) a strong presidential election procedure, (3) strongly linked presidential and legislative elections, and (4) a strong legislative election procedure – then the situation is this: There is a single non-divisible and very powerful office, elected under rules that typically allow at most two viable candidates at the national level. The election of this officer, moreover, is strongly linked to the legislative elections, which themselves tend to local bipartism. Under these conditions, there are two viable legislative candidates in each legislative district, and two viable presidential candidates nationwide. The presidential candidates in this scenario have a pretty clear incentive to recruit supporters among the legislative candidates, and the legislators may have incentives to ride presidential coattails or court presidential favor. Presidential ambition may thus lead to the organization of legislators from each district into two nationwide electoral alliances, or parties.

In pursuit of the premiership

If would-be presidents must necessarily gather votes nationwide and might plausibly seek to organize cross-district alliances of would-be legislators to this end, what of would-be premiers? They are not directly elected but they do face a sort of indirect election procedure that argues the necessity of gathering support nationwide. And they of course have even stronger incentives than presidents to build specifically *legislative* coalitions as vehicles for their ambition, since legislators form something like an ongoing electoral college for purposes of selecting the prime minister. One might think, then, that considerations analogous to those advanced above concerning presidential powers, presidential election rules, and the linkage of presidential and legislative elections, are apt here as well:

1. *Prime ministerial power.* Just as presidents in different systems have varying degrees of power, so too do prime ministers. At some times complaints have been voiced in Britain about the emergence of "prime ministerial government," suggesting that executive power has been substantially concentrated in that single office. In other systems, the premier is merely *primus inter pares,* and the system looks more like a plural executive (cf. Sartori 1993).
2. *Strength of the prime ministerial election procedure.* In addition to directly electing legislators, parliamentary elections also indirectly elect prime ministers: The freshly elected members of parliament must choose which government to support, and in the process act essentially as do delegates to an electoral college charged with selecting a president. What is the strength of such indirect selection procedures? It all depends on the rules or norms by which prime ministers are chosen *in parliament.* If the leader of the largest party always has the first opportunity to form a government, as is true in many polities, and he or she usually succeeds, then the system looks (ignoring malapportionment, asymmetries in the wastage of votes, etc.) like a plurality election. If the leader of a smaller party sometimes gets the first crack at forming a government, or if the politics of government formation are such that the first chance often fails, then the system is less like a plurality election, and provides weaker incentives to be the largest party. If the prime minister is weak and the system is really more like a plural executive, then the selection procedure will typically be a proportional (hence even weaker) one.
3. *Executive-legislative electoral linkage.* Prime ministerial elections are always held concurrently with legislative elections. And voters always have only a single vote with which to affect both the election of legislators from a given constituency and the election of the premier.[5] Thus, executive and legislative elections are always firmly connected in parliamentary systems.

[5]In a sense, then, they have a special kind of fused vote (one whose ultimate impact on the election of the prime minister may be more or less clear).

Given this connection of executive and legislative elections in parliamentary systems, the strength of the cross-district incentives toward bipartism depends on whether the process of selecting a premier looks like a plurality contest for an elective dictatorship, on the one hand, or a proportional contest for a plural executive, on the other. The first pole is similar to the classic Westminster model, the latter to the classic Consensus model (Lijphart 1984). The closer to the first pole, the more likely it will be that the pursuit of prime ministerial ambition will push the system toward bipartism. The closer to the latter pole, the more likely it will be that prime ministerial ambition, while still serving to link legislators across districts, will not lead to national bipartism.

In pursuit of upper tier seats

Another reason to form cross-district alliances of politicians has to do with the existence of upper tiers. Typically laws implementing upper tiers require an explicit legal linkage of the lists or candidates that wish to pool their votes at the regional or national level (see the discussion of Belgium in Chapter 3). Often, such laws are written specifically to promote the formation of broadly-based parties.[6] In principle, one could allow participation in the upper tier only for parties that were "viable" (e.g., won seats or were runner-ups) in every district in the country, which would obviously provide a substantial incentive toward fully nationalized parties, depending on how many seats were allocated there. In practice, no system is this manipulative but there is still some variation along this dimension (as can be seen in Appendix C).

In pursuit of campaign finance

Finally, let us briefly consider three ways in which the necessities of raising money might lead to cross-district linkage. First, if a peak labor (e.g., the Trades Union Congress in Britain) or business (e.g., the *Keidanren* in Japan) association is actively financing electoral campaigns with an eye to affecting national policy, then they may require or encourage the beneficiaries of their largesse to be members of a single party. Second, national regulation of campaign finance could in principle severely discriminate against unlinked politicians, for example, by providing public

[6] Several recent Eastern European electoral laws have features of this kind. For example, article 92 of the Slovenian law doubly restricts the parties that can win seats allocated in the national upper tier. First, no party that does not run lists in at least two of the eight primary electoral districts can get any of the upper tier seats. Second, no party that would not win at least three seats, were all seats allocated on the basis of national vote totals by the d'Hondt method of PR, is eligible to receive upper tier seats.

funds or free TV time to candidates from national parties but denying these to independents. Third, if the market for campaign contributions is one in which businesses and special interests seek particularistic favors in return for their money, then the parties that can best deliver such benefits will have an advantage. (The potential importance of this advantage can be gauged by the substantial realignment of campaign finance that has occurred in the United States, pursuant to the Democrats' loss of power in Congress. In 1993, roughly two-thirds of all political action committee contributions reported to the Federal Elections Commission went to Democrats; in 1995, roughly two-thirds of such contributions went to Republicans.[7]) The source of the advantage in delivering benefits is typically "being in government," something that usually requires a certain minimum size (although there are exceptions, such as the religious microparties in Israel). Thus, raising campaign funds may be substantially easier for larger parties.

The interaction of social and electoral structure at the national level

This section has noted five factors that might push the process of linkage across legislative districts. The first of these factors pertains to social structure at the national level, while the last four pertain to electoral structure at the national level. In this subsection I stress that, just as the district-level logic of electoral coordination suggests an interaction between social and electoral structure, so too does the national logic suggest such an interaction. Consider first a polity in which there are strongly organized peak labor and business organizations but a weak executive choice procedure. It is conceivable that these peak associations possess an array of sanctions needed to solve whatever collective action problems they face. These sanctions might then be sufficient to hold together a national two-party system, even though the electoral system itself is permissive. Consider next a polity with a fractionated and diverse structure of interest groups at the national level but a strong executive choice procedure (e.g., a nationwide plurality election of a strong president). In this case it is plausible that the various interest groups will sort themselves out into two large alliances, driven to this by the necessities of presidential politics. Thus, just as at the district level, one might argue that a large number of separate parties will arise only if there is both social diversity and electoral proportionality (see Chapter 7). In other words, the number of parties at the national level should depend on the interaction of social and electoral structure.

[7]See the November 6, 1995 issue of *U.S. News and World Report.*

10.3 LINKAGE AND STRATEGIC VOTING

In this section, I assume that a desire to compete more effectively for executive office drives the linkage of legislators across districts. In pursuit of this goal, politicians face a coordination problem similar in form to that they face within legislative districts: If too many leftist candidates seek the presidency, or too many leftist parties demand too large a share of portfolios, then no leftist government may be able to form to begin with. Just as the coordination problem posed by winning legislative seats engenders strategic voting and entry, so too does the coordination problem posed by winning executive office; but the main purpose of strategic coordination shifts from affecting the allocation of seats within a given district (seat maximization) to affecting who controls the government (portfolio maximization). In this section, I focus on three species of "portfolio-maximizing" strategic voting: strategic sequencing, or voting so as to affect which party gets the first opportunity to form a government; strategic balancing, or voting so as to deny a single party control of all branches of government (in presidential or bicameral systems); and strategic threshold insurance, or voting so as to keep a prospective coalition partner's vote above some threshold mandated by the electoral code. Empirical examples of these possibilities are provided from the Israeli, United States, and German literatures.

Strategic sequencing

In this section, I shall initially consider a parliamentary system in which (1) voters care solely about which parties participate in government; and (2) legislative elections are held under highly proportional rules. How will beliefs about which government coalition will form affect strategic voting in the constituencies?

Let us consider an example in which there are three parties – A, B, and C – competing for seats. Everyone believes that (1) no party will secure a majority of parliamentary seats on its own; (2) either A or C will be the largest party; and (3) whichever of these two parties is the largest will have the first opportunity to form a government and will succeed in forming a coalition with B. *Given* these beliefs, the only likely way in which voters can affect the outcome (i.e., which government forms) is by determining whether A or C is the largest party, hence which of these has the first opportunity to form a government, hence whether an AB or a CB coalition assumes office.

How will those who most prefer B behave? By assumption, there is no reason to vote against B in order to avoid a wasted vote at the district level: The system is highly proportional and so it will not be clear that anyone is out of the running for the last-allocated seat. But B supporters who strongly prefer an AB coalition to a BC coalition will have an incentive to vote strategically for A, while B supporters who strongly prefer a BC coalition will have an incentive to vote strategically for C. Thus, B may suffer a loss of votes even though it is locally viable, in favor of parties that have a shot at forming a government. If the local electoral system is permissive, then Leys' claim that strategic voting occurs in favor of nationally competitive parties is more plausible.

There is very little empirical work that explores whether this kind of strategic sequencing, or voting so as to affect which party has the first opportunity at forming a government, is common. But there is one system with highly proportional elections for which there is some evidence: Israel. Israel elects all 120 members of the Knesset from a single nationwide constituency. Thus, it is plausible that Israeli voters do not worry about wasting their votes in the conventional sense of that phrase. But Felsenthal and Brichta (1985), based on a survey of 1,024 Israelis, suggest that about 12% of Israelis cast coalitionally strategic votes. And Nixon et al. (1996) also suggest, based on survey evidence, that Israelis have voted in coalitionally strategic ways; in particular, some *Tzomet* supporters appear to have voted against *Tzomet* in favor of *Likud,* presumably in an effort to give *Likud* the first chance at forming a coalition.

I turn now to consider a parliamentary system in which voters again care solely about which parties participate in government, but in which legislative elections are held under plurality rule. Can strategic sequencing appear here too? I have already noted that the strong version of Leys' argument does not work, but there is nonetheless a way in which being nationally competitive may help in attaining local viability in an SMSP system. Suppose that the (sincere) local standings of three parties – A, B, and C – put A ahead, with B and C too close to call, while the national standings put C clearly out of the running for majority control. In this case, voting for B is equivalent to voting for C from the point of view of preventing an A majority in parliament; but voting for B also has some chance of converting a hung parliament into a B majority, while voting for C has no analogous chance. Thus, all voters who rank C first but prefer a B majority to a hung parliament (and both to an A majority) will vote strategically, for B. If this class of C supporters is sufficiently numerous, the local tie between B and C will be broken in B's favor. Thus, national viability can serve a "tie-breaking" function in local strategic voting equilibria, removing some otherwise possible non-Duvergerian equilibria.[8]

The practical importance of this theoretical possibility depends on how much information voters possess about local and national standings

[8]For a more extensive discussion of this point, see Cox and Monroe (1995).

(and the nature of voter preferences over national outcomes). If there is no good information about local standings, and electoral history is not seen as a reliable guide to predicting the outcome (perhaps there has been a redistricting, for example), then voters in many districts may perceive all parties as having roughly equal chances of contending for the local seat. If at the same time there is good information about national standings, then national viability can serve an important tie-breaking function in the constituencies, along the lines sketched above. In Chapter 14, I suggest that this may have been part of the explanation for the decline of the Liberal Party in the United Kingdom after the first world war.[9]

Strategic balancing

Some constitutional structures endow multiple elected bodies – lower and upper houses, presidents – with significant legislative power. In any such system, the possibility arises for strategic balancing by voters. Suppose, for example, that there are two main parties, L (on the left) and R (on the right). If L controls body X, then when the time comes to elect body Y, centrist voters, even those closer to L than to R, may wish to moderate the influence of L, by giving R control of Y. If this sort of strategic balancing occurred regularly, then one would expect a negative correlation between control of X and control of Y.

The best-developed case for this kind of balancing is made in the context of U.S. elections. The United States obviously fits the abstract constitutional requirements of the model: The House, the Senate, and the president are all separately elected and all have significant legislative powers. Moreover, the party controlling the presidency is well-known to suffer a regular loss of seats in midterm congressional elections. Alesina and Rosenthal (1989), Alesina, Londregan, and Rosenthal (1993), and Fiorina (1992) have argued that this regularity can be explained by the desire of a relatively small number of sophisticated moderate voters to rein in the party controlling the presidency.

Another case that meets the constitutional requirements of the model is Germany. Germany is a federal system, with both a national govern-

[9] National viability can also be important in determining voters' views of who is locally viable. See Johnston et al. (1992:197–211, 224–225) for evidence of this in the 1988 Canadian election. Yet another way in which lack of national viability may contribute to a party's fall is via a drying up of contributions. Here, the logic may well be more national than local: Favor-seeking contributors have no reason to contribute to locally hopeless candidates, as has been noted many times before; but neither do they have much reason to contribute to locally viable candidates from nationally unimportant parties. In order to get a return on their investment, the candidate must not only win a seat but also be able to do something with that seat once in parliament.

ment and (until 1990) eleven *Land* (or state) governments. The lower house (the *Bundestag*) is directly elected in national elections. The members of the upper house (the *Bundesrat*) are appointed by the *Land* governments, which themselves are elected in *Land* elections held between national elections. Although the system is multiparty, one may still suspect that German voters use the *Land* elections, which indirectly determine the composition of the *Bundesrat,* to counterbalance the senior party of government emerging from the previous *Bundestag* elections. Brady, Lohmann, and Rivers (1995) develop a model of this sort, taking into account the subtleties of German coalition politics, and use it to explain a regularity that is strikingly similar to the U.S. midterm loss phenomenon: The senior party of government in Germany consistently loses votes in the ensuing round of "midterm" *Land* elections.

Threshold insurance

Another species of strategic voting, aimed at preventing a prospective coalition partner from falling below a critical threshold of votes, is also possible under the German electoral system and was discussed briefly in Chapter 4. Recall that German voters have two votes, one which they cast for a candidate in a single-member district and one which they cast for a party list in their *Land.* The candidate votes determine the winners in 248 single-member districts, the list votes the distribution of 248 compensatory seats. The compensatory seats are in practice distributed at the national level using the d'Hondt method of proportional representation, but only parties that secure at least 5% of the national vote (or win at least three constituency seats) are eligible to receive any of these seats. Because the German party system from the 1960s to the 1980s featured two large parties (the Christian Democrats, or CDU/CSU, on the right; the SPD on the left) and one small party (the FDP in the center), the typical situation was for the FDP to be in alliance with one or the other of the large parties in government. The conjunction of the 5% threshold and the FDP's position as perennial junior partner in German governments raised the possibility of voters wishing to take out a "threshold insurance policy" when they voted.

For example, if the CDU/CSU and the FDP are in alliance, and polls show that the former will get 47% of the vote while the latter will get 4%, then the FDP will get no seats. Assuming that the SPD gets the remaining 49% of the votes, they will form the government. Were 1% of the CDU/CSU voters to give their list votes to the FDP, however, then a CDU/CSU government in partnership with the FDP would ensue. In case the logic of the situation might escape the voters, the FDP has in most elections since 1969 explained it quite directly in their electoral propaganda. Consider the following leaflet distributed when the FDP was in alliance with the CDU/CSU (from Roberts 1988:326):

CDU-CSU 47 + FDP 4 = 47	(and no CDU-CSU government!)
CDU-CSU 46 + FDP 5 = 51	(and a CDU-CSU&FDP coalition!)

This puts the point compactly and is an open appeal to threshold insurance voters.

Do German voters actually buy any of the threshold insurance that the FDP offers? The overall rate of split voting (a list vote for the FDP, a candidate vote for some other party's nominee) in a given election does depend on the FDP's strategy in a sensible fashion: The rate of FDP splits started to trend up in 1969; fell back in 1976 when the FDP decided to appeal for both candidate and list votes, rather than focus on the latter; then picked up again thereafter, when the FDP returned to and stuck with a list vote strategy (Roberts 1988). Moreover, it is mostly voters who give their constituency votes to candidates of the FDP's coalition partner that give their list votes to the FDP (e.g., Jesse 1988; Roberts 1988). This pattern is of course consistent with FDP supporters voting strategically in the constituencies, rather than CDU/CSU supporters voting strategically in the *Land.* But there is no reason to expect the aggregate level of split voting to follow the FDP's strategy of appealing for list votes, if split voting is produced solely by FDP supporters who wish not to waste their candidate votes.[10]

10.4 LINKAGE AND ENTRY

National entry markets. The existence of cross-district links between politicians can affect entry at the district level profoundly. Entry in a single district considered in isolation is essentially a Battle of the Sexes or Chicken game (which game it is depending on details of preference), whereas entry in a multiplicity of districts considered together tends to be a bargaining game, in which concessions in one district lead not to dispreferred equilibria (as in the single-district case) but to gains in another district.

Perhaps the most important point to note is that there are potential gains from trade that would go unaccrued were all parties purely local, but that can in principle be captured if parties are national in scope (or at least multidistrict). Consider the simplest case of a system in which all districts are single-member and in which the Left is divided into two kinds of person, type A and type B. Type A voters from one district have

[10]McCuen (1995) finds some coalitionally strategic action in laboratory experiments intended to capture electoral incentives similar to those facing German voters.

an easier time agreeing on policy options with type A voters from other districts than with type B voters from their own district. If entry proceeds as a series of isolated contests between the type A and type B forces, then a certain number of double entries may be expected in (the mixed-strategy) equilibrium. The result is that the Left as a whole loses a certain number of seats. If two national factions form, and bargain at the national level, then a series of reciprocal withdrawals may be negotiated. The Left as a whole gains seats. Those factions who must withdraw in a particular district can accept either payment in kind in another district or other compensations. Because bargaining proceeds at the national level, there may be a broader array of potential side payments to allocate to those who withdraw. The whole market for entry is simply more liquid when conducted at the national level, with the consequence that more gains from trade are accrued.[11]

In a sense, then, the expected loss of seats (were entry to proceed as a series of isolated events) can be taken as part of the collective incentive to form national parties. Even were these gains negligible in a particular situation, there would still be an incentive for national leaders to take over the market for entry as much as they could. Not only does it provide another coin in which they might trade – making the national market for political deals of all kinds more liquid – but of course it also gives them more power.

The importance of organization. It is important to note that the gains from trade that can potentially be accrued by linking districts together are more easily captured by more organized groups than by less organized groups. Thus, just as the politics of coordination within districts privileges more organized groups over less organized groups, so does the politics of vote- and withdrawal-trading across districts favor such groups.

Let me give an example of this from the work of Ray Christensen. Christensen (N.d.) studies electoral cooperation among the noncommunist opposition parties in Japan – the Democratic Socialist Party (DSP), the Japan Socialist Party (JSP), and the Clean Government Party (CGP)

[11]Linkage between politicians from different districts may also lead to higher barriers to entry at the local level. If entry is purely a local matter, then the primary advantage a nominating group has is the advantage of being obviously focal: Its candidates have won or done well before. If entry is a matter of national imprimaturs, then receipt of the label typically confers an advertising subsidy (the candidate benefiting from national publicity for the party), a credibility boost (candidates affiliated with national parties can secure policy benefits more effectively than can mavericks), and possibly a financial subsidy (from party or factional coffers). Knowledge of this package of subsidies ought to discourage entry.

– during the period 1958-1990. The intent of such cooperation from the point of view of the national parties was clear enough: If they could agree that each of them would not run candidates in certain districts, and could direct their supporters in those districts to support their alliance mate's candidate(s), then all of them might win more seats. As Christensen points out, however, there was a series of problems that might in principle be expected to arise, and did in practice. For example, local party leaders might not be willing to cooperate with a scheme in which they were the ones stuck with the role of supporter of another party's candidate; and local voters might not be very predictable, in which case the value of one party stepping down in another's favor might be hard to verify and subject to debate.

In solving these problems, the CGP was in a better position than either of the other parties because of its close association with *Soka Gakkai,* a large and well-organized lay organizational affiliate of a fundamentalist Buddhist sect in Japan. Because the party was launched as an outgrowth of *Soka Gakkai,* it had a very strong national party organization which was in a position to tell its local affiliates what to do. Thus, the CGP had more flexibility in where and when it withdrew its candidates. It was also more flexible and more credible when it promised to deliver some number of votes in a given district, as it had a good count on *Soka Gakkai* membership and those members could be relied on to take the party leadership's advice on whom to vote for.

The CGP took the lead in innovating better terms of trade for itself by insisting that vote trades across district lines be structured in ways that made the other parties' delivery of votes more observable and credible. For example, if a CGP candidate needed support in a district with many telephone union workers, then the CGP would throw their support behind a JSP candidate from that union in another district. Sometimes, the CGP would negotiate directly with the local union, rather than with the national party, and would ask for the names of the union members who had agreed to trade their votes and even visit their workplaces or homes to verify their support. Obviously, in making cross-district trades, the ability to "deliver the goods" could not be taken for granted, and social actors who could direct local candidates and voters effectively were at a substantial advantage. One can only imagine the range of cross-district deals that were not consummated, due to lack of an appropriate organizational base for the relevant interests.

10.5 CONCLUSION

This chapter has in a sense ended the discussion of Duverger's Law that began in Chapters 2 and 4. Duverger clearly recognized that both the wasted vote argument and the prudent withdrawal argument operated only at the district level. He thus acknowledged that the "true effect" of plurality elections was to promote local bipartism but argued that local bipartism would "project" into national bipartism when parties nationalized. Sartori later clarified and developed this argument but I have argued that the argument simply begs the real questions: Why do would-be legislators from different districts find it necessary or valuable to link together in national parties? *To what extent* will they do so?

If all candidates find it necessary to join a party that runs candidates in all districts, then local bipartism will indeed turn into national bipartism. But if the extent of linkage stops short of this extreme, then the system may have more than two parties that can field viable candidates in at least some districts. So whether Duverger's Law works at the system level depends crucially on the factors that drive linkage. These factors, however, are absent from the theoretical statement "plurality election rules at the district level tend to produce national bipartism." Thus, the systemic version of Duverger's Law is incomplete as a theoretical proposition, whatever its merits as an empirical generalization.

In attempting to complete the theoretical argument, I have focused on the role of executive (presidential or prime ministerial) ambition. Would-be executives have an incentive to orchestrate cross-district coalitions of would-be legislators that are big enough to place them in office, especially when executive and legislative elections are held concurrently. Thus the Duvergerian logic may reappear at the national level, if executive power is highly concentrated in one office and that office is awarded by something like plurality rule. On the other hand, if executive power is dispersed among several portfolios and those portfolios are awarded by a proportional method, then executive ambition may still push the process of linkage among legislative candidates but there is no reason to expect it to push all the way to national bipartism.

If one were to rewrite Duverger's Law in light of these objections, it would look something as follows: "If a system (1) elects legislators by plurality rule in single-member districts; (2) elects its chief executive by something like nationwide plurality rule; and (3) holds executive and legislative elections concurrently, then it will tend to (a) have at most two viable candidates in each legislative district, (b) have at most two viable candidates for executive office, and (c) have a national two-party or one-party-dominant system." More generally, the discussion in this chapter suggests that studies of national party systems need to take both district-level legislative and national-level executive electoral rules into account, a suggestion that is pursued in Chapter 11.

The creation of national parties that compete for control of executive office can also affect strategic voting calculations, if voters' attention is diverted from purely local considerations – e.g., which candidate (or list) in my constituency do I like better? – to more national considerations – e.g., which party has the best chance of forming a government? If voters care only about who forms the government and the legislative election procedure is highly proportional, then strategic voting will, if it arises at all, occur in favor of *nationally* competitive parties, rather than in favor of *locally* competitive parties. This suggests a quite different species of strategic voting (portfolio-maximizing rather than seat-maximizing) about which we know very little empirically or theoretically.

Linkage can also radically affect the politics of entry, by converting a series of independent single-constituency entry games into a nationally brokered multi-constituency entry game. The result can be not only a gain in "efficiency" for the politicians who establish the cross-district links but also an important centralization of power within parties, again often with would-be executives playing the main entrepreneurial role.

11

Electoral institutions, cleavage structures, and the number of parties[1]

There does not exist a sustainable scientific proposition of high informative content concerning the effects of electoral systems that can be derived in complete isolation from social and political relations. The social, ethnic or religious homogeneity or heterogeneity of a society are very important for the structure of the party system.

Nohlen 1993:27

Thus far in this book I have considered two levels at which political actors may face incentives to coordinate their actions. First, within individual legislative constituencies, voters or parties may need to coalesce in order to convert their votes into legislative seats more efficiently. Second, within the nation as a whole, would-be legislators and would-be executives may need to cooperate in order to convert their resources into executive office more efficiently. I have also stressed two broad influences on the outcome of the electoral coordination game, whether at the district or the national level: First, the nature of the electoral procedure pertinent to each level (the local electoral system by which legislators are elected, the national electoral procedure by which executives are elected); second, the nature of the social actors and cleavages involved at each level.

Chapter 10 suggested that coordination at both levels would be pertinent to explaining the number of parties at the national level: coordination at the district level by affecting the number of parties within each district, coordination at the national level by affecting the degree to which the local party systems cumulated into a national party system. Chapter 10 also reasserted a point at the national level that had previously been developed at the district level: The number of parties should

[1]This chapter is based directly on my work with Octavio Amorim Neto (Cox and Amorim Neto N.d.).

be an interactive function of social diversity and electoral permissiveness. In this chapter, I develop a cross-sectional model of the effective number of parties (at the national level) in 54 polities that addresses these points.

The main purpose of this model is to investigate whether the hypothesized interaction between social and electoral structure appears in practice. The structure of the investigation is similar to that in a recent pair of works (Powell 1982; Ordeshook and Shvetsova 1994) that have included both sociological and institutional variables in regression analyses of cross-national variations in the number of parties. I put particular emphasis on testing Ordeshook and Shvetsova's main finding, that there is a significant *interaction* between social heterogeneity and electoral structure. In order to put this claim to a stringent test, I employ a substantially different dataset, one that includes about twice as many countries as have previous studies, including a large number of third-world democracies.

A second purpose of the model is to follow up on the suggestion made in Chapter 10 that the number of national parties in a system will depend interactively on (1) the degree of integration of executive and legislative elections; and (2) the strength of the executive choice procedure. The importance of variables affecting the degree of integration – in particular, whether presidential and legislative elections are held concurrently – has been stressed in recent work by Shugart and others (see below). My approach follows this earlier work but specifies the key relationships differently. In particular, I do not model presidential election rules as having a direct impact on the legislative party system. Instead, there is a two-step process: (1) Presidential election rules combine interactively with social diversity to produce an effective number of presidential candidates; (2) the effective number of presidential candidates affects the effective number of legislative competitors, with the size of the impact depending on the proximity of the presidential and legislative elections.

A final purpose of the model is to assess the importance of another national-level variable suggested in Chapter 10: The existence of upper tiers. Here too my operational approach differs somewhat from that in the previous literature, in that I have separate variables that reflect the nature of the upper tier (if any) and the lower tier of the electoral system, rather than trying to combine these two considerations into a single measure, such as Taagepera and Shugart's "effective magnitude."

The outline of the chapter is as follows. Section 11.1 reviews the previous work of Powell and of Ordeshook and Shvetsova. Section 11.2 explains how my data and methods differ from, and complement, these previous efforts. Section 11.3 presents the empirical results. Section 11.4 concludes.

11.1 THE PREVIOUS LITERATURE

Studies of the effective number of elective or legislative parties rarely investigate the impact of both social cleavages and electoral laws on party system fractionalization. Among quantitative studies I am aware of only two that do. The first of these, Powell (1982), looks only at legislative fractionalization while the second, Ordeshook and Shvetsova (1994), looks at both elective and legislative fractionalization.[2]

Powell's work focuses on a set of 84 elections held in 27 mostly European countries during the period 1965-1976. The dependent variable, legislative fractionalization, is measured by Rae's index (that is, $1 - \Sigma s_i^2$, where s_i is the seat share of the ith party). The independent variables of primary interest are three measures of social heterogeneity:

- ethnic fractionalization as measured by Rae's index (that is, $1 - \sum g_i^2$, where g_i is the proportion of the population in ethnic group i);
- an index of agricultural minorities (coded 3, 2, or 1 if the agricultural population comprises 20–49%, 50–80%, or 5–19% of the total population); and
- an index of Catholic minorities (coded similarly to the agricultural index);

and two measures of electoral structure:

- the "strength" of the electoral system for legislative elections (coded 3 for single-member plurality elections, 2 for the Japanese, German, and Irish systems, and 1 for proportional systems); and
- a dummy variable indicating whether or not the system is presidential (1 if yes, 0 if no).[3]

Regressing the independent variables just listed on the legislative fractionalization scores for each election, Powell (p. 101) finds that "fractionalization is encouraged above all by ... nonmajoritarian electoral laws, but also by all of the heterogeneity measures, and discouraged by presidential executives."

Ordeshook and Shvetsova (1994) consider several different datasets: Lijphart's (1990) sample of 20 Western democracies from 1945-85 (representing 32 distinct electoral systems); an extension of this

[2]Other studies that share the same basic conception, but do not run regressions with explicit measures of both electoral and social structure, include Nagel (1994) and Coppedge (1995).

[3]Two control variables, population (in millions, as of 1965) and GNP per capita (as of 1965), are also included.

dataset covering elections in 23 Western democracies from 1945-90 (representing 52 distinct electoral systems); and a further extension that includes Continental elections in the period 1918-39. The dependent variables that Ordeshook and Shvetsova investigate are four: the effective number of elective parties (ENPV = $1/\sum v_i^2$, where v_i is party i's vote share); the effective number of legislative parties (ENPS = $1/\sum s_i^2$, where s_i is party i's seat share); the number of parties that receive at least 1% of the vote in two or more successive elections; and the number of parties that secure one or more seats in two or more successive elections. They measure social structure chiefly in terms of ethnicity, calculating the effective number of ethnic groups (ENETH = $1/\sum g_i^2$, where g_i is the proportion of the population in ethnic group i); and measure electoral system properties by the average district magnitude and by Taagepera and Shugart's "effective magnitude" measure. They then use OLS regression to explain variations in their dependent variables (here I shall look just at ENPV), considering three basic specifications: (1) the institutionalist specification: ENPV as a function solely of the log of district magnitude, as in Taagepera and Shugart (1989); (2) the sociological specification: ENPV as a function solely of ethnic heterogeneity; and (3) the interactive specification: ENPV as a function of the *product* of ethnic heterogeneity and district magnitude. They find that the interactive model does best in explaining the data, summarizing their findings as follows:

> ... if the effective number of ethnic groups is large, political systems become especially sensitive to district magnitude. But if ethnic fractionalization is low, then only especially large average district magnitudes result in any "wholesale" increase in formally organized parties. Finally, if district magnitude equals one, then the party system is relatively "impervious" to ethnic and linguistic heterogeneity ... (Ordeshook and Shvetsova 1994:122).

Thus, whereas Powell (1982:81) had success with an additive specification, Ordeshook and Shvetsova find an interactive model to be superior.

Why should an interactive model work well? The answer suggested in previous chapters runs as follows. A polity will have many parties only if it *both* has many cleavages *and* has a permissive enough electoral system to allow political entrepreneurs to base separate parties on these cleavages. Or, to turn the formulation around, a polity can have few parties either because it has no need for many (few cleavages) or poor opportunities to create many (a strong electoral system). If these claims are true, they would rule out models in which the number of parties depends only on the cleavage structure, or only on the electoral system, or only on an additive combination of these two considerations.[4]

Plausible though this formulation might be, it still leaves several questions unanswered. First, and most important, is the question of empirical evidence. Thus far we have one study in which an additive specification seems to work well (Powell) and one study in which an interactive specification proves superior (Ordeshook and Shvetsova). The latter study, moreover, is based largely on European evidence, and one might well ask what would happen if India (or other socially diverse third-world countries with strong electoral systems) were added. Since India appears to have lots of social cleavages and also to have lots of parties, would the addition of this (kind of) case to the analysis not bolster the importance of social heterogeneity and, perhaps, point more toward an additive rather than an interactive specification? Second, there is also the issue of what the form of the interaction between electoral and cleavage structure is. Perhaps the effective number of elective parties (ENPV) should equal the minimum of (1) the number of parties that the cleavage structure will support (loosely following Taagepera and Grofman [1985], we might say this number was $C + 1$, where C is the number of cleavages); and (2) the number of parties that the electoral system will support (following the "generalized Duverger's Law" of Taagepera and Shugart [1989], we might say this number was $2.5 + 1.25\log_{10}M$, where M is the district magnitude). That is, perhaps the equation should be something like $\text{ENPV} = \text{MIN}[2.5 + 1.25\log_{10}M, C + 1]$. Or, perhaps the form of the interaction is as Ordeshook and Shvetsova specify it, a simple product of factors reflecting electoral strength and number of cleavages. In Sections 11.2 and 11.3, I investigate both these questions, especially the first.

11.2 DATA AND METHODS

In considering the interaction between social heterogeneity and electoral permissiveness, my analytical strategy is to look at different data than did Ordeshook and Shvetsova (1994), using different operational measures of key variables. The notion is that, if their basic finding of a significant interaction is robust to these changes, then we can have more confidence in it. The most important differences between the present analysis and Ordeshook and Shvetsova's are as follows: I include a larg-

[4]An additive combination model, such as Powell's, allows the number of parties to be large either because there are many cleavages (regardless of how strong the electoral system is) or because the electoral system is very permissive (regardless of how few cleavages there are).

er number of countries, including many third-world democracies; I measure the strength of an electoral system by employing separate measures of lower-tier district magnitude and upper-tier characteristics, rather than combining these two factors (in an "effective magnitude") or ignoring upper tiers (by taking a simple average of the district magnitudes); and I include variables tapping the influence of presidential elections (if any) in the system. Let us consider each point in turn.[5]

Case selection: I have taken as a case every polity with an election in the 1980s (defined as 1980-1990 inclusive) that qualifies as "free" by Freedom House's score on political rights (either a 1 or a 2); if a polity has multiple such elections in the 1980s, I have taken the one closest to 1985.[6] These criteria of selection yield a substantially more diverse sample than that used by Ordeshook and Shvetsova (or Powell before them), one including India, Venezuela, Mauritius, and many other third-world countries (see Appendix C). The total number of countries included is 54. As there is only one observation per country, the sample can also be described as having observations on 54 electoral systems.

Measuring electoral structure. I differ from Ordeshook and Shvetsova and most of the previous literature in that I do not use average magnitude or Taagepera and Shugart's "effective magnitude" to indicate the strength of an electoral system. Instead, I use two variables, one to describe the magnitude of the lower-tier districts, one to describe the impact of the upper tier.

The lower-tier variable is based on the magnitude of the median legislator's district. An example may help to clarify why I use this variable rather than simply the average district magnitude. Suppose an electoral system has just two districts, one returning a single member and one returning 100 members. The average district magnitude in this system is (100+1)/2 = 50.5. But this process of averaging, in which each district counts equally, does not correspond to the usual way in which the effective number of parties is calculated. To see this, suppose that there are 100 voters in the 1-seat district, who split equally between two parties, while there are 10,000 voters in the 100-seat district, who split equally among ten parties. In this case, the effective number of parties in the 1-seat district, the 100-seat district, and the

[5]A copy of the full dataset, along with SAS code that reads and analyzes the data, can be found under the "publication-related datasets" heading of the Lijphart Elections Archive at http://dodgson.ucsd.edu/lij.

[6]The only exceptions to these rules are as follows. First, I have not included any of the Pacific Island states (e.g., Tuvalu) because I could not get complete data. Hungary (1990) is excluded for the same reason. Finally, I take the 1990 Brazilian election rather than the (unusual) 1986 election and the 1981 French election (held under the traditional runoff system) rather than the 1988 election (held under PR).

nation as a whole are respectively 2, 10, and almost 10. The national effective number of parties is much closer to the effective number of parties in the large district because the votes from both districts are simply added to arrive at the national vote totals, and there are 100 times more voters in the large district than in the small. The national effective number of parties, in other words, is a weighted average of the district figures, in which larger districts get more weight. Accordingly, it seems natural to use a similarly weighted measure of the central tendency in district magnitudes. I weight each district by the number of legislators from that district (which, if there is no malapportionment in the system, and turnout is equal across districts, will correspond to the weights used in calculating the national effective number of parties). I also use medians rather than means. In the example at hand, this yields a figure of 100: There are 101 legislators, of whom 100 are elected from a district of magnitude 100; the magnitude of the median legislator's district is thus 100. As it turns out, using the average of the legislators' district magnitudes, rather than the median, has virtually no impact on the results that follow. Finally, I follow Taagepera and Shugart (1989) and take the logarithm of the median legislator's district's magnitude, to produce a variable I call LML.

The upper tier variable that I use, denoted UPPER, equals the percentage of all assembly seats allocated in the upper tier(s) of the polity. It ranges from zero for polities without upper tiers to a maximum of 50% for Germany. The idea here is that instead of attempting to deduce how the existence of an upper tier affects the "effective magnitude" of a system, I simply let the upper tiers speak for themselves. Because all but one of the upper tiers in my sample are compensatory – designed specifically to increase the proportionality of the overall result – I can avoid some of the complexities of Taagepera and Shugart's "effective magnitude," which attempts to put the effects of compensatory and additional seats on a common metric (Taagepera and Shugart 1989, ch. 12).[7]

Presidentialism. Several previous studies, e.g., Powell (1982), Lijphart (1994), Jones (1994), Mainwaring and Shugart (1996), have included a code for presidential elections in investigations of legislative fractionalization. So do I. As my coding of this variable differs from these previous studies, however, I discuss it at some length.

The simplest way to code presidentialism is with a dummy variable (1 for presidential systems, 0 for parliamentary), as do Lijphart and Powell.

[7]The South Korean upper tier is designed to ensure that the largest party can secure a majority, or a near-majority, in the legislature, and thus in principle it *reduces* proportionality. The results do not change appreciably depending on how one codes South Korea. Nor do they change if South Korea is simply omitted from the analysis.

The problem with this approach is that there are different kinds of presidential elections (runoff, plurality), held at different times relative to the legislative elections (concurrently, non-concurrently), and these factors plausibly matter. Thus, other scholars, such as Shugart and Carey (1992), Jones (1994), Shugart (1995), and Mainwaring and Shugart (1996), have developed more elaborate schemes. My approach, which follows Shugart and Carey in general conception but differs in the details of implementation, takes the influence a presidential election exerts on a legislative election as depending on two factors: the proximity of the two elections; and the degree of fractionalization of the presidential election.

Proximity is a matter of degree. If the presidential and legislative elections are concurrent, then proximity is maximal. Here, I take the maximum value of proximity to be unity (so concurrent elections are "100% proximal," so to speak). At the other end of the scale are legislative elections held in complete isolation from presidential elections, i.e., in non-presidential systems.[8] Such legislative elections are not at all proximal to a presidential election, so they are coded as of zero proximity. In between these two extremes are presidential systems with nonconcurrent elections. If we denote the date of the legislative election by L_t, the date of the preceding presidential election by P_{t-1}, and the date of the succeeding presidential election by P_{t+1}, then the proximity value is

$$\text{PROXIMITY} = 2* \left| \frac{L_t - P_{t-1}}{P_{t+1} - P_{t-1}} - \frac{1}{2} \right|.$$

This formula expresses the time elapsed between the preceding presidential election and the legislative election ($L_t - P_{t-1}$), as a fraction of the presidential term ($P_{t+1} - P_{t-1}$). Subtracting 1/2 from this elapsed time fraction, and then taking the absolute value, shows how far away from the midterm the legislative election was held. The logic of the formula is as follows: The least proximal legislative elections are those held at midterm. This particular formula gives a proximity value of zero to these elections, which equates them with the totally isolated elections of non-presidential systems.[9] The most proximal nonconcurrent elections are

[8]In deciding whether a system is presidential or not, I have followed Shugart and Carey (1992, ch. 8). Ireland, for example, in which the president has neither legislative nor governmental powers, is coded as non-presidential. All systems in which the president has either legislative, or governmental, or both kinds of powers are coded as presidential.

[9]It is possible to include an additional parameter to test whether midterm elections are significantly more affected by presidential politics than elections occurring in non-presidential systems. I have done so and found that one cannot reject the hypothesis that midterm and nonpresidential elections are equally unaffected by presidential elections.

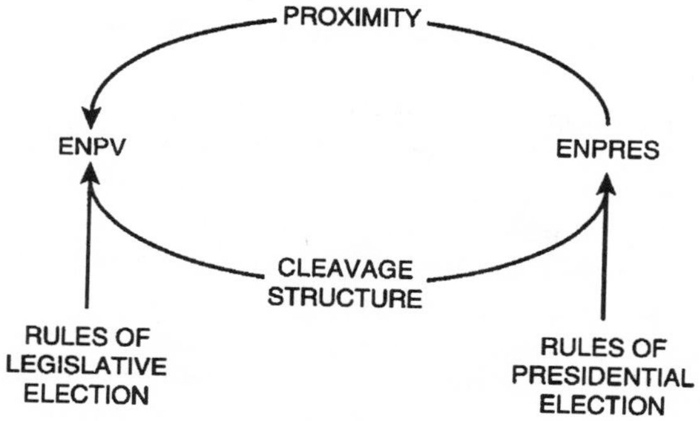

Figure 11.1. A schematic representation of the relationship between social cleavages, rules of election, and number of competitors in presidential and legislative elections

those held just before or just after a presidential election. The formula above gives them a proximity value that approaches one, the same value given to concurrent elections.[10]

The proximity of the presidential election to the legislative election is a necessary condition for the former to influence the latter. But the nature of that influence depends on the nature of the presidential election. One approach to coding the nature of the presidential election is institutional. Mainwaring and Shugart (1996), for example, introduce variables that distinguish three classes of presidential elections: concurrent plurality, majority runoff, and other. Although I report some results in a footnote that follow this route, my approach is different.

My point of departure is the notion that both presidential and legislative election results convey information about the impact of social cleavages and electoral laws. To put it another way, if one denotes the effective number of presidential candidates by ENPRES, and the effective number of elective parties in the legislative election by ENPV, then both ENPRES and ENPV may be thought of as dependent variables – products of social and electoral structure – along the lines of Figure 11.1.

There are three things to note about Figure 11.1. First, the picture assumes that the effect of the presidential election on the legislative elec-

[10]With the current dataset, it is difficult to test Shugart's (1995) hypothesis that there is a jump between nearly concurrent and exactly concurrent elections, with the depressive effect of presidential elections being much larger in the latter, since there are only five observations on concurrent elections. Some limited exploration – replacing the value "2" in the definition of PROXIMITY given in the text by "1.9" and other lower values – suggests that the main results of the paper do not depend on how one handles this issue.

tion dominates that of the legislative election on the presidential: Thus there is an arrow from ENPRES to ENPV but not one going in the reverse direction. In reality, there no doubt are reverse causal arrows of the kind omitted from Figure 11.1. But I believe that the direction of influence is primarily from executive to legislative elections, and making this assumption facilitates econometric estimation of the system of equations implied by Figure 11.1. In particular, one can first estimate an equation determining ENPRES and then estimate an equation, in which ENPRES appears as a regressor, determining ENPV (see below). (One can estimate a fully simultaneous pair of equations for ENPV and ENPRES but I do not believe that this is necessarily the best way to go econometrically and, in any event, the results do not change appreciably from those reported for the recursive model.[11])

The second thing to note is that the influence of presidential on legislative elections is mediated through the effective number of presidential candidates, ENPRES, and does not include a direct impact of presidential rules on legislative fractionalization, as does the Mainwaring and Shugart formulation. The justification for this runs as follows. Imagine a presidential election held under runoff rules that nonetheless – perhaps because the country is dominated by a single cleavage, perhaps for reasons idiosyncratic to the particular election – ends up as a two-way race. Given that there are just two candidates in the presidential race, I expect the same kind of influence as would be produced by a plurality race with two candidates. The nature of the coattail opportunities that face legislative candidates should be similar, the nature of the advertising economies of scale that might be exploited should be similar, and so forth. It is hard to see why the presidential rules themselves, having failed to produce the expected result in the presidential race, would nonethe-

[11]Estimating the equations using two-stage least squares rather than recursively substitutes a measurement error problem (because of the poor quality of the instruments that 2SLS produces in this case) for a simultaneity bias problem. It is true that asymptotically the measurement error problem goes away but in the present case I have only 51 observations, so it is not obvious that the tradeoff is favorable. The results, as noted in the text, do not change when two-stage least squares is used to estimate the main equation (in which the dependent variable is the effective number of elective parties). Probably this is so because there are only 16 presidential democracies in the sample of 51. This is hardly a standard simultaneous model in that the endogenous variables appear in interacted form, so that a substantial subset of the cases, those where PROXIMITY=0, are separably estimable. The results of the second equation, in which the effective number of presidential candidates is estimated, are changed substantially by using 2SLS. This is not too surprising, given that there are only 16 observations and one is adding two more variables to the specification. In any event, appealing to the asymptotic properties of the 2SLS estimator in this case seems even less justifiable, and so I prefer the OLS results.

less exert some direct influence on the legislative race. Thus, I prefer to include ENPRES as a regressor in the equation for ENPV, rather than including descriptors of presidential election rules (these rules, of course, do have an indirect impact via their influence on ENPRES). All told, my expectation is that legislative elections that are highly proximal to presidential elections should have a lower effective number of parties, but how much lower should depend on ENPRES. Thus I include both PROXIMITY and PROXIMITY*ENPRES in the analysis.[12]

A final point to note about Figure 11.1 is that it presupposes an interaction between electoral and social structure, both in the production of ENPV and in the production of ENPRES. If there is such an interaction in legislative elections, then there should also be an interaction in presidential elections, as argued in the last chapter.[13]

Specifying the equations. Having discussed the main differences of data and operationalization between my analysis and Ordeshook and Shvetsova's, I can turn to the issue of how I specify the relations of interest. I shall consider first the effective number of legislative parties (ENPS), then the effective number of elective parties (ENPV), and finally the effective number of presidential candidates (ENPRES).[14]

In investigating the first of these dependent variables (ENPS), I am interested in the purely mechanical features of how the legislative electoral system translates votes into seats. Accordingly, I include ENPV on the right-hand side (cf. Coppedge 1995). Indeed, the proper formulation is one in which ENPS would equal ENPV, were the electoral system perfectly proportional, with stronger electoral systems reducing ENPS below ENPV. Thus, I run the following regression:

$$\text{ENPS} = \alpha + \text{ENPV}^{*}(\beta_0 + \beta_1\text{LML} + \beta_2\text{UPPER}) + \varepsilon$$

If the electoral system employs single-member districts (so LML = 0) and has no upper tier (so UPPER = 0), then it is maximally strong, and only a fraction β_0 of ENPV is added to α to give the predicted effective number of

[12]My data on presidential structure are culled from Jones (1995), Mackie and Rose (1991), Nohlen (1993), and Santos (1990).

[13]In principle I would be happy to include the "effective number of prime ministerial candidates," if I could. In practice, I do not have the knowledge of each system that would be needed to code such a variable. Just taking the leader of each party as if he or she were an active candidate would not do; the whole point would be to see if there is widespread recognition that there are really only two (or three, four ...) viable contenders.

[14]My data on votes and seats (at the national level) were culled from Arms and Riley (1987), Brazil-Tribunal Superior Eleitoral (1990), Gorwin (1989), Mackie and Rose (1991), Nohlen (1993), Singh and Bose (1986), and Wightman (1990).

legislative parties in the system. As LML and UPPER increase, the system becomes more permissive and the fraction of ENPV that translates into seats should be greater. That is, the coefficients on ENPV*LML (i.e., β_1) and on ENPV*UPPER (i.e., β_2) should both be positive. One way to interpret this regression is simply as a check on the validity of the measures LML and UPPER. If LML properly measures the central tendency in lower-tier district magnitudes and UPPER really catches the impact of upper tiers, then the coefficients associated with both should be significant!

In the analysis of ENPV, I run five specifications: a pure institutionalist specification, with only variables pertaining to the legislative electoral system or the impact of presidential elections; a pure sociological model, with only a variable tapping into social heterogeneity (specifically, ENETH, the effective number of ethnic groups, used by Ordeshook and Shvetsova);[15] an additive model in which both sets of variables are included; an additive/interactive model in which an interaction term (between LML and ENETH) is added to the previous specification; and an interactive model in which the linear terms for LML and ENETH are omitted but the interaction term LML*ENETH is kept.

Finally, the analysis of ENPRES is as suggested in Figure 11.1. The main regressors are a dummy variable identifying runoff systems (RUNOFF), the effective number of ethnic groups (ENETH), and their interaction (RUNOFF*ENETH).

11.3 RESULTS

The main results are displayed in Tables 11.1, 11.2, and 11.3. Table 11.1 shows, not surprisingly, that a fair amount of the variance (93%) in ENPS can be explained by just ENPV and interactions between ENPV and two indicators of the strength of the electoral system – LML and UPPER. All variables have the expected sign and are statistically discernible from zero at about the .001 level or better. One way to explain the substantive impacts implied by the results in Table 11.1 is to compare two hypothetical systems, in neither of which there is an upper tier. System A has single-member districts, hence LML = 0. System B has ten-seat districts, hence LML = 2.3. Suppose that both systems have ENPV = 3 in a particular election. The stronger system (A) is predicted to reduce this number of elective parties by almost a full (effective) party, to

[15]I have also investigated the impact of the effective number of language groups and the effective number of religious groups, and various combinations of ethnic, religious, and linguistic heterogeneity, without finding significantly stronger results than those reported. My data on ethnic groups, language groups, and religious groups come from Olga Shvetsova (thank you!), the CIA *World Factbook* (1990, 1994), Vanhanen (1990), and the *Worldmark Encyclopedia of the Nations* (1984).

Table 11.1. *The determinants of the effective number of legislative parties in 54 democracies, circa 1985*

Dependent variable: ENPS *Independent variables*	*Estimated coefficients*	*Standard errors*
Constant	.582	.135
ENPV	.507	.048
ENPV*LML	.080	.012
ENPV*UPPER	.372	.111
Adjusted R^2 =	.921	
N of Obs =	54	

Table 11.2. *The determinants of the effective number of electoral parties in 51 democracies, circa 1985*

Dependent variable: ENPV

Independent variables	*Model* 1	2	3	4	5
Constant	2.44	2.76	1.61	2.45	2.40
	(.25)	(.66)	(.47)	(.55)	(.21)
LML	.48	—	.52	−.23	—
	(.11)		(.11)	(.31)	
UPPER	3.64	—	3.95	3.46	3.51
	(1.52)		(1.48)	(1.40)	(1.37)
PROXIMITY	−5.98	—	−5.95	−6.01	−6.04
	(.97)		(.94)	(.89)	(.88)
PROXIMITY * ENPRES	2.18	—	2.14	2.05	2.09
	(.29)		(.28)	(.26)	(.26)
ENETH	—	.49	.51	.01	—
		(.40)	(.25)	(.30)	
LML*ENETH	—	—	—	.53	.39
				(.21)	(.07)
Adjusted R^2 =	.613	.01	.639	.679	.686
N =	51	51	51	51	51

Table 11.3. The determinants of the effective number of presidential candidates in 16 democracies, circa 1985

Dependent variable: ENPRES		*Model*	
Independent variables	1	2	3
Constant	2.26	4.30	2.68
	(.87)	(1.23)	(.36)
RUNOFF	.63	-2.49	—
	(.61)	(1.56)	
ENETH	.37	-.98	—
	(.50)	(.77)	
RUNOFF*ENETH	—	2.01	.58
		(.94)	(.29)
Adjusted R^2 =	−.015	.202	.171
N =	16	16	16

Table 11.4. Predicting the number of parties in Japan, 1960–90

Dependent variable: N OF PARTIES$_{it}$ *Independent variables*	*Coefficient estimates (std err)*	*Coefficient estimates (std err)*
Constant	0.30 (.11)	1.02 (.29)
N OF PARTIES$_{i,t-1}$	0.55 (.02)	0.55 (.02)
MAGNITUDE$_{it}$	0.20 (.02)	0.01 (.07)
PURBE$_{it}$	.012 (.001)	0.15 (.41)
MAGNITUDE$_{it}$*PURBE$_{it}$	—	0.28 (.10)
ADJUSTED R^2	.60	.60
NUMBER OF OBS	1323	1323

Notes: N OF PARTIES$_{it}$ is the number of parties running candidates in district i, election t. MAGNITUDE$_{it}$ is the number of members elected from district i, election t. PURBE$_{it}$ is the percentage of all electors in district i, as of year t, who reside in urban areas. The estimation was performed using OLS and the unstandardized regression coefficients are reported in the table. Year dummies (as in Table 9.2) not reported. Results similar if EXCESS variable included.

Table 11.5. Predicting the effective number of parties in Japan, 1960–90

Dependent variable: $ENPV_{it}$ *Independent variables*	*Coefficient estimates (std err)*	*Coefficient estimates (std err)*
Constant	0.03 (.06)	0.41 (.17)
$ENPV_{i,t-1}$	0.76 (.02)	0.76 (.02)
DISTRICT $MAGNITUDE_{it}$	0.06 (.01)	-.04 (.04)
$PURBE_{it}$	.007 (.001)	0.15 (.24)
$MAGNITUDE_{it}$*$PURBE_{it}$	—	0.14 (.06)
ADJUSTED R^2	.80	.80
NUMBER OF OBS	1323	1323

Notes: $ENPV_{it}$ is the effective number of elective parties in district *i*, election *t*. The other variables are as defined in the notes to Table 11.4.

2.09 (shades of the United Kingdom in the 1980s!). The weaker system (B) is predicted to reduce the three effective parties competing in the election by much less, to 2.64 legislative parties. The substantive importance of this difference might vary from situation to situation, but it certainly suggests an important change from essentially a two-party legislative system with mostly single-party governments to a two-and-a-half or three-party legislative system with coalition governments as the norm.[16]

The results in Table 11.2 show the results for the five ENPV equations outlined in the Section 11.2. In running these regressions, I have omitted electoral systems with fused votes, that is, systems in which the voter casts a single vote for a slate that includes candidates for executive and legislative offices. The reason for omitting such systems is that they change the meaning of essentially all the institutional regressors. For example, do voters in such systems respond to the district magnitude at the legislative level or at the presidential level? Fused-vote systems really need to be analyzed separately (see Shugart [1985] for the case of Venezuela, which has a fused vote for senate and house races) but I do not attempt to do so here: I just omit the three cases of executive-leg-

[16]Because the translation of legislative votes into legislative seats is not affected by the existence (or not) of presidential elections in the system, nor by the number and character of social cleavages, these variables should not affect ENPS once ENPV is included. I have verified that they do not. I also note that a model that excludes the intercept term works slightly less well than the model with the intercept, in terms of the root mean squared error (.47 versus .40).

islative fused votes in the sample: Bolivia, Honduras, and Uruguay.[17] This reduces the number of observations to 51 for the regressions in Table 11.2. We shall discuss each briefly in turn.

The first model, with only institutional variables, explains about 61% of the variance in ENEP values. All coefficients are of the expected sign and significant at the .05 level or better. The second model, with only the effective number of ethnic groups (ENETH) as a regressor, produces a poor fit (an adjusted R^2 of .01) and an insignificant coefficient and regression. The third model, which combines the regressors from the first two, shows little change in the coefficients of the institutional variables but produces a coefficient on ENETH that is statistically significant at the .05 level. Apparently, proper controls for electoral structure are important in discerning any independent additive effect due to ethnic heterogeneity. The fourth model, which adds to the third an interaction term, LML*ENETH, reduces the coefficients on LML and ENETH to statistically insignificant values, while producing a substantial and statistically significant positive coefficient on the interaction term (LML*ENETH), together with little change in the coefficients of the remaining variables. Finally, the fifth model, in which the variables LML and ENETH are omitted, but their interaction is retained, produces a somewhat smaller interaction coefficient (but a substantially smaller interaction standard error), with other coefficients largely unchanged. If one chooses among specifications according to which produces the largest adjusted R^2 (not necessarily recommended; see the discussion in Kennedy [1994]), then the last specification, with an adjusted R^2 of .69, is the best.

I have also investigated a different formulation for the interactive term, using the minimum of LML and ENETH instead of their product. Substituting this minimum term for LML*ENETH in the last model produces little change in any of the other coefficients or in the overall fit of the equation. It is thus difficult on the basis of this study to say much one way or another about whether the form of the interaction should be thought of as a product or a minimum.[18]

[17]These cases did not need to be omitted in the first regressions because, once the votes are given, the translation to seats is via the legislative electoral system, so the variables LML and UPPER retain their meaning. Omitting these cases does not in any event change any of the previous results.

[18]Other variations in the model that I have explored include: introducing a dummy variable to identify the majoritarian systems in the sample (France and Australia) or, alternatively, coding them as $M = 2$ on the argument that they are similar to top-2 runoff systems; introducing a dummy variable to identify systems with primary elections (i.e., the United States); and introducing a population variable as another possible indicator of social diversity. None of these changes yields statistically significant results on the newly introduced variables and none of them changes the pattern of results described in the text.

Finally, Table 11.3 displays results for three regressions that take ENPRES as the dependent variable. The first model is additive, using RUNOFF and ENETH as regressors. As can be seen, neither regressor is statistically significant and the regression as a whole sports a negative adjusted R^2 (regressions with just RUNOFF and just ENETH are also insignificant). The second model adds the interaction term, RUNOFF*ENETH, to the first. The linear terms remain insignificant (albeit reversing sign) but the interaction term is appropriately signed and significant. The last model drops the linear terms, keeping only the interaction; the coefficient on the interaction term is again positive and statistically discernible from zero in a one-tailed test at the .05 level.

11.4 THE INTERACTION OF SOCIAL AND ELECTORAL STRUCTURE IN JAPAN

The evidence presented in the last section shows a substantial interaction between a national-level measure of electoral permissiveness (the magnitude of the median legislator's district) and a national-level measure of social diversity (the effective number of ethnic groups). Does this interaction work because the national-level variables reflect the typical situation in the districts, and the logic plays out at the district level (with especially large numbers of parties appearing within districts that combine high magnitudes with social diversity)? Does it work because the measure of electoral permissiveness in legislative elections covaries with the permissiveness of the executive choice procedure in each polity, and the logic plays out at the national level (with especially large numbers of executive candidates, hence especially low levels of cross-district legislative linkage, in countries that combine permissiveness in the executive choice procedure with social diversity)? Or is it some combination of effects at both levels that produces the result?

In this section, I address this issue by examining district-level evidence (on the number of parties, social diversity, and district magnitude) from Japan 1960–90. In Japan at this time, the big cities and countryside alike were carved up into a number of medium-magnitude districts (the range was from 1 to 6, with the vast bulk of districts between 3 and 5). Importantly for present purposes, there were districts of any given magnitude in both urban and rural areas. One can thus hope to tease out any interaction effects between social and electoral structure that there might be at the district level.

Operationally, I use two different measures of the number of parties: a simple count of the number of parties fielding candidates in each district; and the effective (or vote-weighted) number of candidates. The independent variables of primary interest are two. First, I use the district magnitude to assess the permissiveness of the local electoral system. Second, I use the percentage of each district's registered electorate that lives in urban places to measure social heterogeneity, assuming (in accord with conventional wisdom in the literature) that the more urban districts are also the more heterogeneous ones. I also include, as controls, dummy variables for each year (except the first) and the lagged dependent variable (to deal with autocorrelation). I use multiple regression to estimate the specified relationship, using data from elections occurring in the 1960–90 period.

The results displayed in Table 11.4 take the scalar number of parties as the dependent variable. As can be seen, one can explain about 60% of the variance with the percent urban, district magnitude, lagged dependent variable, and year effects (Model 1). Increasing district magnitude by one seat increases the number of parties by .2.[19] Increasing the urbanness of a district by ten percent increases the number of parties by .12. As both effects are statistically significant, there is some evidence here for the importance of both electoral and social structure.

Model 2 in Table 11.4 adds the interaction of district magnitude and urbanness. As can be seen, the additive terms are no longer statistically significant but the interactive term is, while the overall statistical "fit" of the model is unaffected. That is, it appears to be the *product* of social heterogeneity (proxied by the urbanness of the registered electorate) and electoral permissiveness (proxied by the district magnitude) that produces a large number of parties, not the *sum* of these factors.

Similar results are obtained when the effective number of elective parties (ENEP) is used as the dependent variable. Model 1 in Table 11.5 shows that a model with district magnitude and urbanness modeled as having additive effects explains about 80% of the variance in ENEP, with both additive effects statistically significant. Model 2 shows that, when one allows for an interactive effect, both additive terms fall to insignificance and only the interactive term is significant.

11.5 CONCLUSION

In this chapter I have developed an econometric model that predicts the effective number of parties at the national level based on variables drawn from both the district and the national levels, and from both institutional and sociological perspectives. The discussion in Part II of the book

[19]One might ask why district magnitude does not have a bigger impact. After all, would not the $M + 1$ rule suggest that increasing district magnitude by one should increase the number of parties by one, i.e., that the coefficient on district magnitude should equal one, instead of about a fifth as reported in Table 11.4? There are two answers to this. First, the $M + 1$ rule refers to *candidates,* not parties. Second, the rule only imposes an upper bound in any event, so there is no necessary prediction of growth with M.

suggested district magnitude as the key indicator of the nature of the district-level electoral system. The discussion in Chapter 7 suggested that the district-level number of parties would be an interactive function of social diversity and electoral permissiveness. Both of these district-level considerations are embodied in the model. At the national level, the key institutional variables outlined in Chapter 10 pertained to the executive choice procedure and the existence of upper tiers. And, again, I suggested that there should be an interaction between social and electoral structure in determining the effective number of executive candidates. Both of these national considerations are also embodied in the model.

The results presented in the previous sections are remarkably similar to those generated by Ordeshook and Shvetsova (1994). Despite using a different data set – one that included many new and developing democracies rather than concentrating on the long-term democracies – and despite several differences in operationalization and specification, the basic result holds up: The effective number of parties appears to depend on the product of social heterogeneity and electoral permissiveness, rather than being an additive function of these two factors.[20] The intuitive formulation of this finding is that a polity can tend toward bipartism either because it has a strong electoral system or because it has few cleavages. Multipartism arises as the joint product of many exploitable cleavages and a permissive electoral system.

If this general conclusion is valid, it ought to hold, not just for elections to the lower house of the national legislature, but also for other elections. And there is a bit of evidence consistent with the notion that the effective number of presidential candidates is an interactive product of social and electoral structure. In particular, elections that are *both* held under more permissive rules (runoff rather than plurality) *and* occur in more diverse societies (with a larger effective number of ethnic groups) are those that tend to have the largest fields of contestants for the presidency.

The model also further documents the impact of two national-level variables on the legislative party system: the existence and nature of upper tiers; and the existence, nature, and timing of presidential elections. Here, I model the effect of executive choice rules as being indirect, rather than direct, as in the previous literature.

A second model that I explore in this chapter concerns district-level data from Japan. My results provide additional support for the hypothesis of this chapter, that multipartism arises as a joint product of social diversity and electoral permissiveness.

[20]Or, to take account of the results with the minimum of LML and ENETH just mentioned, perhaps one should say that the effective number of parties depends on an interaction between electoral and social structure.

PART V

Coordination failures and democratic performance

12

Coordination failures and representation

Most of this book has focused on successful electoral coordination and the conditions that facilitate such successes in practice. Coordination failures have certainly been noted but thus far not much has been said about their consequences. In this part of the book, I investigate how coordination failures affect various aspects of democratic performance, including those that touch on the representativeness of government policy (this chapter), the maintenance of dominant parties (Chapter 13), and the politics of realignment (Chapter 14).

I center the discussion in the present chapter on the following question of electoral engineering: How will democratic performance be affected when the electoral system broadly conceived (including both the legislative and executive election procedures) becomes stronger?[1] This is a classic question in electoral studies to which there is a traditional (albeit contested) answer: Increasing the strength of the electoral system will decrease the representativeness of the polity's legislative and executive branches but will increase government stability. In the standard view, then, there is a grand trade-off entailed in any strengthening of the electoral system.[2] I shall focus on the representational side of this tradeoff, investigating how the quality of representation changes with the politics of electoral coordination.

The chapter proceeds as follows. First, I discuss some of the various kinds of representation that an electoral system might affect. Representation is often defined as having one's views voiced in the legislative decision-making process. Here I define representation as having

[1] Recall that electoral system A is said to be stronger than system B if the upper bound on the number of viable competitors that A imposes is lower than the upper bound that B imposes.

[2] Much of the best work on constitutional engineering addresses this trade-off, both positively and normatively. For example, the whole line of argument in three recent and very important books, Powell (1982); Lijphart (1984); and Shugart and Carey (1992), is to a substantial degree organized around the representation/stability trade-off.

one's views reflected in the final product of the legislative decision-making process, that is, in enacted policy. As will be seen, policies under this definition are more representative of electoral opinion when they are more centrist. Thus, the question becomes: What kinds of electoral systems, under what conditions, reliably produce centrist outcomes?

As a first step toward answering this question, I consider how election-seeking politicians will respond to the electoral incentives posed by stronger electoral systems, in terms of the policies that they advocate during election campaigns and pursue while in office. These results establish how candidates and lists will array themselves in equilibrium but do not say who will win the seats at stake, nor what final policy will look like.

Accordingly, I next discuss how strengthening an electoral system affects the representativeness of elected legislators, and hence government policy (Sections 12.3 and 12.4). The main point is that the impact of strengthening is different, depending on parties' success at coordination. If parties can consistently solve the coordination problems that stronger electoral systems pose, then these systems will consistently produce centrist results, and may outperform more permissive systems (depending on how one thinks the process of government formation will play out). On the other hand, if parties frequently fail to coordinate, then stronger electoral systems can yield fairly noncentrist results and are more likely to be outperformed by permissive systems.

12.1 REPRESENTATION

There are many different notions of representation in the literature (cf. Pateman 1970). I shall focus on just one: How well actually enacted policy represents the opinions of the national electorate. In order to clarify what is captured and what is lost with this particular definition of representation, it will help to start with a more traditional definition of policy representation.

Typically, policy representation is defined in terms of policy advocacy. If one thinks of each voter as having preferences among the available policy options that face the government, then one natural measure of how well represented a particular voter is would be the distance between that voter's most-preferred package of policies and the package *advocated* by the elected representative whose views are most consonant with that voter's.[3] Natural measures of the aggregate quality of representation

[3]If one does not require that the elected representative actually hail from the same constituency as the voter, then one is talking in terms of "virtual representation." If one instead confines the search for a good policy advocate to those representatives elected from the voter's constituency, then one is talking in terms of a more conventional representational relationship.

would be, for example, how far the most poorly represented voter is from the nearest elected representative, or how far voters are on average from their nearest elected representative. To put it another way, if representation is defined in terms of policy advocacy, then representation is better the more closely the distribution of opinion in the legislature reflects the distribution of opinion in the electorate.

The nature of the representational problem is quite different when one talks of enacted rather than advocated policy. Ultimately, the government must choose a single policy to pursue.[4] And voters who have their views advocated but never acted upon may not feel very well represented. From this perspective, the actual policy that the government pursues is an important aspect of representation.

What single policy is the most representative of a diversity of opinions in the electorate? Suppose one wants to minimize the distance between the most poorly represented voter and the government's policy. If the "distance" between a voter's ideal policy and the government's policy is defined as the percentage of the electorate with ideal points between these two points, then the minmax standard just suggested amounts to a demand that the government adopt the policy most preferred by the median voter.[5] Similarly, minimizing the average distance between voters' ideal points and the government's policy also requires choosing the median position, if distance is defined in terms of the percentage of voters between a given voter and government policy. Thus, whereas representation through advocated policy requires that the legislature be a mirror, representation through enacted policy requires that policy be centrist.

This way of looking at the issue of representation is potentially favorable to stronger electoral systems. The literature is unanimous in viewing SMSP as a poor method of producing elected representatives who reflect the full diversity of constituents' opinions. But if being more representative just means choosing a centrist policy, then perhaps strong electoral systems will look better than more permissive systems. In Section 12.2, I begin to investigate whether this is so.

[4]There is a semantic problem to avoid here. I use the term "government policy" to mean the set of actions taken by the government. Thus, even if different parts of the government are at odds and pursue what in one sense of the term might be considered different policies, the government as a whole still undertakes a certain set of actions – prudent or imprudent, coherent or incoherent – and that is "government policy" in the sense meant here.

[5]If policy distance is defined in terms of the metric used in the policy space itself, whatever that may be, then minimizing the average squared distance will correspond to choosing the average voter's position rather than the median voter's position. I shall not pursue that avenue here. See, e.g., Hinich (1977).

12.2 THE SPATIAL MODEL

One choice that candidates and parties face in electoral competition concerns the ideological stance with which they will associate themselves. The standard spatial model of Hotelling (1929) and Downs (1957) analyzes the position-taking choice that faces two candidates competing under plurality rule, when there is a single ideological dimension upon which the candidates must place themselves. The well-known conclusion of their work, enshrined in the median voter theorem, states that the optimal position to adopt, from the perspective of maximizing the probability of winning the seat, is that of the median voter.

In previous work (Cox 1987c, 1990a), I have generalized the Hotelling-Downs model to cover electoral competition under a wide range of electoral rules. The explanandum of the generalized model is the same as in the original: the position-taking incentives of election-seeking candidates (or lists).[6] But the electoral system, hence what election-seeking candidates (or lists) must do to get elected, is allowed to vary. The conclusions of the generalized analysis are, as in Hotelling's and Downs' work, statements about the equilibrium locations of the various contestants in the race (whether candidates or lists). Will all candidates/lists end up bunched together at or near the position of the median voter, compelled by strong centripetal incentives set in train by the electoral rules of the game? Or will the incentives produced by some electoral systems instead prompt candidates/lists to disperse across the ideological spectrum?

The nature of the incentives that candidates face depend on three broad considerations: what competitors' goals are; how competitors think voters will react to any given choice with which they are faced; and what the rules of election are. I shall assume here that candidates seek to maximize the probability that they will win a seat, that lists seek to maximize the expected number of seats that they win, and that the rules of election are either SNTV (including the $M = 1$, or SMSP, case) or closed-list PR (whether largest remainders or divisors), with no upper tiers. As far as voters are concerned, I shall initially assume that they vote sincerely (i.e., for whichever competitor is closest to their ideal point). This, as it turns out, is not crucial to the results sketched below, concerning the dispersion of candidates and lists in equilibrium. But whether one assumes that voters are sincere or strategic does affect the quality of representation, as will be seen.

Given that elections are held under single-tier SNTV or PR, the strength of the system is determined solely by the district magnitude, M. Accordingly, the key issue is how changing M affects the location patterns of candidates and lists. I present two conditions that location patterns must satisfy in equilibrium.

The first condition puts a lower bound on the range of competitors' locations, expressed in terms of the percentiles of the distribution of voter ideal points. I denote by $Q[z]$ the ideological position such that a proportion z of the voters' ideal points are to the left of $Q[z]$, with $1-z$ to the right. Thus 10% of the electorate has an ideal point to the left of $Q[.1]$, 20% have ideal points to the left of $Q[.2]$, and so forth. Denoting competitor i's location by x_i, for $i = 1, \ldots, K$; the furthest-left competitor's location by x_L; and the furthest-right competitor's location by x_R; one has:

Minimal range condition:

(a) If $K > M$ candidates compete for M seats under SNTV, each seeking to maximize the probability of winning a seat, then any equilibrium set of locations $x = (x_1, \ldots, x_K)$ must be such that $x_L \leq Q[1/(M + 1)]$ and $x_R \geq Q[M/(M + 1)]$.

(b) If K lists compete for M seats under PR, each seeking to maximize the number of seats it wins, then any equilibrium set of locations $x = (x_1, \ldots, x_K)$ must be such that either every list wins at least one seat or both $x_L \leq Q[1/(M + 1)]$ and $x_R \geq Q[M/(M + 1)]$.

The proof of part (a) is as follows. If $K > M$, then not all candidates' probabilities of victory can be unity. If $x_L > Q[1/(M + 1)]$ then any candidate whose probability of victory is less than 1 can move to $Q[1/(M + 1)]$ and win a seat with certainty. So x cannot be an equilibrium in this case (with a similar argument working in case $x_R < Q[M/(M + 1)]$).[7]

The proof of part (b) is similar. A stronger result holds for the case of PR if one allows entry. For then, if a set of locations x is such that every list wins at least one seat but $x_L > Q[1/(M + 1)]$, a new list could enter at $Q[1/(M + 1)]$ and guarantee itself a seat. Assuming that the certain prospect of a seat is sufficient to cover any costs of entry, a necessary condition for equilibrium would be $x_L \leq Q[1/(M + 1)]$ and $x_R \geq Q[M/(M + 1)]$.

For both SNTV and PR (with entry), then, the range of competitors' locations must extend from at or below $Q[1/(M + 1)]$ to at or above $Q[M/(M + 1)]$ and, hence, must cover at least $(M - 1/M + 1) \times 100\%$ of

[7]What if voters can coordinate? If they can coordinate only a little, then the result in the text may not hold: A candidate who moves to a niche with at least $1/(M + 1)$ of the voters in it may not be able to count on all these voters switching, if the voters themselves are unsure that the other voters will. Alternatively, if voters can coordinate a lot, then the result in the text still holds: Candidates can be confident that the voters in an "empty niche" will coordinate properly, were they to occupy the niche; thus, there will be no empty niches (of sufficient size to guarantee a seat).

the ideological spectrum. Thus, *the larger is the district magnitude, the larger is the lower bound on the range of competitors' locations.*[8]

A second necessary condition requires that there not be any large interior gaps in the distribution of candidates' or lists' positions. If competitors are labeled so that $x_1 \leq x_2 \leq \ldots \leq x_K$, then a gap exists between x_i and x_{i+1} whenever $x_i < x_{i+1}$. This gap is said to offer a niche of size λ if there exists a position between x_i and x_{i+1} such that a competitor adopting this position would win a vote share of λ.

Interior gaps condition:

(a) If $K > M$ candidates compete for M seats under SNTV, each seeking to maximize the probability of winning a seat, then any equilibrium set of locations $x = (x_1, \ldots, x_K)$ must be such that no gap exists that offers a niche of size $\lambda > 1/(M + 1)$.

(b) If K lists compete for M seats under PR, each seeking to maximize the number of seats it wins, then any equilibrium set of locations $x = (x_1, \ldots, x_K)$ must be such that either every list wins at least one seat or no gap exists that offers a niche of size $\lambda > 1/(M + 1)$.

Part (a) follows because not all candidates can be certain of winning seats ($K > M$) but any candidate can find a position in a gap of size $\lambda > 1/(M + 1)$ that guarantees a seat. Part (b) follows along similar lines and, as above, the conclusion can be strengthened if entry is allowed.

For both SNTV and PR (with entry), then, no gaps in the distribution of competitors' locations can exist that offer niches of size greater than $1/(M + 1)$, in equilibrium. Thus, *the larger the district magnitude, the smaller the gaps between competitors must be.*

The minimal range and interior gaps conditions show that representation measured in terms of the quality of policy advocacy improves as the district magnitude gets larger. Or, to put the point more precisely, if one analyzes the purely electoral incentives that face candidates and lists under SNTV and PR, one finds that as M increases these incentives induce candidates and lists to disperse more or less uniformly across the percentiles of the distribution of voters, hence improving the quality of policy advocacy. In Section 12.3, I consider how increasing (or decreasing) M might affect the policy ultimately chosen by the government.

[8] If candidates are vote or margin-of-victory maximizers, then multicandidate equilibria typically do not exist (cf. Cox 1990b:183; Osborne 1993). With seat-maximizing candidates, multiple equilibria often exist (I am generalizing from the results for the one-seat three-candidate case in Soskice and Bhaskar 1992).

12.3 COORDINATION, STRENGTH, AND REPRESENTATION

Does strengthening the local electoral system worsen global policy representation, in the sense of pushing enacted policy away from the global median? Or does it improve global policy representation, by nudging enacted policy closer to the global median? Theoretically, one might expect SMSP electoral systems to produce centrist results, if there are two parties, for then Downsian competition should push them toward the position of the median voter. On the other hand, PR electoral systems might also be expected to produce centrist results if more centrist parties have better bargaining positions than more extremist parties, hence are more likely to get into and have influence in government (see Huber and Powell 1994). Theoretically, then, which system performs better depends on how closely local elections approximate the conditions of the standard Downsian model, on the one hand, and on the process of government formation, on the other.

The first of these issues, how closely local elections approximate the conditions of the Downsian model, relates directly to issues of coordination. If coordination follows a Duvergerian logic, then in an SMSP system there will be two candidates in each district. Hence (from Downs) competition in each district will pull the candidates to the district median. Global policy will be centrist as well, since regardless of which party gets into government, it will be composed of centrists.[9] On the other hand, if local coordination fails, and there are three or more candidates in most constituencies, then the victor in each district can be far from the district median and a noncentrist result at the global level can result.

The United Kingdom in the 1980s is a good example of this last possibility. Due to the split in the center-left vote, Conservative candidates in many districts were able to win with about 40% of the vote. And, at the global level, Huber and Powell find that the British Conservatives were relatively far from the median respondent in national surveys. During the period of pre-Thatcherite consensus politics, in contrast, there were typically only two viable candidates in each district and the parties' policies were, according to conventional wisdom, both closer to the national median. Thus, the centrism of national policy in a strong electoral system is sensitive to how the politics of electoral coordination plays out in the districts.

To see this point in more detail consider how district-level outcomes are affected when voters are strategic rather than sincere, when candi-

[9]Technically, this conclusion holds only if constituencies are sufficiently alike. If there is a large set of leftist districts, and a large set of rightist districts, then one party may return a bunch of candidates who, although locally moderate, are nationally pretty far left, while the other party returns a bunch of local moderate/national conservatives.

dates anticipate rather than ignore strategic voting, and when parties are farsighted rather than myopic about getting into government. Each of these different kinds of strategic coordination leads, in various senses, to more centrist results.

Voters' strategy. How is the outcome of an election affected when voters are strategic rather than sincere? The general result of allowing voters to be strategic is to enhance the uniformity of the distribution of winners across the ideological spectrum, given any set of locations by candidates. When voters are sincere, it is possible for leftists to win no seats in an *M*-seat district, if they run far too many candidates/lists and split their vote more or less equally among them. When voters are strategic, in contrast, overcrowding is "solved" by strategic voting: Votes transfer away from the weaker candidates and lists to the stronger ones, until an efficient translation of votes into seats is achieved (in Duvergerian equilibria). Thus, no niche of opinion that is sufficiently large can fail to get representation due to overcrowding, when voters are strategic (and the more "optimistic" coordination equilibria are selected).

That the set of winners is more uniformly distributed when strategic voting is assumed to reach its Duvergerian equilibrium implies a limit on the dispersion of victors' positions. When voters are sincere, if overcrowding is more severe in the center than on the extremes, then candidates on the far left and/or far right may win. When voters are strategic, in contrast, overcrowding in the center is "solved" by an increase in strategic voting. Thus, a fair share of centrists win seats and fewer seats are won by the far left and far right candidates.

An example of this kind of effect can be given in the case of a single-member district with five candidates competing under plurality rule. Suppose that voters' ideal points are distributed uniformly on the [0,1] interval, that four of the candidates have adopted the position of the median voter, and that the fifth candidate has adopted the most extreme possible rightist position (*viz.*, 1). If voters are sincere, then the three-fourths of the electorate whose ideal points lie to the left of the point 3/4 will be indifferent among the four candidates at the median, and will distribute their votes among them randomly. Each of these four candidates will thus have an expected vote share of one-fourth of three-fourths, or 3/16. The one-fourth of the electorate with ideal points to the right of the position 3/4 prefer the extreme candidate (at 1) to the median candidates (at .5), and so the extremist will get a vote share of 1/4. This vote share being larger than 3/16, the extremist candidate will (almost certainly) win.

The outcome is very different if voters are presumed capable of thinking strategically and solving coordination problems. If the three-fourths of the electorate with ideal points to the left of 3/4 recognize that the extremist will win unless they concentrate their votes on one of the centrists, then they will seek to do so. If they succeed, then a centrist candidate will win, not the extremist. Thus, the relative centrism or extremism of victors' locations is sensitive to what one assumes about voters' abilities to coordinate.

This point echoes standard criticisms of the performance of plurality rule in the social choice literature and of single-winner electoral procedures in the traditional comparative literature. Part of Brams and Fishburn's (1983) argument in favor of approval voting, to take a social choice example, is precisely that ordinary plurality rule performs poorly in multicandidate contexts. Part of the dominant critique of presidentialism, to take a comparative example, is that single-winner elections can lead to the victory of either outsiders (e.g., Fujimori in Peru) or minority candidates (e.g., Allende in Chile), with disastrous consequences for democracy (cf. Linz and Valenzuela 1993).

In the example developed and the literature reviewed above the focus is on the strongest possible system: single-member plurality. But a similar point holds for more permissive systems: It is possible for quite extreme candidates, more extreme than should have a chance of victory under ordinary circumstances, to win under such systems, if the center is sufficiently overpopulated. But if one asks how overpopulated the center must be in order for a given percentage of the seats, say 100%, to go to the extremes, the answer is that the required degree of overpopulation is less under stronger systems. In other words, the outcome under stronger systems is more sensitive to the politics of electoral coordination, because the coordination problems posed by these systems are greater.

All told, then, the effect of strengthening depends crucially on how one thinks the politics of electoral coordination will play out. When voters are strategic and adept at coordinating, strengthening limits the degree of extremism possible. But when voters are sincere and poor at coordinating, strengthening increases the degree of extremism possible.

Candidates' strategy. Strategic entry as envisioned by Duverger will lead to the non-entry of candidates and lists that would have been weak and therefore targets of strategic voting. Allowing strategy in entry thus decreases the number of competitors, thereby decreasing dispersion.

This observation leads to the same conclusion about how electoral coordination conditions the impact of strengthening as drawn above. If potential candidates are assumed to be strategic and proficient at coordinating, then strengthening an electoral system will not lead to lots of coordination failures, with their attendant increase in the probability of extremist victors. But if potential candidates are assumed not to care solely about winning the current election, or to disagree about who it is that will bear the brunt of strategic voting, then more of them may enter than the electoral system can carry, putting the onus of coordination on the voters.

Parties' strategy. Political forces need to coordinate at the district level in order to convert votes efficiently into legislative seats. At the national level, political forces may need to coordinate in order to convert their seats efficiently into executive office(s). How does the latter necessity affect policy centrism?

Schofield (1993) develops a model in which parties take positions with an eye not just to the payoff in seats that they will get, but also to the payoff in portfolios. This latter payoff depends on parties' anticipations of the coalition formation process. Schofield adopts as an axiom the notion that parties are more likely to form coalitions with one another the more compatible are their policy platforms.[10] Using this assumption, Schofield shows that the politics of getting into government entails being more centrist than a seat-maximizer would be. The key to this result is that the legislative and executive choice procedures both come into play. Parties that might find a niche on the extreme left attractive from a purely seat-maximizing perspective look forward to the government formation stage and discover that they will be further from all the other parties than is the party immediately to their right, hence by assumption less likely than this party to make it into government. The best-positioned parties are those in the center, as they are closer to all the right-wing parties than are any of the left-wing parties, and vice versa. Thus, anticipation of the coalition formation process brings centrist incentives from that process to bear on parties' choices of spatial positions and produces a contraction in the field of competitors toward the median.[11]

12.4 THE IMPACT OF STRENGTHENING IN ELECTIONS WITH LONG-TERM COORDINATION

In this section, I shall reconsider the issue of policy centrism. The analysis holds everything constant from Section 12.3 except that voters and potential candidates are assumed to be interested not only in the current

[10]In particular, he assumes that the probability of two parties cooperating with one another in government is proportional to the inverse of the square of the policy distance separating them. But this particular functional form is not crucial for the qualitative result described in the text.

[11]Schofield's model is actually more general than suggested by the wording in the text, in that he does not impose unidimensionality. The centrism of the electoral result is judged by reference to a solution concept dubbed the "heart," a subset of the "uncovered set," which is centrally located in the distribution of voter ideal points.

election but also in future elections. The politics of coordination is assumed, in other words, to be a repeated game. In repeated coordination games, centrism is not the unanswerable card that it sometimes is in one-shot games. It may be trumped by intensity of preference or the perception thereof.

Most of the coordination games encountered previously in this book have been one-shot affairs. Intensity of preference in these models has determined who is most likely to desert a candidate or list perceived to have inferior chances of winning seats: Those who only slightly prefer these weaker candidates/lists are more likely to desert them than are those who strongly prefer them. But there is another way in which intensity of preference might affect the outcome in a one-shot game that has been ignored heretofore.

To see this, consider an example in which a divided left faces a unified right in a single-member district. The left can agree either on a candidate from the far left (FL), or a candidate from the moderate left (ML), or fail to agree (in which case both will put up candidates). Supposing that either FL or ML could win in a straight fight against the rightist candidate, which leftist will back down? In a one-shot strategic voting game, the answer given in previous chapters has essentially been that the group with the larger block of first-preference supporters in the district should be able to induce the other group's voters to strategically desert it (if both enter). If the moderate leftists are the larger group, then only ML will in fact enter, FL prudently withdrawing.

But what if it is common knowledge that moderate left voters only slightly prefer the moderate- to the far-left candidate, while far-left voters greatly prefer the far- to the moderate-left candidate (who is viewed as not much better than the right-wing candidate)? In this case, the far left could credibly threaten to enter regardless of what the moderate left did. If the moderates did not enter, then of course this would be the best outcome for the far left. If the moderates did enter, then the far left would suffer only a small loss by obstinately sticking to their plan and fielding a candidate: By sticking, they get the right-wing candidate; by blinking, they get the almost equally bad moderate. In contrast, the moderates would face a large incentive to back down. By entering, they get the right-wing candidate; by withdrawing they get the much better far-left candidate.

The reason that I have not highlighted this possibility earlier in the book is that it is hard for intensities of preference to become common knowledge. Precisely because intensity confers a bargaining advantage, it is not credible for either the far or the moderate left simply to assert that they have intense preferences. So it is hard to see how, in the context of a one-shot interaction, either agent could convince the other that they had the more intense preferences.

If electoral politics is viewed as a repeated coordination game, however, then the situation changes. Now both agents have available a costly action that can demonstrate their intensity of preference: They can refuse to withdraw their candidate and suffer through a legislative term in which the seat goes to the right-wing party. The side that truly has more intense preferences will be more willing to give a victory or two to the right-wing than the side with less intense preferences. Thus, the willingness to suffer coordination failure can credibly communicate intensity of preference in a repeat-game context. And the possibility of such communication can mean that smaller but more intense groups may get their way, whereas they would not in one-shot interactions.[12]

Suppose that the state of the world changes from time to time, in such a way as to change voters' preferences. After each such "preference shock" voters and politicians would be faced with a new repeated coordination game, in which intensity of preference would have to be signaled via coordination failures. From this perspective, one should expect repeated episodes of failure to coordinate, followed by equilibrium. In permissive systems, these cycles would not make much difference, in that coordination failures lead to relatively small seat penalties. In stronger systems, however, these coordination cycles might be rather more consequential, as periodic battles for the "heart and soul" of the Republican party, to take a recent example, erupt to the detriment of the party's short-term chances of success. This suggests that the realignment phenomenon much studied in the American literature ought to be a general feature of stronger systems, a notion that I pursue in Chapter 14.

12.5 CONCLUSION

If representation is defined in terms of whether each voter can find a legislator who advocates similar views, then larger district magnitudes obviously enhance representation. If representation is defined in terms of how close the government's policy is to each voter's ideal, then the case in favor of larger-magnitude districts is less immediate and depends crucially on how one thinks the politics of coordination will play out.

If Duvergerian results obtain everywhere, then a single-member simple plurality electoral system will (1) produce two-candidate competition in every district, hence strong centripetal incentives in each district

[12]A classic problem in democratic theory, posed most pointedly by Dahl (1956), concerns how to design democratic institutions that are sensitive to intensity of preference. Can one design a method of decision that will give intense minorities their way over apathetic majorities, without at the same time allowing apathetic minorities to get their way over intense majorities? It is interesting to note that bargaining in the context of a repeated coordination game meets Dahl's abstract requirements.

(Downs 1957); and (2) produce bipartism at the national level, with both major parties offering essentially the same centrist policies. Hence, regardless of which party wins the election, the government's policy will be centrist as well. In a Duvergerian world, then, the strongest electoral system (i.e., SMSP) would perform well were representation defined in terms of centrism.

If non-Duvergerian results crop up at various levels, however, then a strong electoral system can perform quite erratically. If the center fails to coordinate properly, relatively extreme candidates can win in the constituencies, and a party composed of such extremists can pull national policy fairly far from the national median.

More permissive systems are less sensitive to coordination failures in legislative elections. If coordination is poor, then (in a highly permissive system) a few seats are lost out of many, typically without seriously affecting the balance of power in the legislature. Thus, these systems are less variable in the way they translate votes into seats. Assuming that centrist parties are well-positioned in coalition bargaining, permissive systems should regularly produce governments that are fairly centrist, regardless of whether coordination failures occur at earlier stages or not.

Putting these two observations together, one sees that the comparison between strong and permissive systems depends on what one assumes about coordination. If coordination is more likely to fail at the electoral stage, then stronger systems will be more erratic. If coordination is more likely to fail at the government formation stage, then feebler systems will be more erratic.

13

Coordination failures and dominant parties

In this chapter I continue to investigate how coordination failures affect democratic performance, this time considering the role of such failures in sustaining dominant party systems. Dominant parties are those that are uninterruptedly in government, either alone or as the senior partners of a coalition, for a long period of time (say three to five decades). Such parties are problematic for democratic theory in at least two ways.

First, are systems that support dominant parties really democratic or not? If a party is always the sole or senior party of government, then a key feature of democracy – the possibility of peaceful alternation in power – is called into doubt. Is there something in the structure of the system (whether intentionally or unintentionally contrived) that gives the dominant party an unfair electoral advantage? Would the dominant party actually step down were the electorate to vote it out?

Second, even if one believes that a particular dominant party would step down if they ever lost an election, and also believes that the electoral system is basically fair, there is still the worry that a long tenure in power may corrupt. The Italian Christian Democrats and the Japanese Liberal Democrats are two signal examples in this regard. Both parties' long reigns ended recently in part through a series of devastating disclosures about how corrupt each had become. This returns one to the question of how they continued to be elected: Do some systems facilitate corrupt but nonetheless successful politics more than others?

In this chapter I argue that the answer is "yes." I begin with a brief review of relevant theories in comparative politics. One of these theories highlights failure to coordinate at the electoral stage as a key to explaining the existence of dominant parties in developed democracies, while two emphasize failure to coordinate at the government formation stage.

The succeeding three sections explore the Japanese dominant party system (1955-1993) at greater length. I argue that coordination failure did underpin the LDP's long rule but that (1) it was in large part a failure to coordinate at the electoral stage, rather than at the government formation stage; and (2) such failures by the opposition are probably inherent in the SNTV electoral procedure itself, rather than peculiar to the Japanese case. To put the point another way, the SNTV system seems well-calculated to support machine-style politics in government and divisions in the opposition. Section 13.5 provides some corroborating evidence from Taiwan, the only other democratic country in which SNTV is used at national elections and for which data are available.

13.1 COORDINATION FAILURES AND DOMINANT PARTIES

A survey of the literature reveals that coordination failure, either at the seat-winning or at the portfolio-winning stage, is thought by several scholars to play a key role in sustaining dominant party systems. Consider the following examples:

1. *Riker on India.* Twenty years ago, Riker (1976) sought to explain why India did not obey Duverger's Law, despite having an electoral system that has relied exclusively on single-member districts since 1953. His answer was essentially that the Congress Party, due to its central ideological location, was proof against coalitions of its opponents. These opponents, scattered to the right and left of Congress, would have had to create an ends-against-the-center coalition in most districts in order to unseat Congress MPs, followed by an ends-against-the-center coalition in the *Lok Sabha* to unseat Congress ministers. The difficulty of pulling off this kind of coordination kept Congress in power.[1]
2. *Sartori on polarized pluralism (Chile, Italy, Weimar, France IV).* At about the same time, Sartori (1976) elaborated a model of polarized pluralism part of which was essentially similar to Riker's model of India, although pitched at the national parliamentary rather than at the district level. Sartori emphasized that systems with large center parties facing numerous competitors to the left and right tended to perpetuate the center in government: The left and right could never agree on an alternative to the centrists, as each was further from the other than from the government. Thus, although these center parties did not necessarily govern alone, they did govern continuously, because their competitors could never coordinate on an alternative that excluded them.

[1]Soon after Riker published his article, the ends did manage to combine against the center under the added stimulus of martial law, throwing Congress out of office in 1977. Congress revived its fortunes soon thereafter, however.

3. *Laver and Schofield on Italy.* Laver and Schofield (1990:80) have a similar but more clearly articulated story about the dominance of Italy's Christian Democrats. They note (theoretically) that if parties care only about policy, and politics really are unidimensional, then the party that controls the median legislator will be in a dominant bargaining position and always end up in government. They claim (empirically) that the Christian Democrats have often been in something like this position in Italy.
4. *Pempel on dominant party systems.* Finally, a somewhat similar story is told by Pempel (1990). In explaining why the LDP of Japan, the Labour Party of Israel, and the Social Democrats of Sweden, none centrally located, have been able to dominate their respective systems, Pempel points among other things to the opposition's failure to coordinate. *Why* the opposition on the left in Japan, and on the right in Israel and Sweden, should have had difficulty in coordinating is not as clear as in the cases above, where policy incompatibilities separated the opposition. But failure to coordinate is again seen as important to explaining dominance.

The first three of the theories reviewed above assume, with varying degrees of clarity, that political competition is unidimensional and that parties care mostly about policy. Riker and Sartori further postulate the existence of a (large) center party. But in all three models the key is that the left and right cannot put together an ends-against-the-middle coalition, and this coalition failure, which the parties in the model can hardly escape, perpetuates the center party in power.

This model may capture elements of the situation in Italy, Chile, or India. But what of Japan, Israel, and Sweden? In Section 13.2, I consider the case of Japan in more detail, arguing that the LDP's dominance arose not because it had a dominant bargaining position in the government formation process (it typically formed single-party majority governments during its heyday) but rather because of the particular coordination problems posed by SNTV.

13.2 SNTV AND COORDINATION FAILURES[2]

Problems. Under SNTV, parties face two problems of coordination. First, they must decide how many candidates to run in each constituency. A large party in a four-seat district may need to decide whether it has enough support to elect three candidates or should instead stick with just two. A small party may need to decide whether to run a candidate at all

[2]This and the next two sections are based on Cox (N.d).

or instead withdraw in favor of another party's nominee. Decisions of both kinds can lead to coordination failure and consequent seat loss.[3]

A second problem that parties (or alliances of parties) face under SNTV is that of dividing their vote optimally among their nominees. This problem arises whenever a party or alliance runs more than one candidate in a given district. Because candidates are elected in order of the votes that they receive, and each voter casts a single vote, a party that nominates two candidates cannot be confident that both will be elected, even if it has enough followers. For, if all of the party's supporters vote for one of the party's two nominees, then that candidate will win handily while the other loses. In order for both candidates to win, the party's votes must be distributed more or less equally between its nominees.

Solutions. How can parties solve the two problems identified above? First, how can they assure that they nominate the correct number of candidates, avoiding both undernomination (fewer nominees than can win seats) and overnomination (more nominees than can win seats)? The brief answer is: by conducting regular negotiations on a national scale, in which withdrawals in one constituency are compensated either in kind (withdrawals in other constituencies) or in other coin. The LDP's factions have conducted such negotiations through the LDP's Electoral Strategy Committee since the party's inception in 1955 (Cox and Rosenbluth N.d.). The negotiations were probably helped by the availability of other resources – cabinet posts, positions in the Policy Affairs Research Council, and so forth – that could be traded as well. The noncommunist opposition parties have conducted less comprehensive but still regular negotiations over reciprocal withdrawals since 1972 (Christensen N.d.). As they do not have the other resources that the LDP factions have to trade, they are greatly concerned with verifying specific trades, for example: Will a withdrawal by party X from the race in *Shiga* transfer enough votes to party Y so that its candidate wins a seat? Can X guarantee delivery of the votes? Can Y reciprocate in kind in another district?

Once the problem of nomination is resolved, how can votes be equalized across a party's (or alliance's) nominees? Various solutions are theoretically possible (McCubbins and Rosenbluth 1995). If the party can dictate how its supporters vote, then this ability provides an obvious

[3]The LDP often found that its factions were unwilling to leave a particular district to their intraparty competitors, with the result that too many LDP candidates split the conservative vote too thinly, and the party as a whole won fewer seats than it would have, had a smaller number of candidates entered the fray. Similarly, the small parties making up the noncommunist opposition in Japan sometimes failed to coordinate their candidacies, splitting the opposition vote too thinly and giving the LDP more seats than it would otherwise have won. Cf. Cox and Niou (1994).

solution. Absent the ability simply to tell its voters how to vote, however, a party must seek a more decentralized solution.

One possibility here is to let candidates carve out different policy niches for themselves, advocating different versions of conservatism, for example. The problem with this strategy from the party's perspective is that open differences of opinion between its members will dilute the value of the party label, by making it harder for voters to figure out what the party stands for.

Another decentralized solution to the vote division problem is to let candidates provide particularistic services of various sorts to their constituents. For example, one might facilitate backbench members' efforts at pork-barreling. Alternatively, one might facilitate backbench members' efforts to provide machine-style welfare services and traditional gifts to their constituents.

The LDP followed both of these strategies in its heyday. It facilitated its members' pursuit of pork by creating the Policy Affairs Research Council, an elaborate committee system in which only LDP members participated and which afforded them a position from which to dole out and credibly claim credit for pork.[4] And it supported its members' generous provision of gifts and personal services to their constituents by ensuring that campaign finance laws did not get in the way of the important business of raising money.[5] Of course the two were intimately related: Pork benefited businesses that contributed to LDP members' coffers, thus enabling them to give gifts (and fueling a long series of scandals).

Resources. Having discussed possible solutions to the problems of nomination and vote division, the next question concerns the resources that are necessary to implement the solutions. Two key resources in this regard are access to pork-barrel projects and access to money. Pork and money help solve the problem of nomination by making the market in which national leaders trade withdrawals and endorsements more liquid. They help solve the problem of vote equalization because allowing general access to pork and money, then letting candidates compete in delivering pork and maintaining personal machines, tends to yield roughly equal vote shares (and more predictably equal shares than would competition based on policy differentiation).

Which parties will have access to distributive projects and to money? Generally speaking, governing parties should have better access to pork. And if they are willing to "sell" the pork to high bidders, then they

[4]MPs from the New Liberal Club were also given appointments in the Policy Affairs Research Council in the years just before the party was reabsorbed into the LDP.

[5]The laws predated the LDP but the party did not change them.

should have access to money as well. To the extent that government parties do control pork and money, they should solve the coordination problems posed by SNTV better, hence convert a given level of voting support into seats more efficiently.

Section 13.3 develops this "government advantage argument" by making some of its preconditions more explicit. In particular, one needs to recognize that there are resources other than those that flow from being in government that may help in solving coordination problems – a committed religious membership, for example – and that the difficulty of coordination tasks differs across electoral situations.

13.3 HOW SNTV ADVANTAGES GOVERNING PARTIES

The difficulty of the coordination problem that parties must solve under SNTV increases with the number of candidates they should run. More precisely, under SNTV it is harder for any given party, with a given technology of nomination and vote division, to (1) turn votes enough for n seats into n seats, than to (2) turn votes enough for $n - 1$ seats into $n - 1$ seats.

To unpack this statement a bit, note that it is very easy to turn votes enough for zero seats into zero seats. It does not matter what the party does. It is a bit harder to turn votes enough for one seat into one seat: The party must agree on a single nominee. It is harder still to turn votes enough for two seats into two seats: The party must avoid both undernomination and overnomination, and then allocate the party vote between its nominees equally enough so that they both win. Things get even harder to manage if three, four, or more seats are winnable.

The implication of the observations just made is that a party's **seat loss rate,** defined as the number of seats that a party falls short of the maximum it could have won, expressed as a proportion of the number of winnable seats, should increase with the number of winnable seats.[6] To express this more formally, I shall take a party's seat loss rate (SLR) in a particular district to be a function of (1) the maximum number of seats that the party could, with optimal performance, win in that district, denoted n;[7] (2) the flow of particularistic benefits that the party's

[6]More formally, the seat loss rate equals (MAXSEATS – SEATSWON)/MAXSEATS, where MAXSEATS is the maximum number of seats that the party could have won in the focal district and SEATSWON is the number of seats the party actually won.

[7]There are two ways to define the maximum number of seats that a party can win in a district (cf. Cox and Niou 1994). First, one might take the actual vote totals garnered by all candidates as fixed, and calculate how many seats a given party could have won had its candidates, and its candidates alone, been able to trade votes so as to maximize the party's seat total. Second, one might take the actual vote totals and allow all parties to optimize the allocation of votes among their candidates. The first

candidates running in the district enjoy, denoted b; and (3) other factors, denoted z. These other factors might reflect, for example, the innate organizational strength of the party. In terms of the notation just introduced the claim about SNTV made above can be restated as follows:

> (P0) Under SNTV, a party's seat loss rate is, *ceteris paribus,* an increasing function of n, the number of seats it could have won with optimal performance. More formally, if $n_1 < n_2$, then $SLR(n_1,b,z) < SLR(n_2,b,z)$.

In words, the greater difficulty of turning votes enough for n seats into n seats, as n increases, should mean that seat loss rates increase with the number of winnable seats.

Given assumption (P0), the major premises of a general argument about SNTV's effects can be stated as follows:

> (P1) Under SNTV, a party's seat loss rate is, *ceteris paribus,* a decreasing function of b, the flow of particularistic benefits to which the party's candidates have access. More formally, if $b_1 < b_2$, then $SLR(n,b_1,z) > SLR(n,b_2,z)$.

> (P2) Governing parties have superior access to particularistic benefits.

From (P0), (P1) and (P2), I conclude:

> (C) Under SNTV, governing parties typically have lower seat loss rates, difficulty of task (i.e., n) held constant, than do opposition parties.

The logic behind the conclusion runs as follows. Holding the difficulty of the task (i.e., n) constant, the seat loss rate is a function of b and z. Governing parties enjoy a systematically larger flow of particularistic benefits (b), by postulate (P2). Hence, if one takes z as random, with no systematic bias in favor of either government or opposition, the conclusion follows from (P1): Typically, governing parties will have lower seat loss rates, n held constant.

allow all parties to optimize the allocation of votes among their candidates. The first definition takes the view that parties should be able to exploit the errors of their opponents; the second that parties should assume optimal behavior by their adversaries. In what follows, I adopt the first definition of what the maximum number of winnable seats is. If one adopts the second definition, one finds that sometimes the conservative camp wins more than the "maximum number of winnable seats"!

13.4 EVIDENCE FROM JAPAN

Having clarified the logic of the government advantage argument, I can turn now to some evidence from Japan. I shall focus on the electoral efficiency of two broad camps in the Japanese party system: The conservative camp, composed of the LDP, LDP-affiliated independents, and the NLC; and the noncommunist opposition camp, composed of the JSP, DSP, and CGP. Similar analyses can be conducted of the electoral efficiency of more narrowly defined groups – just the LDP, for example – and they show similar results.

To assess the task-held-constant success of the conservative and noncommunist camps, Table 13.1 displays the average number of seats that each camp won when it faced each possible task (winning 0 seats, winning 1 seat, and so on).[8] As can be seen, the conservative camp did better than the noncommunist opposition at any given task. When both camps had votes enough for two seats, for example, the conservatives won on average 1.80 seats while the noncommunist opposition won only 1.60 seats. Had the noncommunist opposition performed as efficiently at each task as the conservatives did, they would have won 169 more seats over the 1958–1990 period than they actually did, or about 14 more per election.[9] Looked at from the other way around, had the conservatives performed as efficiently at each task as the noncommunist opposition did, they would have won 198 *fewer* seats over the 1958–90 period than they actually did, or about 16.5 fewer per election.

In order to assess the statistical significance of these figures, I ran a series of simple probit analyses, one for each column in Table 13.1 (that is, one for each task or number of winnable seats). First I created a dummy variable, SHORTFALL_{jct}, equal to 1 if camp c fell short of the maximum number of seats it could have won in district j at election t, equal to 0 otherwise. I then regressed this variable on a constant term and a dummy variable, CAMP_{jct}, equal to 1 when c was the conservative camp, and equal to 0 for the noncommunist opposition (I excluded the communist/other camp from the analysis). The results of these probit analyses (not shown) gibe with what one would think just looking at the averages in Table 13.1: When only one seat is winnable, there is not much difference between the camps in the efficiency with which they

[8]The raw data upon which this analysis is based are available in the Lijphart Elections Archive at http://dodgson.ucsd.edu/lij.

[9]The calculation, crude and first-order, is as follows. In 558 districts, the noncommunists could win at most one seat. Had they won the conservative average (of .97) rather than their actual average (of .94) this would have meant .03×558 = 16.74 more seats. Performing similar calculations for all tasks, one gets .03×558 + .2×555 + .13×291 + .1×35 = 169. There were 12 elections in the period 1958–90, so 169/12 yields about 14 more seats per election.

Table 13.1. Average seats won by conservatives and noncommunist opposition in Japan, 1958–90

	Maximum Number of Seats Winnable											
	0		1		2		3		4		5	
	Con	*Opp*	*Con*	*Opp*	*Con*	*Opp*	*Con*	*Opp*	*Con*	*Opp*	*Con*	*Opp*
Avg. seats won	—	0	.97	.94	1.80	1.60	2.51	2.38	3.19	3.09	3.84	—
N of observations	0	66	149	558	490	555	538	291	258	35	63	0
% of observations	0	4.4	9.9	37.1	32.6	36.9	35.8	19.3	17.1	2.3	4.2	0

Notes: This table aggregates data from all elections 1958–90. It is read as follows: The conservative camp, when faced with a situation in which the most they could have won was 1 seat (of which there were 149 cases, constituting 9.9% of all situations faced by the conservatives) won .97 seats on average.

win, but what difference there is favors the conservatives. The coefficient on CAMP is negative in this case, indicating that the conservatives were less likely to fall short of one seat than the noncommunist opposition, and the *t*-statistic on this coefficient was –1.46. When two or three seats were winnable, the conservative advantage was larger and attained statistical significance (*t*'s of –6.39 and –2.98). Finally, when four seats were winnable (something that happened for the noncommunist camp only 35 times), the conservative advantage was more modest and fell short of conventional levels of significance (t = -1.54).

All told, these results show that the conservative camp was *always* more efficient than the noncommunist opposition, task held constant, and sometimes significantly so.[10] This conclusion, moreover, holds not just for the entire 1958–90 period but also for the subperiods 1958–69 (during which the noncommunist opposition did not normally attempt to cooperate) and 1972–90 (during which they did).[11]

13.5 EVIDENCE FROM TAIWAN

Although the Japanese evidence is supportive, the conclusion (*C*) articulated above is by no means obviously established as a general proposition about SNTV as an electoral system. Perhaps the conservative camp had a natural advantage in electoral efficiency and the figures reflect this advantage rather than the one asserted to derive from governmental status. Or perhaps there is some other feature of the Japanese case that explains the observed patterns.

From the point of view of analysis, it would be nice if many (and diverse) nations held national elections under SNTV. One could then look at them all with similar methods and see what came of it. Unfortunately for analysis, only four other nations currently hold SNTV elections at the national level: Jordan, Malawi, Taiwan, and Vanuatu. In this section, I investigate the 1992 Legislative *Yuan* elections in Taiwan,

[10]Christensen and Johnson (N.d.) report that the *overall* conservative error rate exceeds the *overall* noncommunist error rate. This is correct and follows because the conservatives more often faced difficult tasks than did the noncommunists (see rows 2 and 3 of Table 13.1). Fully 37.1% of all districts were such that the noncommunists could have won at most one seat, which poses a relatively easy coordination task. In contrast, only 9.9% of all districts fell into the comparable category for the conservatives. On the other end of the scale, 17.1% of all districts were such that the conservatives could have won four seats, while only 2.3% of districts fell into this category for the noncommunists. Thus, the conservatives were more efficient at any given task but they were less efficient overall because they faced a harder mix of tasks as the largest party.

[11]The conservative camp's efficiency advantage was typically larger in the earlier period. See Cox (N.d.).

Table 13.2. Average seats won by KMT and DPP in Taiwan, 1992

	Maximum Number of Seats Winnable													
	1		2		3		4		5		6		7	
	KMT	*DPP*	*KMT*	*DPP*	*KMT*	*DPP*	*KMT*	*DPP*	*KMT*	*DPP*	*KMT*	*DPP*	*KMT*	*DPP*
Avg. seats won	1	.78	1.50	1.83	2.40	2.00	3.50	3.00	4.50	3.00	6.00	3.00	4.00	—
N of observations	7	9	4	6	5	3	4	1	2	1	2	1	1	0
% of observations	28.0	42.9	16.0	28.6	20.0	14.3	16.0	4.8	8.0	4.8	8.0	4.8	4.0	0

Notes: See the notes to Table 13.1 for instructions on how to read this table (which is read analogously).

the first truly general election (all seats being at stake) in which opposition parties could legally compete.[12]

Table 13.2 displays the average number of seats won by the Kuomintang (KMT) and Democratic Progressive Party (DPP), for each number of winnable seats. The data look similar to those from Japan: The KMT was more efficient in converting votes into seats than the DPP in all but one case (when two seats were winnable).

As to the statistical significance of the KMT's apparent task-held-constant advantage in efficiency, I can say the following. If one simply regresses the seat loss rate for a camp on a constant term, the maximum number of winnable seats for that camp, and a dummy variable identifying the KMT, one finds a negative coefficient on the dummy (indicating that the KMT seat loss rate was generally lower, i.e., that it was more efficient) with a t of -1.6 (almost significant at the .05 level in a one-tailed test). There is thus another smidgen of support in the Taiwanese data for the notion that SNTV inherently advantages governing parties.

13.6 CONCLUSION

The argument in this chapter has two parts. First, differences in the ability of political forces to coordinate often contribute to the maintenance of dominant-party systems. From this perspective, ordinary competitive party systems are those in which coordination tends to be symmetric while dominant-party systems are those in which coordination tends to be asymmetric.

Second, the SNTV electoral system seems particularly likely to produce asymmetric coordination, hence one-party dominance. SNTV creates difficult coordination problems that governing parties typically have the resources, access to pork and money, to solve. Opposition parties, on the other hand, must rely on their own innate organizational wherewithal. This is a recipe for a corrupt machine-style governing coalition facing a divided opposition.

For this argument to work it is not necessary to claim that SNTV would produce patron-client relations in a society otherwise devoid of them, or to deny that preexisting social norms may be an important element determining the success of machine-style politics. It may even be that politicians yearning to build personal political machines influenced the creation (doubtful in Japan on my reading of Ramseyer and Rosenbluth 1995) or maintenance (plausible) of the electoral system

[12] I thank Emerson Niou for providing the data upon which the analysis to follow is based.

itself. As long as the electoral system has some independent impact once in place, as I think it clearly does, the argument goes through.

The more general argument that this chapter suggests is that the more difficult the coordination problems that an electoral system presents, the more factors other than citizens' preferences matter in determining who wins seats. It may be possible to interpret a pure PR system as a more or less neutral method of translating votes into seats but under SNTV the translation is heavily influenced by the ability to coordinate. I have stressed here that governing parties have this ability due to their access to pork and money. I might just as well have focused on the Clean Government Party's ability to "dictate" how its fundamentalist Buddhist followers vote. Social groups that are already highly cohesive should do better under any electoral system but their relative advantage over unorganized interests should be even greater under SNTV and other systems that pose difficult coordination problems.

14

Coordination failures and realignments

Since V.O. Key's seminal work in the 1950s, the study of critical realignments has formed an important part of American political studies.[1] Definitions of what critical realignments are vary from author to author but certain features recur in the literature: First, there are "short-lived but very intense disruptions of traditional patterns of voting behavior" in which "large blocks of the active electorate ... shift their partisan allegiance"; second, there are disruptions of "the party nominating and platform-writing machinery," leading to "transformations in the internal loci of power in the major party most heavily affected by the pressures of realignment"; and third, there are "transformations in large clusters of policy" (Burnham 1970:6, 7, 9). Critical realignments thus feature abrupt changes in voting, nominating, and policy-making strategy on the part of elites and voters.

The most dramatic examples of realignment entail the disintegration of a major party. When the Whig party fell apart in the 1850s and was rapidly replaced by the Republican party, large numbers of voters and politicians switched their allegiance, with profound consequences for the nation's politics. When the Liberal party in the United Kingdom fell apart in the 1920s and was rapidly replaced by Labour, again large numbers of voters and politicians switched their allegiance, and again the consequences for the nation's politics were profound.

The abruptness of the change in voter and elite strategies in these cases, and the patterned nature of the changes – with virtually all former Whigs going either into the new Republican or the reconstituted Democratic party, for example – indicates the element of coordination in realignment politics. As soon as a sufficient mass of erstwhile Whigs have announced their intention to form a new party, the rest are presented with a choice of joining the new party or joining the evolving

[1]See Key (1955). For an introduction to the subsequent literature, see e.g. Burnham (1970), Brady (1988), and the cites therein.

Democrats. Any attempt to continue the Whig party is doomed, in the short run at least, to failure; it is little better than launching a third party.

Viewing realignments as outcomes of electoral coordination games may provide a theoretical framework within which to analyze these phenomenona, a framework that has repeatedly been proclaimed absent in the literature itself. In this chapter, I do not have the space to develop all the implications that might follow from such a view. Instead, I shall focus on just one, relatively neglected, aspect of the realignment phenomenon: failure.

Battles for the heart and soul of a party, and even a party system, may occur at any time. But the agents of change in these battles need not always be successful. Realignments can fail.

This point might seem obvious but it is not one that is stressed in the traditional literature on realignment, which focuses almost exclusively on successful realignments. Nor would it necessarily follow if one thought of realignments as simply "big" changes of policy. There is nothing in the standard multidimensional spatial model, for example, that suggests that changing policy is particularly difficult, costly, or prone to failure. Indeed, changes of policy are usually taken to entail no transactions costs at all, and the central problem that spatial theory highlights is not that attempts to change policy might fail but that they might succeed, leading to instability (cf. McKelvey 1976; Schofield 1978).

In this chapter I assume that realignment projects are costly not just in the sense that they must be researched, negotiated, and publicized, but also in the sense that they entail costs if they fail. I focus on how alterations in the costs of failure affect the timing and size of realignments (Section 14.1). I then provide an extended discussion of one particular failed coordination project, David Lloyd George's attempt to reinvent British politics in the period from 1910 to 1930 (Section 14.2). The discussion has two main themes: First, Lloyd George seemed thoroughly to understand the logic of the coordination problem that faced him; second, although he had arguably identified a profitable realignment of British politics and was supremely well-positioned to publicize the main elements of his scheme, he failed: Coordination is not easy.

In the third section, I consider how the costs of Lloyd George's failure ramified into the constituencies. This relates to one of the key points raised in the first section, that the costs of coordination failure are greater in strong than in weak electoral systems. Section 14.4 concludes.

14.1 REALIGNMENT AND THE COSTS OF FAILURE

Realignment projects require that a large number of politicians and voters change their behavior in a coordinated fashion. Take as an example the project of constructing a new major party in an SMSP system in which party A currently holds a majority and runs the government. If only a few politicians and voters bolt from A, then they do not bring down the government and are just another third party, too small to do any damage. If a somewhat larger group bolts from A, they may be able to throw the next election to the other major party, B. The pain of electoral defeat may convince A to accommodate their policy interests, but that is not clear and the immediate impact of dissent is simply to benefit B. If an even larger group bolts from A, A may fall apart, making the new party viable on its own. It may even be able to win the next election and immediately implement the new policies that it desires. Thus, potential dissidents do reasonably well by not bolting at all, do better if they bolt *en masse* and succeed in convincing the rest of the party to adapt to their action, but do poorly if they fall somewhere in-between, launching a dissent that is large enough to hurt but not large enough to succeed. In realignment projects, as in coordination games in general, half measures yield poor payoffs.

The higher are the anticipated costs of coordination failures, the harder it should be to realign a system, because the high costs of failure mean that prospective changers must be more certain that enough others will also be changing, before they are willing to take the plunge themselves.[2] One should thus expect realignments to be less frequent in high-cost systems. High perceived costs of realignment also ensure that any realignments that do come will be more consequential. This is merely as a consequence of selection bias: Political agents will be willing to risk the high costs of coordination only for realignments that really bring large changes. So the realignments in a system with high costs of coordination failure will be "bigger" than the realignments in a system with lower costs of failure.

When will the costs of coordination failure be high? Suppose that one accepts the following premise: (P) Other things equal, the stronger an electoral system is, the higher are the costs of coordination failure under that system. The idea here is that failures under strong electoral systems entail, quite regularly, a significant loss of legislative seats, while failures under more proportional electoral systems do not. If the Left party or coalition splits in two (at the national level) in an SMSP system, then the split ramifies through all the constituencies and redounds considerably to the benefit of the Right (think of the Labour-SDP/Liberal split in the United Kingdom). If the Left splits in a high-magnitude PR system, then each part may end up winning just as many seats as it had formerly. The

[2] A Hobbesian view of *regime* change takes the costs of coordination failure (a visit to the state of nature) to be quite high; and so the recommendation is to stick with the current order rather than risk transiting to another. Cf. Hardin (1991).

split may incur a cost in lost portfolios, but these costs can arise just as much under SMSP systems.

Thus, elites who seek to realign politics in a strong electoral system must get voters into the act from the beginning. If they do not, if voters vote sincerely rather than strategically after elites make their moves, then seats will be lost, at least in the short term. In contrast, elites acting under proportional electoral rules can contemplate the prospect of sincere voting with relative equanimity. Their seats are not at stake.[3]

If one accepts the premise (P), then one should expect realignments in stronger electoral systems to be *less frequent* and *more consequential.* These conclusions fit with the stylized picture of realignment presented in the U.S. case (and reviewed in the introduction to this chapter): Voter allegiances change abruptly simply because voters have to be brought into any realignment in a strong electoral system; elite competition for control of nominations increases abruptly because of the importance of focalness in strong systems and the scarcity of viable labels; finally, "transformations in large clusters of policy" occur because realignments can typically be pushed through successfully in stronger systems only when the payoffs are large enough.

Whether the approach sketched here can shed light on the nature of realignment battles in other systems, so that a truly comparative study of realignment politics is possible, I do not know. Nor do I propose to pursue that project here. My present aim is much more modest: to investigate a particular case of failed coordination in a strong electoral system, with an eye to assessing the plausibility of the theoretical account given above. Did the elites pushing the coordination project see it as a coordination problem or act as if they did? Did the failure of the project entail significant loss of seats in the constituencies? Sections 14.2 and 14.3 take up these questions in the context of the fall of the Liberals in the United Kingdom.

14.2 LLOYD GEORGE AND THE COLLAPSE OF THE LIBERALS IN THE 1920S

David Lloyd George was a British politician of the first importance in the opening decades of the twentieth century. As Chancellor of the Exchequer (1908–1915), he presided over budgets that played an impor-

[3]More precisely, they are not at risk of losing their seats *due to strategic voting.* Elites who break off from a pre-existing party may of course find that it is difficult to overcome habitual voting patterns. That is, voters who truly prefer the dissidents and would vote for them were they fully informed, may not realize who has bolted the party, and thus continue supporting the old label. This threat to realignment projects exists under any electoral system, however.

tant role both in introducing the welfare state to Britain and in provoking a watershed constitutional crisis with the House of Lords (culminating in two successive general elections in 1910 and the Parliament Act of 1911). As prime minister (1916–1922) he vigorously prosecuted the war, in the process splitting his own party (the Liberals) and facilitating its replacement by Labour as the second major party in Britain. It is the latter role that I shall emphasize here.[4]

There is of course a vast literature focusing on the dramatic fall of the Liberal Party in Britain. How could a party that had won three consecutive general elections, been in sole possession of power from 1906 to 1915, and then held the prime ministership from 1915 to 1922, become a minor party by the early 1930s? There are answers aplenty, from those that emphasize the pressures that war put on the Liberal coalition (Wilson 1966), to those that emphasize the importance of the fourth Reform Act's expansion of the electorate (Matthew, McKibbin, and Kay 1976), to those that emphasize the lessening importance of the religious cleavage in British politics (Wald 1983). Here I consider Lloyd George's role, casting him as would-be heresthetician (Riker 1986) or focal arbiter (Schelling 1960).

Both these terms, heresthetician and focal arbiter, were coined as a way of dramatizing the possibility of manipulating the choice of equilibrium in coordination games. Focal arbiters are those that have a privileged communication position. They can, merely by publicizing the availability and popularity of a given alternative, make it the focal alternative upon which to coordinate, without actually changing anyone's preferences, only their perceptions of what is viable. Herestheticians "set up the situation in such a way that other people will want to join them – or will feel forced by circumstances to join them – even without any persuasion at all" (Riker 1986:ix).

Lloyd George's primary heresthetical project was to realign British politics along a socialist/antisocialist axis, especially if this could be done by creating a Centre Party of which he would be the chief. This was not his only idea for realignment (he flirted briefly with Labour as well) but it was a project he pursued intermittently from 1910 to 1923, a period spanning almost all his years in the front ranks of politics. His heresthetical maneuvers, consisting largely of attempts to manipulate his colleague's perceptions of the future viability of the Liberal party, form an important part of the story of the Liberals' decline.[5]

[4]I cannot claim any originality in the narrative that follows. Most of it is based on Wilson (1966), Cook (1984), and Searle (1992).

[5]I do not claim that Lloyd George's maneuvers were in some unproblematic sense the cause of the Liberal Party's demise: As will be seen, part of the argument is that he sought realignment on his own terms because he believed that realignment on some terms was inevitable.

Let me begin by discussing why Lloyd George might have anticipated a realignment of the old order. The answer, I believe, lies in his perceptions of the rise of socialism and Labour. By 1909 it was his view that "a split between Liberalism and Labour" had "destroyed Liberalism in Germany and elsewhere" (quoted in McLean 1987; Murray 1980:207). Assuming that Lloyd George was familiar with recent Australian political history, he would have known that politics there had realigned decisively away from a free-trade/protectionist axis and toward a socialist/antisocialist axis. This realignment, moreover, had occurred rapidly after independence in 1901, culminating in 1909 with the final dismemberment of the Protectionist Party and the subsequent formation of the Liberal Party (which was really an anti-Labour vehicle, rather than a proponent of classical liberalism).

In the United Kingdom, there were two approaches that the Liberals might have taken toward Labour. One approach, that they had been following since the 1880s, was to prevent Labour's rise by proactive advocacy of policies favorable to the working class (such as Asquith's Old Age Pension scheme in 1908) and by electoral cooperation with Labour against the Conservatives. Proactive advocacy stole some of Labour's thunder. Electoral cooperation deprived them of experience as an independent electoral force.

The traditional Liberal approach to managing the working class vote did not prevent the formation of the Labour Representation Committee in 1900, nor the election of Labour (as opposed to Lib-Lab) MPs in 1906. If one entertained the thought that Labour would eventually grow so strong that politics in the United Kingdom would realign in reaction, as it had in Australia, then the option of "managing" the labor movement by judicious concessions, while maintaining essentially liberal principles, might have begun to appear thoroughly chimerical. There were certainly some objective indicators of Labour's rise with which Lloyd George was probably familiar; and many of his actions are consistent with the notion that he sought to respond proactively to Labour's rise.

Consider first the objective indicators, of which Lloyd George (and others) may be presumed to have been aware. First, the number of trade unionists roughly doubled between 1914 and 1919. As very few opted out of the political levy that was part of their dues, this greatly enriched the Labour party, which was flush with funds by 1918 (Searle 1992:137). Second, a natural part of the Labour voting coalition, the Irish working class, had voted Liberal as long as the Liberals were the best hope for Irish Home Rule. After the onset of war pushed Home Rule off the political agenda, moderate Irish leaders were rapidly superseded by Sinn Fein and the independence movement. By the Easter Rebellion of 1916, it might have been clear that the Irish vote in England was no longer tied firmly to the Liberal Party, and was therefore free to gravitate to Labour. In any event, "in many industrial constituencies after 1918 Labour successes owed much to the capture of the Irish vote" (Howard 1983:68). Third, by 1917 the wartime coalition government had agreed on a further expansion of the electorate, in time for an election in 1918. Matthew, McKibbin, and Kay (1976) have shown, using contemporary statistics, that a substantial portion of the working class stood to gain the vote in 1918. Although the political importance of this has been contested (see McKibbin 1990:66), what else could a politician at the time have thought, other than that it would help Labour?[6]

Consider next the sequence of attempts by Lloyd George to form a Conservative-Liberal coalition of one kind or another. As early as 1910, we find him publicly declaring that the old issues of politics were dead and secretly urging a grand coalition upon Balfour, the Conservative leader. The coalition's immediate purpose was to dispose of the troublesome Irish but it would also have left Labour out in the cold.[7]

With the onset of the war, one finds Lloyd George seeking an end to Herbert Asquith's Liberal government (of which he was a part) in favor of a coalition (cf. Wilson 1966:52-53). The Liberal government did fall in May 1915, when Bonar Law (the Conservative leader) presented Asquith with a choice between coalition and a frontal Conservative assault on the Liberal government. Bonar Law not only delivered his ultimatum with Lloyd George at his side but (according to Churchill) the latter threatened to resign if Asquith did not accept the proposal of coalition.

The coalition thus formed was not what Lloyd George had proposed in 1910, as it included Labour. And of course it was still headed by

[6]In addition to the growing strength of Labour, one might also point to the growing strains within the Liberal party. The gist of Wilson's (1966) argument is that the war necessitated policies, such as conscription and trade sanctions against Germany, that were anathema to voluntarist, free-trade liberals. The inevitable consequence was a division of opinion within the party, with some willing to sacrifice liberal principles to the efficient prosecution of the war, while others were not. It was not inevitable that this division of opinion should have turned into an organized split (as it did), but certainly the materials for such a split were at hand for the politician ready to use them.

[7]After the first of the two general elections held in 1910, the Irish Nationalists held the balance of power in the House of Commons. The price that they exacted from the Liberals in return for their support of the "People's Budget" was that Home Rule for Ireland be put on the political agenda again and that the way for its passage be cleared by removing the House of Lords' ability to veto legislation (a proposal that some Liberals favored, many others preferring merely a change in the Lords' composition). In the summer of 1910 the Liberals convened a constitutional conference (to which the Irish were not invited) and considered various proposals that would have entailed backing out of their deal with the Irish. In the course of the conference, Lloyd George secretly approached Balfour to propose a coalition. See Searle (1992:88–89).

Asquith, Lloyd George's senior in the Liberal party. His actions thereafter seem calculated to remedy both of these problems.

Take the issue of the leadership first. Wilson (1966:66) notes that "from early in its existence it was widely believed that Lloyd George intended to break up the government and seize the premiership himself." By December 1916 he had succeeded in this suspected intent and emerged as prime minister, supplanting Asquith.

Eight months later came Lloyd George's "foolish expulsion of Henderson [the key Labour Minister] in the so-called 'doormat incident'" (Searle 1992:126). Although this incident has been seen as rather abrupt and pointless, it did lead to Labour's eventual withdrawal from the coalition. Thus, Lloyd George had created by 1918 a version of the coalition he had proposed in 1910, with Asquithian Liberals, Labour, and the Irish in opposition.

Nor did Lloyd George stop at merely establishing the appropriate governing coalition. Although Asquith did not actively oppose the new coalition, apparently seeking to prevent an open split in the party, Lloyd George nonetheless proceeded to appoint his own whips in the Commons, to set up his own electoral headquarters in London, and to seek control of one of the major Liberal newspapers as his official mouthpiece (Wilson 1966:106, 112, 113). By mid-July 1918 the notion of an electoral alliance between the Coalition Liberals and their Conservative allies was canvassed in a memorandum to Lloyd George from his chief whip, and this initiative in due course resulted in the (in)famous Coupon Election of December 1918. Letters of endorsement, known as coupons, were sent out over the signature of Lloyd George and Bonar Law to selected Liberals and Conservatives. The result was a crushing defeat for the Asquithian Liberals and (to a lesser extent) Labour, and an overwhelming victory for the coalition candidates.

When the new parliament met, in February 1919, the Asquithian Liberals and the Coalition Liberals, after a brief and unsuccessful attempt at reconciliation (in which Lloyd George played no role), set up separate parliamentary groups. This parliamentary break ramified into the constituencies when Lloyd George sought to turn his electoral alliance into a new Centre Party. Evidence of his intent came first in by-elections, where he continued to oppose Asquithians in favor of Conservative and Coalition Liberal candidates. As Wilson (1966:193) describes it:

> Such conduct could have only one objective: a final severance from the Liberal party and the 'fusion' of Coalition Liberals with Conservatives. Churchill gave warning of what was afoot when on 16 July 1919 he publicly advocated the formation of a Centre party, arguing that 'no deep division of principle' now separated the two wings of the coalition. He was recognised as speaking for Lloyd

George as well as himself, for he had spent the previous week-end with the prime minister, and in his speech he made the first public reference to Lloyd George's Centre party scheme of 1910, which he would scarcely have done without the Premier's consent. Shortly after, Lloyd George began sounding his Liberal colleagues on the subject of 'forming a new progressive party' ('Liberalism,' he warned them, 'has no future'). And in the months between December 1919 and March 1920 he set about launching his new party.

His first move was a speech at Manchester on 6 December 1919. It ... consisted largely of a fierce attack on Labour and condemnation of 'socialism' ...

Lloyd George's next step was to get the consent of the two wings of the coalition to fusion. The Conservatives looked easy, for their leaders had signified their agreement, and the rank and file had given no warning of hostility. But the Coalition Liberals were plainly more difficult .... He spent a good deal of January and February 1920 urging the scheme on Liberal members of the government ....

Lloyd George's strategy in convincing his colleagues was a canny one, full of heresthetical appeal, and calculated to leave his followers no better choice than to do what he wished them to. Here I shall discuss his attempt to manage perceptions of the political situation both in the large and in the small.

Lloyd George had a clear two-pronged strategy in manipulating perceptions of the lay of the political land. The first component of the strategy was to activate the socialism/antisocialism cleavage. He pursued this strategy not only in the Manchester speech cited above but as early as his final election address in 1918, in which he likened the Labour leaders to the Bolsheviks. The second, and complementary, component of his global strategy was to proclaim the death of Liberalism. This was something he had articulated as early as January of 1918, and many times thereafter (Wilson 1966:149). The joint effect of these pronouncements was clearly to underline that the most important choice lay between socialism and antisocialism and that the Liberal party was not viable as an antisocialist vehicle. Such pronouncements, moreover, had a self-fulfilling character to them in that, if his audience believed his analysis of the drift of events, then they really were left with only one viable political strategy: Antisocialist Liberals, even if they really cared more about the old issues that separated them from the Conservatives, should follow Lloyd George into a permanent alliance with the Conservatives. The alternative was to be left irrelevant and impotent.

At a smaller level of detail, Lloyd George pursued a similar coordination strategy. It was his intent to meet on March 18th with the Liberal rank and file and push for a decision to fuse with the Conservatives. Before that meeting, however, he wished to secure the support of those holding ministerial appointments, and then lead these gentlemen into the meeting. This of course would be a classic ploy in coordinating expectations among the backbenchers. The appearance would be that most if not all of the Coalition Liberals were planning to go along with Lloyd George, which appearance would, if believed, increase the number who would find it in their interests to go along.

Despite his carefully laid plans, however, Lloyd George was not able to convince his ministerialists to join the Conservatives, and thus was not able to lead a unified body into the March 18th meeting with his backbenchers. The reason seems to be that he was ahead of his time, and could not convince his colleagues of his two global premises – that Labour's advance was inevitable, that Liberalism was dead. In any event, the result was that he backed off pushing for fusion at the meeting on March 18th, lacking his solid phalanx of ministerialists. Thanks to a leak to the *Times,* there was a fairly complete account of his failure.

Lloyd George never again came so close to achieving the kind of coalition after which he strove. But he did not give up. Instead his proposals became increasingly contingent on electoral reform. Here too he seems to have missed his chance.

In 1918, when Lloyd George was still prime minister, a Speaker's Conference had unanimously recommended that Britain switch to some version of proportional representation (PR). While not actively hostile to the proposal, Lloyd George gave it little time in the government's agenda and certainly did not push it, with the consequence that the proposal died. His inaction at this time makes sense when one remembers that he was at that time actively pursuing fusion with the Conservatives which, if successful, would have left it in his best interest to preserve the plurality system.

After fusion with the Conservatives had failed, however, Lloyd George increasingly discovered the charms of electoral reform. One incident that illustrates this progression occurred during the Cabinet crisis of March 1922, shortly before Lloyd George's fall from the Premiership. Sir Alfred Mond, one of Lloyd George's closest associates, had a report prepared on PR on his own initiative.

> News of this report leaked out early to the press, which used it to support rumours of the formulation of a new centre party – a union of a body of Liberals with the non-die-hard Conservatives; electoral reform, it was suggested, was a prerequisite to such a party's success. The idea was explored on 1 and 3 March in the *Daily Chronicle,* at the time reputed to be a semi-official mouthpiece of Mr. Lloyd George. But the flurry came to nothing (Butler 1953:42).

Soon thereafter, Lloyd George's coalition with the Conservatives fell apart, prompting an election in late 1922. Afterwards, Lloyd George found himself both out of office and leading a much-reduced band of Coalition Liberals. It was only at this point that reconciliation with the Asquithian branch of the party seems to have become attractive. But even after such a reconciliation had been patched together in 1923, one still finds Lloyd George pursuing coalition with the Conservatives in November of that year (Cook 1984:92). He did not become a full-fledged advocate of PR until 1924, by which time he must finally have given up hopes of achieving his Centre Party ideal.

The narrative account just given cannot do justice to the twists and turns of Lloyd George's policy and no doubt paints a clearer picture than was visible at the time. Nonetheless, the outlines of the picture are pretty clear.

Did Lloyd George seek a realignment? He floated the idea of a coalition with the Conservatives as early as 1910. Wilson (1966) opines that he was after fusion from the early years of the war, and in any event it was clearly a full-time preoccupation in 1919–20, and intermittently thereafter.

Did he have reasons to seek a realignment? The growth of trade unionism, the situation in Ireland, and the expansion of the electorate all suggested an Australian outcome.

Was his strategy for securing a favorable realignment heresthetical? Every element of his strategy was thoroughly top-down, as if he perceived the situation as a vast coordination game in which larger players could present smaller players with *faits accomplis,* leaving them no better strategy than to join new forces. Thus, he attempted to lead his ministers into fusion first, with their aid to lead the backbenchers, and to let things in the constituencies sort themselves out later. In addition, his strategy at the elite level was not so much persuasion as coordination. He sought to manipulate his colleagues' perceptions of the objective forces at work in the polity, arguing that the real choice they faced was between joining Labour and joining the Conservatives, rather than to persuade them on given policy issues one way or the other (although deemphasizing policy differences with the Conservatives was a part of his strategy).

14.3 NATIONAL COORDINATION AND THE CONSTITUENCIES

The possibility of realignment can arise in any polity. In strong electoral systems, however, realignments must involve coordination both at the national level, in choosing governments, and at the district level, in choosing legislators. In this section, I continue the discussion of Lloyd

George's realignment project by considering how its failure affected events in the constituencies.

Lloyd George's strategy was not entirely a matter of high politics, even if as shown above it was thoroughly top-down. He took the trouble, for example, to amass a very sizable and notorious fund, largely by selling honors while prime minister (Searle 1992), and this of course was quite useful in financing candidates and organization in the constituencies. In this section, I shall not concentrate on his direct attempts to influence the constituencies. Instead, I consider how his strategy of pursuing alliance with the Conservatives, especially as it played out in the Coupon Election of 1918, affected the ability of Labour to establish its viability (and thereby to impugn the Liberals' viability) in the constituencies.

The argument is fairly simple. In 1918 there were entirely new constituencies and a greatly expanded electorate going to the polls for the first time. This produced a substantial amount of uncertainty. Although Labour had been only a minor electoral force before the war, one could be less sure that it was obviously out of the running in the new world of 1918 than one might have been in the old world of 1910 (the date of the last election with the old districts and electorate). The situation was thus favorable for a previously small party to make a move.

In addition to the increased uncertainty of the first postwar election, Labour also disposed of greatly increased funds, thanks to the growth of union membership and the political levy. Labour accordingly was able to increase the number of constituencies it contested sevenfold, fielding 361 candidates all told (versus 56 in 1910). This was an important contributor to the more than tripling of Labour's national vote share, from 6.4% in 1910 to 20.8% in 1918.

In this context, Lloyd George's strategy of bestowing a coupon upon some Liberals and not others produced a substantial and essentially permanent contraction in the number of districts in which Liberal candidates appeared viable, and a substantial and essentially permanent increase in the number of districts in which Labour appeared viable. The broad outlines of this change in the London boroughs can be seen in Figure 14.1, which graphs the percentage of London districts in which the Liberals (respectively, Labour) finished either first or second.

Before the war, the percentage of all districts in which the Liberals fielded viable candidates (those finishing first or second) was about 90%. In the election of 1910 in London, the figure was 93%. In contrast, Labour prior to the war was a minor force restricted to a handful of districts. In London, a relatively favorable area, Labour was viable in only 7 districts (12%) in 1910, and in 3 of these there were Lib-Lab (jointly endorsed) candidates.

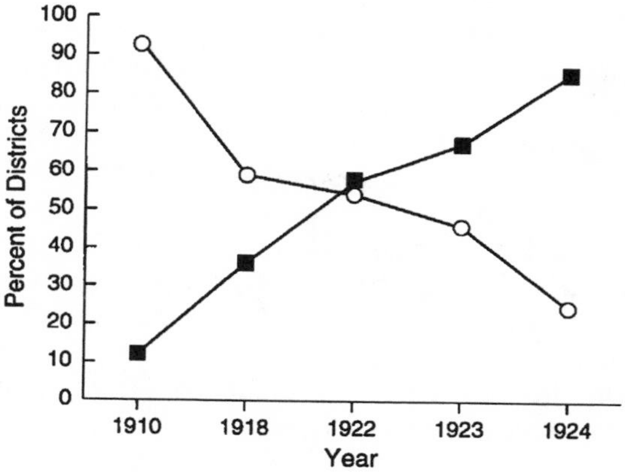

Figure 14.1. The battle of London

The situation in 1918 was starkly different. The Coalition Liberals refrained from running candidates in all but 159 districts, in return for the Conservatives' withdrawal in those districts. But the Asquithian Liberals did not have the funds to contest all of the districts left without a Coalition Liberal. Thus, a substantial number of districts had either no Liberal at all or only a weak one. In London, the Liberals fielded viable candidates in only 36 districts, 59% of the total. This represented a drop of fully 34 percentage points from their 1910 figure of 93%. Meanwhile, Labour fielded viable candidates in 22 districts (36%), of whom none were Lib-Labs. They thus tripled the percentage of districts in which they might be perceived as viable.

As Figure 14.1 shows, the Liberal fall and the Labour rise continued after 1918. By 1924, an election at which the Liberals had great difficulty funding candidates, the Liberals and Labour have essentially switched places in terms of the percentage of London districts in which each is viable.

These figures suggest the importance of getting off to a good early start. Another way to suggest the point is to look at how the subsequent electoral history of each London district relates to the result in 1918. The Liberals won 15 London districts in 1918; in one of these (6.7%) their subsequent fate was disastrous: They never again did better than third place. The comparable percentages in districts in which the Liberals finished second, finished below second, and failed to field any candidate were, respectively, 43.8%, 53.9%, and 76.5%.

Presumably, these figures line up in the way they do in part because Lloyd George chose to withdraw from districts in which he thought the

Liberals were weak in any event, and to insist on a coupon for one of his followers in districts in which he thought the Liberals were strong. But such predictions could rapidly become self-fulfilling. By not fielding a candidate at all, or a weak one, the Liberals gave Labour a chance to post a good showing. Voters whose primary goal was to stop the Conservatives then saw Labour as the best vehicle to that end, while voters whose primary goal was to stop Labour fled to the Conservatives. Lloyd George's rhetoric, which highlighted the fight against socialism, was of course likely to increase the percentage of the electorate that fell into one of the two categories described above, hence to accelerate the process of Liberal dismemberment.

Finally, it should also be noted that the uncertainty of electoral politics in the early 1920s was ideal for the translation of national into local viability, along the lines suggested by Leys (1959) and in Chapter 10. Given the newness of the district lines and the electorate, and the flux in the number and names of the parties competing in the districts, many districts must have been hard to handicap with much confidence. The decision by Asquith in 1924 to let Labour form a minority government lent credibility to Labour as the second viable party of government. But voters who saw a national contest between Labour and the Conservatives for control of parliament, and an unclear free-for-all in their own districts, in which a Conservative-Labour tie was at least as likely as any other, would have been led to vote for either Labour or the Conservatives, even if they preferred the Liberals. From this perspective, Asquith's decision, which has often been second-guessed, looks to have been a poor one.

14.4 CONCLUSION

In the context of the perennial debate about great leaders and their impact on history, the notion of a coordination game is an intriguing one. The key feature of such a game is that there are multiple possible equilibria and that which one is chosen depends crucially on which one people expect to be chosen. Moreover, the more people there are who act in accord with a given equilibrium (e.g., that the two major parties are Labour and the Conservatives), the more it is in the interest of others to act in accord with that equilibrium. The consequence of these two features is that manipulating expectations – something that great leaders, with their bully pulpits, are in a position to do – can powerfully affect the course of events, leading to fairly rapid and important changes in regime.

Nonetheless, even with all the advantages of focalness, realignments are not easy to bring about, and there are costs to failure. In strong electoral systems, the costs of failed coordination are particularly high. This very fact makes it harder to realign such systems, simply because people fear the costs. It also means that any realignments that do occur are more consequential, purely as a selection phenomenon: Only really important issues can force realignments in stronger systems, whereas smaller issues can motivate realignments in proportional systems.

The narrative presented in this chapter can be read as a case study of the costs of forming a new coalition in a strong electoral system. Lloyd George hoped that he could engineer a new equilibrium, with a center party of which he was the chief ruling the country. In order to push the project along he had to convince one and all that the old Liberal party was no longer viable. He convinced some people, but not others, and not all at the same time. And that missed timing was enough to turn into substantial coordination costs in a large and growing number of constituencies, eventually leading to the demise of the party and the project.

PART VI

Conclusion

15

Conclusion

In a world without transaction costs, democratic politics is inherently unstable. There is always another deal that might be offered to a majority coalition comprising some current winners and some current losers, which makes all members of that coalition better off.[1] But typically there are lots of new deals that can beat the old deal, and people will differ over which of them is best. If only a few voters "defect" from the current political equilibrium and vote for a new party or policy, the old equilibrium will be undisturbed. In order for a new deal to come about, it takes the coordinated actions of large numbers of politicians and voters. Thus, the inherent instability of politics implies that coordination problems will be omnipresent.

One way to think of the problem of democratic coordination dealt with in this book is in terms of a sequence of choices whereby a government is chosen from the mass of citizens. In a stylized parliamentary system, the sequence includes a procedure to decide which citizens will appear on the ballot as candidates, then a procedure to decide which candidates will be elected to serve in parliament, then a procedure to decide which MPs will form the government. At each of these stages, there may be more people of a given ideology or type seeking a spot on the ballot, a seat in the legislature, or a portfolio in the government than there are spots, seats, or portfolios to be had. If these "people of a given ideology or type" cannot somehow agree on which of them will get the prize(s) at stake, then the niche that they seek to represent may win fewer spots, seats, or portfolios than it has the support to win. Their votes will not count.

In order to make their votes count, some coordination is required. Elites can attempt to ensure that the number of those seeking spots,

[1]This is the lesson of the instability theorems – e.g., McKelvey (1976), Schofield (1978), Schwartz (1986).

seats, or portfolios is not too large to begin with, for example, by forming a party whose nomination becomes a focal cue to a particular segment of the electorate. Voters can attempt to coordinate their signatures (in the case too many seek access to the ballot) or votes (in the case too many seek election to the legislature), while MPs can analogously attempt to coordinate their support (in the case too many seek selection to the government).

The procedures used to choose who wins spots, seats, and portfolios can be more or less strong – and the stronger they are, the bigger the coordination problem that political actors face at that stage. In this book, I have focused on the last two stages, at which the legislature and executive are chosen, dividing the discussion between coordination success (Parts II, III, and IV) and coordination failure (Part V). When electoral coordination succeeds, the most readily observable consequence is a reduction in the number of electoral players: The number of lists or candidates appearing on the ballot is decreased when elites agree to a merger of parties, or a joint list, or a fusion candidacy; the effective number of lists or candidates is decreased when voters strategically concentrate their votes on the more viable lists and candidates. When electoral coordination fails, the most readily observable consequence is that the maladroit find themselves underrepresented, while the better-coordinated find their representation magnified. In this conclusion, I will first review some of the findings in each of the two main segments of the book, and then turn briefly to some ideas for future research.

15.1 COORDINATION SUCCESSES AND ELECTORAL LAW

Strategic voting. Duverger did not adapt his model of plurality rule to PR and runoff systems and then deduce that strategic voting in the latter systems would be unimportant. He simply dismissed the possibility of strategic voting in PR and runoff systems out of hand.[2] Leys (1959) and Sartori (1968) chastised him for this dismissal, both asserting that a version of the wasted vote logic should reappear in certain kinds of PR systems. But neither of these scholars arrived at their common conclusion by developing a general model, any more than did Duverger. The Leys-Sartori conjecture is just that: a conjecture, based on keen but largely unarticulated insight. Thus, the electoral studies literature does not say anything very precise about *how much* strategic voting there should be under different kinds of PR, and how much this should constrain the party system.

[2]The tendency to assume that strategic voting has no place under PR has not entirely disappeared. Bowler and Lanoue (1992:486), for example, advance the erroneous thesis that "under proportional representation ... voting sincerely is a dominant strategy."

Nor can help on this score be found in the social choice literature. Although the Gibbard-Satterthwaite theorem is both general, covering all democratic choice procedures, and rigorous, it merely asserts the existence of incentives to vote strategically. It does not specify how much strategic voting there should be or how much such voting will constrain the party system.

Part II of this book has reexamined the district-level logic of strategic voting, holding constant assumptions about voters while varying the institutional context within which those voters act. The two key assumptions about voters concern their preferences and beliefs.[3] As regards preferences, I assume that voters are short-term instrumentally rational (i.e., they care only about who wins the seats in their district at the present election). As regards beliefs, I assume that voters possess rational expectations (i.e., expectations that are consistent with rational behavior on the part of all voters). The results of the analysis, for any given electoral system, are then *equilibrium* results, in which no one has an incentive to change their behavior, given their preferences (over outcomes) and expectations (about the behavior of others).

What does such a model tell one about the number of candidates or lists that can appear in equilibrium under alternative electoral institutions? The most general result is that all three of the systems in which Duverger was originally interested, single-member simple plurality (SMSP), top-M majority runoff, and PR, obey what I have called the $M + 1$ rule: Typically, no more than $M + 1$ *candidates* can be viable in SMSP or top-M runoff elections; and no more than $M + 1$ *lists* can be viable in PR elections. (Recall that M denotes the district magnitude, in the case of SMSP and PR, but the number of candidates who can advance to the second round, in the case of runoff elections.) The same result obtains also for elections held under some electoral procedures that Duverger did not consider, such as the single nontransferable vote (SNTV).[4]

Classic results in the literature, or district-level versions thereof, emerge as special cases of the general $M + 1$ rule: (1) In SMSP elections, for which $M = 1$, the rule asserts that there can be no more than two viable candidates. This is a version of Duverger's Law, stated at the district level. It does *not* say that there will be exactly two parties, as the typical formulation would have it. It says only that there cannot typically be more than two. And this is all that the wasted vote logic yields, properly understood. (2) In multimember elections held under SNTV, the

[3]Other important assumptions of the model are reviewed in Chapter 4.

[4]All systems have other possible equilibria, of varying plausibility, as discussed in detail in the relevant chapters. The runoff system in particular would seem to have equilibria that support more than $M + 1$ viable competitors in the first round.

rule asserts that there can be no more than $M + 1$ viable candidates. This is a version of Reed's (1991) extension of Duverger's Law to the Japanese case, with the same caveat: The logic implies an upper bound, not a point prediction. (3) In multimember elections held under PR rules, the rule asserts that there can be no more than $M + 1$ viable lists. This is a formalized version of the Leys-Sartori conjecture.

In addition to the results that generalize classic propositions, the model also yields insight into other modalities of strategic voting. In some systems, strategic voting can arise even if the number of competitors falls below the $M + 1$ upper bound. This is the case under open-list PR, for example, where strategic voting can take the form of "raids" on another party's list. In other systems, such as that used in Mauritius, there is no upper bound imposed on the effective number of candidates to begin with. Strategic voting in these systems entails not avoiding hopeless candidates, but instead seeking them out as safe havens for votes that might otherwise harm candidates whom the voter favors.

The types of strategic voting just reviewed are all of the "seat-maximizing" variety, intended to make votes count in the allocation of legislative seats. If voters look ahead to the government formation stage, and the coordination problems that arise at that stage, they may face incentives to cast "portfolio-maximizing" strategic votes, intended to make votes count in the allocation of government portfolios. The recognition of this species of strategic voting follows naturally from the view of electoral coordination as occurring in stages, with abstractly similar consequences at each stage. Part IV of the book investigates three subspecies of portfolio-maximizing strategic voting: strategic sequencing, or voting so as to ensure that a particular party has the first opportunity to form a government; strategic balancing, or voting so as to take advantage of constitutional separations of power in order to check the power of the current government; and threshold insurance, or voting so as to ensure that a coalition partner clears a legally mandated electoral threshold.

Beyond the greater generality that the approach taken here affords, there are also the usual advantages of rigor attendant on formal analysis. First, the assumptions undergirding the analysis are clearly stated, so it should be easy to spot those one dislikes in a particular application. Many in the electoral studies literature have taken for granted that the wasted vote argument works for SMSP elections. Sartori (1985:54), for example, writes:

> [N]obody has ever denied that the plurality formula conditions the voter. It will also be conceded, I trust, that the manipulative conditioning in question is a *constraining-restraining effect*. This means that the voter's choice (unless he prefers to waste his vote) is concretely restricted, very often, to the front-runners.

If indeed nobody has ever denied that the plurality formula restrains the voter, then nobody has ever doubted either that the voter is short-term instrumentally rational, or that the voter has enough information about the prospects of the various candidates in order to identify those that are clearly trailing. In some situations, however, voters may have long-term goals to pursue (the Perotistas in the United States?), or very poor ideas about who is really likely to win (the citizens of Papua New Guinea), and then the restraining effect of plurality rule can be expected to fail.[5]

A second advantage of rigor comes in the form of a clearer statement of what can be concluded from the logic of the wasted vote. Virtually all previous scholars have viewed strategic voting as pushing a system toward a *unique equilibrium number* of *parties*. But the analysis here shows that strategic voting only imposes an *upper bound* on the number of *competitors*. Recognizing this point has a number of further-on advantages, of which I shall mention just three here.

First, recognizing that the direct effect of strategic coordination falls on electoral competitors – that is, candidates or lists – rather than on parties, helps to clarify our understanding of systems that allow joint lists or fusion candidacies. In these systems, the number of viable parties may well exceed the number of viable lists or candidates, because more than one party can support a given competitor.

Second, recognizing that strategic voting only imposes an upper bound on the number of competitors, rather than establishing an equilibrium number, helps to clarify a classic debate about the "multiplying power" of PR. Duverger's original proposition was that PR should promote multipartism. As an empirical generalization, this was fair enough. But as a theoretical proposition, the claim seemed to be that each electoral system had a well-defined equilibrium number of parties, one that grew with the proportionality of the system. This may be the right way to think about the matter – there may be a compelling model in which the equilibria line up in this way – but there was no formal argument to this effect in Duverger's work, nor has there been any since. The only conclusion that one can draw at present, from a careful analysis of strategic voting, is that each system has a maximum carrying capacity: If the party system gets too populous, with too many candidates and lists sent forth to compete, there should be a winnowing out. Given that this is all that one can conclude, proportional systems such as Austria's,

[5]The first of these possibilities, that voters have long-term goals, might be captured under a "preference for wasting votes" suggested in the passage quoted from Sartori in the text, although that would be an odd way to put it. The second possibility, that voters have inconsistent expectations, has nothing to do with such a preference.

Malta's, or Colombia's, which have supported two-party systems for long periods, do not violate the $M + 1$ rule, whereas they do violate Duverger's PR hypothesis as originally stated, and the various reformulations of it that have since appeared.

Finally, recognizing that strategic voting only imposes an upper bound also changes how one thinks about the relation between electoral and social structure. Social cleavages are free to determine the number of competitors below the upper bound. It is only when the number of cleavages suggests a number of competitors that exceeds the upper bound that the electoral rules are constraining. Thus, systems may have few parties because there are few cleavages or because the upper bound is low; but systems should have many parties only when there are many cleavages combined with a permissive electoral system.

Strategic entry. All of the results generated in Part II (and those sections of Part IV dealing with strategic voting) belong to a model that includes only voters as actors. Part III brings potential candidates for office more fully into view, considering in particular their decisions to enter the political fray or not. Just as in studies of strategic voting, so in studies of strategic entry, there is a substantial divergence between traditional electoral studies and formal mathematical studies.

Duverger, and many others after him, have taken for granted that political parties constrain and structure entry opportunities for potential candidates. From this perspective, if a system is prone to strategic voting, there is little doubt as to who will bear the brunt of that strategic voting: Third parties and independents will, major parties will not. Thus, the entry side of Duverger's logic was simple: Third-party candidates, anticipating that they will be strategically deserted by their supporters in single-member simple plurality elections, will not bother to enter in the first place; but as such candidates need not fear strategic desertion under PR, they will enter.

In contrast to the traditional approach in electoral studies, recent formal models of entry have not assumed the preexistence of "major parties" and "minor parties." In these models, it is not clear *ex ante* who will bear the brunt of strategic voting, and the entry-deterring effect of anticipations of such voting is consequently removed. As is frequently the case, formal models take as problematic and to be explained what others see as a given of the situation.

As in the study of strategic voting, I think that both formal and traditional studies have something to contribute. The formal models, in which no parties have established labels with viability advantages, *are* sometimes approximated in the real world: in brand new polities with no democratic experience, for example; or in polities that do not, in Sartori's

(1968) sense, have "structured" party systems.[6] The traditional models, in which party labels are taken as given, correspond to the situation in most developed polities. Most of Part III considers rational entry models with exogenously given labels, wedding the substantive assumptions of the electoral studies literature with the modeling approach (decision theory only!) of the more formal literature.

Systemic coordination. Part IV of the book brings systemic considerations into view. Both Duverger and Sartori have argued that the rules governing legislative elections might have an impact at the national level. I have argued that there is no real sense in which the local effect of electoral rules translates to the national level. There is one (well-understood) logic that drives local results. There is another (little-explored) logic that drives cross-district alliance formation, thereby combining a variety of district-conditioned patterns of party competition into a larger national aggregate.

Why do legislators from different electoral districts link together to form national parties? The general answer given here is that legislators link together when by doing so they can better compete for control of the presidency or premiership. As soon as a set of rules, formal or informal, is in place for electing the executive, legislators face a coordination problem similar in general character to that faced by voters in legislative elections. This is especially clear in parliamentary systems, where MPs select the premier. But it is also true in presidential systems, to the extent that legislative and executive elections are tied together.

The coordination problem posed by the selection of an executive gives rise, as does the coordination problem posed by the selection of legislators, both to strategic voting phenomena and to strategic entry phenomena. I have already reviewed strategic voting in the context of executive choice above.[7]

Strategic entry in the context of executive choice refers to the formation of multiparty alliances to support a presidential candidate, as in Chile; to the creation of national parties to support presidential candidates, as in the United States after 1824 and France after 1962; to the preannouncement of governing pacts, as by the FDP in post-war Germany; and so forth. The general rule is the same at the executive as at the legislative level: The stronger the executive choice procedure, the fewer the number of viable executive candidates that there can typically

[6] Indeed, one might view the entry models as *formalizations* of Sartori's notion of an unstructured party system.

[7] Note that the species of strategic voting discussed above was engaged in by voters, not MPs. Although it is logically possible for MPs too to face strategic voting incentives, my assumption is that strategic coordination within the legislature occurs mostly in the form of advancing and withdrawing executive candidacies.

be. Thus, for example, if there are fifteen executive positions of roughly equal power allocated proportionally to the number of seats that each governing party controls in the legislature, then the number of viable competitors for executive office can be rather large. If, on the other hand, there is one president to be elected by plurality rule, then the number of competitors for executive office will typically be limited to two.

Whether upper bounds on the number of viable executive candidates affect the number of legislative parties depends on how closely related legislative and executive elections are. Elections of prime ministers are always intimately related to legislative elections, held concurrently and with something like a fused vote. Elections of presidents can also be held concurrently and with a fused vote. But it is also possible to have nonfused votes and nonconcurrent elections, in which case upper bounds on the number of presidential candidates may not much affect the legislative party system.

When executive and legislative elections *are* closely related, one can expect executive ambition to be a prime force in linking legislative candidates across district lines into national parties. Thus, the number of legislative parties at the national level is best thought of as a joint product of legislative and executive electoral rules, both interacting with the social cleavage structure. I developed a model along these lines in Chapter 11.

15.2 COORDINATION FAILURES AND DEMOCRATIC PERFORMANCE

Duverger's Law can be viewed as an optimistic assessment of the prospects for electoral coordination under SMSP rules. According to this (revised) law, failures to coordinate should be rare, and thus there should generally be at most two candidates in any race, and at most two parties in any district.

Any coordination problem, however, has consequences not just for the number of competitors in a system but also for the policy that is advocated or enacted. If one puts greater emphasis on the policy goals of political agents, and views coordination problems as inherently multiperiod rather than one-shot, then the prospects for successful coordination begin to look less promising.

In Part V of the book, I focused on the issue of coordination failure, examining in particular three different possible consequences of such failure. The first has to do with the nature of enacted policy in strong electoral systems (Chapter 12). Such systems by definition face larger coordination problems. One thing that this means is that the incentive to coordinate in such systems is greater, so that there are typically fewer electoral competitors. But it also means that the consequences of failure to coordinate are larger in terms of the balance of seats allocated to different political forces: that is precisely why the incentives to succeed are greater. If coordination fails at a national level in a strong electoral system, then a fair number of seats can be lost by one side (poorly coordinated) and gained by another (better coordinated), with substantial consequences for the nature of government policy. In this sense, then, policy in stronger electoral systems can be more erratic and less centrist than in more proportional systems.

Failures to coordinate can also contribute to the maintenance of dominant-party systems. In some countries, such as India and Italy, dominant parties appear to have a positional advantage, in that politics is largely unidimensional and they are centrally located. In these cases, the opposition is more divided among itself than it is from the government, and cannot coordinate to overthrow the centrists. In other countries, in particular those operating under SNTV, the electoral system creates coordination problems that require specific resources to solve, such as access to pork and money, which governing parties in general have in greater supply. In these systems, coordination failure arises not from the positional advantages of a centrist party but from the resource advantages of a governing party. In Chapter 13 I examined how the resource advantages of governing parties have played out in the Japanese and Taiwanese cases.

Failures to coordinate can also arise as a natural by-product of attempts to realign politics in a country. When realignment projects do fail, they can entail significant loss of seats in strong (as opposed to more permissive) electoral systems. The high costs of failure should mean that successful realignments are less frequent and more consequential in strong electoral systems than they are in more proportional systems. Chapter 14 provided a case history of one coordination failure, Lloyd George's attempt to create a Center Party in the United Kingdom in the 1920s.

15.3 FUTURE RESEARCH

From a normative perspective, the institutional engineering question that this book suggests is: When do we want coordination problems to arise? They will unavoidably arise at some point in the process of translating voters' preferences into public policies. Would it be better that they arise early (in translating preferences into votes and thence into seats) or late (in translating seats into portfolios) or still-later (in translating control over seats and portfolios into specific policy decisions)? Early coordination focuses on mass politics and thus any equilibrium that is achieved is harder to change, as it involves changing the actions of large numbers of voters. Late coordination focuses on the formation of governments and thus any equilibrium that is achieved is easier to change, as it involves (at least in the short run) changing only the actions of elites sitting in the legislature. Still-later coordination problems arise in the context of particular policy debates. For example, there may be several different budgets that a majority might accept; which will be agreed on?

In considering the question of when we want coordination problems to arise, a natural follow-on query concerns the consequences of failure to coordinate at each stage. In some systems, failure to coordinate at the government formation stage can take the form of an inability to form a government (cf. Strom 1994). In other systems, constitutional divisions of power, when combined with political divisions of purpose, lead to an inability to pass a budget in a timely fashion (cf. Cox and Kernell 1991). From the perspective of this book, this is a case in which social divisions are allowed to persist, because neither the legislative nor the executive choice procedure is so strong as to induce another outcome. The consequence of this persistence is not just partisan division of opinion within the society, not just partisan division of opinion within the legislature, but partisan division of opinion within the government. Given that there is a divided government, but that only one budget can be passed, the coordination game that might have played out earlier, when forming the legislature or government, is instead played out at the end of the fiscal year. From a purely administrative perspective, might we not wish that our differences had been settled earlier – avoiding the partial closure of the U.S. government in 1995, for example, but ending up with the same budget? Is it possible to construct a system that gives more or less this outcome?

The answer may well be "no," on the "no pain, no gain" principle. That is, it is precisely the pain of coordination failure that forces coordination success. If it takes a closure of the government to bridge the gap between contending forces, once they have reached the point at which a budget must be passed, then presumably earlier coordination could be forced only if there were an equally painful consequence inducing coordination earlier in the process. On the other hand, coordination earlier in the process necessarily entails a broader perspective, one that encompasses many specific policies, and so perhaps one could engineer stable coordination at less cost.

In addition to asking when we want to incur the risks of coordination failure, we might also ask how much we want the costs of such failure to fall on nonpoliticians (e.g., civil servants furloughed when budgets are not passed on time) as opposed to politicians (e.g., politicians who must face reelection if they bring down the government over a particular policy decision). The principle here would seem to be that the politicians should bear a direct pain that is proportional to the social costs of coordination failure.

Appendix A

Formulaic structures in 77 democracies, circa 1992

Part A: 23 Countries using simple plurality[a]

Country	*Comments*
Bahamas	49-member House of Assembly.
BANGLADESH	330-member Parliament (*Jatiya Sangsad*). 300 members are directly elected; 30 are coopted women's representatives.
Barbados	27-member House of Assembly.
Belize	18-member House of Assembly.
BOTSWANA	40-member National Assembly. 34 members directly elected; 4 coopted and 2 *ex officio* members.
Canada	295-member House of Commons.
Dominica	31-member House of Assembly. 21 members are elected. The Speaker and nine senators are appointed on the advice of the prime minister and Leader of the Opposition.
Gambia	51-member Chamber of Representatives. 36 members are elected, 15 are appointed or *ex officio*.
Grenada	15-member House of Representatives.
JAMAICA	60-member House of Representatives.
Micronesia	14-member Congress.
NEPAL	205-member Parliament (*Pratinidhi Sabha*).
NEW ZEALAND	97-member House of Commons. 4 members elected to represent the Maori population by plurality in single-member constituencies.
P.N.G.	109-member Parliament. Three additional members may be appointed by a two-thirds vote in Parliament but this had never happened as of 1989.
St. Kitts & Nevis	14-member National Assembly. 11 members elected; 3 members appointed.

Part A (cont.)

Country	Comments
St. Lucia	17-member House of Assembly.
St. Vincent	19-member House of Assembly. 13 members elected; 6 members appointed (four on advice of prime minister, two on advice of the Leader of the Opposition).
Solomon Islands	38-member Parliament.
TRINIDAD	36-member House of Representatives.
U.K.	650-member House of Commons.
U.S.	435-member House of Representatives.
Western Samoa	47-member Legislative Assembly (*Fono*). Two seats are reserved for non-indigenous minorities.
ZAMBIA	159-member National Assembly. 150 members elected; 1 member elected by Assembly; 8 members appointed by president.

[a]Countries with populations less than one million are listed with an initial capital letter followed by lower-case letters; larger countries are listed using capital letters throughout. This convention is also followed in part B of this appendix.

Part B: 55 Countries without simple plurality

ARGENTINA	*Primary districts (distritos)*
Lists	PR-d'Hondt. Only lists whose vote exceeds 3% of the registered electorate in the district are eligible to receive seats.
Candidates	List order.

254-member Chamber of Deputies (*Cámara de Diputados*).

AUSTRALIA	*Primary districts*
Candidates	Alternative vote system.

148-member House of Representatives.

AUSTRIA	*Primary districts*	*Secondary districts*
Secondary Lists	—	(3) Seats unallocated in step 1 are aggregated within each secondary district and distributed by PR-d'Hondt, on

		the basis of each secondary list's vote (equal to the sum of the remainder votes of the party's constituency lists in the secondary district). Only parties that have won at least one constituency seat in the secondary district are eligible to receive seats at this stage.
Lists	(1) Each list receives as many seats as its vote contains full Hare quotas.	—
Candidates	(2) Seats awarded to lists in step 1 are reallocated to each list's candidates, mostly in accord with list order.	(4) Seats awarded to secondary lists in step 2 are reallocated to each list's candidates in accord with list order.

183-member National Council (*Nationalrat*).

BELGIUM	*Primary districts (*arrondissements*)*	*Secondary districts (provinces)*
Partisan Cartels	—	(2) Seats unallocated in step 1 are aggregated within each province and distributed by PR-d'Hondt. A cartel must obtain 66% of a Hare quota in one of the *arrondissements* contained in the province, and must also have formally affiliated its various *arrondissement* lists in the province, in order to participate in the secondary seat allocation.
Lists	(1) Each list receives as many seats as its vote contains full Hare quotas.	(3) Seats awarded to partisan cartels in step 2 are reallocated to each cartel's component *arrondissement* lists by PR-d'Hondt.
Candidates	(4) Seats awarded to lists in steps 1 and 3 are reallocated to each list's	—

	candidates, by a transferable vote system that puts most of the emphasis on list order. See Dewachter (1983:99–100) for details.	

212-member Chamber of Representatives (*Chambre de Représentants* or *Kamer van Volksvertegenwoordigers*).

BENIN	*Primary Districts*
Lists	LR-Hare.
Candidates	List order.

64-member National Assembly.

BOLIVIA	*Primary Districts*
Lists	LR-Hare, based on qualifying lists' vote totals only. Only lists whose votes exceed the Hare quota (based on all votes) qualify to participate in the distribution of seats.
Candidates	List order.

130-member Chamber of Deputies (*Cámara de Diputados*).

BRAZIL	*Primary Districts*
Lists	d'Hondt.
Candidates	Plurality.

503-member Chamber of Deputies (*Câmara de Diputados*).

BULGARIA	*Primary districts*	*Secondary district (national)*
Partisan Cartels	—	(2) The total number of seats to which a cartel is entitled is determined on the basis of list votes aggregated to the national level, using LR-Hare with a 4% national threshold. (1991 election.)
Lists	(1) In 1991 at least, votes cast for constituency lists were pooled at the national	(3) Seats awarded to partisan cartels in step 2 are reallocated to each cartel's

	level and no seats were allocated at the constituency level (cf. Kuusela 1994:146). Technically, then, the constituencies did not count as primary electoral districts in 1991, and the system was similar to Holland's. I am not sure whether this system continued in 1994 or not.	component constituency lists by PR-d'Hondt.
Candidates	(4) Seats awarded to constituency lists in step 3 are reallocated to the candidates on those lists by list order.	—

240-member National Assembly (*Sobranie*).

Cape Verde	*Primary districts*
Lists	PR-d'Hondt.
Candidates	List order.

79-member National Assembly, of whom 3 represent nonresidents.

CHILE	*Primary districts*
Lists	PR-d'Hondt
Candidates	Plurality.

120-member Chamber of Deputies (*Cámara de Diputados*).

COLOMBIA	*Primary districts*
Lists	LR-Hare
Candidates	List order.

199-member House of Representatives (*Cámara de Representantes*). Multiple lists from the same party can and frequently do run against one another.

COSTA RICA	*Primary districts*
Lists	LR-Hare. Only parties whose vote exceeds half a Hare quota are eligible to receive seats.
Candidates	List order.

57-member Legislative Assembly (*Asamblea Legislativa*).

Cyprus (Greek)	*Primary districts*
Lists	LR-Hare. Only parties who have either secured (1) one quota seat plus at least 8% of the national vote, or (2) at least 10% of the national vote are eligible to receive remainder seats. Coalitions of two parties that submit joint lists can receive remainder seats only if they garner at least 20% of the national vote. Coalitions of more than two parties can receive remainder seats only if they garner at least 25% of the national vote.
Candidates	Seats allocated to lists are reallocated to the candidates on those lists by plurality rule. Any ties are broken by list order.

56-member House of Representatives.

CZECH REPUBLIC	*Primary districts*	*Secondary district (national)*
National Lists	—	(2) Seats not allocated in step 1 are allocated at the national level to national lists on the basis of the sum of each party's remainders in the constituencies, using LR-Hagenbach-Bischoff. Only parties garnering at least 5% of the national vote are eligible to receive seats at this stage. Coalitions of parties that submit joint lists must satisfy stricter requirements: Coalitions of two, three, and four or more parties must garner at least 7%, 9%, and 11%, respectively.
Lists	(1) Each list gets as many seats as its vote contains full Hagenbach-Bischoff quotas.	(4) Seats allocated to national lists in step 3 are reallocated to the candidates on those lists according to their list order.
Candidates	(3) Seats allocated to constituency lists in step 1 are reallocated to the candidates on those lists according to their list order. However, if at least one tenth of those voting	—

for the list have cast preference votes, then these are taken into account, and candidates receiving preference votes from more than 50% of those casting such votes are moved to the top of the list.

200-member Chamber of Deputies. The system described is that used in the 1992 Czechoslovak elections.

DENMARK	*Primary districts (*storkredse, Amtskredse*)*	*Secondary district (national)*
Partisan Cartels	—	(2) Only cartels that have either (a) won one or more constituency seats, or (b) obtained as many votes as on average were cast per constituency seat in at least two of the three regions, or (c) obtained, in the country as a whole, at least 2% of the valid votes cast, are eligible to participate in the second distribution of seats. The total number of seats to which each cartel is entitled is determined using the LR-Hare method (the quota equals the nationwide sum of the votes of all lists associated with qualifying cartels, divided by the total number of Danish seats, 175). From this total number is then subtracted the number of constituency seats won by associated lists in step 1. The difference gives the number of the forty supplemental seats to which the cartel is entitled.
Lists	(1) 135 constituency seats are distributed by the modified Sainte-Lague method.	(3) Seats awarded to partisan cartels in step 2 are reallocated to each cartel's component constituency lists by a two-step procedure. Seats are first allocated to regions, by the Sainte-Lague method. Then, within regions, they are allocated to constituencies by another divisor method. See Johansen (1979:46) for details.

Candidates	(4) Seats awarded to lists in steps 1 and 3 are reallocated to each list's candidates, by three different procedures. See Johansen (1979:50–54) for details.	—

179-member Parliament (*Folketing*).

DOMINICAN REPUBLIC	*Primary districts*
Lists	PR-d'Hondt
Candidates	List order.

120-member Chamber of Deputies (*Cámara de Diputados*).

ECUADOR	*Primary districts (provincial)*	*Primary district (national)*
Lists	(1a) Seats are allocated by three different methods, depending on district magnitude: in single-member districts, by plurality; in double-member districts, by PR-d'Hondt; in all other districts, by the same procedure as that used at the national level.	(1b) Seats are allocated as follows. Let Q_1 equal half a Hare quota and Q_2 equal a full Hare quota based only on the votes of those lists whose vote exceeds Q_1. If no list's vote exceeds Q_1, then seats are given one to a list in descending order of their vote totals. If exactly one list's vote exceeds Q_1, then that list gets M-1 seats, and the second largest list gets 1 seat. If more than one list's vote exceeds Q_1, then there are two cases. If no list's vote exceeds Q_2, then seats are distributed by LR-Q_1. If at least one list's vote exceeds Q_2, then each list whose vote exceeds Q_1 gets as many seats as its vote contains full quotas (Q_2), with any remaining seats being distributed by largest remainders among all lists whose vote exceeds $.6Q_1$.
Candidates	(2a) Seats allocated to lists in	(2b) Seats allocated to lists in step 1b are reallocated to the candidates on

step 1a are reallocated to the candidates on each list by list order.	each list by list order.	

72-member National Chamber of Representatives (*Cámara Nacional de Representantes*). 12 national deputies (*diputados nacionales*) have four-year terms; 60 provincial deputies (*diputados provinciales*) have two-year terms.

FINLAND	*Primary districts*
Lists	PR-d'Hondt.
Candidates	Plurality.

200-member Parliament (*Eduskunta*).

FRANCE	*Primary districts*
Candidates	Majority-runoff system. All candidates whose vote exceeds 12.5% of the registered electorate may participate in the runoff.

577-member National Assembly (*Assemblée National*).

GERMANY	*Primary districts*	*Secondary districts (*Länder*)*	*Tertiary district (national)*
Partisan Cartels	—	—	(2) The total number of seats to which a cartel is entitled is determined on the basis of list votes (*Zweitstimmen*) aggregated to the national level, using LR-Hare with a 5% national threshold.
Lists	—	(1b) Votes cast for *Land* lists (*Zweitstimmen*) can, at the option of each party, either be used for an allocation of seats within the *Land* by LR-Hare, or be pooled at the national level.	(3) Seats awarded to partisan cartels in step 2 are reallocated to each cartel's component *Land* lists by PR-d'Hondt.

		In practice, all parties take the latter option.	
Candidates	(1a) Constituency seats are awarded by plurality rule on the basis of candidate votes (*Erststimmen*).	(4) Let the number of seats to which a *Land* list is entitled, determined in step 3, be denoted L. Let the number of constituency seats won by the party in that *Land*, determined in step 1a, be denoted C. If L-C > 0, then the first L-C names on the *Land* list, not having already won constituency seats, are awarded seats. If L-C < 0, then no seats are allocated to candidates on the list, but the party does get to keep the surplus seats (*Überhangmandaten*) it has won.	—

496-member Federal Diet (*Bundestag*).

GREECE	*Primary districts* (nomoi)	*Secondary districts (major districts)*	*Tertiary district (national)*	*Secondary district (national)*
National Lists	—	—	—	(6) Votes cast in *nomoi* are aggregated to the national level and 12 "state deputies" chosen by PR-d'Hondt. 3% threshold.
Partisan Cartels	—	(2) All votes cast in *nomoi* for lists passing the 3%	(4) The party with the most national votes wins all	—

		threshold (as in step 1) are aggregated at the major district level, along with seats not allocated at step 1. Each cartel gets as many seats as its vote contains full Hare quotas.	unallocated seats from districts where it ran first. Unallocated seats from other districts are aggregated to the national level, along with all votes cast for lists passing the 3% threshold (as in step 1). Each cartel gets as many seats as its vote contains full Hare quotas. Seats still not allocated go to the largest party.	
Lists	(1) PR-d'Hondt in one- and two-member districts. In larger districts, each list gets as many seats as its vote contains full "plus one" quotas. Only lists from a party/coalition that gets at least 3% of the national vote are eligible	(3) Seats allocated to cartels in step 2 are reallocated to the cartel's component lists according to which *nomos* the seat came from.	(5) Seats allocated to cartels in step 4 are reallocated to the cartel's component lists according to which *nomos* the seat came from.	—

	to receive seats.			
Candidates	(7) Seats allocated to lists in steps 1, 3, and 5 are reallocated to each list's candidates by plurality.	—	—	(8) List order.

300-member Chamber of Deputies. In a final adjustment, any party whose vote exceeds the 3% national threshold, but whose seats fall short of 70% their proportional due (their vote percentage, times the total number of seats), receives extra seats at the expense of the immediately stronger party.

HONDURAS	*Primary districts*
Lists	LR-Hare.
Candidates	List order.

132-member National Assembly (*Congreso*).

HUNGARY (Tóka N.d.)	*Primary districts: single-member*	*Primary districts: multimember (counties)*	*Secondary district (national)*
National Lists	—	—	(3) Votes from steps 1a (first round) and 1b that do not contribute to winning a seat are aggregated to the national level. 58 national compensatory seats, plus seats not allocated in step 1b, are awarded on the basis of these votes by PR-d'Hondt. A 4% national threshold applies, as in step 1b.

Lists	—	(1b) Only lists affiliated with cartels that get 4% or more of the total regional list vote are eligible to receive seats. Qualifying lists get as many seats as their votes contain Hagenbach-Bischoff quotas, plus one more if their remainder exceeds 2/3 of the quota.	—
Candidates	(1a) 176 seats filled by a majority runoff system. Absent a majority winner in the first round, the top three finishers, plus any others whose vote exceeds 15%, can participate in the runoff, when the seat is awarded by plurality.	(2) List order.	(4) List order.

386-member Parliament.

ICELAND	*Primary districts*	*Secondary district (national)*
Partisan Cartels	—	(2) Seats unallocated in step 1 are aggregated at the national level and distributed by PR-d'Hondt, on the basis of the cartels' national vote totals and taking into account seats already won in the constituencies. A cartel must win at least one constituency seat, in order to

		participate in the secondary seat allocation.
Lists	(1) In each constituency [3M/4] seats (where [x] represents the least integer greater than or equal to x) are allocated by LR-Hare. Only parties whose vote exceeds 2/3 of the Hare quota (based on the votes of all parties) can participate in seat allocations. If any parties are eliminated, the quota is recomputed in terms of the votes of qualifying parties only.	(3) Seats awarded to partisan cartels in step 2 are reallocated to each cartel's component constituency lists by a three-step process. See Helgason (1991) for details.
Candidates	(4) Seats awarded to lists in steps 1 and 3 are reallocated to each list's candidates, mostly in accord with list order.	—

63-member General Assembly (*Althing*).

IRELAND	*Primary districts*
Candidates	STV system.

166-member lower house (*Dáil Éireann*).

ISRAEL	*Primary district (national)*
Lists	PR-d'Hondt. Only lists receiving at least 1.5% of the national vote are eligible to receive seats.
Candidates	List order.

120-member Assembly (*Knesset*).

ITALY	*Primary districts*	*Secondary district (national)*
Partisan Cartels	—	(2) Seats unallocated in step 1 are aggregated at the national level and distributed by LR-Hare. Each cartel's vote is equal to the sum of the remainder votes of its associated constituency lists.

		A cartel's associated lists must win at least one constituency seat, and amass at least 300,000 votes nationwide, in order for the cartel to participate in the secondary seat allocation.
Lists	(1) Each list gets as many seats as there are full Imperialii quotas contained in its vote. If this results in more seats being distributed than there are seats in the constituency, then each list gets as many seats as there are full Hagenbach-Bischoff quotas contained in its vote.	(3) Seats awarded to partisan cartels in step 2 are reallocated to each cartel's component constituency lists in decreasing order of each list's remainder vote expressed as a percentage of its constituency's quota (calculated in step 1).
Candidates	(4) Seats awarded to lists in steps 1 and 3 are reallocated to each list's candidates, by plurality rule (based on the candidates' preference votes).	—

630-member Chamber of Deputies (*Camara dei Deputati*).

JAPAN	*Primary districts*
Candidates	Plurality. A candidate's vote total must exceed ¼ of a Hare quota to win a seat.

512-member House of Representatives (*Shugi-in*).

Kiribati	*Primary districts*
Candidates	"Members ... are elected in 23 electoral districts allotted one, two or three seats by absolute majority vote (or simple majority, if the seat is not filled in the first round of voting)" (*Electoral Systems: A Worldwide Comparative Study*, Inter-Parliamentary Union: 1993:51).

41-member House of Assembly (*Maneaba Ni Maungatabu*). One seat is allocated to the Banaban community and one *ex officio* to the Attorney General.

KOREA, SOUTH	*Primary districts*	*Secondary district (national)*
Lists	—	(2) "If a party wins a majority of seats allocated in single-member districts, all 75 nationwide seats are allocated among all parties ... according to their relative shares of district seats. However, if the winning party has only a plurality of district-level seats, then this party receives 38 (just over 50%) of the seats in the nationwide tier, the remaining parties that have won at least 5 district-level seats divide the remaining seats according to their shares of district seats won" (Cheng 1993:16–17).
Candidates	(1) 224 members elected by plurality	(3) Seats awarded to national party lists in step 2 are reallocated to the candidates on those lists by list order.

299-member Parliament.

Liechtenstein	*Primary districts*
Lists	LR-Hare. Only lists receiving at least 8% of the national vote are eligible to receive seats.
Candidates	Plurality.

25-member Diet (*Landtag*).

LITHUANIA	*Primary districts: single-member*	*Primary district (national)*
Lists	—	(1b) 70 members are elected by LR-Hare at the national level, on the basis of list votes. Only lists receiving at least 4% of the national vote are eligible to receive seats.
Candidates	(1a) 71 members are elected by majority runoff. To win in the first round, a candidate must get over 50% of the valid votes, and turnout must exceed 40%.	(2) List order.

Absent a first-round winner, the top two finishers meet in a runoff.

141-member Parliament (*Seimas*).

Luxembourg	*Primary districts*
Lists	PR-d'Hondt.
Candidates	Seats awarded to party lists are reallocated to the candidates on those lists by plurality rule. Each candidate's vote total equals the sum of his or her personal or preference votes and votes cast for the whole list.

64-member Chamber of Deputies (*Chambre des Députées*).

MALI	*Primary districts*
Lists	116 seats are filled in single- and multimember districts as follows. Each party presents a list of M candidates, where M is the district magnitude. Any party garnering a majority of votes in the district wins all the seats. If no party wins a majority, then the top two vote-getting lists are pitted in a runoff election, with the winner taking all M seats.
Candidates	All candidates on any winning list receive seats.

129-member National Assembly. 13 seats are chosen by Malians living in other countries.

Malta	*Primary districts*	*Secondary district (national)*
Parties	—	(2) "Malta introduced a contingent higher tier before the 1987 election: if the party winning a majority of first preference votes does not win a majority of the lower-tier seats, it receives a sufficient number of upper-level adjustment seats to ensure it a parliamentary majority" (Lijphart 1994:36).
Candidates	(1) STV system.	(3) No information on how seats allocated in step 2 are reallocated to individuals within each party.

65-member House of Representatives.

Marshall Islands: No information.

MAURITIUS	*Primary districts*
Candidates	Plurality. 62 members are elected in primary districts. A second allocation of 8 seats seeks to ensure fair representation for the four officially recognized "communities" of Mauritius (Hindu, Muslim, Sino-Mauritian, and General Population) while, at the same time, ensuring that the position of the most successful party in the election is not eroded. For details, see schedule 1 of the Mauritian constitution, in Blaustein and Flanz (1971).

70-member Legislative Assembly.

NAMIBIA	*Primary district (national)*
Lists	LR-Hare.
Candidates	List order.

72-member Constituent Assembly.

Nauru: Election appears to be by a system of preferential voting in multimember districts.

NETHERLANDS	*Primary dstrict (national)*
Lists	PR-d'Hondt. Only lists receiving at least .67% of the national vote are eligible to receive seats.
Candidates	Seats awarded to party lists are reallocated to the candidates on those lists, by a transferable vote system that puts most of the emphasis on list order. See Seip (1979:211) for details.

150-member Second Chamber (*Tweede Kamer*).

NORWAY	*Primary districts (counties)*	*Secondary district (national)*
Lists	(1) 157 county seats are allocated in each country by the modified Sainte-Laguë method.	(2) 8 at-large seats are allocated to those county lists with the highest quotients remaining after the distribution of the county seats. Only registered parties that win more than 4% of

		the national vote are eligible to receive seats at this stage.
Candidates	(3) Seats allocated to county lists in steps 1 and 2 are reallocated to the candidates on each list mostly in accord with list order (voters may change the order of names on a list, but for these changes to have any effect over half the voters must make the same changes).	

165-member Parliament (*Storting*).

POLAND	*Primary districts*	*Secondary district (national)*
National lists	—	(4) 69 seats are awarded by the modified Sainte-Laguë method, on the basis of constituency list votes aggregated to the national level. Only parties whose constituency lists have won seats in at least five constituencies, and whose aggregate vote exceeds 5% of the aggregate national vote, are eligible to receive seats at this stage.
Interparty Cartels	(1a) LR-Hare.	—
Independent Lists	(1b) Independent lists compete with interparty cartels, with seats awarded by LR-Hare.	—
Allied Lists	(2) Seats awarded to interparty cartels in step 1a are reallocated to the cartel's component lists by LR-Hare.	—
Candidates	(3) Seats awarded to lists in steps 1b and 2 are reallocated to the candidates on each list by plurality.	(5) List order.

460-member Parliament (*Sejm*). 391 members are elected in the primary districts, 69 at-large in the nation.

PORTUGAL	*Primary districts*
Lists	PR-d'Hondt.
Candidates	List order.

250-member Assembly of the Republic (*Assembleia da República*).

San Marino	*Primary districts*
Lists	PR-d'Hondt.
Candidates	?

60-member Grand and General Council.

São Tomé and Príncipe	*Primary districts (distritos)*
Lists	List plurality: the list winning the most votes in a given constituency wins all the seats.
Candidates	All candidates on a winning list are elected.

55-member National People's Assembly.

SLOVAKIA	*Primary Districts*	*Secondary District (national)*
National Lists	—	(2) Seats not allocated in step 1 are allocated at the national level to national lists on the basis of the sum of each party's remainders in the constituencies, using LR-Hagenbach-Bischoff. Only parties garnering at least 5% of the national vote are eligible to receive seats at this stage. Coalitions of parties that submit joint lists must satisfy stricter requirements: coalitions of two or three must garner at least 7%, while those of four or more must garner at least 10%.
Lists	(1) Each list gets as many seats as its vote contains full Hagenbach-Bischoff quotas.	(4) Seats allocated to national lists in step 3 are reallocated to the candidates on those lists according to their list order.

Candidates	(3) Seats allocated to constituency lists in step 1 are reallocated to the candidates on those lists according to their list order. However, if at least one-tenth of those voting for the list have cast preference votes, then these are taken into account, and candidates receiving preference votes from more than 50% of those casting such votes are moved to the top of the list.	—

150-member National Council (*Narodna rada*). The system described is that used in the 1992 Czechoslovak elections.

SLOVENIA	*Primary districts*	*Secondary districts*
Partisan Cartels	—	(2) Seats unallocated in step 1 are aggregated at the national level and distributed by PR-d'Hondt, on the basis of each cartel's remainder vote (the sum of all remainders from associated constituency lists). Only cartels that would win at least three seats were all seats allocated at the national level by PR-d'Hondt on the basis of the total vote cast are eligible to participate.
Lists	(1) Each lists gets as many seats as there are whole Hare quotas contained in its vote.	(3) Seats awarded to partisan cartels in step 2 are reallocated to each cartel's component lists as follows. Each constituency list's remainder is expressed as a fraction of the quota in its constituency. The cartel seats are then awarded to constituency lists by the order of their proportional remain-

		ders, ignoring lists from constituencies all of whose seats have already been allocated.
Candidates	(4) Seats awarded to lists in steps 1 and 3 are reallocated to each list's candidates as follows. Each candidate on each list is associated with one (or two) geographically defined subdistricts. The candidates on each list are ranked in terms of the percentage of the total vote each has received in his or her subdistrict. The top candidates on the list get the seats to which their list is entitled.	—

90-member National Assembly. The Italian and Hungarian minorities are each entitled to a single Deputy, with election by a preferential vote system.

SPAIN	*Primary districts*
Lists	PR-d'Hondt. Only lists that get at least 3% in the district are eligible to receive seats.
Candidates	List order.

350-member Congress of Deputies (*Congreso de Diputados*).

SWEDEN	*Primary districts*	*Secondary district (national)*
National Partisan Cartels	—	(2) All votes cast for parties whose vote exceeds 4% of the national total are aggregated to the national level. A hypothetical allocation of all seats, both fixed or constituency seats and additional or national seats, is made by modified Sainte-Laguë. Parties that receive more seats in this hypothetical allocation are allotted additional seats, from the pool of 39 additional seats in the nation.
Intra-district Partisan Cartels	(1b) As in 1a.	(3b) As in 3a.

Lists	(1a) Each constituency has a certain number of "fixed" seats allocated to it, and these are allocated by modified Sainte-Laguë. To receive constituency seats a party must either exceed 4% of the national vote or its list(s) in the constituency must exceed 12% of the constituency vote. (4) Seats allocated to intra-district partisan cartels in steps 1b and 3b are reallocated to the cartel's constituent lists, basically by PR-d'Hondt.	(3a) Additional seats allocated to national partisan cartels in step (2) are reallocated to each cartel's constituent lists/partisan cartels according to which of those lists/ cartels had the largest average in their districts after the allocation of constituency seats.
Candidates	(5) Seats allocated to lists in steps 1a, 3a, and 4 are reallocated to each list's candidates mostly by list order.	—

349-member Parliament (*Riksdag*).

SWITZERLAND	*Primary districts*
Lists	PR-d'Hondt.
Candidates	Plurality.

200-member National Council (*Nationalrat/Conseil National*).

TURKEY	*Primary districts*
Lists	In districts returning at least five members, the party getting the most votes is awarded a bonus seat, with the rest of the

	seats awarded by PR-d'Hondt. In districts returning no more than four members, the system is PR-d'Hondt (and no bonus seats). A party must poll 10% of the national vote, and receive at least a Hare quota in the district, in order to be allocated seats.	
Candidates	List order.	

450-member Grand National Assembly (*Büyük Millet Meclisi*).

Tuvalu	*Primary districts*
Candidates	Plurality.

13-member Parliament. The Attorney General sits *ex officio*.

URUGUAY	*Primary districts*	*Secondary district (national)*
Lemas	(2) Seats awarded to *lemas* at the national level in step 2 are reallocated to the constituency level by PR-d'Hondt, taking into account the constitutional requirement that at least two seats go to each constituency.	(1) Votes cast for lists are aggregated nationally within *lemas*, and seats awarded by PR-d'Hondt.
Sub-lemas	(3) Seats awarded to *lemas* in step 3 are reallocated to *sub-lemas* by PR-d'Hondt.	—
Lists	(4) Seats awarded to *sub-lemas* in step 3 are reallocated to the lists within the *sub-lema* by PR-d'Hondt.	—
Candidates	(5) List order.	—

99-member Chamber of Deputies (*Cámara de Diputados*).

Vanuatu	*Primary districts*
Candidates	Plurality.

46-member Parliament.

Western Samoa	*Primary districts*
Candidates	Plurality.

47-member Legislative Assembly (*Fono*). Two seats are reserved for non-indigenous minorities.

Appendix B

Notation and proofs for Chapter 6

PART 1: THE VOTER'S DECISION PROBLEM

This appendix considers how a voter motivated solely by a desire to affect the outcome of the election decides which candidate to vote for, given that she votes. There are two parameters in the voter's decision (subscript *i*'s are suppressed and the distribution of utility types F is taken as given): First, the voter's preferences over the candidates, given by $u \in U$; second, the voter's expectations about how well each candidate will do at the polls.

I model voter expectations as follows. Each voter i views the candidates' vote totals (exclusive of her own vote) as random variables $V_1, \ldots, V_K$ governed by a joint distribution function, $g_n(v_1, \ldots, v_K)$. I assume that the mean of g_n does not depend on n (the number of voters), although n may affect higher-order moments. It may be, for example, that g_n is the K-nomial distribution with parameters $\pi = (\pi_1, \ldots, \pi_K)$ and $n - 1$. This is the case considered by Palfrey (1989), Cox (1994), and in Chapter 4.

I assume that the joint distribution g_n is common knowledge. This entails common knowledge of the expected vote shares of the candidates, denoted $\pi = (\pi_1, \ldots, \pi_K) = E(V_1/(n-1), \ldots, V_K/(n-1) \mid g_n)$, and of the tie-probabilities relevant in the voter's expected utility calculation.

I also assume that the probability beliefs g_n satisfy a version of Myerson and Weber's (1993:105) *ordering condition*. Supposing without loss of generality that the candidates' numbers refer to their order of expected finish, i.e., that $\pi_1 \geq \pi_2 \geq \ldots \geq \pi_K$, the version of the ordering condition that I shall use says the following: If $\pi_j < \pi_3$ then each voter believes the probability of the event "candidate j is tied for second" is *negligible* in comparison to the probability of the event "candidate 3 is tied for second," for large enough electorates. That is, no voter believes a fourth or lower place candidate really has a non-negligible chance of being tied for second, even conditional on there being a tie for second between some candidates. This condition, which is used below in deriving Proposition 1 but not in deriving Proposition 2, emerges naturally in models in which each voter's decision is statistically independent of every other's and the electorate is large (for then g_n collapses around its mean as n grows without bound; cf. Palfrey 1989; Cox 1994).

Another thing that the ordering condition says is that, if $\pi_1 > \pi_2$ then each voter believes the probability of the event "candidate 1 is tied for second" is *negligible* in comparison to the probability of the event "candidate 2 is tied for second," for large enough electorates. Thus, just as it is unlikely that fourth- or lower-place candidates will end up in a tie for second, relative to the probability that the third-place candidate will, so also it is unlikely that a first-place candidate will end up in a tie for second, relative to the probability that the second-place candidate will. This condition is used only in Proposition 2 and is unnecessary in deriving Proposition 1.

Finally, I also assume that expectations are rational:

Rational expectations condition: The expectation g_n is rational with respect to the distribution F if, for all j:

$$\pi_j = \int_{H_j(g_n)} dF$$

Here, $H_j(g_n)$ is the set of all voters for whom casting a vote for candidate j is optimal, given that g_n describes the distribution of other voters' votes.

I shall denote by $V(u;g_n) \subseteq K = \{1, \ldots ,K\}$ the optimal vote(s) of a voter of type u facing an electorate described by g_n. The purpose of this appendix is to show that the parameters identified are indeed sufficient to yield a well-defined decision problem, and to reveal such of the technical details of solving this problem as are necessary for proving the theorem to come.

By voting for candidate j, the focal voter can affect her utility either by breaking or making ties for second in the first round or by giving a candidate the last vote needed for a majority in the first round. I shall denote the probability (under g_n) that candidate j is one vote shy of a first-round majority, with k in second, by $q^j{}_k$. This gives the probability of putting j over the top rather than facing a jk pairing in the runoff. As far as breaking and making ties, there are two abstract possibilities to consider (if, following Hoffman (1982) and Myerson and Weber (1993), I ignore the possibility of r-way ties, $r > 2$, for the second seat): the voter's vote may put j into a tie with k for the second runoff spot or break a tie for the second spot between j and k. I shall let $q^i{}_{jk}$ equal the probability that candidates j and k end up tied for second, with candidate i in first.

Assuming (again following Hoffman and Myerson and Weber) that the probability of the event "k is in second, tied with j, behind i" equals the probability of the event "k is in second, one vote ahead of j, behind i," then q^i_{jk} equals the probability of *breaking* a tie for second between j and k, with i in first, and it also equals the probability of *making* a tie for second between j and k, with i in first.

In terms of the notation just introduced, the expected utility increment from voting for j rather than abstaining can be written:

$$\xi_j = \sum_{k \neq j} q^j_k (u_j - (p_{jk}u_j + p_{kj}u_k)) + \sum_{i \neq j} \sum_{\substack{k \neq j \\ k \neq i}} q^i_{jk}((p_{ji}u_j + p_{ij}u_i) - (p_{ki}u_k + p_{ik}u_i))$$

where p_{jk} equals the probability that candidate j will defeat candidate k in a runoff pairing of the two. Thus, $V(u;g_n) = \arg\max_{j \in K} \xi_j$.

The terms $\{p_{jk}\}$ can be computed as follows. Let $sgn(x - y) = 1$ if $x - y$ is positive, 0 if $x - y$ is zero, and -1 if $x - y$ is negative. Let $U^i = (u_1, \dots, u_{i-1}, u_{i+1}, \dots u_n)$ be a profile of voter types for voters other than i. Let $C^+ = \{U^i \in U^{n-1}: \sum_h sgn(u_{hj} - u_{hk}) > 1\}$ be the set of profiles in which a plurality larger than 1 of the other voters prefer j to k; $C(a) = \{U^i \in U^{n-1}: \sum_h sgn(u_{hj} - u_{hk}) = a\}$ be the set of profiles in which j is a votes ahead of k, for $a \in \{-1,0,1\}$; and $C^- = \{U^i \in U^{n-1}: \sum_h sgn(u_{hj} - u_{hk}) < -1\}$ be the set of profiles in which a plurality larger than 1 of the other voters prefer k to j. Finally, for voter i let G be the distribution over the $n - 1$ other voters' utility types induced by F:

$$G = \prod_{h=1}^{n-1} F$$

Then, if voter i prefers j to k,

$$p_{jk} = \int_{C^+ \cup C(1) \cup C(0)} dG + \frac{1}{2} \int_{C(-1)} dG$$

If voter i prefers k to j, then

$$p_{jk} = \int_{C^+} dG + \frac{1}{2} \int_{C(1)} dG$$

PART 2: THE ORDERING CONDITION AND PROOF OF PROPOSITION 1

Given a distribution F defined over U, I shall say that the expectation g is a limit of rational expectations if and only if there exists a sequence $\{g_n\}_{n=1}^{\infty}$ of expectations, each rational with respect to F, that converges to g in the Whitney-C^∞ topology. In other words, g is a limit of rational expectations if and only if arbitrarily large electorates can have rational expectations that are arbitrarily close to g. Given this definition, Proposition 1 can be stated as follows:

> *Proposition 1:* Let g be an expectation (i.e., a joint distribution for $V_1, \ldots, V_K$) and let $E(V_1/\Sigma V_k, \ldots, V_K/\Sigma V_k \mid g) = \underline{\pi}$. Assume without loss of generality that $\underline{\pi}_1 \geq \underline{\pi}_2 \geq \ldots \geq \underline{\pi}_K$. Then if $0 < \underline{\pi}_j < \underline{\pi}_3$ for some $j > 3$, g is not a limit of rational expectations.

In order to prove this proposition, I shall need the following definition.

> *The ordering condition:* A sequence of expectations $\{g_n\}_{n=1}^{\infty}$ satisfies the *ordering condition* if and only if

$$(1)\ \pi_j < \pi_3 \rightarrow \lim_{n\rightarrow\infty} \frac{q_{jh}^{(n)}}{q_{\bullet\bullet}^{(n)}} = 0 \text{ for all } h \neq j; \text{ and}$$

$$(2)\ \pi_1 > \pi_2 \rightarrow \lim_{n\rightarrow\infty} \frac{q_{1h}^{(n)}}{q_{\bullet\bullet}^{(n)}} = 0 \text{ for all } h \neq 1. \text{ Here,}$$

$$q_{jh}^{(n)} = \Pr(V_j = V_h \,\&\, V_h < V_k \text{ for exactly one } k \mid g_n), \text{ and } q_{\bullet\bullet}^{(n)} = \sum_{j\in K} \sum_{\substack{h\in K\\ h>j}} q_{jh}^{(n)}.$$

Proof of Proposition 1

Let g be a limit of rational expectations. Then by definition there exists a sequence of expectations $\{g_n\}_{n=1}^{\infty}$ such that each g_n is rational with respect to F, and such that $\{g_n\}_{n=1}^{\infty} \rightarrow g$ in the Whitney–C^{∞} topology. Suppose that $0 < \underline{\pi}_j < \underline{\pi}_3$. Then since $\{g_n\}_{n=1}^{\infty} \rightarrow g$ it follows that $0 < \pi_j < \pi_3$. Thus, from the ordering condition, we know that

$$\lim_{n\rightarrow\infty} \frac{q_{jh}^{(n)}}{q_{\bullet\bullet}^{(n)}} = 0 \text{ for all } h.$$

Thus, in the limit, voting for candidate j is no different from abstaining; the probability of a vote for j affecting the outcome, even given that there is a tie or near-tie of some sort, is virtually nil.

Now consider a voter with arbitrary preferences. In the limit, the only candidates with non-negligible probabilities of being tied for second are some subset of $\{1, 2, \ldots, j-1\}$. Will the voter do better to vote for one of these candidates than abstain? I shall deal with only one of many possible cases here, that in which $K > 4$ and $\pi_1 > \pi_2$ and $\pi_3 = \pi_4 > \pi_5$. Letting q_{hk}^{i} equal the probability (under g) that candidates h and k end up tied for second, with candidate i in first, this case is one in which q_{hk}^{i} is non-negligible only if $i = 1$, $h = 2$, and $k \in \{3,4\}$. Thus, the utility of voting for a candidate $k \in \{3, 4\}$, rather than abstaining, is

$$\xi_k = q^1_{2k}((p_{1k}u_1 + p_{k1}u_k) - (p_{12}u_1 + p_{21}u_2))$$

This will be positive for all voters for whom the utility differential in parentheses is positive. If j is such that $0<\underline{\pi}_j<\pi_3$, then voters who prefer a runoff pairing of 1&3 to 1&2 will not vote for j, preferring to vote for 3. Those who prefer a runoff pairing of 1&4 to 1&2 will not vote for j, preferring to vote for 4. Finally, those who prefer a runoff pairing of 1&2 to both 1&3 and 1&4 will not vote for j, preferring to vote for 2. Thus, any voter with a strict ranking of the three probable runoff pairings – 1&2, 1&3, and 1&4 – will not vote for j. Only voters who are indifferent among all three pairings, a measure-zero set, will vote for j. This, however, contradicts the assumption that $0 < \underline{\pi}_j$. Other cases can be dealt with similarly. *QED*.

Appendix C

Data and sources for Chapter 11

Country	Year	ENPV[1]	ENPS[2]	ML[3]	Upper[4]	Proximity[5]	ENPRES[6]	ENETH[7]
Argentina	1985	3.37	2.37	9.0	0.00	0.55	2.51	1.34
Australia	1984	2.79	2.38	1.0	0.00	0.00	.	1.11
Austria	1986	2.72	2.63	30.0	0.11	0.80	2.27	1.01
Bahamas	1987	2.11	1.96	1.0	0.00	0.00	.	1.34
Barbados	1986	1.93	1.25	1.0	0.00	0.00	.	1.50
Belgium	1985	8.13	7.01	8.0	0.40	0.00	.	2.35
Belize	1984	2.06	1.60	1.0	0.00	0.00	.	3.46
Bolivia	1985	4.58	4.32	17.5	0.00	1.00	4.58	3.77
Botswana	1984	1.96	1.35	1.0	0.00	0.00	.	1.11
Brazil	1990	9.68	8.69	30.0	0.00	0.63	5.69	2.22
Canada	1984	2.75	1.69	1.0	0.00	0.00	.	3.49
Colombia	1986	2.68	2.45	8.0	0.00	0.93	2.13	2.51
Costa Rica	1986	2.49	2.21	10.0	0.00	1.00	2.07	1.08
Cyprus	1985	3.62	3.57	12.0	0.00	0.00	.	1.56
Czech Republic*	1990	3.10	2.04	24.0	0.05	0.00	.	1.12
Denmark	1984	5.25	5.04	11.0	0.00	0.00	.	1.02
Dominica	1985	2.10	1.76	1.0	0.00	0.00	.	1.68
Dominican Republic	1986	3.19	2.53	5.0	0.00	1.00	2.80	1.75
El Salvador	1985	2.68	2.10	4.0	0.00	0.64	3.16	1.25
Ecuador	1984	10.32	5.78	3.0	0.00	1.00	5.18	2.60
Finland	1983	5.45	5.14	17.0	0.00	0.61	3.79	1.13
France	1981	4.13	2.68	1.0	0.00	0.96	4.86	1.17
Germany	1983	3.21	3.16	1.0	0.50	0.00	.	1.15
Greece	1985	2.59	2.14	6.0	0.24	0.00	.	1.04

Country	*Year*	*ENPV*[1]	*ENPS*[2]	*ML*[3]	*Upper*[4]	*Proximity*[5]	*ENPRES*[6]	*ENETH*[7]
Grenada	1990	3.84	3.08	1.0	0.00	0.00	.	1.06
Honduras	1985	3.49	2.80	9.0	0.00	1.00	3.49	1.23
Iceland	1983	4.26	4.07	7.0	0.18	0.41	3.60	1.06
India	1984	3.98	1.69	1.0	0.00	0.00	.	1.72
Ireland	1987	3.46	2.89	5.0	0.00	0.00	.	1.08
Israel	1984	4.28	3.86	120.0	0.00	0.00	.	1.39
Italy	1983	4.51	4.11	24.0	0.11	0.00	.	1.04
Jamaica	1989	1.97	1.60	1.0	0.00	0.00	.	1.65
Japan	1986	3.35	2.57	4.0	0.00	0.00	.	1.01
Korea (South)	1988	4.22	3.56	1.0	0.25**	0.87	3.55	1.01
Liechtenstein	1986	2.28	1.99	15.0	0.00	0.00	.	1.11
Luxembourg	1984	3.56	3.22	21.0	0.00	0.00	.	1.63
Malta	1987	2.01	2.00	5.0	0.00	0.00	.	1.13
Mauritius	1983	1.96	2.16	3.0	0.00	0.00	.	1.86
Netherlands	1986	3.77	3.49	150.0	0.00	0.00	.	1.08
New Zealand	1984	2.99	1.98	1.0	0.00	0.00	.	1.28
Norway	1985	3.63	3.09	10.0	0.00	0.00	.	1.04
Peru	1985	3.00	2.32	9.0	0.00	1.00	2.76	2.76
Portugal	1983	3.73	3.41	16.0	0.00	0.05	1.96	1.02
Spain	1986	3.59	2.81	7.0	0.00	0.00	.	1.65
St. Kitts and Nevis	1984	2.45	2.46	1.0	0.00	0.00	.	1.22
St. Lucia	1987	2.32	1.99	1.0	0.00	0.00	.	.22
St. Vincent & Grenadines	1984	2.28	1.74	1.0	0.00	0.00	.	1.66
Sweden	1985	3.52	3.39	12.0	0.00	0.00	.	1.26

Switzerland	1983	5.99	5.26	12.0	0.00	0.00	.	2.13
Trinidad & Tobago	1986	1.84	1.18	1.0	0.00	0.00	.	2.74
United Kingdom	1983	3.12	2.09	1.0	0.00	0.00	.	1.48
United States	1984	2.03	1.95	1.0	0.00	1.00	1.96	1.36
Uruguay	1989	3.38	3.35	11.0	0.27	1.00	3.38	1.28
Venezuela	1983	2.97	2.42	11.0	0.09	1.00	2.19	1.99

Notes:

*The Czech Republic was not of course an independent state in 1990. We use the Czech results from the Czechoslovak election of that year. Omitting this case does not affect the results.

**South Korea's upper tier is not compensatory and so in the main results I do not handle it in the same way as the other systems with upper tiers.

[1]ENPV = $1/\Sigma v^2_i$, where *vi* is party *i*'s vote share in the legislative election; the effective number of elective parties.

[2]ENPS = $1/\Sigma s^2_i$, where s_i is party *i*'s seat share in the legislature; the effective number of legislative parties.

[3]ML is the magnitude of the median legislator's district. If there are *N* members of a given country's legislature, one can associate with each member the magnitude of the electoral district from which that member was elected. Taking the median of these *N* numbers then gives ML. We take the median rather than the average because the former is a more robust measure of central tendency, although in practice the two measures work similarly. Data to compute ML come mostly from Chapter 3.

[4]UPPER: as defined in text.

[5]PROXIMITY: as defined in text.

[6]ENPRES = $1/\Sigma p^2_i$, where p_i is party *i*'s vote share in the presidential election; the effective number of presidential candidates.

[7]ENETH = $1/\Sigma g^2_i$, where g_i is the proportion of the population in ethnic group *i*; the effective number of ethnic groups.

References

Abramson, Paul R., John H. Aldrich, Phil Paolino, and David W. Rohde. 1995. "Third-Party and Independent Candidates in American Politics: Wallace, Anderson, and Perot." Political Science Quarterly 110:349–367.

Alesina, Alberto, and Howard Rosenthal. 1989. "Partisan Cycles in Congressional Elections and the Macroeconomy." *American Political Science Review* 83:373–98.

Alesina, Alberto, John Londregan, and Howard Rosenthal. 1993. "A Model of the Political Economy of the United States." *American Political Science Review* 87:12–33.

Allen, Chris. 1992. *"Democratic Renewal" in Africa: Two Essays on Benin.* Edinburgh: Centre of African Studies.

Amoroso, Mario. 1979. "Italy." In Geoffrey Hand, Jacques Georgel, and Christoph Sassee, eds., *European Electoral Systems Handbook.* London: Butterworths.

Argersinger, Peter. 1980. "A Place on the Ballot: Fusion Politics and Antifusion Laws." *American Historical Review* 85:287–306.

Arms, Thomas S., and Eileen Riley, eds. 1987. *World Elections on File.* New York: Facts on File.

Aronoff, Myron J. 1978. "Fission and Fusion: The Politics of Factionalism in the Israel Labor Parties." In Frank P. Belloni and Dennis C. Beller, eds., *Faction Politics: Political Parties and Factionalism in Comparative Perspective.* Santa Barbara: ABC-Clio, Inc.

Arrow, Kenneth J. 1951. *Social Choice and Individual Values.* New Haven: Yale University Press.

Aubert, J. F. 1983. "La Composition du Parlement Suisse et Les Systèmes Électoraux." In Jacques Cadart, ed., *Les Modes de Scrutin des Dix-huit Pays Libres de L'Europe Occidentale.* Paris: Presses Universitaires de France.

Austen-Smith, David. 1987. "Sophisticated Sincerity: Voting Over Endogenous Agendas." *American Political Science Review* 81:1323–1330.

Balinski, Michael L., and H. Peyton Young. 1982. *Fair Representation: Meeting the Ideal of One Man, One Vote.* New Haven: Yale University Press.

References

Banks, Jeffrey. 1985. "Sophisticated Voting Outcomes and Agenda Control." *Social Choice and Welfare* 1:295–306.

Barnes, Samuel H., Frank Grace, James K. Pollock, and Peter W. Sperlich. 1962. "The German Party System and the 1961 Federal Election." *American Political Science Review* 56:899–914.

Bartels, Larry M. 1988. *Presidential Primaries and the Dynamics of Public Choice.* Princeton: Princeton University Press.

Bartholdi, John J., and James B. Orlin. 1991. "Single Transferable Vote Resists Strategic Voting." *Social Choice and Welfare* 8:341–354.

Bartolini, Stefano. 1984. "Institutional Constraints and Party Competition in the French Party System." *West European Politics* 7:103–127.

Bawn, Kathleen. 1993. "The Logic of Institutional Preferences: German Electoral Law as a Social Choice Outcome." *American Journal of Political Science* 37:965–989.

Besley, Timothy, and Stephen Coate. 1995. "An Economic Model of Representative Democracy." Working Paper 95-02, Center for Analytic Research in Economics and Social Sciences, University of Pennsylvania.

Beyme, Klaus von. 1985. *Political Parties in Western Democracies.* Translated by Eileen Martin. New York: St. Martin's Press.

Black, Gordon S. 1972. "A Theory of Political Ambition: Career Choices and the Role of Structural Incentives." *American Political Science Review* 66:144–59.

Black, Jerome H. 1978. "The Multicandidate Calculus of Voting: Applications to Canadian Federal Elections." *American Journal of Political Science* 22:609–38.

Black, J. H. 1980. "The Probability-choice Perspective in Voter Decision Making Models." *Public Choice* 35: 565–74.

Blais, André, and R. K. Carty. 1987. "The Impact of Electoral Formulae on the Creation of Majority Governments." *Electoral Studies* 6:99–110.

Blais, André, and R. K. Carty. 1989. "Electoral Formulae." Université de Montréal. Unpublished typescript.

Blais, André, and R. K. Carty. 1991. "The Psychological Impact of Electoral Laws: Measuring Duverger's Elusive Factor." *British Journal of Political Science* 21:79–93.

Blais, André, and Louis Massicotte. N.d. "Electoral Formulas: A Macroscopic Perspective." *European Journal of Political Research,* forthcoming.

Blais, André, and Richard Nadeau. N.d. "Measuring Strategic Voting: A Two-Step Procedure." *Electoral Studies,* forthcoming.

Blais, André, F. Renaut, and R. Desrosiers. 1974. "L'effet en amont de la carte electorale." *Canadian Journal of Political Science* 7: 648–72.

Blaustein, Albert P., and Gisbert H. Flanz, eds. 1971. *Constitutions of the Countries of the World.* Dobbs Ferry, N.Y.: Oceana Publications.

Blondel, Jean. 1972. *Comparing Political Systems.* New York: Praeger.

Bogdanor, Vernon. 1983. "Conclusion." In Vernon Bogdanor and David Butler, eds., *Democracy and Elections: Electoral Systems and Their Political Consequences.* Cambridge: Cambridge University Press.

Bowler, Shaun, and David J. Lanoue. 1992. "Strategic and Protest Voting for Third Parties: The Case of the Canadian NDP." *Western Political Quarterly* 45:485–499.

Brace, Paul. 1984. "Progressive Ambition in the House: A Probabilistic Approach." *Journal of Politics* 46:556–569.

Brady, David. 1988. *Critical Elections and Congressional Policy Making.* Stanford: Stanford University Press.

Brady, David, Susanne Lohmann, and Douglas Rivers. 1995. "Party Identification, Retrospective Voting, and Moderating Elections in a Federal System: West Germany 1961–1989." University of California at Los Angeles. Unpublished typescript.

Brams, Steven J., and Peter Fishburn. 1983. *Approval Voting.* Boston: Birkhauser.

Brams, Steven J., and P. D. Straffin. 1982. "The Entry Problem in a Political Race." In P. C. Ordeshook and K. A. Shepsle, eds., *Political Equilibrium,* Kluwer-Nijhoff.

Brazil - Tribunal Superior Eleitoral. 1990. *Resultado das Eleições de 1990 para a Câmara dos Deputados.* Brasília: Supervisão de Engenharia de Sistemas do Tribunal Superior Eleitoral.

Brody, Richard A., and Benjamin I. Page. 1973. "Indifference, Alienation and Rational Decisions." *Public Choice* 15:1–17.

Buchanan, James, and Gordon Tullock. 1962. *The Calculus of Consent.* Ann Arbor: University of Michigan Press.

Bullock, Charles S., III, and Loch K. Johnson. 1992. *Runoff Elections in the United States.* Chapel Hill: University of North Carolina Press.

Burnham, Walter Dean. 1965. "The Changing Shape of the American Political Universe." *American Political Science Review* 59:7–28.

Burnham, Walter Dean. 1970. *Critical Elections and the Mainsprings of American Politics.* New York: W. W. Norton.

Butler, David E. 1953. *The Electoral System in Britain 1918–1951.* Oxford: Clarendon Press.

Butler, David, and Dennis Kavanagh. 1988. *The British General Election of 1987.* London: Macmillan.

Cairns, A. 1968. "The Electoral System and the Party System in Canada, 1921–1965." *Canadian Journal of Political Science* 1:55–80.

Campbell, Peter. 1958. *French Electoral Systems and Elections 1789–1957.* London: Faber and Faber.

Campbell, Peter, and Alistair Cole. 1989. *French Electoral Systems and Elections Since 1789.* Aldershot: Gower.

Carstairs, Andrew McLaren. 1980. *A Short History of Electoral Systems in Western Europe.* London: George Allen & Unwin.

Catt, Helena. 1989. "Tactical Voting in Britain." *Parliamentary Affairs* 42:548–59.

Catt, Helena. 1991. "What Do Voters Decide?" *Political Science* 43:30–42.

Central Intelligence Agency. 1990. *World Factbook.* Washington, D.C.: Central Intelligence Agency.

Central Intelligence Agency. 1994. *World Factbook.* Washington, D.C.: Brassey's.

Charlesworth, James C. 1948. "Is Our Two-Party System Natural?" *Annals of the American Academy of Political and Social Science* 259:1–9.

Cheng, T. J. 1993. "Constitution-Making in the Republic of Korea." Case Study 93-008, Graduate School of International Relations and Pacific Studies, University of California at San Diego.

Christensen, Raymond. N.d. "Strategic Imperatives of Japan's SNTV Electoral System and the Cooperative Innovations of the Former Opposition Parties." *Comparative Political Studies,* forthcoming.

Christensen, Raymond. 1994. "The 1994 Electoral Reform in Japan: How it was Enacted and Changes it Will Bring." *Asian Survey* 34:589–605.

Christensen, Raymond, and Paul Johnson. N.d. "Toward a Context-Rich Analysis of Electoral Systems: The Japanese Example." *American Journal of Political Science,* forthcoming.

Clogg, Richard. 1987. *Parties and Elections in Greece : The Search for Legitimacy.* Durham: Duke University Press.

Cole, Alistair, and Peter Campbell. 1989. *French Electoral Systems and Elections Since 1789.* Aldershot: Gower.

Cook, Chris. 1984. *A Short History of the Liberal Party 1900–1984.* 2d edn. London: Macmillan.

Coppedge, Michael. 1995. "District Magnitude, Economic Performance, and Party-System Fragmentation in Five Latin American Countries." University of Notre Dame. Unpublished manuscript.

Coughlin, Peter. 1992. *Probabilitistic Voting Theory.* New York: Cambridge University Press.

Cox, Gary W. 1984. "Strategic Electoral Choice in Multi-Member Districts: Approval Voting in Practice?" *American Journal of Political Science* 28:722–738.

Cox, Gary W. 1987a. *The Efficient Secret.* Cambridge: Cambridge University Press.

Cox, Gary W. 1987b. "Duverger's Law and Strategic Voting." University of California, San Diego. Unpublished manuscript.

Cox, Gary W. 1987c. "Electoral Equilibria Under Alternative Voting Institutions." *American Journal of Political Science* 31:82–108.

Cox, Gary W. 1990a. "Centripetal and Centrifugal Incentives in Electoral Systems." *American Journal of Political Science* 34:903–935.

Cox, Gary W. 1990b. "Multicandidate Spatial Competition." In James M. Enelow and Melvin J. Hinch, eds., *Advances in the Spatial Theory of Voting.* Cambridge: Cambridge University Press.

Cox, Gary W. 1991. "SNTV and d'Hondt are 'Equivalent'." *Electoral Studies* 10:118–32.

Cox, Gary W. 1994. "Strategic Voting Equilibria under the Single Non-Transferable Vote." *American Political Science Review* 88:608–621.

Cox, Gary W. N.d. "Is the Single Non-Transferable Vote Superproportional? Evidence from Japan and Taiwan." *American Journal of Political Science,* forthcoming.

Cox, Gary W., and Octavio Amorim Neto. N.d. "Electoral Institutions, Cleavage Structures, and the Number of Parties." *American Journal of Political Science,* forthcoming.

Cox, Gary W., and Michael C. Munger. 1989. "Closeness, Expenditure, Turnout: The 1982 U.S. House Elections." *American Political Science Review* 83:217–232.

Cox, Gary W., and Samuel Kernell, eds. 1991. *The Politics of Divided Government.* Boulder: Westview Press.

Cox, Gary W., and Burt Monroe. 1995. "Strategic Voting Equilibria in Parliamentary Elections." Paper presented at the American Political Science Association meetings in Chicago.

Cox, Gary W., and Scott Morgenstern. 1993. "The Increasing Advantage of Incumbency in the American States." *Legislative Studies Quarterly* 18:495–514.

Cox, Gary W., and Emerson Niou. 1994. "Seat Bonuses Under the Single Non-Transferable Vote System: Evidence from Japan and Taiwan." *Comparative Politics* 26:221–236.

Cox, Gary W., and Frances Rosenbluth. N.d. "Factional Competition for the Party Endorsement: The Case of Japan's Liberal Democratic Party." *British Journal of Political Science,* forthcoming.

Cox, Gary W., and Matthew S. Shugart. 1995. "Strategic Voting Under Proportional Representation." University of California, San Diego. Unpublished manuscript.

Cox, Gary W., and Matthew S. Shugart. N.d. "In the Absence of Vote Pooling: Nomination and Vote Allocation Errors in Colombia." *Electoral Studies,* forthcoming.

Crewe, Ivor. 1987. "What's Left for Labour: An Analysis of Thatcher's Victory." *Public Opinion* 10:52–56.

Curtis, Gerald L. 1971. *Election Campaigning Japanese Style.* New York: Columbia University Press.

Dahl, Robert A. 1956. *A Preface to Democratic Theory.* Chicago: University of Chicago Press.

Dewachter, Wilfried. 1983. "Les Modes De Scrutin en Belgique pour L'élection Des Assemblées Parlementaires." In Jacques Cadart, ed., *Les Modes de Scrutin des Dix-huit Pays Libres de L'Europe Occidentale.* Paris: Presses Universitaires de France.

Dick, Leonard, and Richard Natkiel. 1987. *The Economist World Atlas of Elections.* London: Hodder and Stoughton.

Dorney, Sean. 1990. *Papua New Guinea: People, Politics and History Since 1975.* Sydney: Random House.

Downs, Anthony. 1957. *An Economic Theory of Democracy.* New York: Harper and Row.

Dummett, Michael. 1984. *Voting Procedures.* Oxford: Clarendon Press.

Duverger, Maurice. 1954. Political Parties. New York: Wiley.

Duverger, Maurice. 1986. "Duverger's Law: Thirty Years Later." In Arend Lijphart and Bernard Grofman, eds., *Choosing an Electoral System: Issues and Alternatives.* New York: Praeger.

Eckstein, H. 1963. "The Impact of Electoral Systems on Representative Government." In H. Eckstein and D. Apter, eds., *Comparative Politics: A Reader.* New York: Free Press.

Endersby, James W., and W. D. Thomason. 1994. "Spotlight on Vermont: Third Party Success in the 1990 Congressional Election." Social Science Journal 31:251–62.

Enelow, James, and Melvin Hinich, eds. 1990. *Advances in the Spatial Theory of Voting*. Cambridge: Cambridge University Press.

Epstein, Leon. 1986. *Political Parties in the American Mold*. Madison: University of Wisconsin Press.

Evans, Geoffrey, and Anthony Heath. 1993. "A Tactical Error in the Analysis of Tactical Voting: A Response to Niemi, Whitten and Franklin." *British Journal of Political Science* 23:131–37.

Farquharson, Robin. 1969. *Theory of Voting*. New Haven: Yale University Press.

Farrell, Joseph. 1987. "Cheap Talk, Coordination, and Entry." *Rand Journal of Economics* 18:34–39.

Feddersen, Timothy. 1992. "A Voting Model Implying Duverger's Law and Positive Turnout." *American Journal of Political Science* 36:938–962.

Feddersen, Timothy, I. Sened, and S. G. Wright. 1990. "Rational Voting and Candidate Entry under Plurality Rule." *American Journal of Political Science* 34:1005–1016.

Felsenthal, Dan S., and Avraham Brichta. 1985. "Sincere and Strategic Voters: An Israeli Study." *Political Behavior* 7:311–323.

Ferejohn, John, and Roger Noll. 1988. "Three's a Crowd: Duverger's Law Reconsidered." Stanford University. Unpublished typescript.

Fey, Mark. 1995. "Stability, Polls and Duverger's Laws." University of California at Irvine. Unpublished manuscript.

Fiorina, Morris P. 1977. "An Outline for a Model of Party Choice." *American Journal of Political Science* 21:601–625.

Fiorina, Morris P. 1992. *Divided Government*. New York: Macmillan.

Fishburn, Peter. 1973. *The Theory of Social Choice*. Princeton: Princeton University Press.

Fisher, Steven L. 1973. "The Wasted Vote Thesis." *Comparative Politics* 5: 293–99.

Fisichella, D. 1984. "The Double-ballot as a Weapon against Anti-system Parties." In Arend Lijphart and Bernard Grofman, eds., *Choosing an Electoral System: Issues and Alternatives*. New York: Praeger.

Forsythe, Robert, Roger Myerson, T. A. Rietz, and Robert Weber. 1993. "An Experiment on Coordination in Multi-Candidate Elections: the Importance of Polls and Election Histories." *Social Choice and Welfare* 10:223–247.

Franco, Rolando. 1986. "El Sistema Electoral Uruguayo en un Perspectivo Comparada." In Rolando Franco, ed., *El Sistema Electoral Uruguayo: Peculiaridades y Perspectivas*. Montevideo: Fundación Hanns-Seidel.

Freedom House. 1980–1991. *Freedom in the World*. New York: Freedom House.

Fukui, Haruhiro. 1988. "Electoral Laws and the Japanese Party System." In Gail Lee Bernstein and Haruhiro Fukui, eds., *Japan and the World*. London: Macmillan.

Galbraith, John W., and Nocol C. Rae. 1989. "A Test of the Importance of Tactical Voting: Great Britain, 1987." *British Journal of Political Science* 19:126–137.

Gibbard, Alan. 1973. "Manipulation of Voting Schemes: A General Result." *Econometrica* 41:587–601.

Gilmour, J. B., and P. Rothstein. 1993. "Early Republican Retirement—A Cause of Democratic Dominance in the House of Representatives." *Legeslative Studies Quarterly* 18:345–365.

Gonzalez, Luis E. 1991. *Political Structures and Democracy in Uruguay.* Notre Dame: University of Notre Dame Press.

Gorwin, Ian, ed. 1989. *Elections Since 1945. A Worldwide Reference Compendium.* Essex: Longman.

Greenberg, Joseph, and Kenneth Shepsle. 1987. "The Effect of Electoral Awards in a Multiparty Competition with Entry." *American Political Science Review* 81:525–537.

Grimm, Dieter. 1983. "Les Modes de Scrutin en Allemagne." In Jacques Cadart, ed., *Les Modes de Scrutin des Dix-huit Pays Libres de L'Europe Occidentale.* Paris: Presses Universitaires de France.

Groseclose, Timothy, and Keith Krehbiel. 1994. "Golden Parachutes, Rubber Checks, and Strategic Retirements from the 102d House." *American Journal of Political Science* 38:75–99.

Grumm, J. G. 1958. "Theories of Electoral Systems." *Midwest Journal of Political Science* 2:357–376.

Gunther, Richard. 1989. "Electoral Laws, Party Systems, and Elites: The Case of Spain." *American Political Science Review* 83:835–858.

Gunther, Richard, and José Ramón Montero. 1994. "Sistemas 'Cerrados' y Listas 'Abiertas': Sobre Algunas Propuestas de Reforma del Sistema Electoral en España." In *La Reforma Del Régimen Electoral: Debate Celebrado en el Centro de Estudios Constitucionales.* Madrid: Centro de Estudios Constitucionales.

Gutowski, William E., and John P. Georges. 1993. "Optimal Sophisticated Voting Strategies in Single Ballot Elections Involving Three Candidates." *Public Choice* 77:225–247.

Hamilton, Howard. 1967. "Legislative Constituencies: Single-member Districts, Multi-member Districts, and Floterial Districts." *Western Political Quarterly* 20:321–340.

Hardin, Russell. 1991. "Hobbesian Political Order." *Political Theory* 19:156–180.

Harrop, Martin, and William L. Miller. 1987. *Elections and Voters: A Comparative Introduction.* London: Macmillan.

Hartigan, J. A., and P. M. Hartigan. 1985. "The Dip Test of Unimodality." *The Annals of Statistics* 13:70–84.

Hartz, Louis. 1955. *The Liberal Tradition in America: An Interpretation of American Political Thought Since the Revolution.* New York: Harcourt, Brace.

Heath, Anthony, Roger Jowell, John Curtice, Geoff Evans, Julia Field, and Sharon Witherspoon. 1991. *Understanding Political Change: The British Voter 1964–1987.* Oxford: Pergamon Press.

Helgason, Thorkell. 1991. "Apportionment of Seats in the Icelandic Parliament." University of Iceland. Unpublished typescript.

Hill, K. 1974. "Belgium: Political Change in a Segmented Society." In Richard Rose, ed., *Electoral Behaviour: A Comparative Handbook*. London: Free Press.

Hinich, Melvin J. 1977. "Equilibrium in Spatial Voting: The Median Voter Result is an Artifact." *Journal of Economic Theory* 16:208–19.

Hinich, Melvin, Otto Davis and Peter Ordeshook. 1970. "An Expository Development of a Mathematical Model of the Electoral Process." *American Political Science Review* 64:426–448.

Hoffman, Dale T. 1982. "A Model for Strategic Voting." *SIAM Journal of Applied Mathematics* 42:751–761.

Hotelling, Harold. 1929. "Stability in Competition." *Economic Journal* 39:41–57.

Howard, Christopher. 1983. "Expectations Born to Death: Local Labour Party Expansion in the 1920s." In Jay Winter, ed., *The Working Class in Modern British History*. Cambridge: Cambridge University Press.

Howe, Stephen. 1987. "The Maltese General Election of 1987." *Electoral Studies* 6:235–247.

Hsieh, John Fuh-sheng, Emerson M. S. Niou, and Philip Paolino. 1995. "Condorcet Winner, Strategic Voting, and Vote Choice: The Case of the 1994 Mayoral Election in the City of Taipei." Paper presented at the Annual Meeting of the American Political Science Association, Chicago, August 31–September 3.

Huber, John, and G. Bingham Powell. 1994. "Congruence Between Citizens and Policymakers in Two Visions of Liberal Democracy." *World Politics* 46:291–326.

Hughes, Colin A., and B. D. Graham. 1968. *A Handbook of Australian Government and Politics 1890–1964*. Canberra: Australian National University.

Hughes, Colin A. 1993. "Bicameralism and Alternate Electoral Systems." University of Queensland. Unpublished typescript.

Inter-Parliamentary Union. 1993. *Electoral Systems: A World-wide Comparative Study*. Geneva: Inter-Parliamentary Union.

Jacobson, Gary C., and Michael A. Dimock. 1994. "Checking Out: The Effects of Bank Overdrafts on the 1992 House Elections." *American Journal of Political Science* 38:601–624.

Jaensch, Dean. 1983. *The Australian Party System*. Sydney: Allen and Unwin.

Jesse, Eckhard. 1988. "Split-voting in the Federal Republic of Germany: An Analysis of the Federal Elections from 1953 to 1987." *Electoral Studies* 7:109–124.

Jesse, Eckhard. 1990. *Elections: The Federal Republic of Germany in Comparison*. Translated by Lindsay Batson. New York: St. Martin's.

Johansen, Lars Nørby. 1979. "Denmark." In Geoffrey Hand, Jacques Georgel, and Christoph Sasse, eds., *European Electoral Systems Handbook*. London: Butterworths.

Johnston, R. J., and C. J. Pattie. 1991. "Tactical Voting in Great Britain in 1983 and 1987: An Alternative Approach." *British Journal of Political Science* 21:95–108.

Johnston, Richard, André Blais, Henry E. Brady, and Jean Crête. 1992. *Letting the People Decide: Dynamics of a Canadian Election.* Stanford: Stanford University Press.

Jones, Mark P. 1994. "Presidential Election Laws and Multipartism in Latin America." *Political Research Quarterly* 47:41–57.

Jones, Mark P. 1995. "A Guide to the Electoral Systems of the Americas." *Electoral Studies* 14:5–21.

Katz, Richard. 1986. "Intraparty Preference Voting." In B. Grofman and A. Lijphart, eds., *Electoral Laws and Their Political Consequences.* New York: Agathon.

Kennedy, Peter. 1994. *A Guide to Econometrics.* 3rd edition. Cambridge: MIT Press.

Key, V. O., Jr. 1955. "A Theory of Critical Elections." *Journal of Politics* 17:3–18.

Key, V. O., Jr. 1964a. *Southern Politics in State and Nation.* New York: Knopf.

Key, V. O., Jr. 1964b. *Politics, Parties and Pressure Groups.* 5th ed. New York: Crowell.

Kiewiet, D. R., and L. Zeng. 1993. "An Analysis of Congressional Career Decisions, 1947–1986." *American Political Science Review* 87:928–941.

Kim, Jae-On, and Mahn-Geum Ohn. 1992. "A Theory of Minor-Party Persistence: Election Rules, Social Cleavage, and the Number of Political Parties." *Social Forces* 70:575–599.

Kirschner, William R. 1995. "Fusion and the Associational Rights of Minor Political Parties." *Columbia Law Review* 95:683–723.

Klain, Maurice. 1955. "A New Look at the Constituencies: The Need for a Recount and a Reappraisal." *American Political Science Review* 49:1105–1119.

Kohno, Masaru. 1992. "Rational Foundations for the Organization of the Liberal Democratic Party in Japan." *World Politics* 44:369–97.

Körösényi, András. 1990. "Hungary." *Electoral Studies* 9:337–45.

Kramer, Michael. 1996. "Rescuing Boris." *Time,* July 15.

Kuusela, Kimmo. 1994. "The Founding Electoral Systems in Eastern Europe, 1989–91." In Geoffrey Pridam and Tatu Vanhanen, eds., *Democratization in Eastern Europe: Domestic and International Perspectives.* London: Routledge.

Laakso, Marku, and Rein Taagepera. 1979. "Effective Number of Parties: A Measure with Application to West Europe." *Comparative Political Studies* 12:3–27.

Lagos, Marta. 1996. "Elecciones y Partidos en Chile." Opinión Pública Latinoamericana. Unpublished typescript.

Laitin, David. 1994. "The Tower of Babel as a Coordination Game: Political Linguistics in Ghana." *American Political Science Review* 88:622–35.

Lakeman, Enid. 1970. *How Democracies Vote.* London: Faber and Faber.

Lanoue, David J., and Shaun Bowler. 1992. "The Sources of Tactical Voting in British Parliamentary Elections, 1983–1987." *Political Behavior* 14:141–157.

LaPalombara, Joseph, and Myron Weiner, eds. 1966. *Political Parties and Political Development.* Princeton: Princeton University Press.

Lavau, G. E. 1953. *Partis Politiques et Réalités Sociales*. Paris: A. Colin.

Laver, Michael. 1987. "The Logic of Plurality Voting in Multi-Party Systems: Strategic Voting in Liverpool Elections." In M. J. Holler, ed., *The Logic of Multiparty Systems*. Dordrecht: Martinus Nijhoff.

Laver, Michael, and Norman Schofield. 1990. *Multiparty Government: The Politics of Coalition in Europe*. Oxford: Oxford University Press.

Levine, Stephen, and Nigel S. Roberts. 1991. "Elections and Expectations: Evidence from Electoral Surveys in New Zealand." *The Journal of Commonwealth and Comparative Politics* 29:129–152.

Lewis, David. 1969. *Convention: A Philosophical Study*. Cambridge: Harvard University Press.

Leys, Colin. 1959. "Models, Theories and the Theory of Political Parties." *Political Studies* 7:127–146.

Lijphart, Arend. 1984. *Democracies*. New Haven: Yale University Press.

Lijphart, Arend. 1990. "The Political Consequences of Electoral Laws, 1945–85." *American Political Science Review* 84:481–96.

Lijphart, Arend. 1994. *Electoral Systems and Party Systems: A Study of Twenty-Seven Democracies, 1945–1990*. Oxford: Oxford University Press.

Lijphart, Arend, and R. W. Gibberd. 1977. "Thresholds and Payoffs in List Systems of Proportional Representation." *European Journal of Political Research* 5:219–44.

Linz, Juan J., and Arturo Valenzuela, eds. 1993. *The Failure of Presidential Democracy*. Baltimore: The Johns Hopkins University Press.

Lipset, Seymour Martin, and Stein Rokkan, eds. 1967. *Party Systems and Voter Alignments: Cross-National Perspectives*. New York: Free Press.

Lipson, Leslie. 1953. "The Two-Party System in British Politics." *American Political Science Review* 47:337–58.

Lipson, Leslie. 1959. "Party Systems in the United Kingdom and the Older Commonwealth: Causes, Resemblances, and Variations." *Political Studies* 7:12–31.

Lipson, Leslie. 1964. *The Democratic Civilization*. New York: Oxford University Press.

Ludwin, William G. 1978. "Strategic Voting and the Borda Method." *Public Choice* 33:85–90.

Mackenzie, W. J. M. 1957. "The Export of Electoral Systems." *Political Studies* 5:240–257.

Mackerras, Malcolm. 1970. "DLP Preference Distribution 1958–1969." University of Sydney. Occasional Monograph No. 3.

Mackie, Thomas T., and Richard Rose. 1991. *The International Almanac of Electoral History*. 3rd. ed. Washington, D.C.: Congressional Quarterly.

Magaloni Kerpel, Beatriz. 1994. "El voto estratégico: el dilemma del elector de oposición." *Cuadernos de Nexos* 73:11–15.

Magleby, David B., and Joseph Q. Monson. 1995. "If You Can't Win, Change the Rules: Strategic Voting, Expressive Voting, and a Proposed Runoff Election in Utah." Brigham Young University. Unpublished typescript.

Mainwaring, Scott. 1991. "Politicians, Parties, and Electoral Systems: Brazil in Comparative Perspective." *Comparative Politics* 24:21–43.

Mainwaring, Scott, and Matthew S. Shugart. 1996. "Conclusion: Presidentialism and the Party System." In Scott Mainwaring and Matthew S. Shugart, eds., *Presidentialism and Democracy in Latin America.* New York: Cambridge University Press.

Mannick, A. R. 1989. *Mauritius: The Politics of Change.* Mayfield: Dodo Books.

Marsh, Michael. 1985. "The Voters Decide?: Preferential Voting in European List Systems." *European Journal of Political Research* 13:365–78.

Matthew, H. C. G., R. I. McKibbin, and John Kay. 1976. "The Franchise Factor in the Rise of the Labour Party." *English Historical Review* 91:723–752.

Mazmanian, Daniel A. 1974. *Third Parties in Presidential Elections.* Washington, D.C.: Brookings Institution.

McAllister, Ian, Malcolm Mackerras, Alvaro Ascui, and Susan Moss. 1990. *Australian Political Facts.* Melbourne: Longman Cheshire.

McCormick, Richard P. 1975. "Political Development and the Second American Party System." In William N. Chambers and Walter Dean Burnham, eds., *The American Party Systems.* 2d ed., 90–116. New York: Oxford University Press.

McCubbins, Mathew D., and Frances Rosenbluth. 1995. "Party Provision for Personal Politics: Dividing the Vote in Japan." In Peter F. Cowhey and Mathew D. McCubbins, eds., *Structure and Policy in Japan and the United States.* Cambridge: Cambridge University Press.

McCuen, Brian. 1995. "Strategic Voters and Coalitions." Paper presented at the American Political Science Association meetings in Chicago.

McKelvey, Richard. 1976. "Intransitivities in Multidimensional Voting Models, and Some Implications for Agenda Control." *Journal of Economic Theory* 2:472–482.

McKelvey, Richard, and Peter Ordeshook. 1972. "A General Theory of the Calculus of Voting." In J. F. Herndon and J. L. Bernd, eds., *Mathematical Applications in Political Science,* vol. 6. Charlottesville: University Press of Virginia.

McKelvey, Richard and Richard Niemi. 1978. "A Multistage Representation of Sophisticated Voting for Binary Procedures." *Journal of Economic Theory* 18:1–22.

McKibbin, Ross. 1990. *The Ideologies of Class: Social Relations in Britain 1880–1950.* Oxford: Clarendon Press.

McLean, Iain, 1987. "Coalition Building and Disequilibrium." University College, Dublin. Unpublished typescript.

Meehl, P. E. 1977. "The Selfish Voter Paradox and the Thrown-away Vote Argument." *American Political Science Review* 61:11–30.

Meisel, John. 1963. "The Stalled Omnibus: Canadian Parties in the 1960s." *Social Research* 30: 383–4.

Meisel, John. 1974. *Cleavages, Parties and Values in Canada.* Beverly Hills: Sage Publications.

Miller, Nicholas. 1980. "A New Solution Set for Tournaments and Majority Voting." *American Journal of Political Science* 24:68–96.

Miranda Pacheco, Mario. 1986. "Bolivia: Reglas del Juego Electoral y Juego sin Reglas de la Representatividad Política." In *Sistemas Electorales y*

Representación Política en Latinoamerica. Instituto de Cooperación Iberoamericano. Madrid: Fundación Friedrich Ebert.

Mueller, Dennis C. 1989. *Public Choice II*. New York: Cambridge University Press.

Murray, B. K. 1980. *The People's Budget 1909/10: Lloyd George and Liberal Politics*. Oxford: Clarendon Press.

Myerson, Roger, and Robert Weber. 1993. "A Theory of Voting Equilibria." *American Political Science Review* 87:102–14.

Myerson, Roger. 1994. "Incentives to Cultivate Favored Minorities Under Alternative Electoral Systems." *American Political Science Review* 87:856–869.

Nagel, Jack H. 1994. "Predicting the Political Consequences of Electoral Reform: How Many Parties Will New Zealand Have Under Proportional Representation?" Paper presented at the annual meeting of the American Political Science Association, New York.

Niemi, Richard. 1984. "The Problem of Strategic Voting Under Approval Voting." *American Political Science Review* 78:952–958.

Niemi, Richard G., Guy Whitten and Mark N. Franklin. 1992. "Constituency Characteristics, Individual Characteristics and Tactical Voting in the 1987 British General Election." *British Journal of Political Science* 23:131-137.

Niemi, Richard, Guy Whitten, and Mark Franklin. 1993. "People Who Live in Glass Houses: A Response to Evans and Heath's Critique of Our Note on Tactical Voting." *British Journal of Political Science* 23:549–63.

Nilson, Sten S. 1983. "Elections Presidential and Parliamentary: Contrasts and Connections." *West European Politics* 6:111–124.

Nixon, David, Dganit Olomoki, Norman Schofield, and Itai Sened. 1996. "Multiparty Probabilistic Voting: An Application to the Knesset." Political Economy Working Paper 186, Washington University in St. Louis.

Nohlen, Dieter, ed. 1993. *Enciclopedia Electoral Latinoamericana y del Caribe*. San José: Instituto Interamericano de Derechos Humanos.

Nohlen, Dieter. 1981. *Sistemas Electorales Del Mundo*. Translated by Ramon Garcia Cotarelo. Madrid: Centro de Estudios Constitucionales.

Noiret, Serge, ed. 1990. *Political Strategies and Electoral Reforms: Origins of Voting Systems in Europe in the 19th and 20th Centuries*. Baden-Baden: Nomos Verlagsgesellschaft.

Nurmi, Hannu. 1987. *Comparing Voting Systems*. Dordrecht: D. Reidel.

Olson, Mancur. 1965. *The Logic of Collective Action*. Cambridge: Harvard University Press.

Ordeshook, Peter C. 1986. *Game Theory and Political Theory*. Cambridge: Cambridge University Press.

Ordeshook, Peter, and Thomas Schwartz. 1987. "Agendas and the Control of Political Outcomes." *American Political Science Review* 81:179–199.

Ordeshook, Peter, and Olga Shvetsova. 1994. "Ethnic Heterogeneity, District Magnitude, and the Number of Parties." *American Journal of Political Science* 38:100–123.

Osborne, Martin J. 1993. "Candidate Positioning and Entry in a Political Competition." *Games and Economic Behavior* 5:133–151.

Osborne, Martin, and Al Silvinski. 1995. "A Model of Political Competition with Citizen Candidates." Working Paper 95-04, Department of Economics, McMaster University.

Ostrogorski, M. 1902. *Democracy and the Organization of Political Parties,* vol. I. Translated from the French by Frederick Clark. London: Macmillan.

Palfrey, Thomas. 1984. "Spatial Equilibrium with Entry." *Review of Economic Studies* 51:139–156.

Palfrey, Thomas. 1989. "A Mathematical Proof of Duverger's Law." In Peter C. Ordeshook, ed., *Models of Strategic Choice in Politics.* Ann Arbor: University of Michigan Press.

Pateman, Carole. 1970. *Participation and Democratic Theory.* Cambridge: Cambridge University Press.

Pempel, T. J., ed. 1990. *Uncommon Democracies: The One-Party Dominant Regimes.* Ithaca: Cornell University Press.

Popkin, Samuel L. 1991. *The Reasoning Voter: Communication and Persuasion in Presidential Campaigns.* Chicago: University of Chicago Press.

Powell, G. Bingham. 1982. *Contemporary Democracies: Participation, Stability and Violence.* Cambridge: Harvard University Press.

Rae, Douglas. 1971. *The Political Consequences of Electoral Laws,* rev. ed. New Haven: Yale University Press.

Ramseyer, J. Mark, and Frances M. Rosenbluth. 1995. *The Politics of Oligarchy: Institutional Choice in Imperial Japan.* Cambridge: Cambridge University Press.

Reed, Steven R. 1991. "Structure and Behaviour: Extending Duverger's Law to the Japanese Case." *British Journal of Political Science* 29:335–356.

Reeve, Andrew, and Alan Ware. 1992. *Electoral Systems: A Comparative and Theoretical Introduction.* London: Routledge.

Reynolds, Andrew. 1995. "The Effect of Ballot Paper Symbols on Voting Behavior." University of California at San Diego. Unpublished typescript.

Reynolds, Lisa. 1995. "Reassessing the Impact of Progressive Era Ballot Reform." University of California at San Diego. Unpublished Ph.D. dissertation.

Riker, William H. 1976. "The Number of Political Parties: A Reexamination of Duverger's Law." *Comparative Politics* 9:93–106.

Riker, William H. 1982. "The Two-Party System and Duverger's Law: An Essay on the History of Political Science." *American Political Science Review* 76:753–766.

Riker, William H. 1986. *The Art of Political Manipulation.* New Haven: Yale University Press.

Ritter, Gerhard A., and Merith Niehuss. 1987. *Wahlen in der Budesrepublik Deutschland: Bundestags- und Landtagswahlen 1946–1987.* Munich: Verlag C. H. Beck.

Roberts, Geoffrey K. 1988. "The 'Second Vote' Campaign Strategy of the West German Free Democratic Party." *European Journal of Political Research* 16:317–337.

Rohde, David. 1979. "Risk-Bearing and Progressive Ambition: The Case of Members of the United States House of Representatives." *American Journal of Political Science* 23:1–26.

Rokkan, Stein. 1970. *Citizens, Elections, Parties.* New York: Mackay.

Romer, Thomas, and Howard Rosenthal. 1979. "Bureaucrats versus Voters: On the Political Economy of Resource Allocation by Direct Democracy." *Quarterly Journal of Economics* 93:563–587.

Rose, Richard. 1983. "Elections and Electoral Systems: Choices and Alternatives." In Vernon Bogdanor and David Butler, eds., *Democracy and Elections.* Cambridge: Cambridge University Press.

Rosenthal, Howard. 1974. "Game-Theoretic Models of Bloc-Voting Under Proportional Representation." *Public Choice* 18:1–23.

Rusk, Jerrold G. 1970. "The Effects of the Australian Ballot Reform on Split-ticket Voting, 1876–1908." *American Political Science Review* 64:1220–1238.

Rydon, Joan. 1989. "Two- and Three-Party Electoral Politics in Britain, Australia and New Zealand." *The Journal of Commonwealth and Comparative Politics* 27:127–142.

Santos, Wanderley Guilherme dos, ed. 1990. *Que Brasil é Este? Manual de Indicadores Políticos e Sociais.* São Paulo: Vértice.

Särlvik, Bo. 1983. "Scandinavia." In Vernon Bogdanor and David Butler, eds., *Democracy and Elections: Electoral Systems and Their Political Consequences.* Cambridge: Cambridge University Press.

Sartori, Giovanni. 1968. "Political Development and Political Engineering." In John D. Montgomery and Albert O. Hirschman, eds., *Public Policy.* Cambridge: Cambridge University Press.

Sartori, Giovanni. 1976. *Parties and Party Systems: A Framework for Analysis.* Cambridge: Cambridge University Press.

Sartori, Giovanni. 1985. "The Influence of Electoral Systems: Faulty Laws or Faulty Method?" In Bernard Grofman and Arend Lijphart, eds., *Electoral Laws and Their Political Consequences.* New York: Agathon Press.

Sartori, Giovanni. 1993. "Neither Presidentialism nor Parliamentarism." In Juan J. Linz and Arturo Valenzuela, eds., *The Failure of Presidential Democracy.* Baltimore: The Johns Hopkins University Press.

Sartori, Giovanni. 1994. *Comparative Constitutional Engineering.* New York: New York University Press.

Satterthwaite, Mark A. 1975. "Strategy-Proofness and Arrow's Conditions: Existence and Correspondence Theorems for Voting Procedures and Social Welfare Functions." *Journal of Economic Theory* 10:1–7.

Scarrow, Howard A. 1986. "Cross-Endorsement and Cross-Filing in Plurality Partisan Elections." In Arend Lijphart and Bernard Grofman, eds., *Choosing an Electoral System: Issues and Alternatives.* New York: Praeger.

Schansberg, D. E. 1994. "Moving Out of the House: An Analysis of Congressional Quits." *Economic Inquiry* 32:445–456.

Schattschneider, Elmer Eric. 1960. *The Semisovereign People: A Realist's View of Democracy in America.* New York: Holt, Rinehart and Winston.

Schelling, Thomas. 1960. *The Strategy of Conflict.* Oxford: Oxford University Press.

Schelling, Thomas. 1978. *Micromotives and Macrobehavior.* New York: W. W. Norton.

Schmidt, Gregory D. 1996. "Fujimori's 1990 Upset Victory in Peru: Electoral Rules, Contingencies, and Adaptive Strategies." *Comparative Politics* 28:321–354.

Schmidt, Gregory D. N.d. *From Tidal Wave to Earthquake: Alberto Fujimori and the Peruvian Presidential Elections of 1990 and 1995.* Gainesville: University Press of Florida, forthcoming.

Schofield, Norman. 1978. "Instability of Simple Dynamic Games." *Review of Economic Studies* 45:575–594.

Schofield, Norman. 1993. "Political Competition and Multiparty Coalition Government." *European Journal of Political Research* 23:1–33.

Schwartz, Thomas. 1982. "No Minimally Reasonable Collective Choice Process Can be Strategy-Proof." *Mathematical Social Sciences* 3:57–72.

Schwartz, Thomas. 1986. *The Logic of Collective Choice.* New York: Columbia University Press.

Searle, G. R. 1992. *The Liberal Party: Triumph and Disintegration, 1886–1929.* New York: St. Martin's Press.

Seip, Dick. 1979. "The Netherlands." In Geoffrey Hand, Jacques Georgel, and Christoph Sasse, eds., *European Electoral Systems Handbook.* London: Butterworths.

Sen, Amartya. 1970. *Collective Choice and Social Welfare.* San Francisco: Holden-Day.

Shamir, Michal. 1985. "Changes in Electoral Systems as 'Interventions': Another Test of Duverger's Hypothesis." *European Journal of Political Research* 13:1–10.

Shepsle, Kenneth, and Barry Weingast. 1984. "Uncovered Sets and Sophisticated Voting Outcomes with Implications for Agenda Control." *American Journal of Political Science* 28:49–74.

Shepsle, Kenneth. 1991. *Models of Multiparty Electoral Competition.* Chur: Harwood Academic Publishers.

Shugart, Matthew Soberg. 1985. "The Two Effects of District Magnitude: Venezuela as a Crucial Experiment." *European Journal of Political Research* 13:353–64.

Shugart, Matthew Soberg. 1995. "The Electoral Cycle and Institutional Sources of Divided Presidential Government." *American Political Science Review* 89:327–43.

Shugart, Matthew Soberg, and John M. Carey. 1992. *Presidents and Assemblies: Constitutional Design and Electoral Dynamics.* New York: Cambridge University Press.

Shugart, Matthew Soberg, and Rein Taagepera. 1994. "Plurality Versus Majority Election of Presidents: A Proposal for a 'Double Complement Rule'." *Comparative Political Studies.*

Shvetsova, Olga. 1995. "Design of Political Institutions in Divided Societies." Ph.D. dissertation, California Institute of Technology.

Silverman, B. W. 1981. "Using Kernel Density Estimates to Investigate Multimodality." *Journal of the Royal Statistical Society,* ser. B 43:97–99.

Singh V. B., and Shankar Bose. 1986. *Elections in India: Data Handbook on Lok Sabha Elections, 1952–85.* 2d ed. New Delhi: Sage Publications.

Solari, Aldo E. 1986. "El Sistema de Partidos y Régimen Electoral en el Uruguay." In Rolando Franco, ed., *El Sistema Electoral Uruguayo: Peculiaridades y Perspectivas*. Montevideo: Fundación Hanns-Seidel.

Soskice, David, and V. Bhaskar. 1992. "Equilibria with Three or More Parties in Single-Seat Plurality Elections Without Entry." Stanford University. Unpublished typescript.

Squire, Peverill. 1989. "Competition and Uncontested Seats in United States House Elections." *Legislative Studies Quarterly* 14:281–295.

Stellman, Henri. 1993. "Israel: The 1992 Election and After." *Parliamentary Affairs* 46:121–132.

Strom, Kaare. 1994. "The Presthus Debacle: Intraparty Politics and Bargaining Failure in Norway." *American Political Science Review* 88:112–127.

Taagepera, Rein, and Bernard Grofman. 1985. "Rethinking Duverger's Law: Predicting the Effective Number of Parties in Plurality and PR Systems – Parties Minus Issues Equals One." *European Journal of Political Research* 13:341–352.

Taagepera, Rein, and Matthew Soberg Shugart. 1989. *Seats and Votes: The Effects and Determinants of Electoral Systems*. New Haven: Yale University Press.

Tagle, Andrés. 1993. "Comentario en Torno a los Trabajos de Jose Maria Fuentes y Peter Siavelis." *Estudios Publicos* 51:325–330.

Taylor, Phillip B. 1955. "The Electoral System in Uruguay." *Journal of Politics* 17:19–42.

Tóka, Gábor. N.d. "Seats and Votes: Consequences of the Hungarian Election Law." In Gábor Tóka, ed., *The 1990 Election to the Hungarian National Assembly: Analyses, Documents and Data*. Berlin: Edition Sigma.

Tsebelis, George. 1986. "A General Model of Tactical and Inverse Tactical Voting." *British Journal of Political Science* 16:395–404.

Turan, İlter. 1994. "Evolution of the Electoral Process." In Metin Heper and Ahmet Evin, eds., *Politics in the Third Turkish Republic*. Boulder: Westview.

Vanhanen, Tatu. 1990. *The Process of Democratization. A Comparative Study of 147 States (1980–88)*. New York: Crane Russak.

Vengroff, Richard. 1994. "The Impact of the Electoral System on the Transition to Democracy in Africa: The Case of Mali." *Electoral Studies* 13:29–37.

Vincent, John. 1966. *The Formation of the British Liberal Party*. New York: Scribner.

Vowles, Jack, and Peter Aimer. 1993. *Voter's Vengeance: The 1990 Election in New Zealand and the Fate of the Fourth Labour Government*. Auckland: Auckland University Press.

Wada, Junichiro. N.d. "A Game Theoretical Study of 'Duverger's Law.'" University of Maryland. Unpublished typescript.

Wald, Kenneth. 1983. *Crosses on the Ballot: Patterns of British Voter Alignment Since 1885*. Princeton: Princeton University Press.

Weber, Sholmo. 1990. "On the Existence of a Fixed-number Equilibrium in a Multiparty Electoral System." *Mathematical Social Sciences* 20:115–130.

Weber, Shlomo. 1992a. "On Hierarchical Spatial Competition." *Review of Economic Studies* 59:407–425.

Weber, Shlomo. 1992b. "An Equilibrium in Electoral Competition with Entry Costs." York University. Unpublished typescript.

Wightman, Gordon. 1990. "Czechoslovakia." *Electoral Studies* 9:319–326.

Wildavsky, Aaron. 1959. "A Methodological Critique of Duverger's *Political Parties.*" *Journal of Politics* 21:303–318.

Wilson, Frank L. 1980. "Sources of Party Transformation: The Case of France." In Peter H. Merkl, ed., *Western European Party Systems*. New York: Free Press.

Wilson, Trevor. 1966. *The Downfall of the Liberal Party 1914–1935*. Ithaca: Cornell University Press.

Worldmark Encyclopedia of the Nations. 1984. New York: John Wiley.

Wright, Stephen G., and William H. Riker. 1989. "Plurality and Runoff Elections and Numbers of Candidates." *Public Choice* 60:155–76.

Subject Index

Subject Index

Author's Index